Volume 3
by Meca Tanaka

HAMBURG // LONDON // LOS ANGELES // TOKYO

Pearl Pink Volume 3
Created by Meca Tanaka

Translation - Adrienne Beck
English Adaptation - Jamie S. Rich
Retouch and Lettering - Star Print Brokers
Production Artist - Vicente Rivera, Jr.
Graphic Designer - Jason Milligan

Editor - Katherine Schilling
Digital Imaging Manager - Chris Buford
Pre-Production Supervisor - Erika Terriquez
Art Director - Anne Marie Horne
Production Manager - Elisabeth Brizzi
Managing Editor - Vy Nguyen
VP of Production - Ron Klamert
Editor-in-Chief - Rob Tokar
Publisher - Mike Kiley
President and C.O.O. - John Parker
C.E.O. and Chief Creative Officer - Stuart Levy

A **TOKYOPOP** Manga

TOKYOPOP and 🐾 are trademarks or registered trademarks of TOKYOPOP Inc.

TOKYOPOP Inc.
5900 Wilshire Blvd. Suite 2000
Los Angeles, CA 90036

E-mail: info@TOKYOPOP.com
Come visit us online at www.TOKYOPOP.com

ISBN: 978-1-59816-777-1

First TOKYOPOP printing: September 2007
10 9 8 7 6 5 4 3 2 1
Printed in the USA

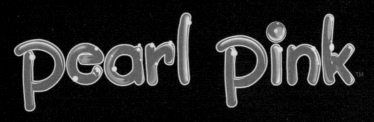

Pearl Pink

Volume 3

Meca Tanaka

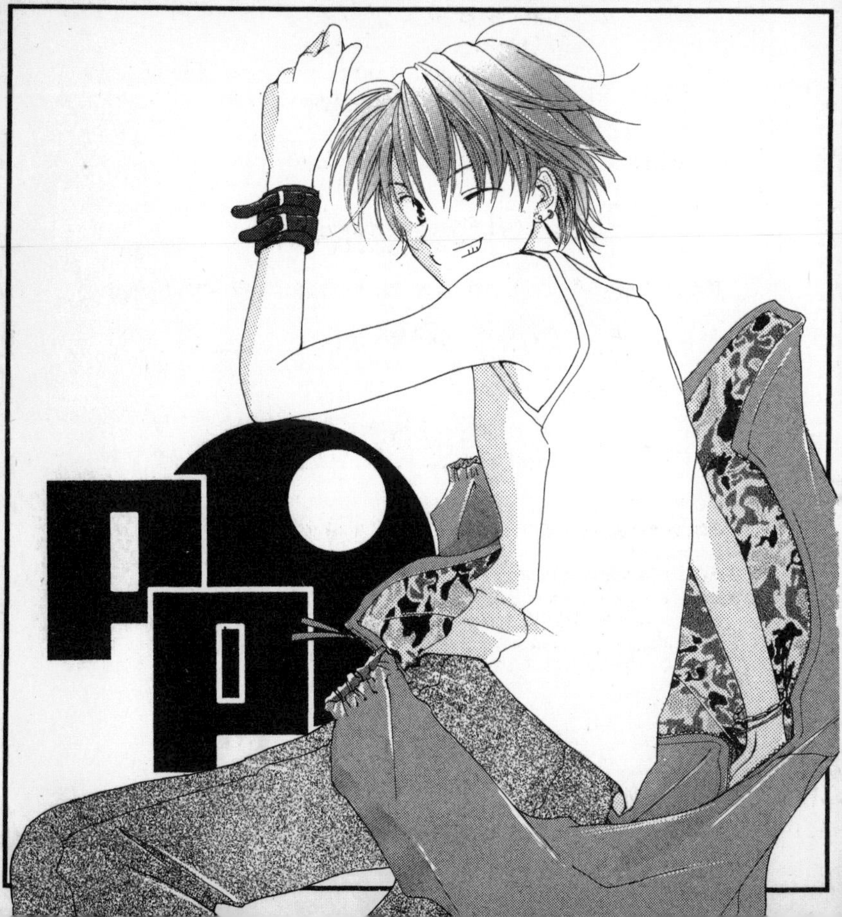

Contents

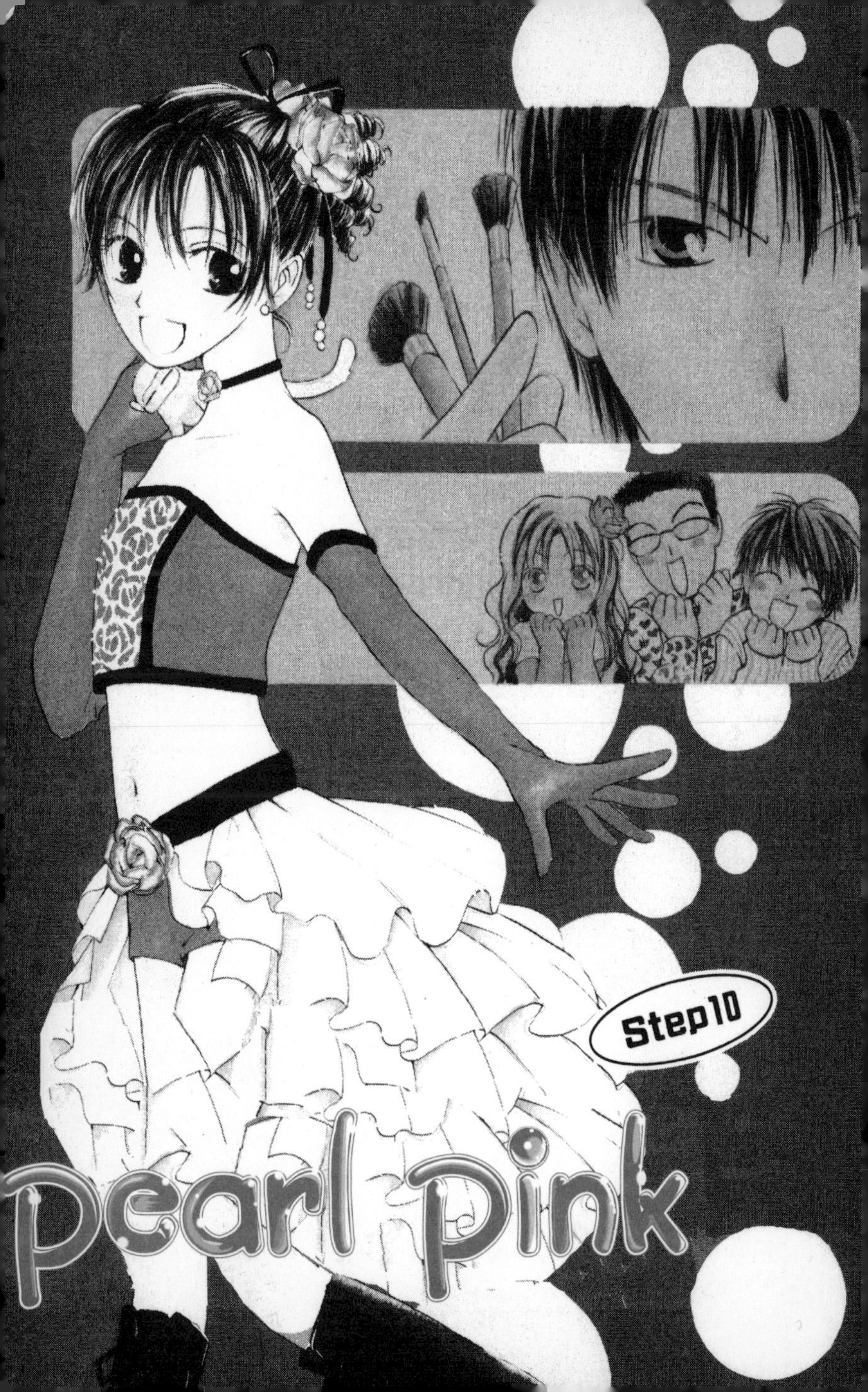
Step 10
Pearl Pink

Pearl Pink

CHARACTER INTRODUCTIONS

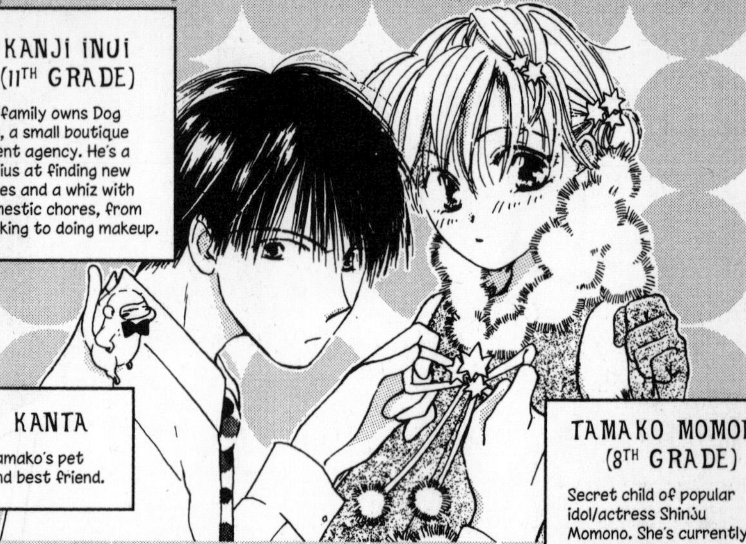

KANJI INUI (11TH GRADE)

His family owns Dog Run, a small boutique talent agency. He's a genius at finding new faces and a whiz with domestic chores, from cooking to doing makeup.

KANTA

Tamako's pet and best friend.

TAMAKO MOMONO (8TH GRADE)

Secret child of popular idol/actress Shinju Momono. She's currently living with the Inui family and has a crush of galactic proportions on Kanji. Limber and athletic as a monkey.

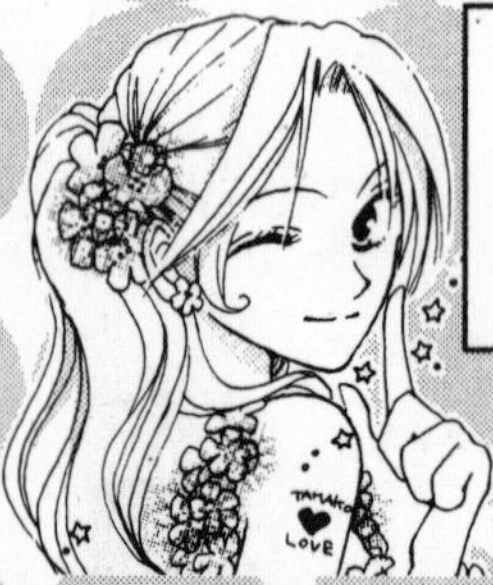
TAMAKO
LOVE

SHINJU MOMONO

Tamako's mother and a famous idol/actress. Her real first name is "Mako." Star of the mega-hit TV drama "Idol P.I."

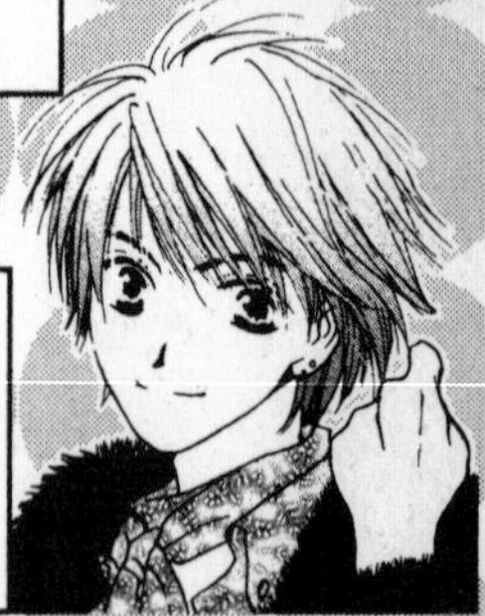

RAIZO HISHIKAWA

Member of the boy band Rain. Scouted by Kanji and hence has pledged his life to pleasing the man who gave him success.

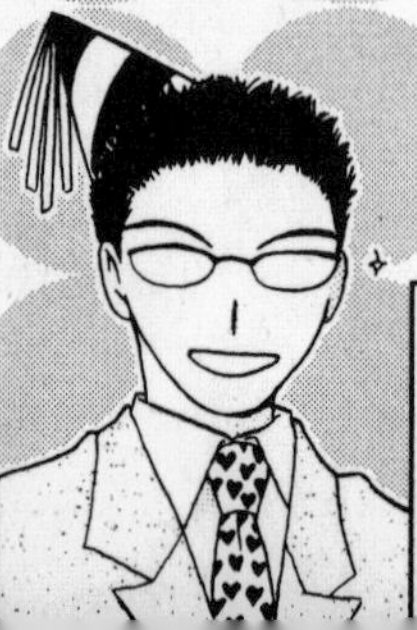

KINICHI INUI

Chief owner of the tiny Dog Run talent agency, in addition to being Kanji's father. A wacky, but nice, middle-aged guy.

Catch the beginning of the story in *Pearl Pink* Volumes 1 & 2, currently on sale from TOKYOPOP!

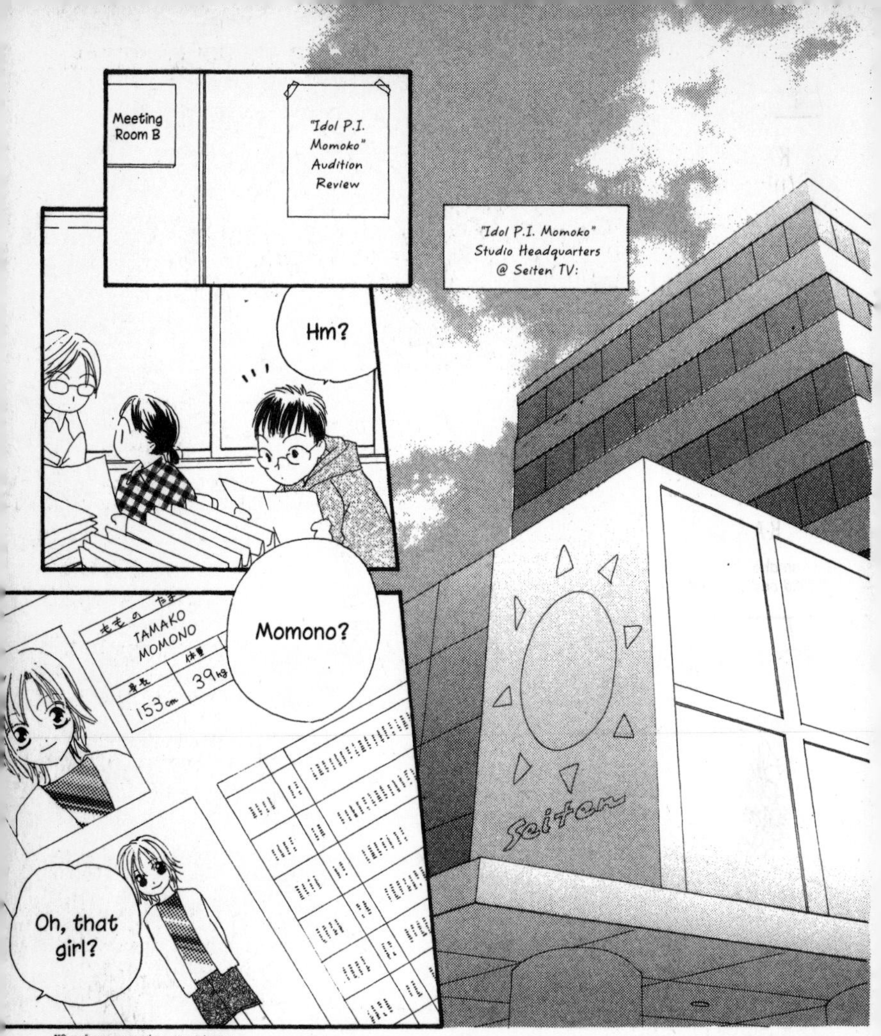
"Idol P.I. Momoko" Studio Headquarters @ Seiten TV:
seiten
Meeting Room B
"Idol P.I. Momoko" Audition Review
Hm?
TAMAKO MOMONO
153 cm
39 kg
Momono?
Oh, that girl?

*"Omiai" = an arranged marriage interview

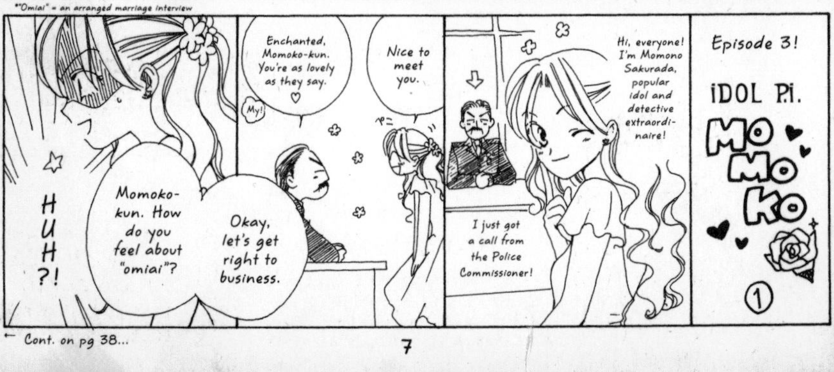
Episode 3!
IDOL P.I. MOMOKO
①
Hi, everyone! I'm Momono Sakurada, popular idol and detective extraordinaire!
I just got a call from the Police Commissioner!
Nice to meet you.
Enchanted, Momoko-kun. You're as lovely as they say. ♡
My!
Okay, let's get right to business.
Momoko-kun. How do you feel about "omiai"?
HUH?!

← Cont. on pg 38...

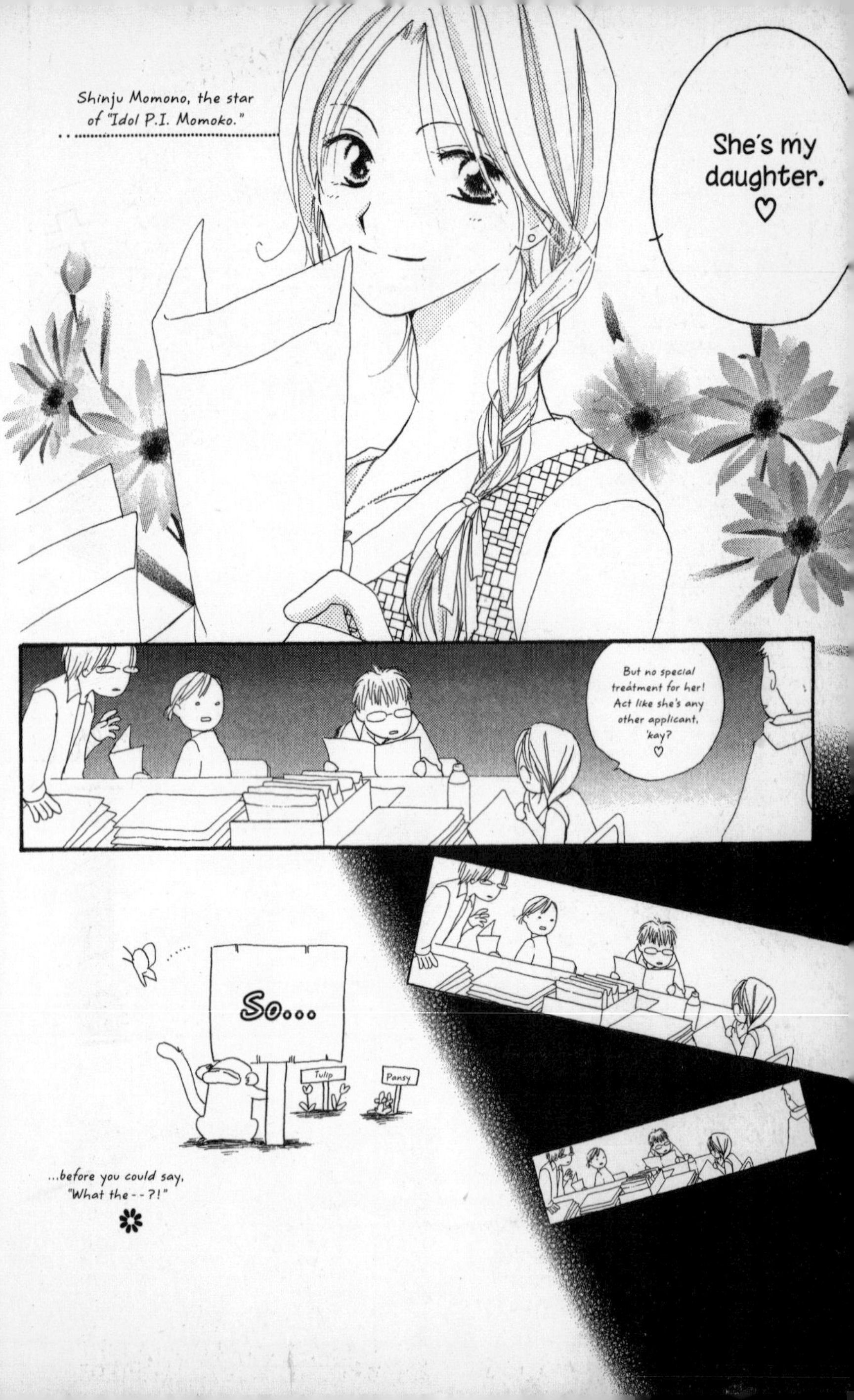
She's my daughter. ♡
Shinju Momono, the star of "Idol P.I. Momoko."
But no special treatment for her! Act like she's any other applicant, 'kay? ♡
So...
Tulip
Pansy
...before you could say, "What the--?!"

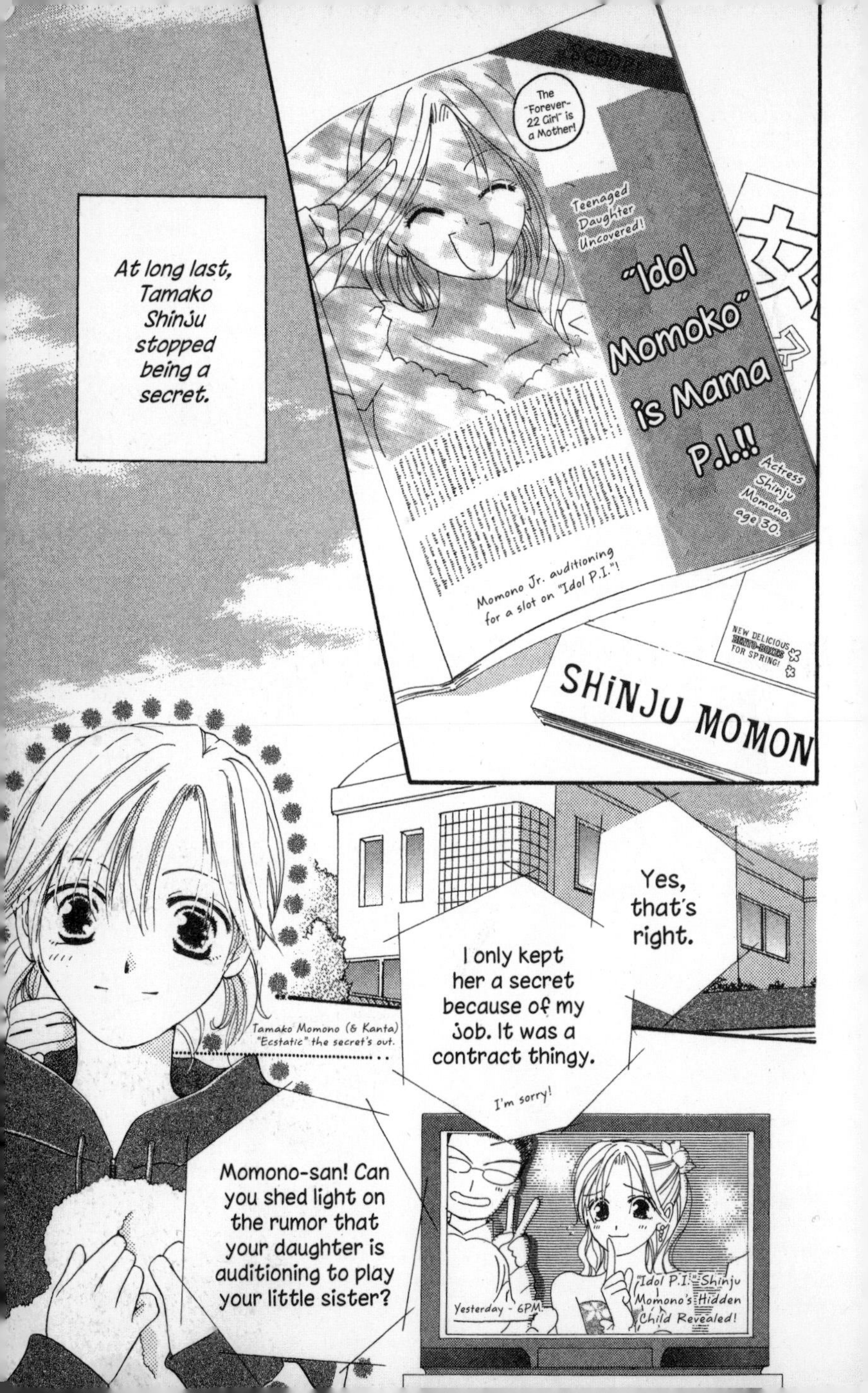
The "Forever-22 Girl" is a Mother!
Teenaged Daughter Uncovered!
"Idol Momoko" is Mama P.I.!!
Actress Shinju Momono, age 30.
Momono Jr. auditioning for a slot on "Idol P.I."!
NEW DELICIOUS BENTO-BOXES FOR SPRING!
SHINJU MOMON
At long last, Tamako Shinju stopped being a secret.
Yes, that's right.
I only kept her a secret because of my job. It was a contract thingy.
I'm sorry!
"Idol P.I." Shinju Momono's Hidden Child Revealed!
Yesterday - 6PM.
Momono-san! Can you shed light on the rumor that your daughter is auditioning to play your little sister?
Tamako Momono (& Kanta) "Ecstatic" the secret's out.

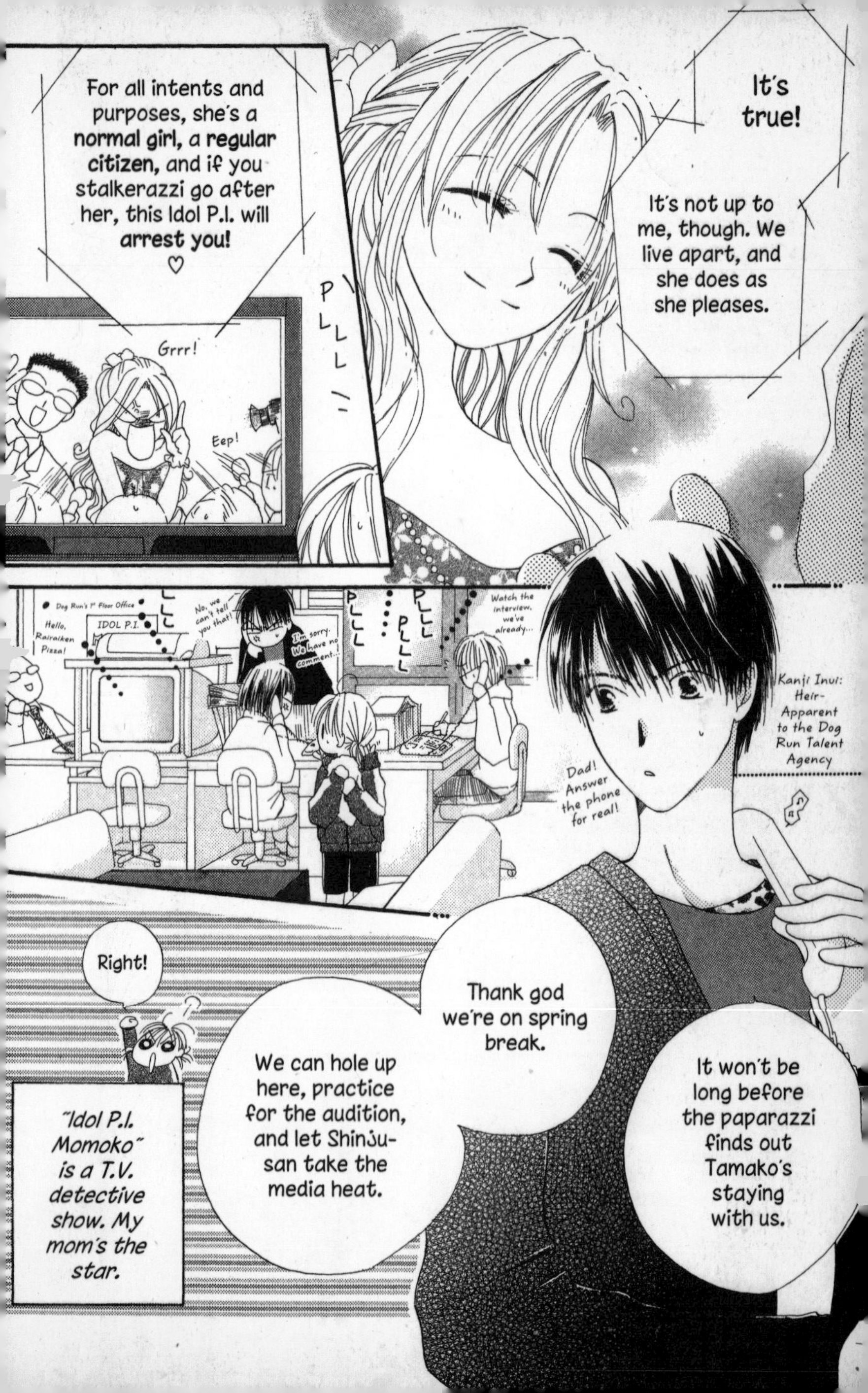
It's true!
It's not up to me, though. We live apart, and she does as she pleases.
PLLL
For all intents and purposes, she's a normal girl, a regular citizen, and if you stalkerazzi go after her, this Idol P.I. will arrest you! ♡
Grrr!
Eep!
Kanji Inui: Heir-Apparent to the Dog Run Talent Agency
Dad! Answer the phone for real!
Watch the interview, we've already...
PLLL
PLLL
I'm sorry. We have no comment...!
No, we can't tell you that!
LLL
Dog Run's 1st Floor Office
IDOL P.I.
Hello, Rairaiken Pizza!
It won't be long before the paparazzi finds out Tamako's staying with us.
Thank god we're on spring break.
We can hole up here, practice for the audition, and let Shinju-san take the media heat.
Right!
"Idol P.I. Momoko" is a T.V. detective show. My mom's the star.

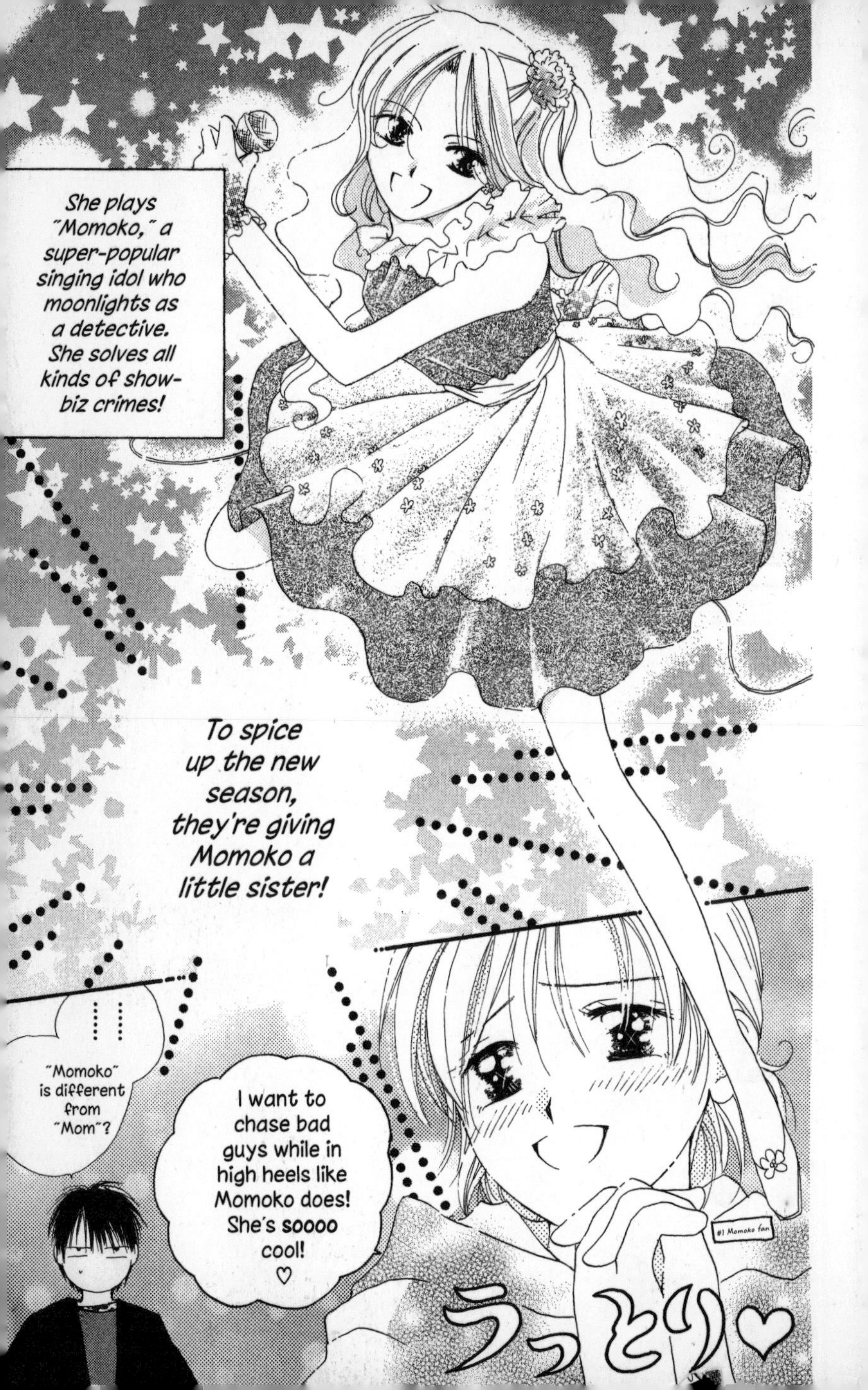

She plays "Momoko," a super-popular singing idol who moonlights as a detective. She solves all kinds of show-biz crimes!
To spice up the new season, they're giving Momoko a little sister!
#1 Momoko fan
I want to chase bad guys while in high heels like Momoko does! She's soooo cool! ♡
うっとり♡
……
"Momoko" is different from "Mom"?

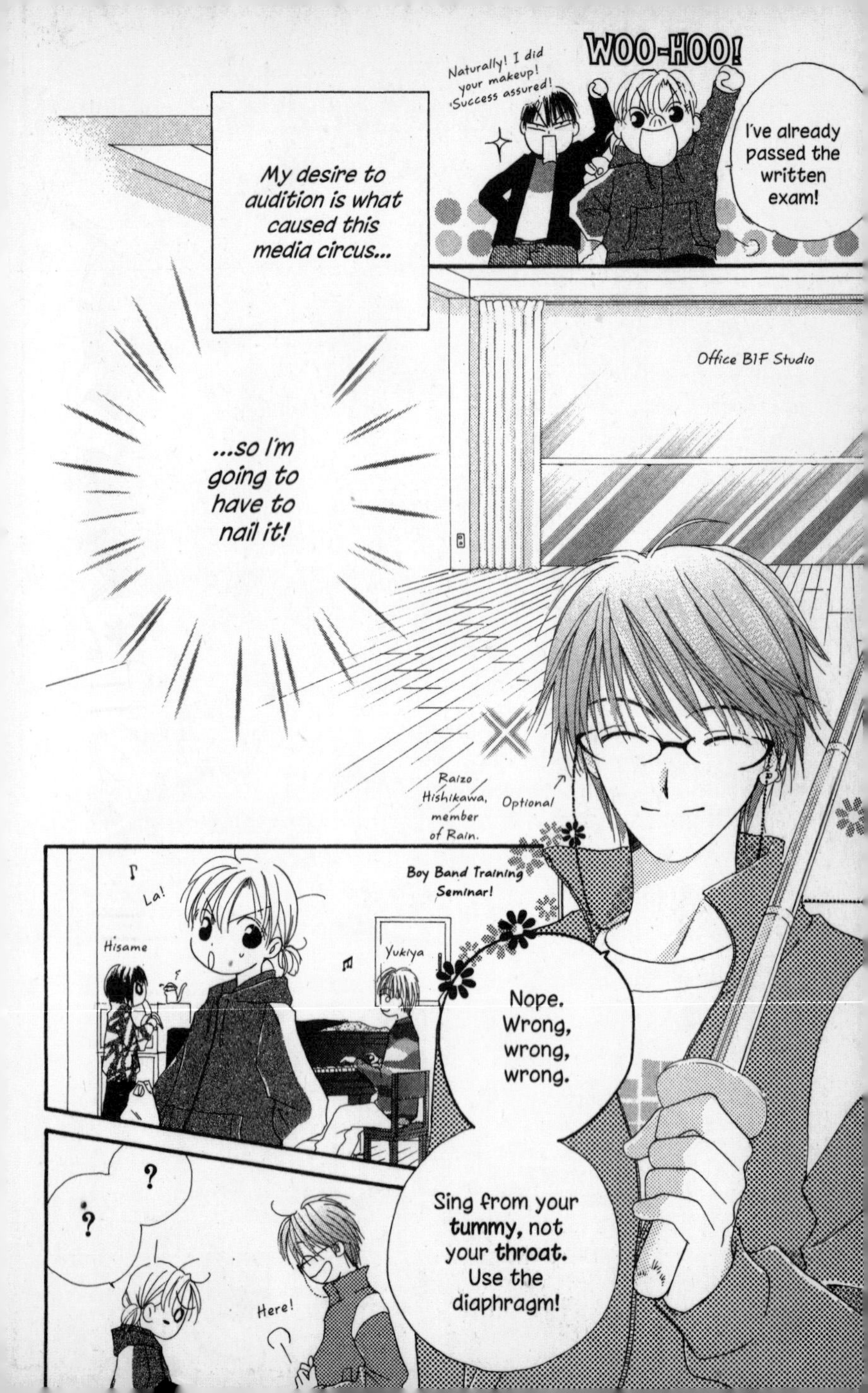
WOO-HOO!
I've already passed the written exam!
Naturally! I did your makeup! Success assured!
My desire to audition is what caused this media circus...
Office B1F Studio
...so I'm going to have to nail it!
Raizo Hishikawa, member of Rain.
Optional
Nope. Wrong, wrong, wrong.
Sing from your tummy, not your throat. Use the diaphragm!
Boy Band Training Seminar!
La!
Hisame
Yukiya
? ?
Here!

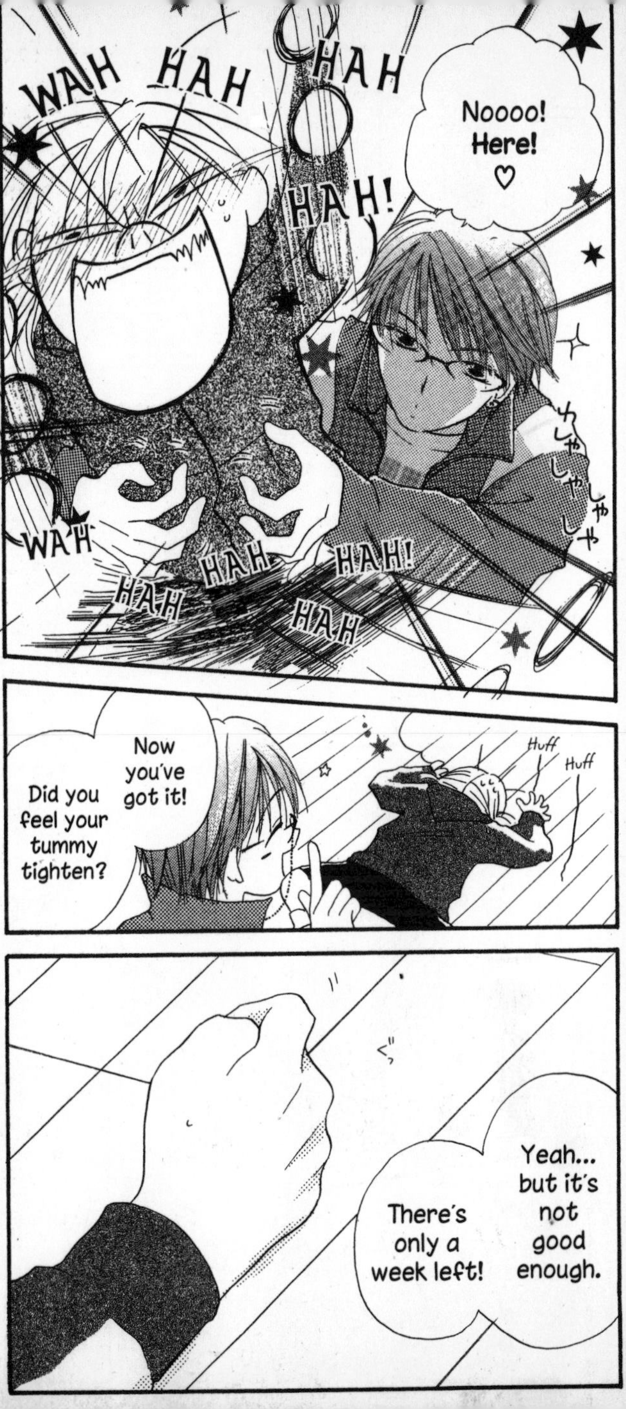
Noooo! Here! ♡
HAH HAH HAH!
WAH HAH
HAH!
WAH HAH HAH HAH HAH
Now you've got it!
Did you feel your tummy tighten?
Huff
Huff
Yeah... but it's not good enough.
There's only a week left!

8TH VOLUME

Hello, everyone! Tanaka here. Boy, time sure does go fast, doesn't it? It feels like I've only just started, but now, all of a sudden, it's time to start the countdown to my 10th published manga volume. Of course, I couldn't have done it without the help and support of all my fans. Thank you so much!!

Pearl Pink is now on its 3rd volume, and the "Audition Arc" of the storyline is starting to gather steam. You wouldn't think it, but this part of the story necessitated a lot more little details. I had to invent more about the society Tamako and Kanji live in. I was having a pretty hard time sorting it out, but thanks to some help from a bunch of friends and colleagues, I somehow managed to put it all together. I even got to tour a television studio as research. I'll write more about it at the end of this volume. Those of you who are curious, feel free to skip to the end and read all about it. And in the remaining space, as always, I shall doodle.

Go!

I'm flying!

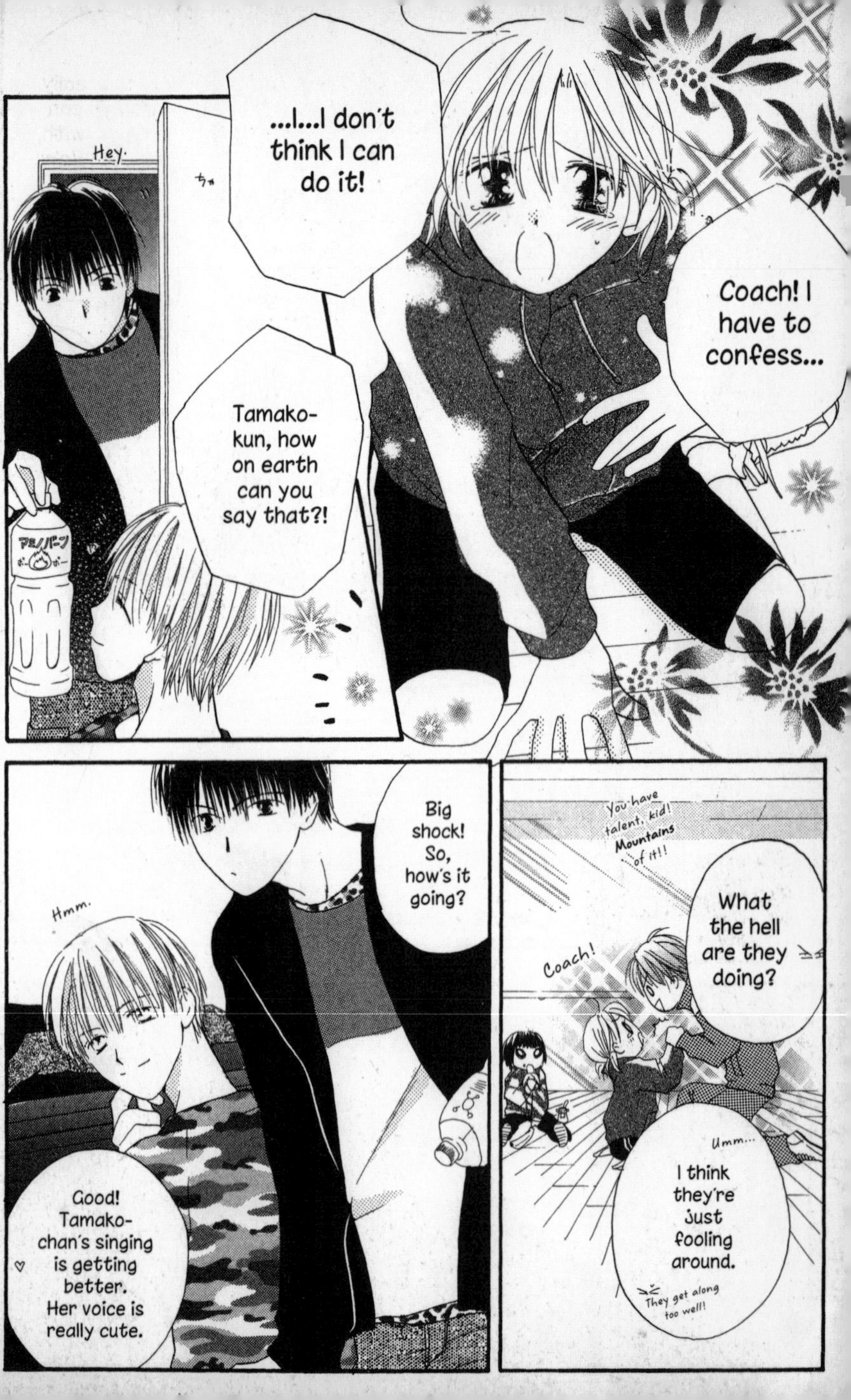
Coach! I have to confess...
...I...I don't think I can do it!
Hey.
Tamako-kun, how on earth can you say that?!
You have talent, kid! Mountains of it!!
What the hell are they doing?
Coach!
Umm...
I think they're just fooling around.
They get along too well!
Big shock! So, how's it going?
Hmm.
Good! Tamako-chan's singing is getting better. Her voice is really cute.

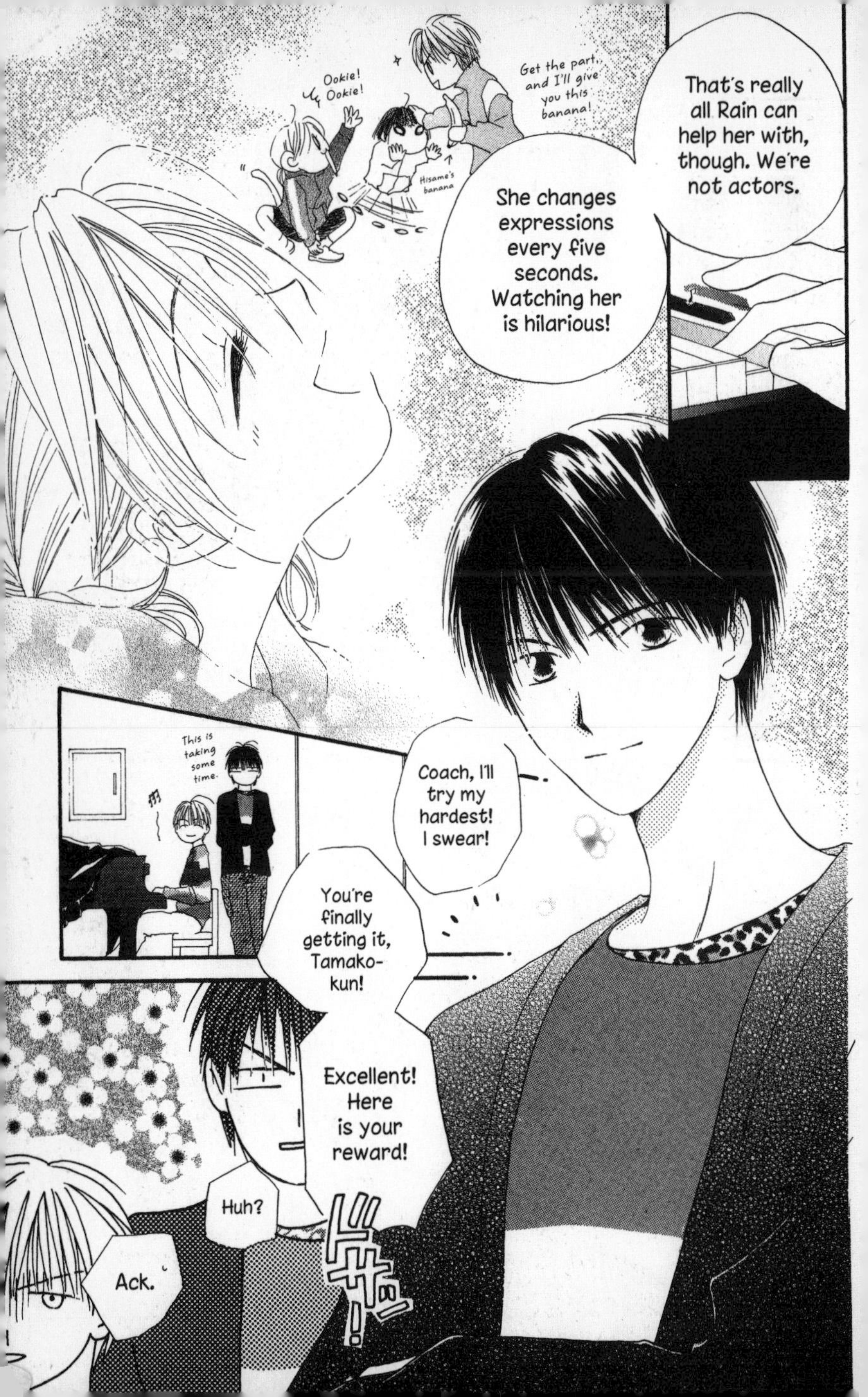
That's really all Rain can help her with, though. We're not actors.
She changes expressions every five seconds. Watching her is hilarious!
Get the part, and I'll give you this banana!
Ookie! Ookie!
Hisame's banana
Coach, I'll try my hardest! I swear!
You're finally getting it, Tamako-kun!
This is taking some time.
Excellent! Here is your reward!
Huh?
Ack.

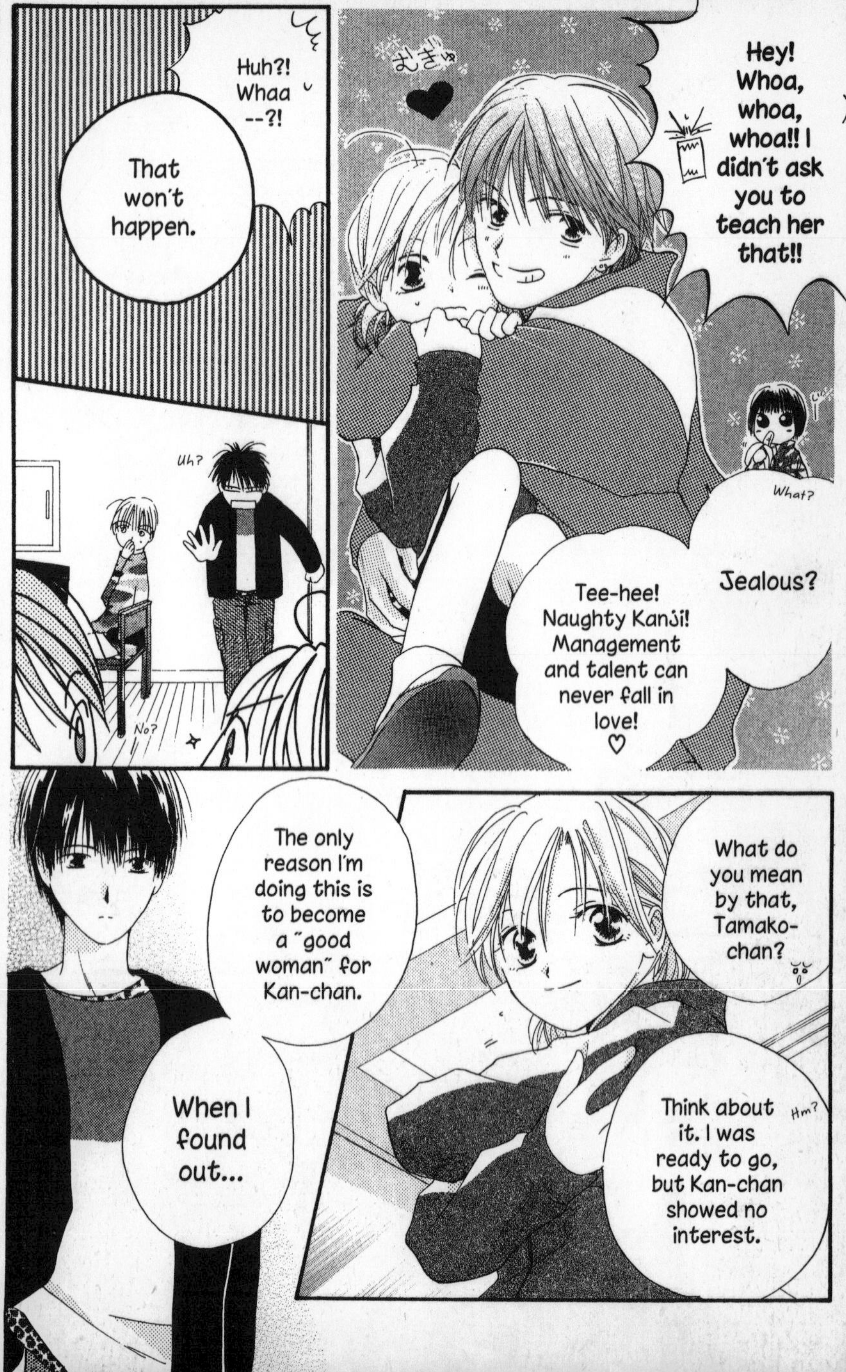

Hey! Whoa, whoa, whoa!! I didn't ask you to teach her that!!
むぎゅ
What?
Jealous?
Tee-hee! Naughty Kanji! Management and talent can never fall in love! ♡
Huh?! Whaa --?!
That won't happen.
Uh?
No?
What do you mean by that, Tamako-chan?
Hm?
Think about it. I was ready to go, but Kan-chan showed no interest.
The only reason I'm doing this is to become a "good woman" for Kan-chan.
When I found out...

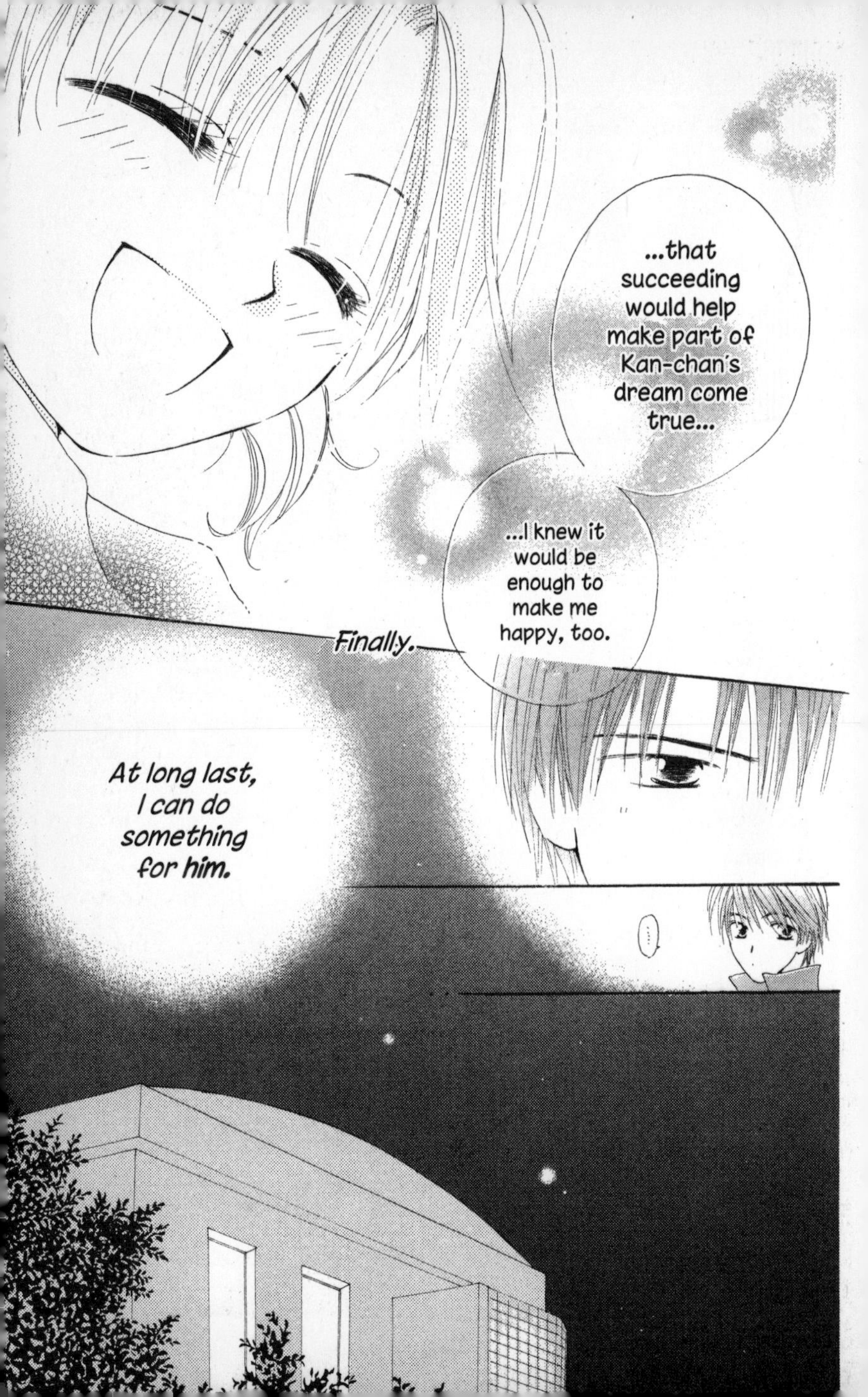
...that succeeding would help make part of Kan-chan's dream come true...
...I knew it would be enough to make me happy, too.
Finally.
At long last, I can do something for him.
...!

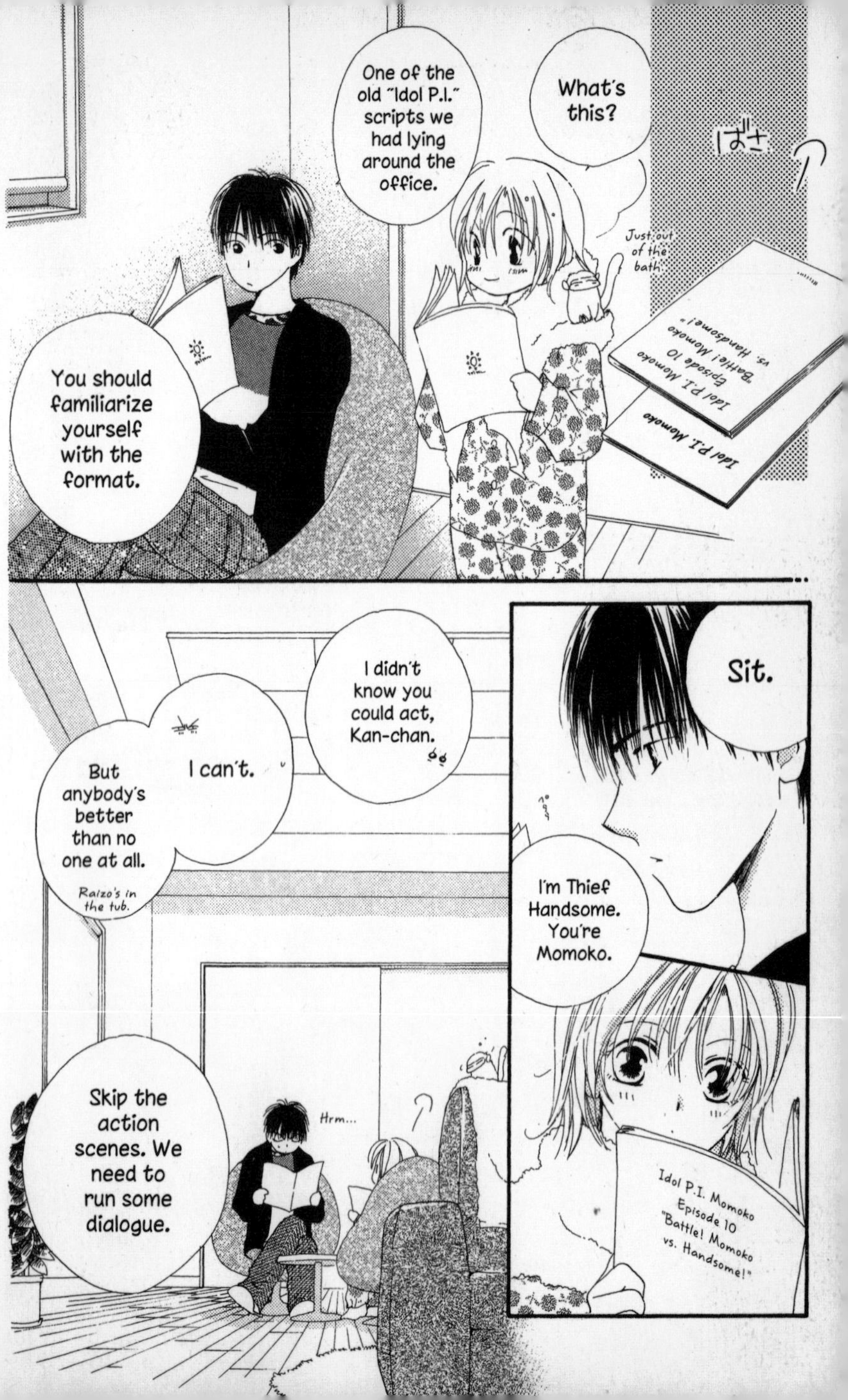
What's this?
One of the old "Idol P.I." scripts we had lying around the office.
ばさ
Just out of the bath.
Idol P.I. Momoko Episode 10 "Battle! Momoko vs. Handsome!"
Idol P.I. Momoko
You should familiarize yourself with the format.
Sit.
I'm Thief Handsome. You're Momoko.
Idol P.I. Momoko Episode 10 "Battle! Momoko vs. Handsome!"
I didn't know you could act, Kan-chan.
I can't.
But anybody's better than no one at all.
Raizo's in the tub.
Hrm...
Skip the action scenes. We need to run some dialogue.

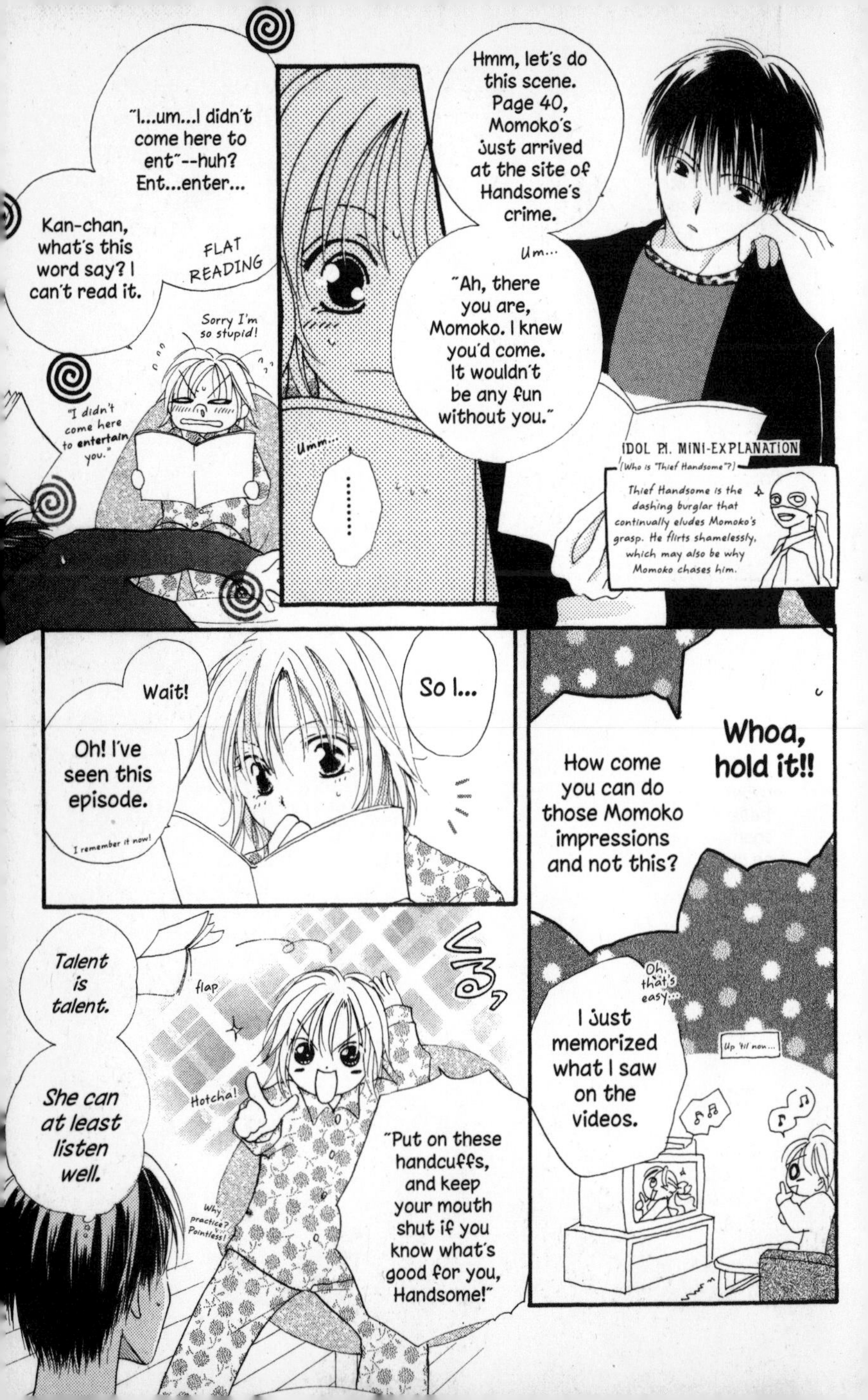
Hmm, let's do this scene. Page 40, Momoko's just arrived at the site of Handsome's crime.
Um...
"Ah, there you are, Momoko. I knew you'd come. It wouldn't be any fun without you."
IDOL P.I. MINI-EXPLANATION
[Who is "Thief Handsome"?]
Thief Handsome is the dashing burglar that continually eludes Momoko's grasp. He flirts shamelessly, which may also be why Momoko chases him.
Umm...
....
"I...um...I didn't come here to ent"--huh? Ent...enter...
Kan-chan, what's this word say? I can't read it.
FLAT READING
Sorry I'm so stupid!
"I didn't come here to entertain you."
Whoa, hold it!!
How come you can do those Momoko impressions and not this?
So I...
Wait!
Oh! I've seen this episode.
I remember it now!
Oh, that's easy...
I just memorized what I saw on the videos.
Up 'til now...
くるっ
flap
Hotcha!
"Put on these handcuffs, and keep your mouth shut if you know what's good for you, Handsome!"
Talent is talent.
She can at least listen well.
Why practice? Pointless!

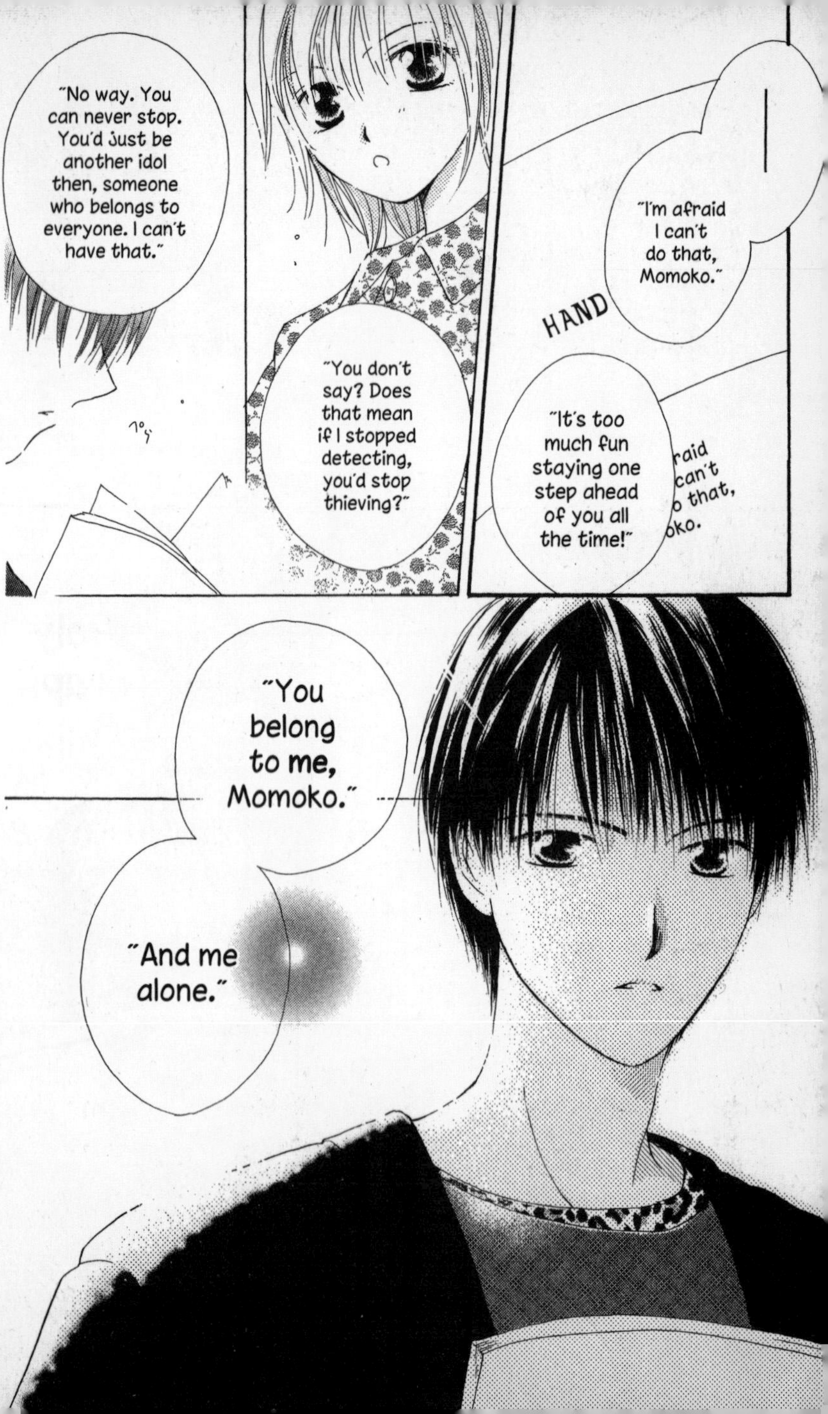
"I'm afraid I can't do that, Momoko."
HAND
"It's too much fun staying one step ahead of you all the time!"
"You don't say? Does that mean if I stopped detecting, you'd stop thieving?"
"No way. You can never stop. You'd just be another idol then, someone who belongs to everyone. I can't have that."
"You belong to me, Momoko."
"And me alone."

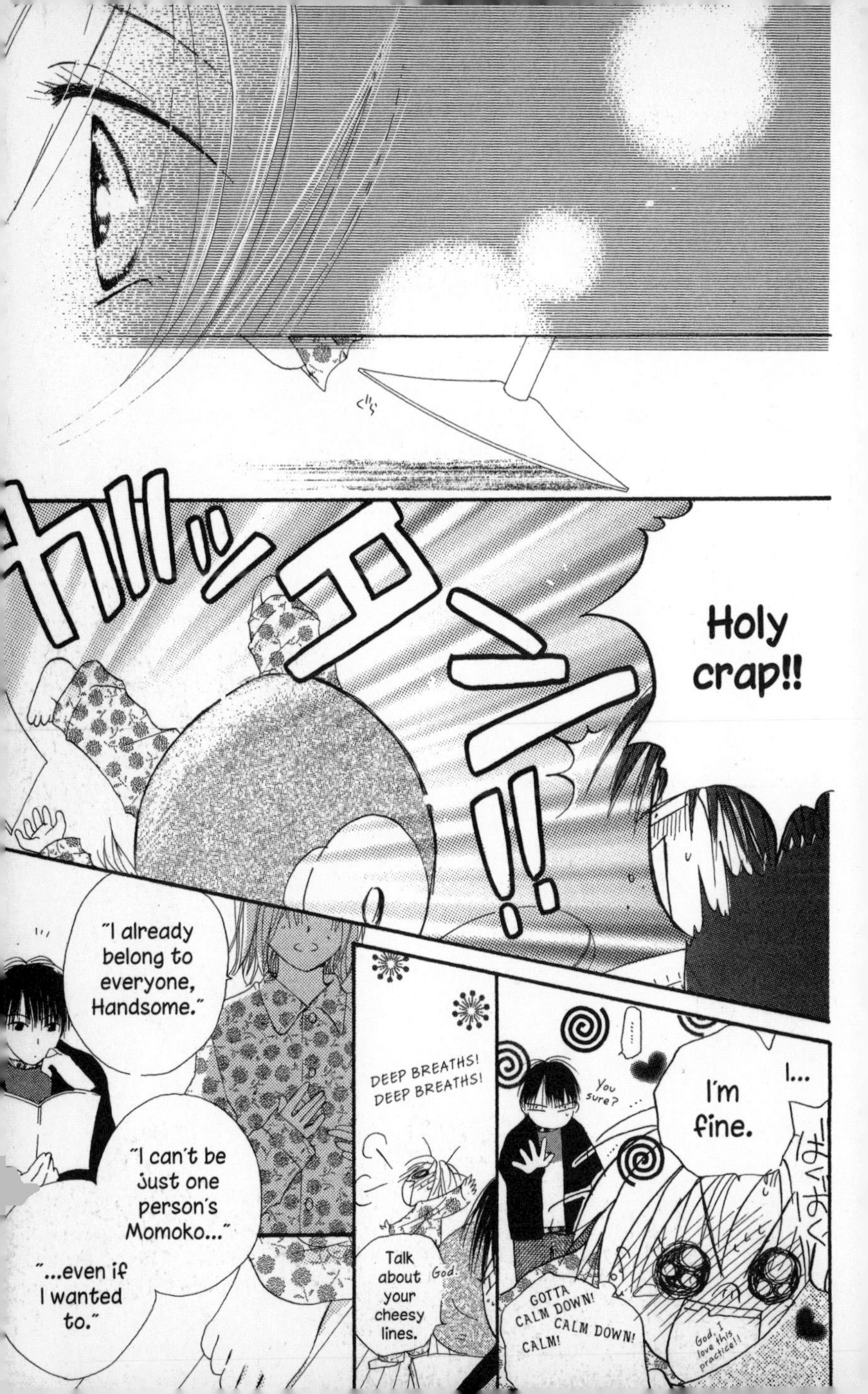
Holy crap!!
I...
I'm fine.
You sure?
GOTTA CALM DOWN! CALM DOWN! CALM!
God, I love this practice!!
DEEP BREATHS! DEEP BREATHS!
Talk about your cheesy lines.
God.
"I already belong to everyone, Handsome."
"I can't be just one person's Momoko..."
"...even if I wanted to."

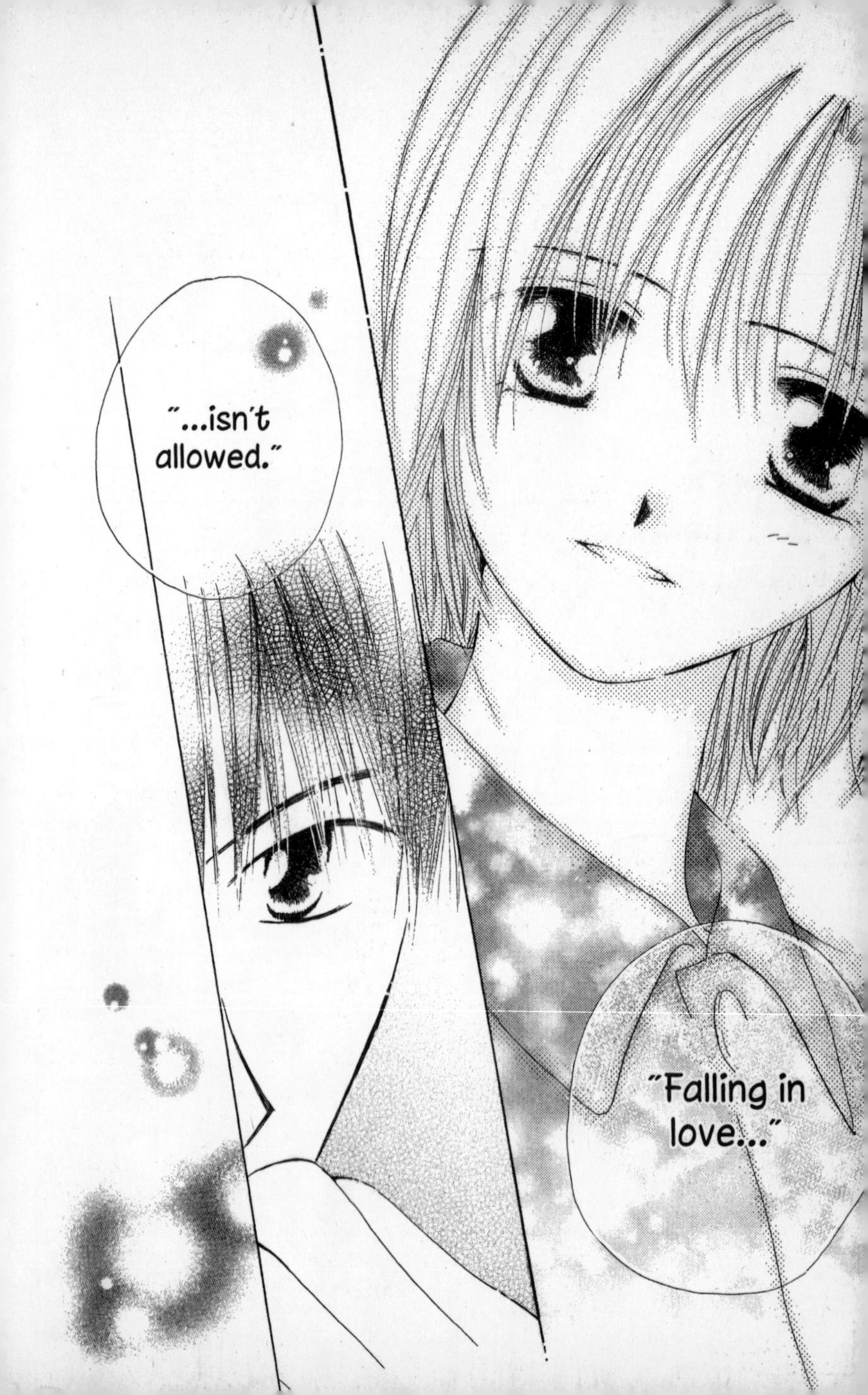
"Falling in love..."
"...isn't allowed."

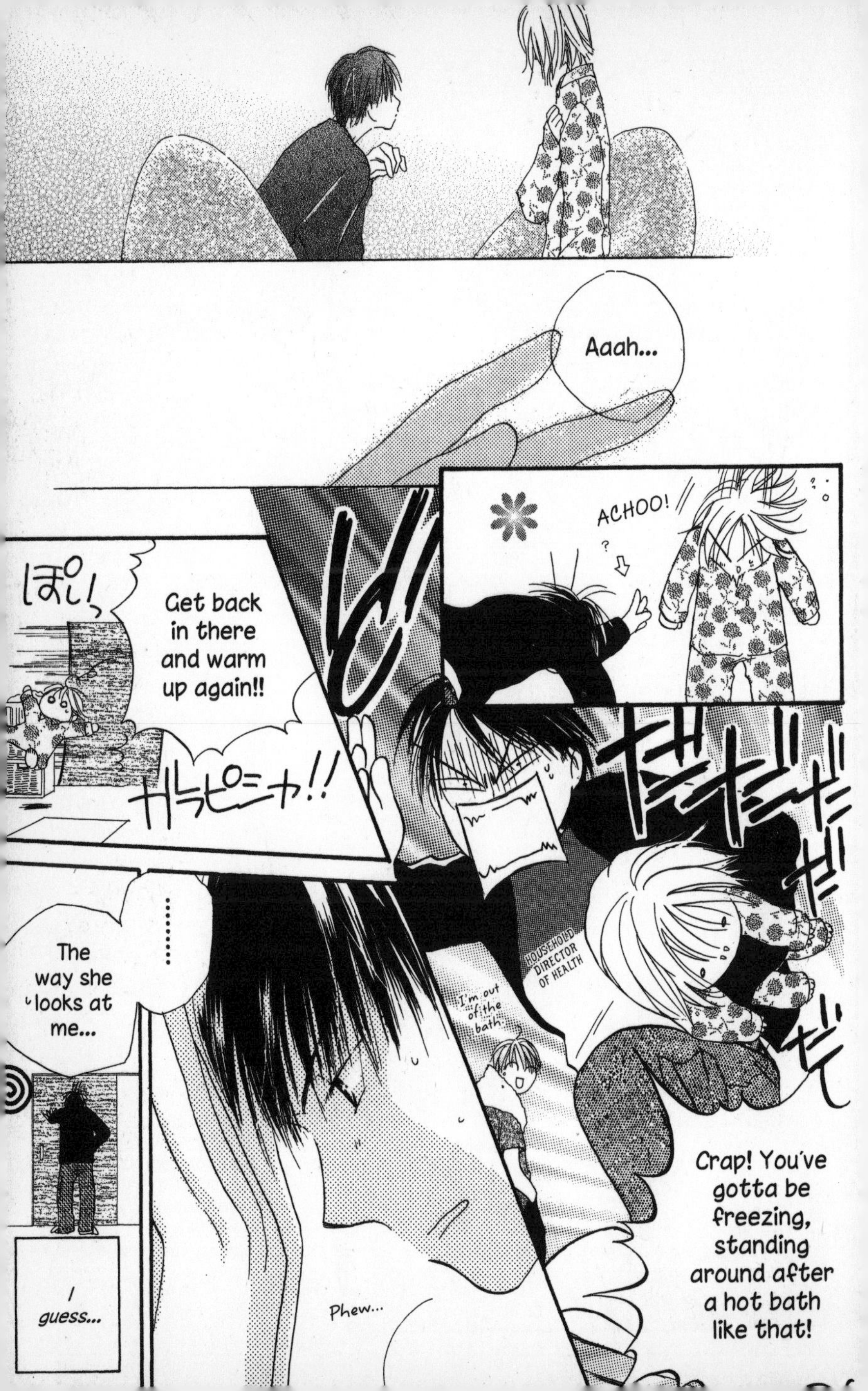

Aaah...
ACHOO!
Crap! You've gotta be freezing, standing around after a hot bath like that!
HOUSEHOLD DIRECTOR OF HEALTH
I'm out of the bath.
Get back in there and warm up again!!
ぽい!
カラピシャ!!
......
Phew...
The way she looks at me...
I guess...

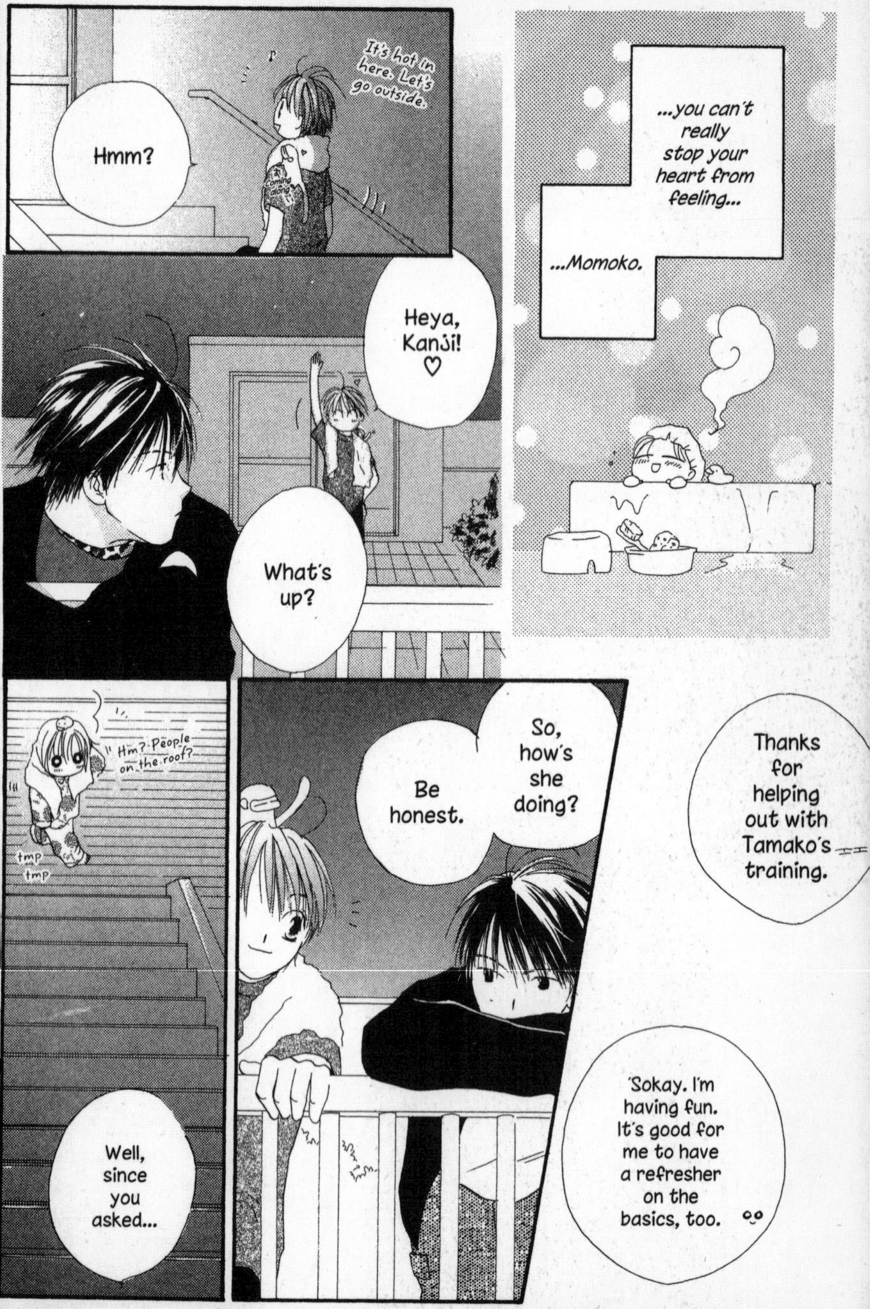
...you can't really stop your heart from feeling...
...Momoko.
It's hot in here. Let's go outside.
Hmm?
Heya, Kanji! ♡
What's up?
Thanks for helping out with Tamako's training.
'Sokay. I'm having fun. It's good for me to have a refresher on the basics, too.
So, how's she doing?
Be honest.
Hm? People on the roof?
tmp tmp
Well, since you asked...

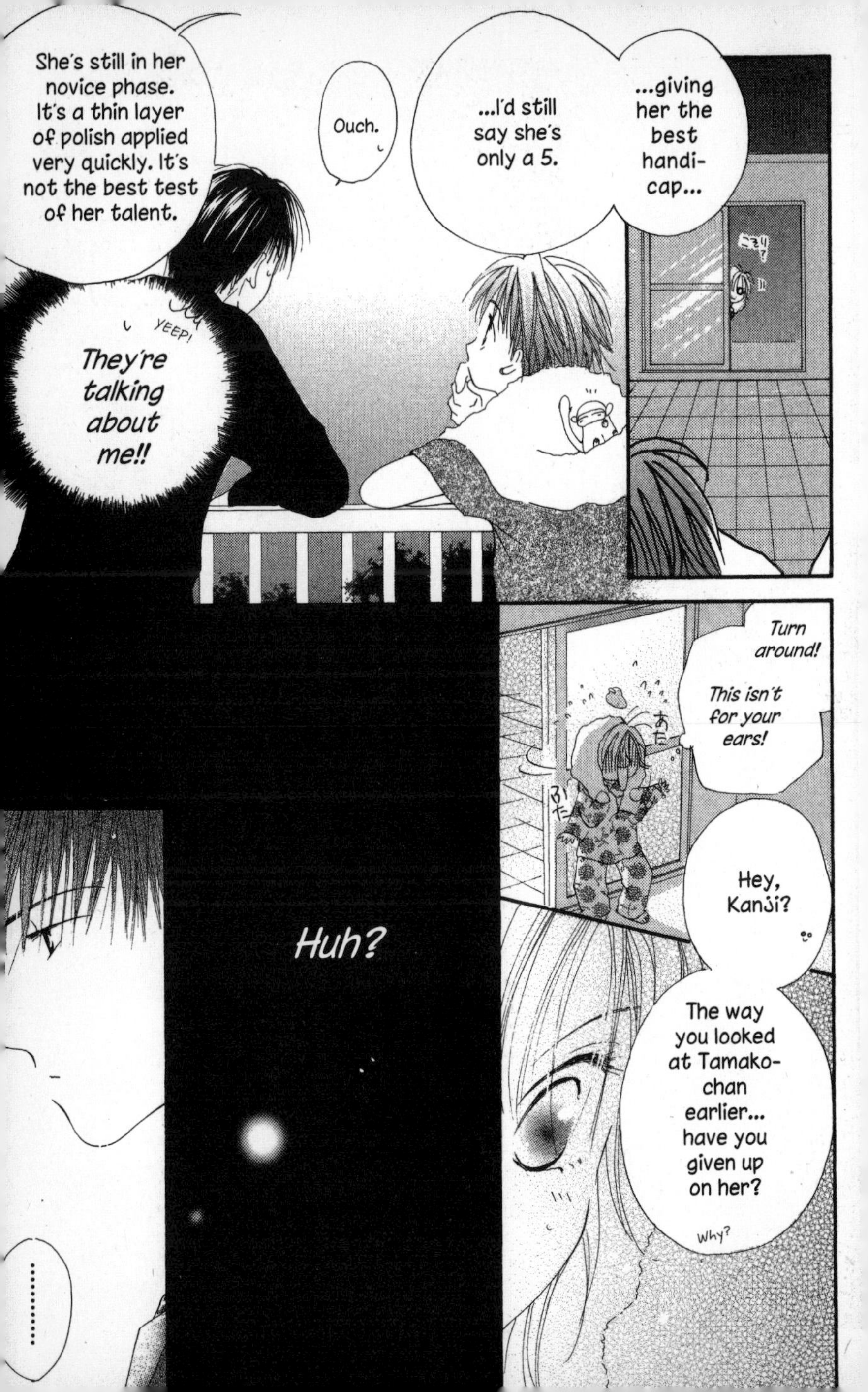
...giving her the best handi-cap...
...I'd still say she's only a 5.
Ouch.
She's still in her novice phase. It's a thin layer of polish applied very quickly. It's not the best test of her talent.
YEEP!
They're talking about me!!
Turn around!
This isn't for your ears!
Hey, Kanji?
The way you looked at Tamako-chan earlier... have you given up on her?
Why?
Huh?
......

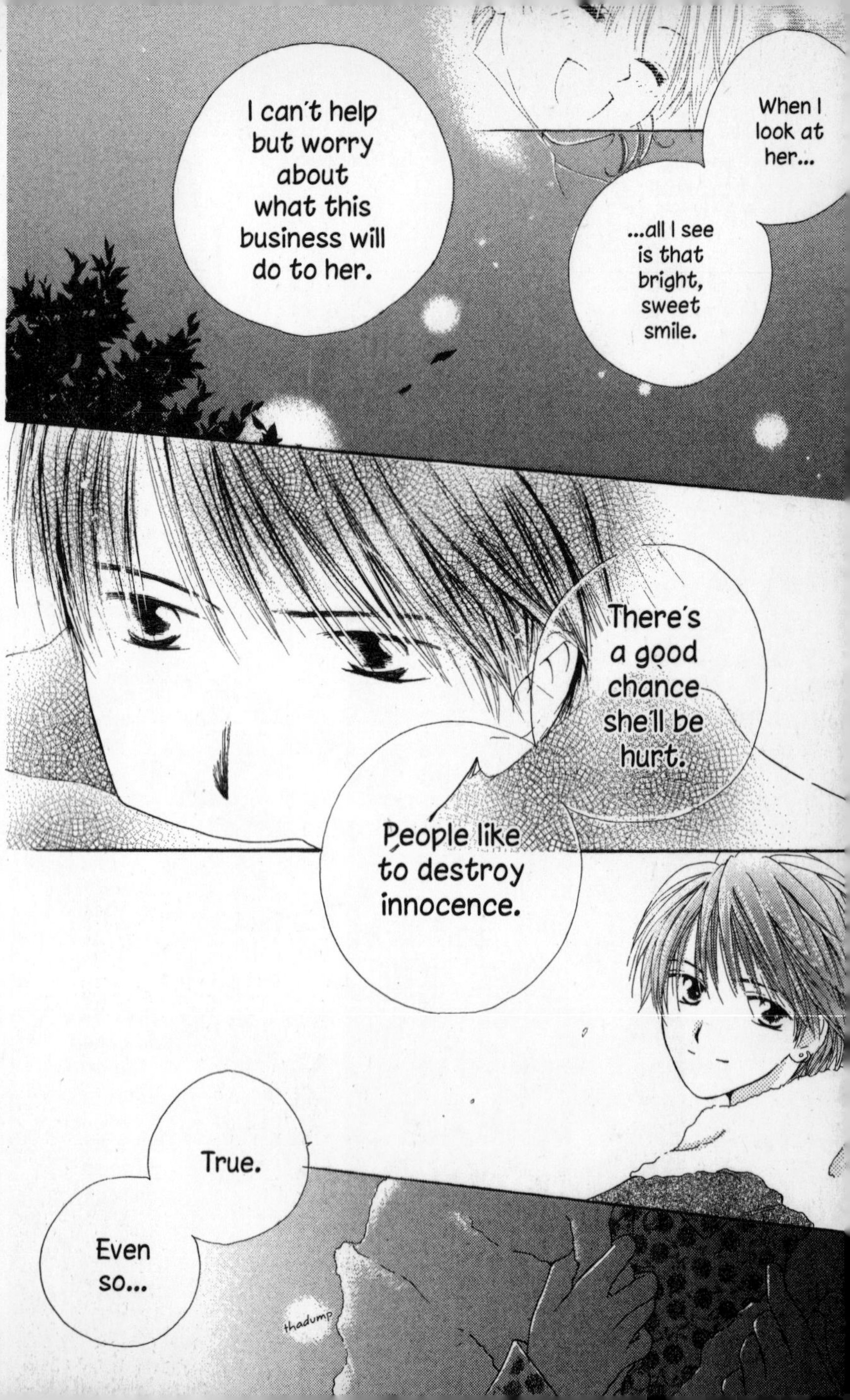
When I look at her...
...all I see is that bright, sweet smile.
I can't help but worry about what this business will do to her.
There's a good chance she'll be hurt.
People like to destroy innocence.
True.
Even so...
thadump

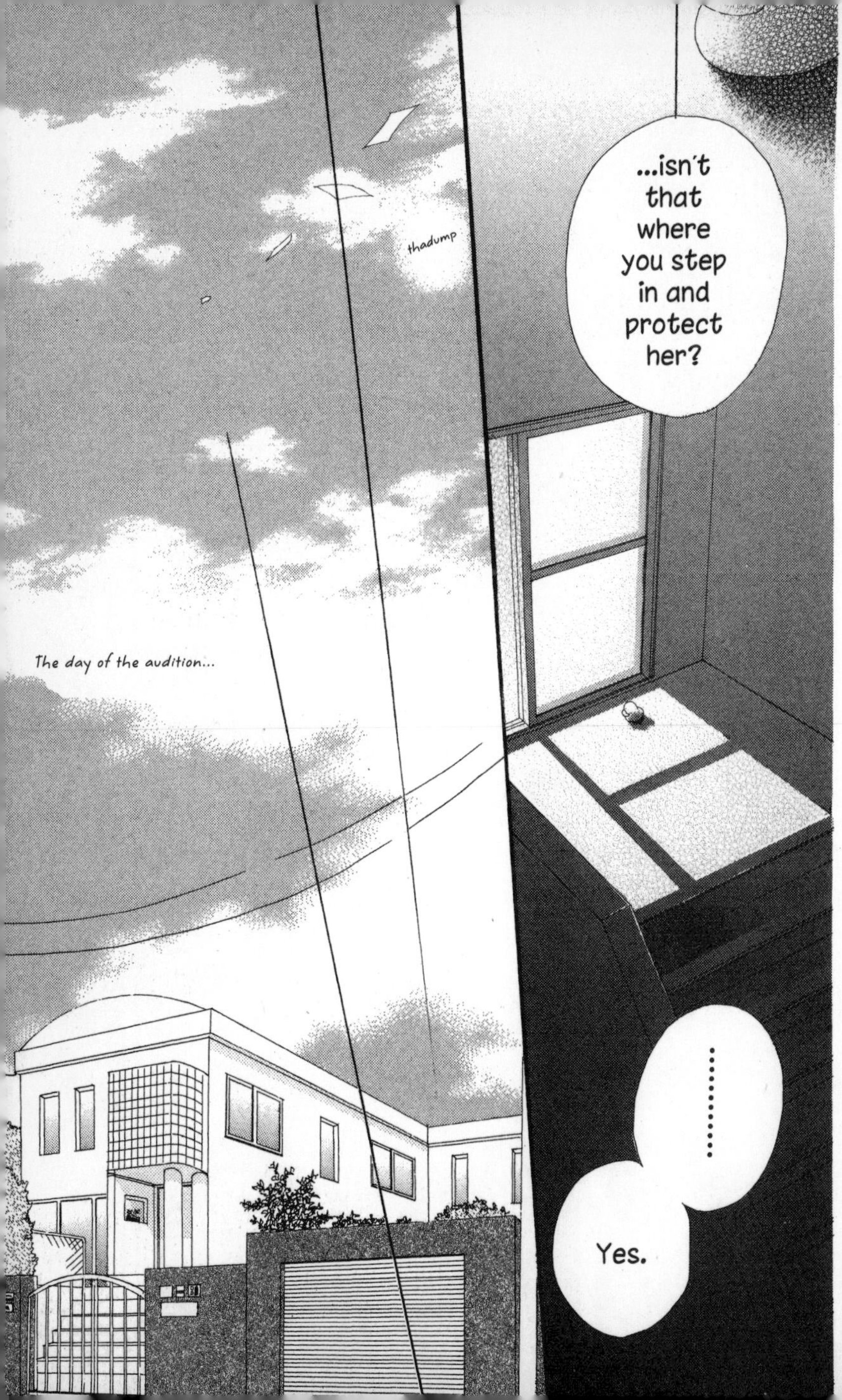
...isn't that where you step in and protect her?
....
Yes.
thadump
The day of the audition...

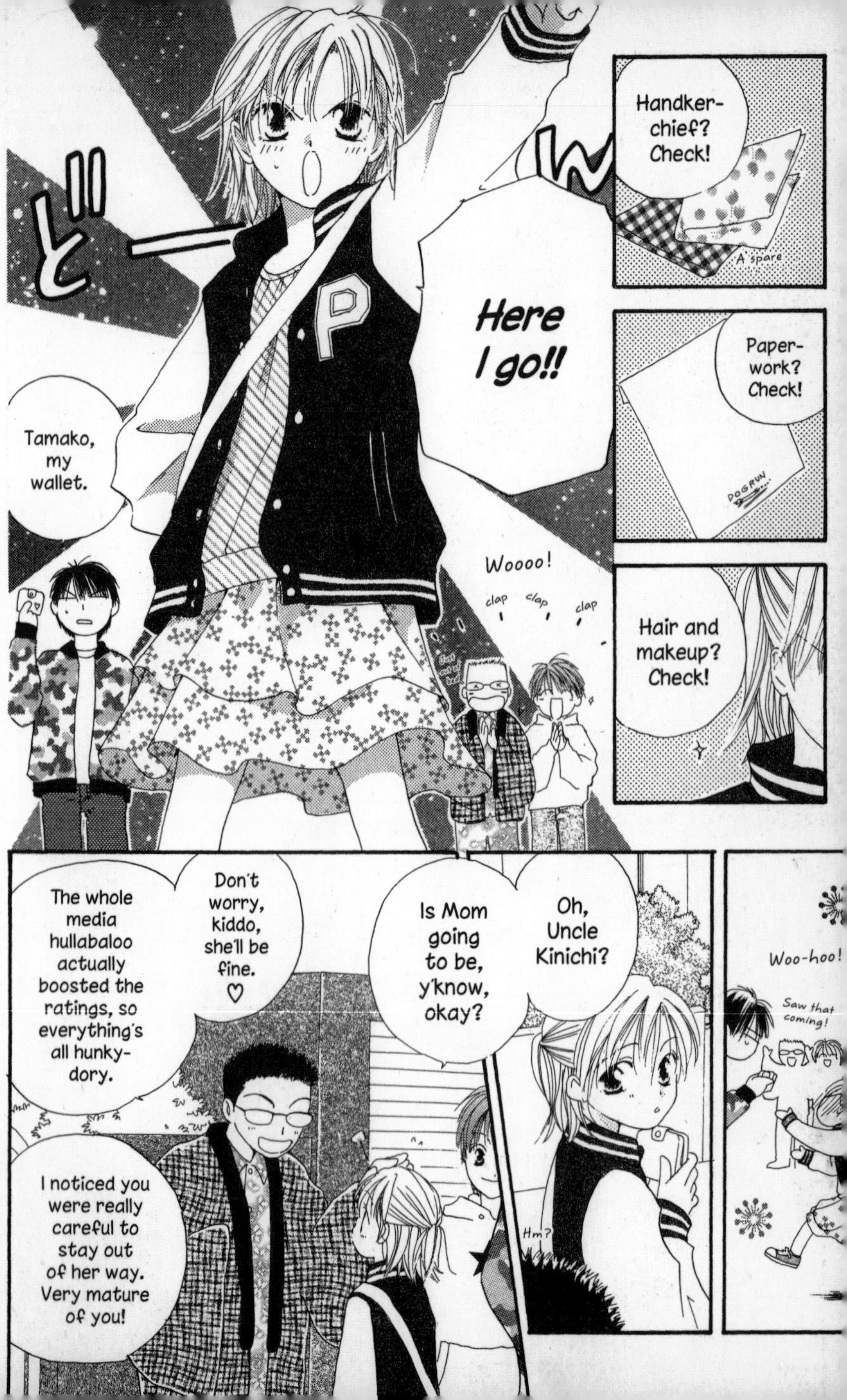
Handker-chief? Check!
A spare
Paper-work? Check!
DOGRUN
Hair and makeup? Check!
Here I go!!
Woooo!
clap clap clap
Tamako, my wallet.
Woo-hoo!
Saw that coming!
Oh, Uncle Kinichi?
Is Mom going to be, y'know, okay?
Hm?
Don't worry, kiddo, she'll be fine. ♡
The whole media hullabaloo actually boosted the ratings, so everything's all hunky-dory.
I noticed you were really careful to stay out of her way. Very mature of you!

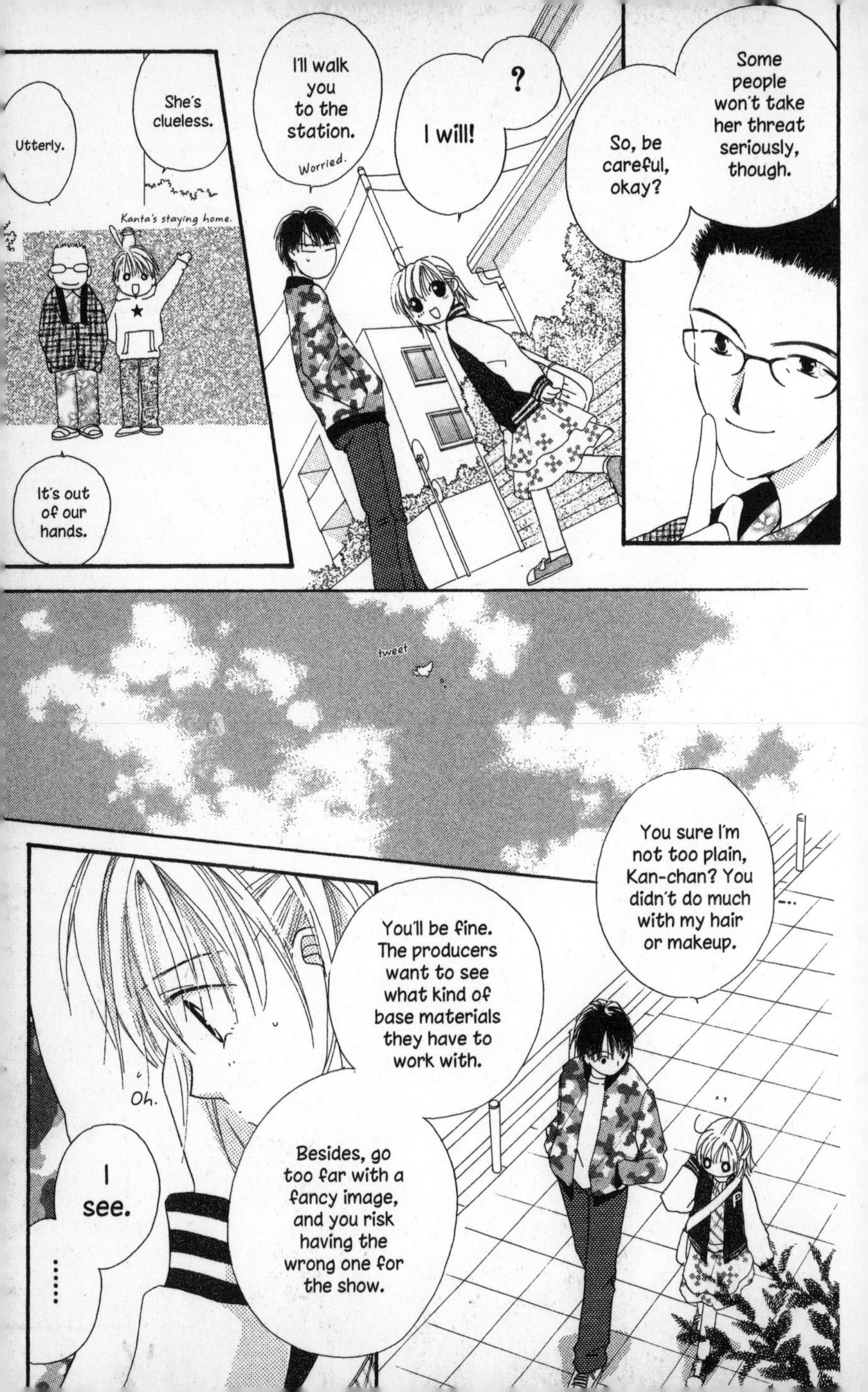
Some people won't take her threat seriously, though.
So, be careful, okay?
?
I will!
I'll walk you to the station.
Worried.
She's clueless.
Utterly.
Kanta's staying home.
It's out of our hands.
tweet
You sure I'm not too plain, Kan-chan? You didn't do much with my hair or makeup.
...
You'll be fine. The producers want to see what kind of base materials they have to work with.
Besides, go too far with a fancy image, and you risk having the wrong one for the show.
Oh.
I see.
......

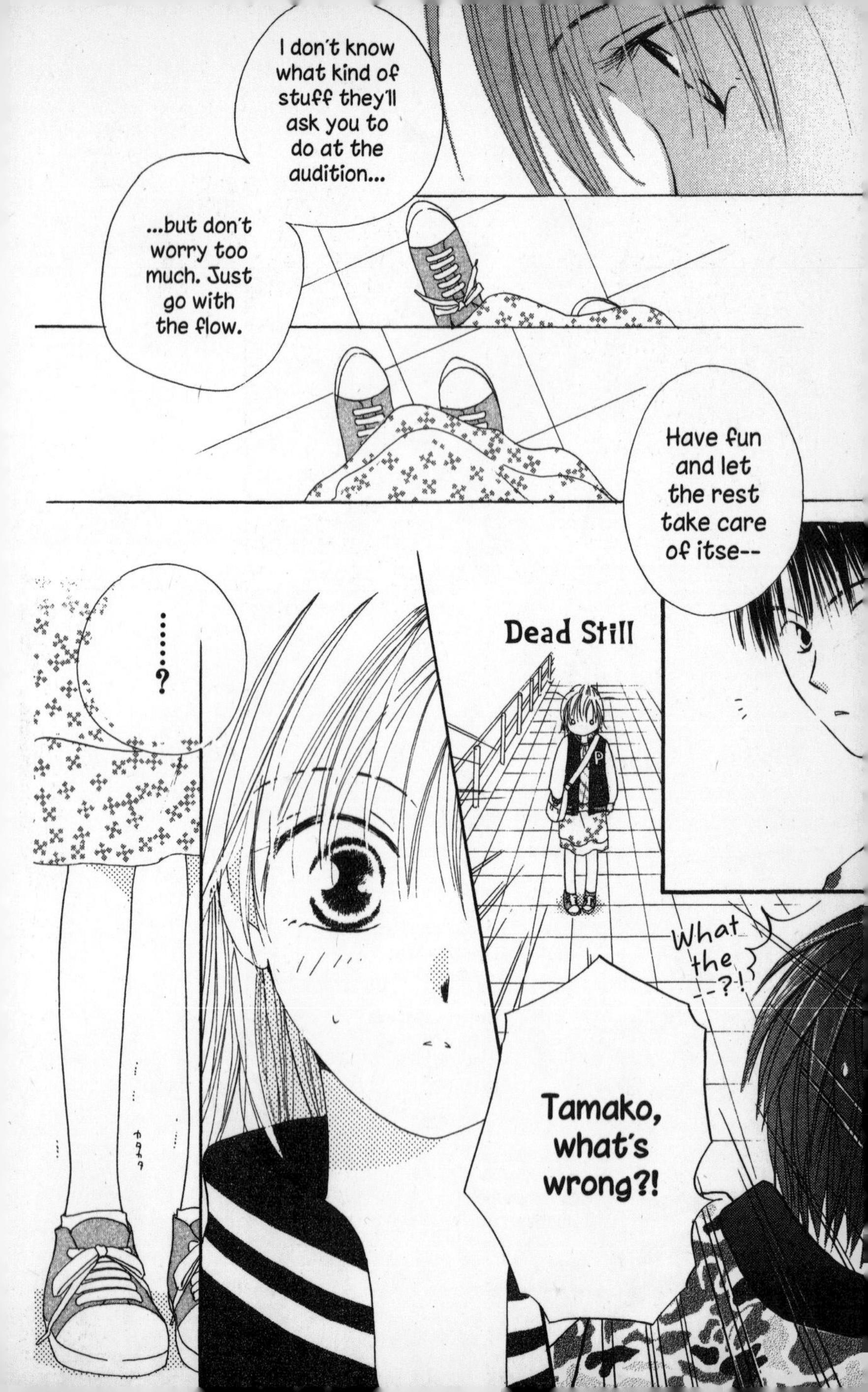
I don't know what kind of stuff they'll ask you to do at the audition...
...but don't worry too much. Just go with the flow.
Have fun and let the rest take care of itse--
Dead Still
What the--?!
Tamako, what's wrong?!
......?

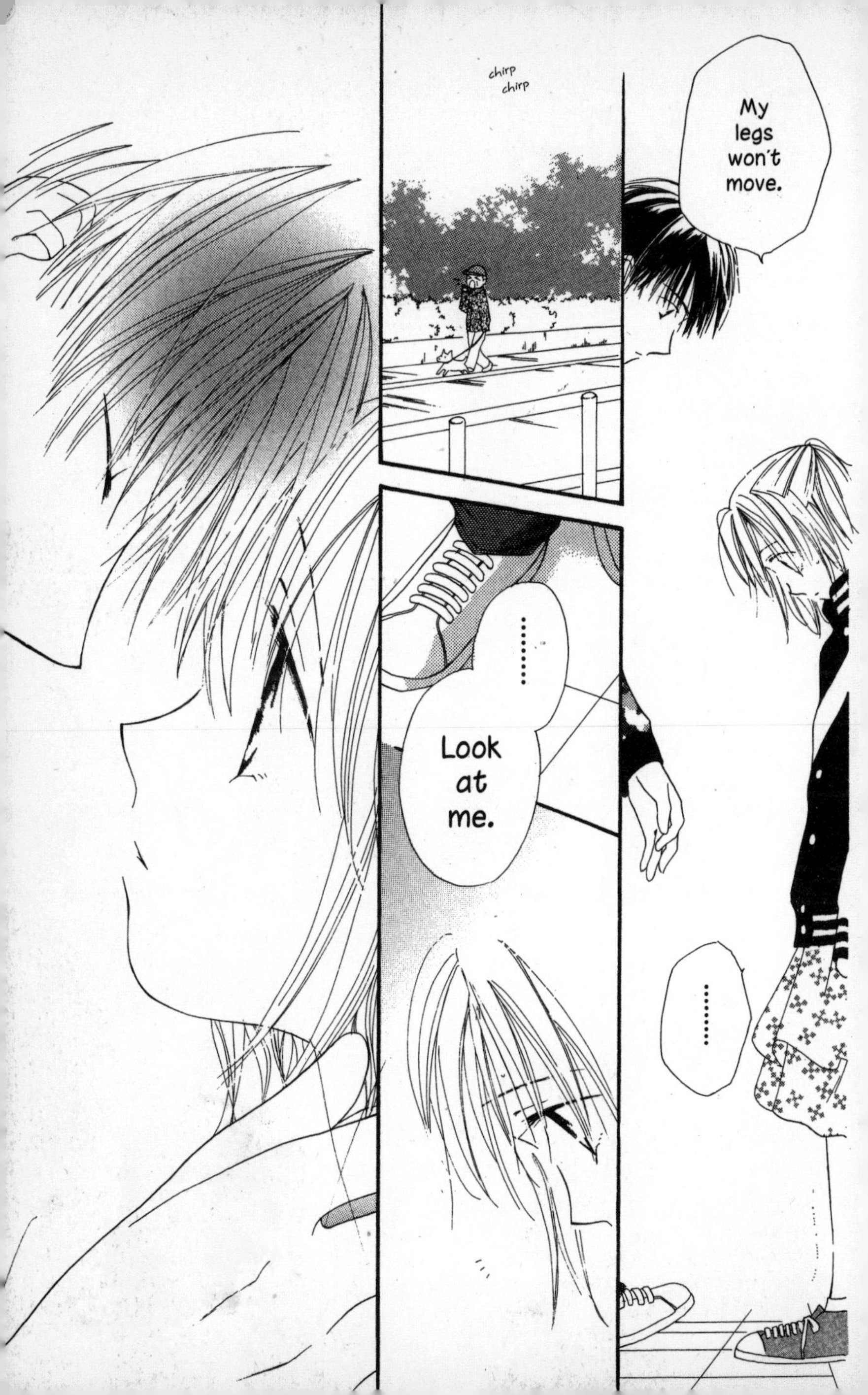
My legs won't move.
......
chirp chirp
......
Look at me.

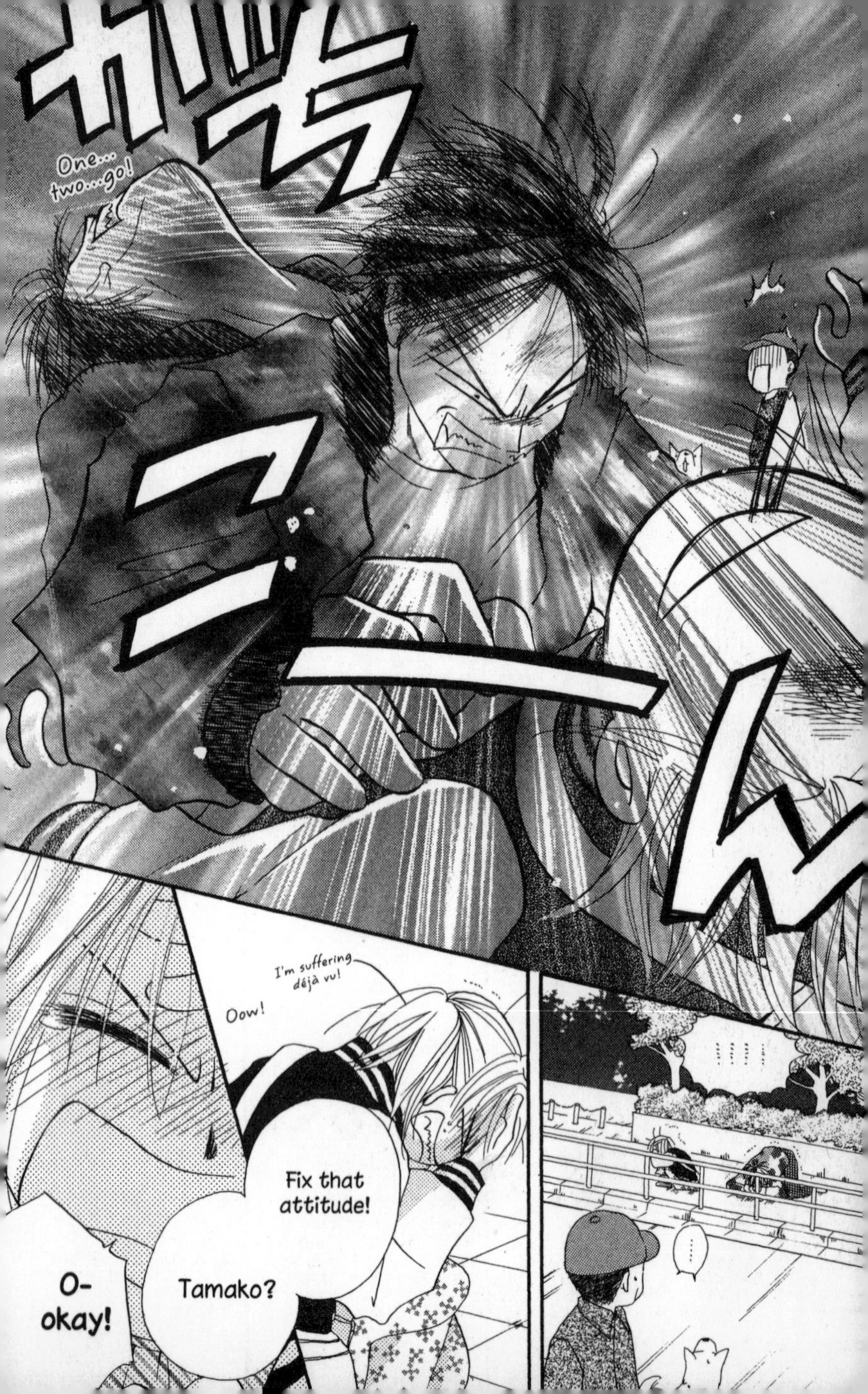

One... two...go!
I'm suffering déjà vu!
Oow!
Fix that attitude!
Tamako?
O- okay!

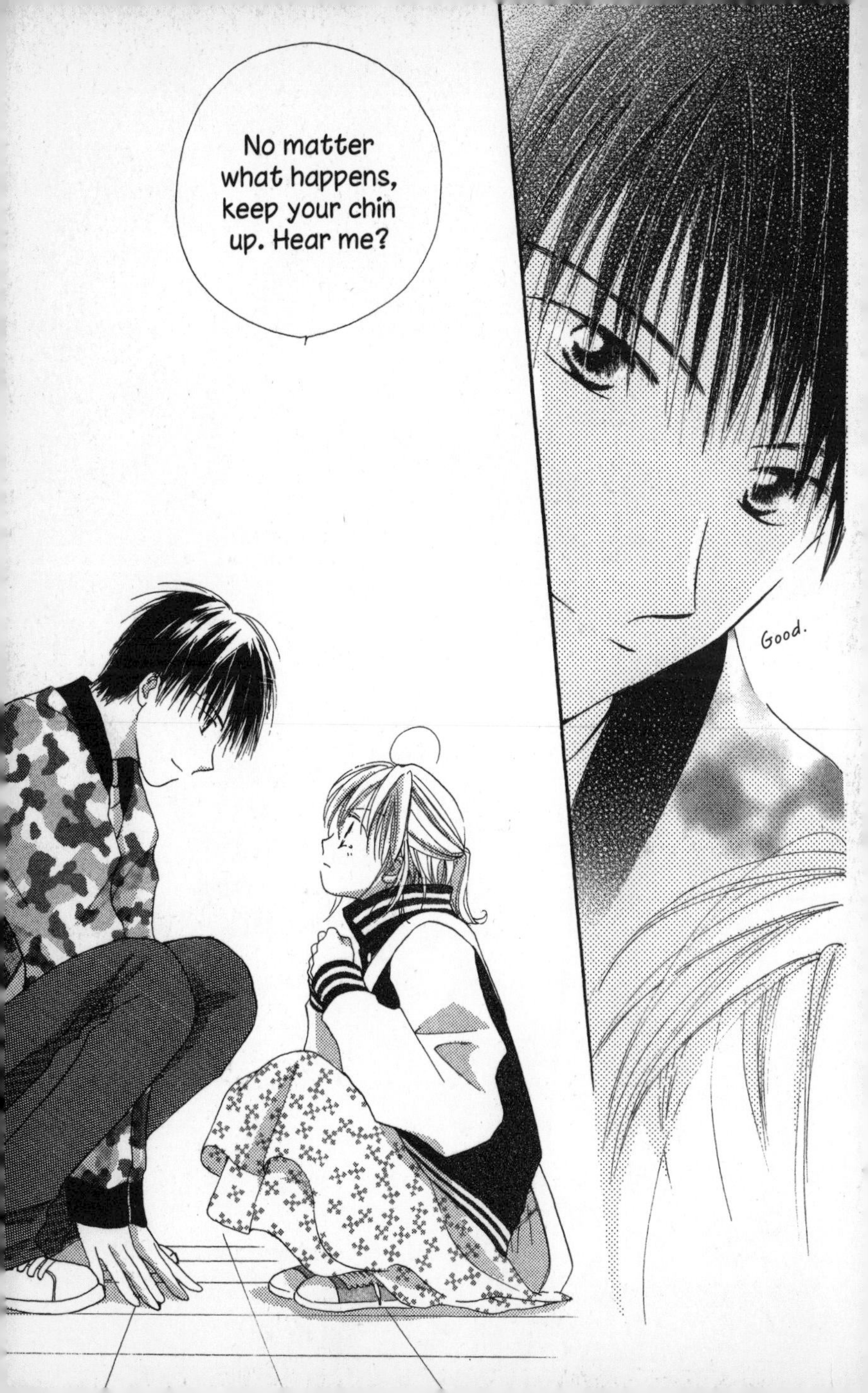
Good.
No matter what happens, keep your chin up. Hear me?

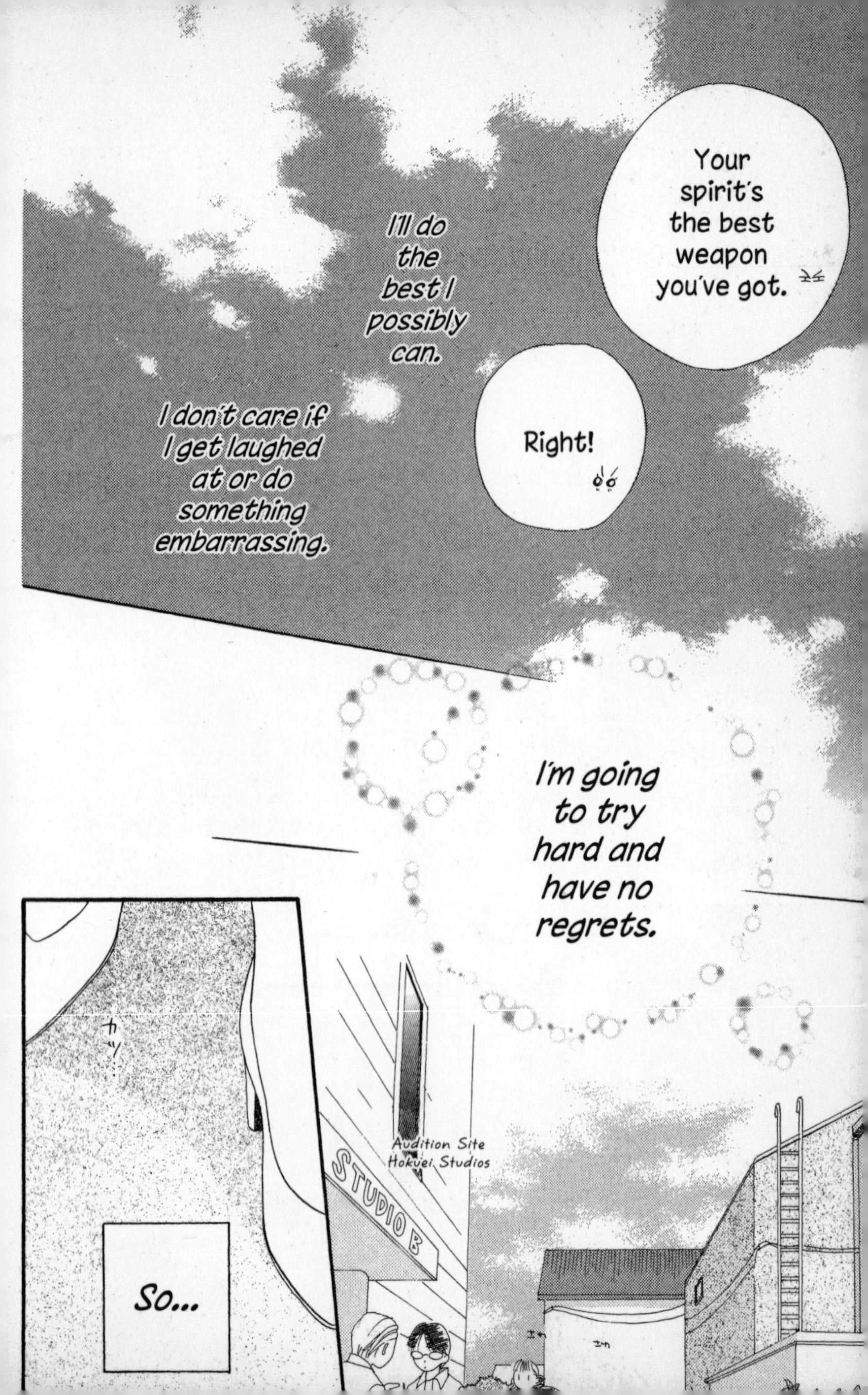
Your spirit's the best weapon you've got.
Right!
I'll do the best I possibly can.
I don't care if I get laughed at or do something embarrassing.
I'm going to try hard and have no regrets.
Audition Site
Hokuei Studios
STUDIO B
So...

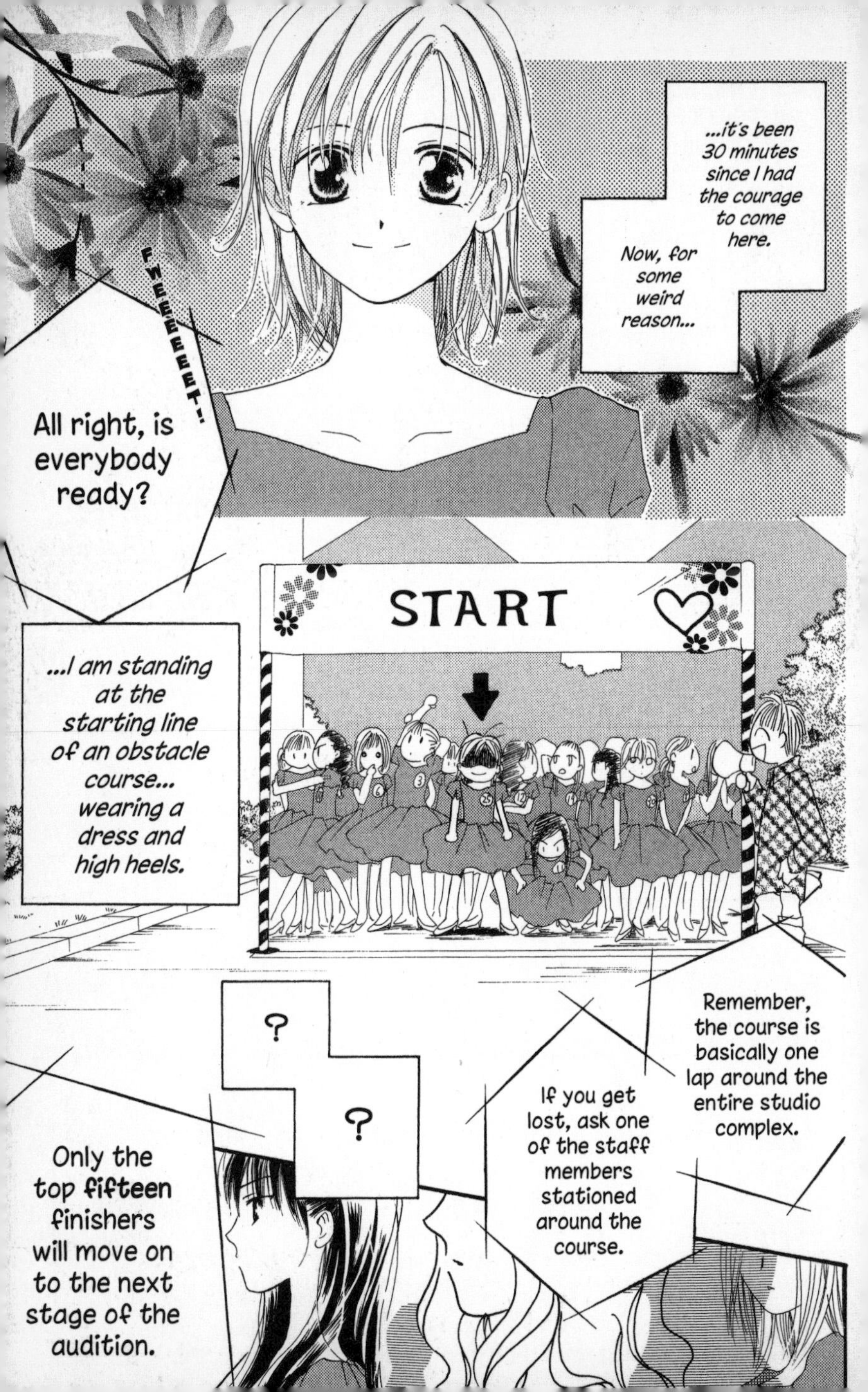
...it's been 30 minutes since I had the courage to come here.
Now, for some weird reason...
FWEEEEEEET!
All right, is everybody ready?
START
...I am standing at the starting line of an obstacle course... wearing a dress and high heels.
Remember, the course is basically one lap around the entire studio complex.
If you get lost, ask one of the staff members stationed around the course.
?
?
Only the top fifteen finishers will move on to the next stage of the audition.

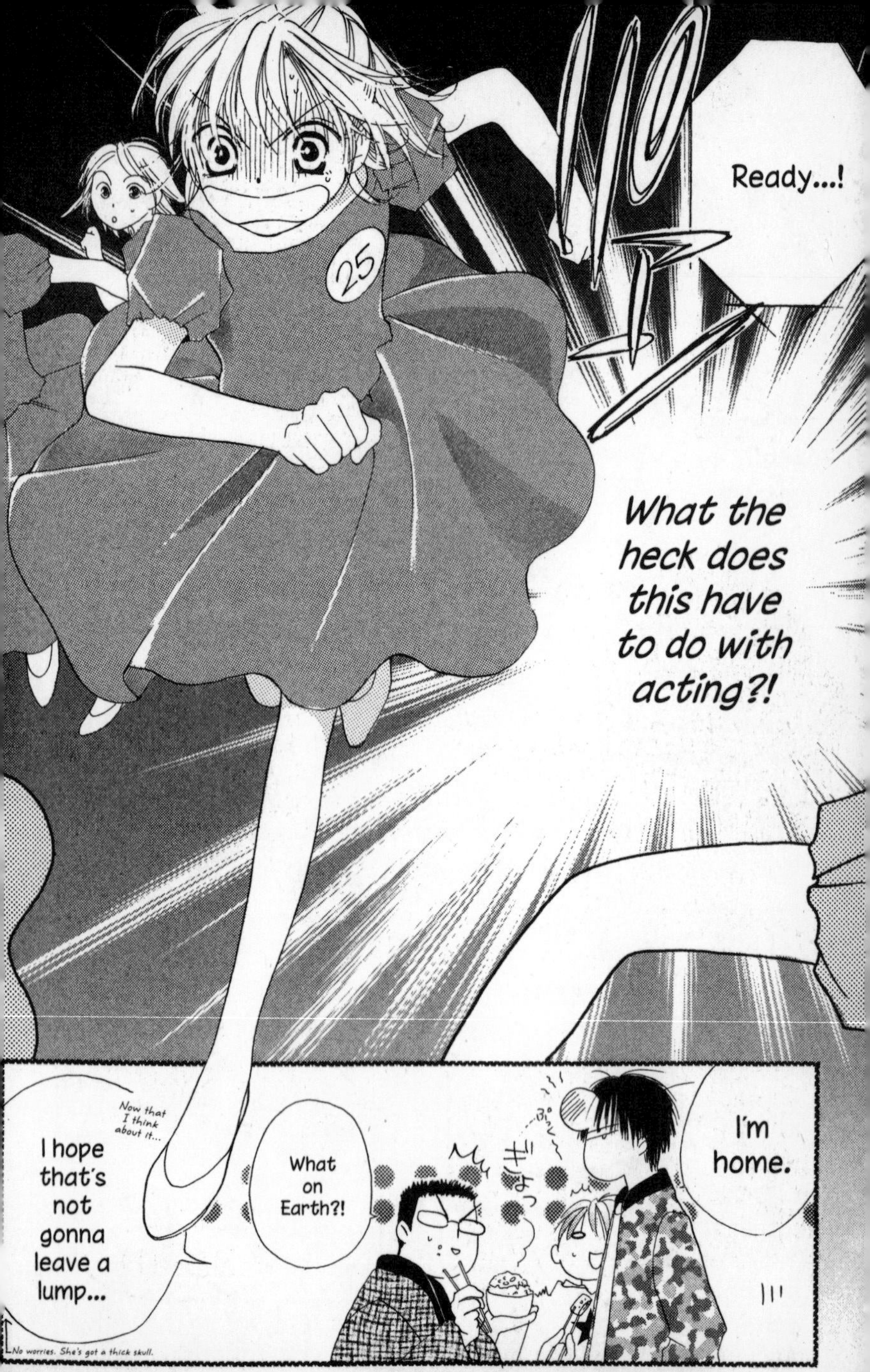

Ready...!
What the heck does this have to do with acting?!
I'm home.
ぎょっ
What on Earth?!
Now that I think about it...
I hope that's not gonna leave a lump...
No worries. She's got a thick skull.

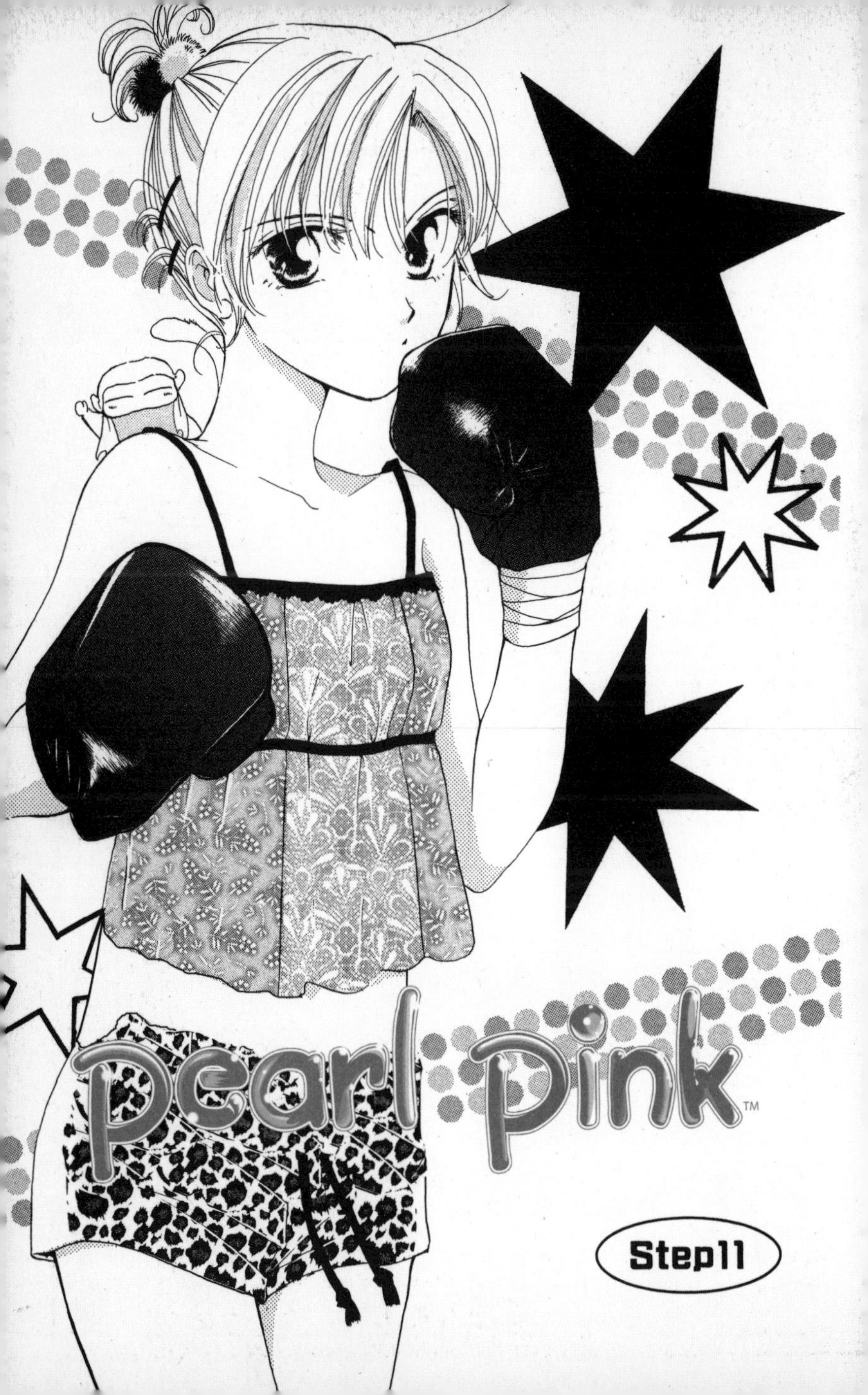
pearl pink™
Step11

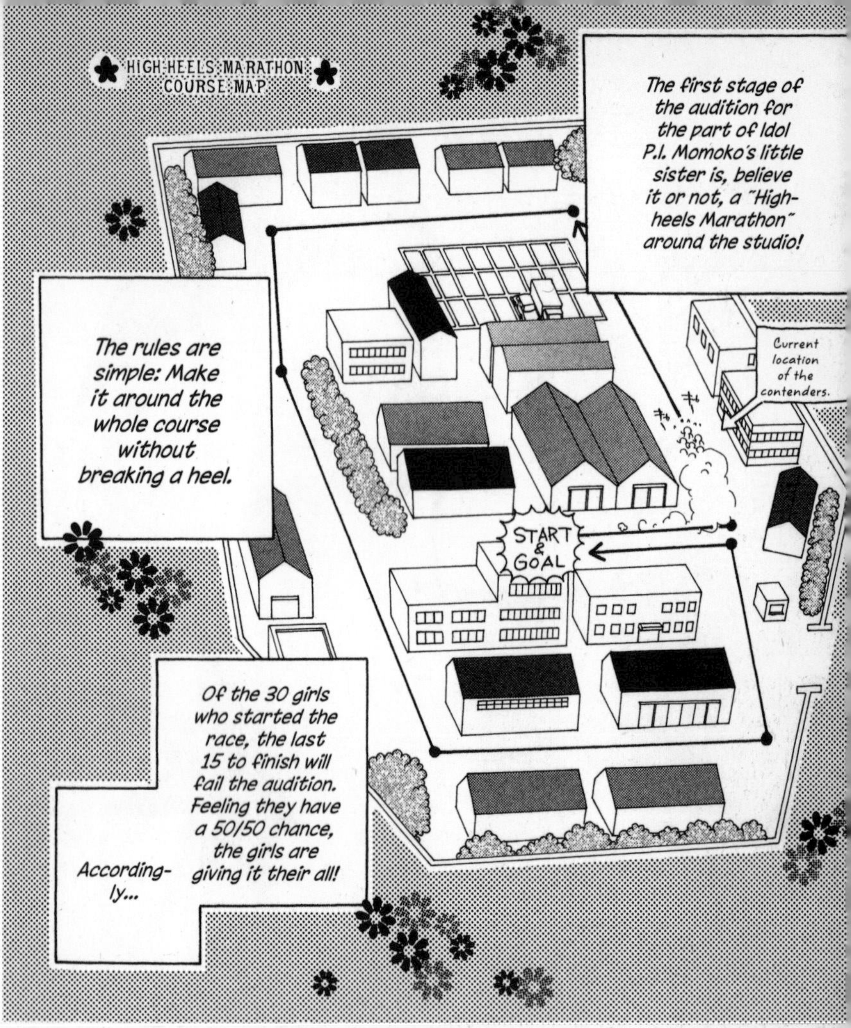
HIGH-HEELS MARATHON COURSE MAP
The first stage of the audition for the part of Idol P.I. Momoko's little sister is, believe it or not, a "High-heels Marathon" around the studio!
The rules are simple: Make it around the whole course without breaking a heel.
Current location of the contenders.
START & GOAL
Of the 30 girls who started the race, the last 15 to finish will fail the audition. Feeling they have a 50/50 chance, the girls are giving it their all!
According-ly...

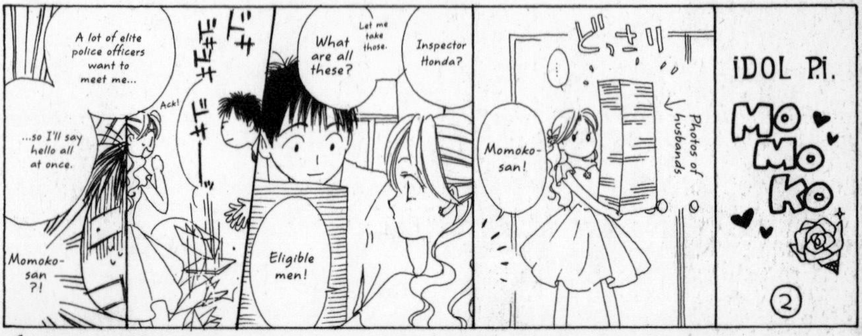
IDOL P.I.
MOMOKO
②
...
Momoko-san!
Photos of husbands
Inspector Honda?
What are all these?
Let me take those.
Eligible men!
A lot of elite police officers want to meet me...
...so I'll say hello all at once.
Ack!
Momoko-san ?!

←Cont. on pg 69...

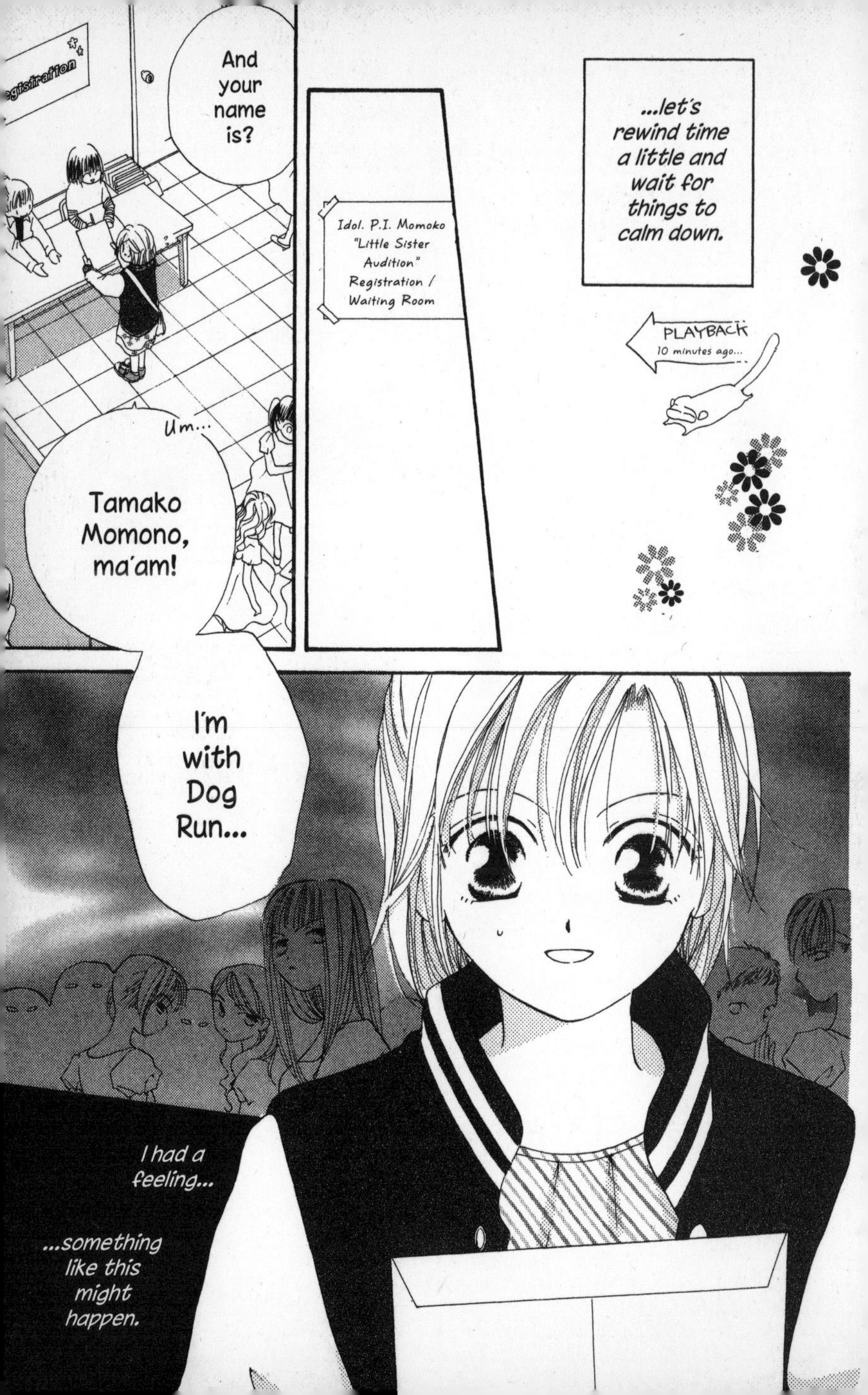
...let's rewind time a little and wait for things to calm down.
PLAYBACK
10 minutes ago...
Idol. P.I. Momoko "Little Sister Audition" Registration / Waiting Room
And your name is?
Um...
Tamako Momono, ma'am!
I'm with Dog Run...
I had a feeling...
...something like this might happen.

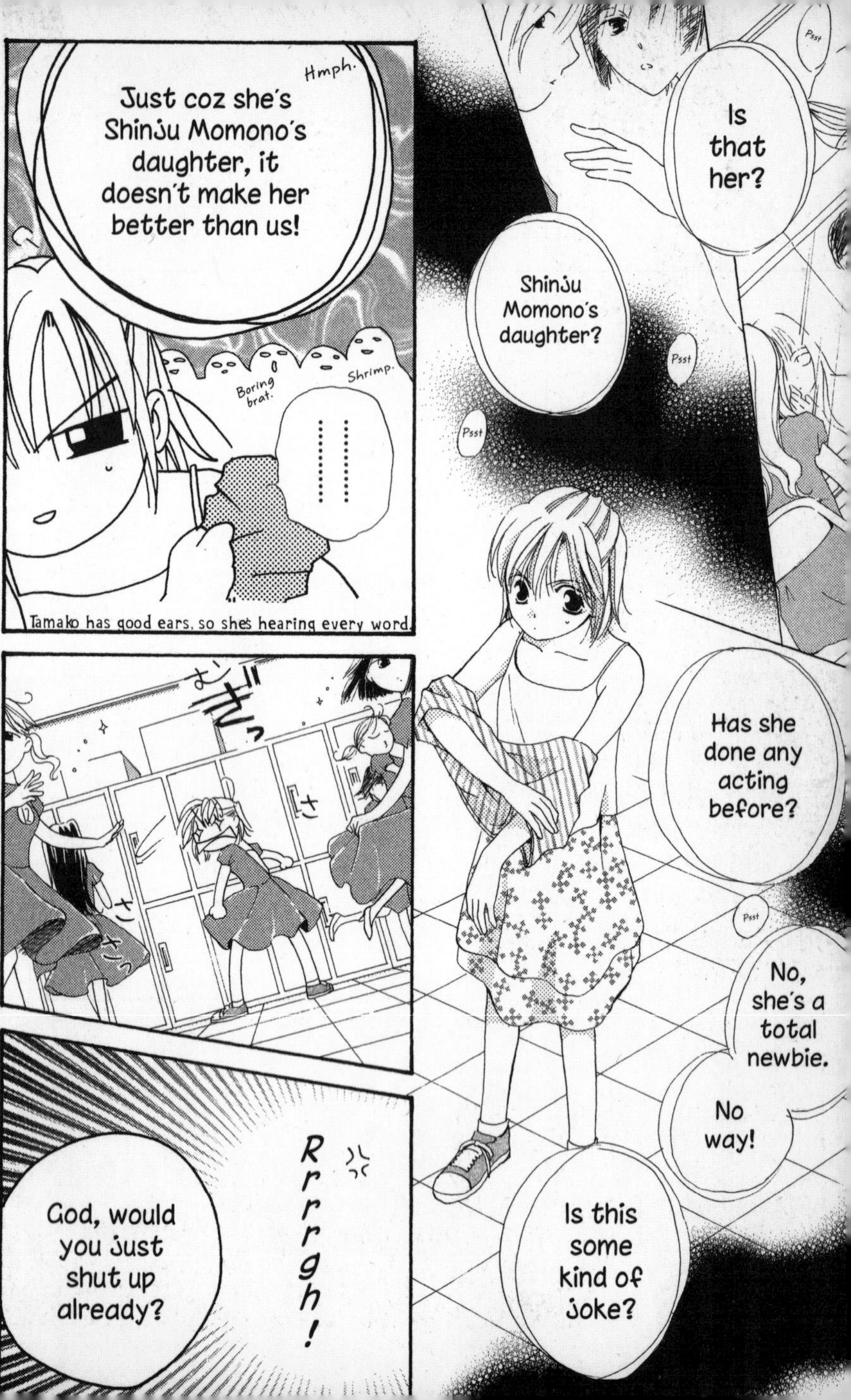
Psst
Is that her?
Shinju Momono's daughter?
Psst
Psst
Has she done any acting before?
Psst
No, she's a total newbie.
No way!
Is this some kind of joke?
Hmph.
Just coz she's Shinju Momono's daughter, it doesn't make her better than us!
Shrimp.
Boring brat.
......
Tamako has good ears, so she's hearing every word.
Rrrrgh!
God, would you just shut up already?

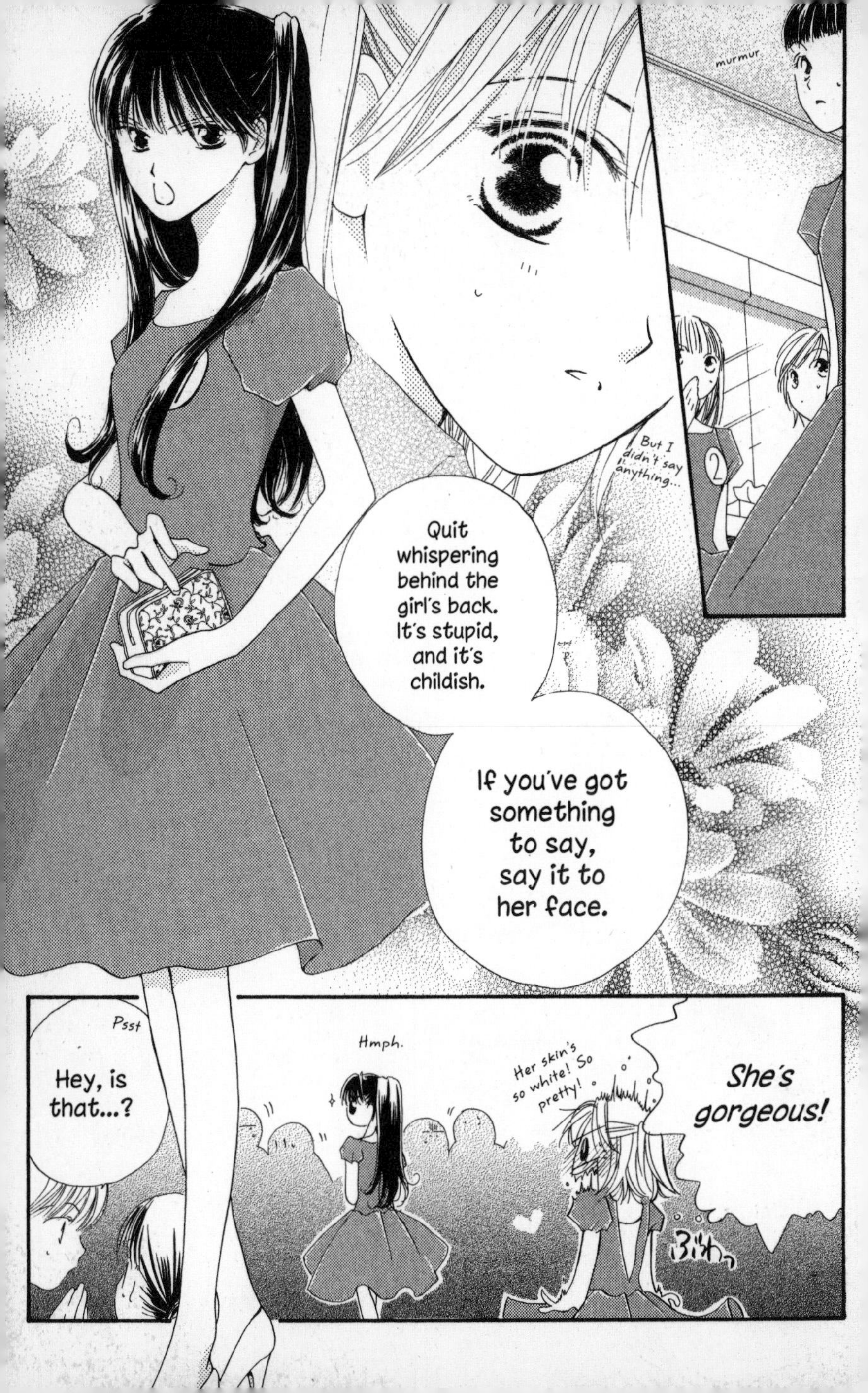
murmur
But I didn't say anything...
2
Quit whispering behind the girl's back. It's stupid, and it's childish.
If you've got something to say, say it to her face.
She's gorgeous!
ふわっ
Her skin's so white! So pretty!
Hmph.
Psst
Hey, is that...?

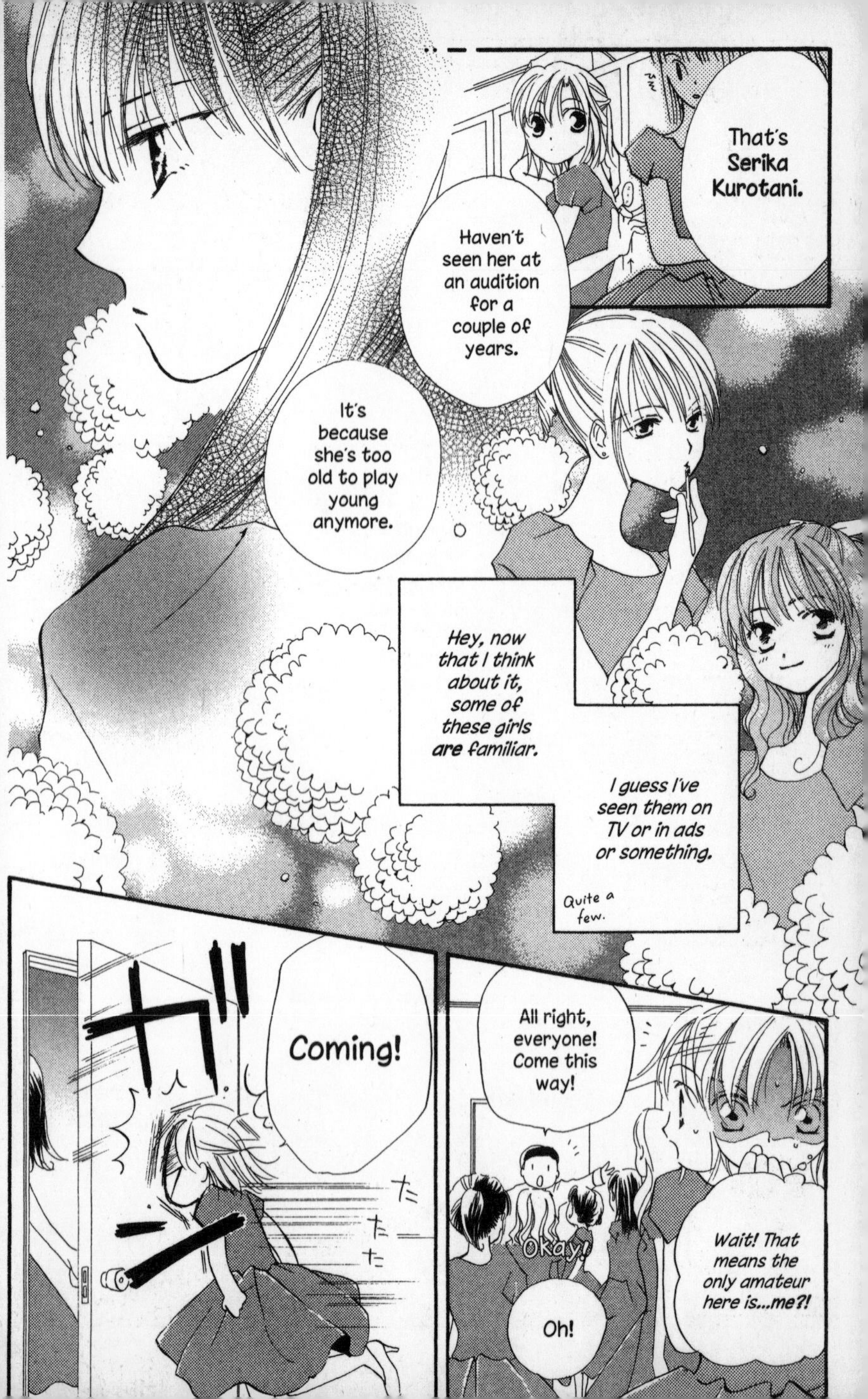
That's Serika Kurotani.
Haven't seen her at an audition for a couple of years.
It's because she's too old to play young anymore.
Hey, now that I think about it, some of these girls are familiar.
I guess I've seen them on TV or in ads or something.
Quite a few.
All right, everyone! Come this way!
Okay!
Oh!
Wait! That means the only amateur here is...me?!
Coming!

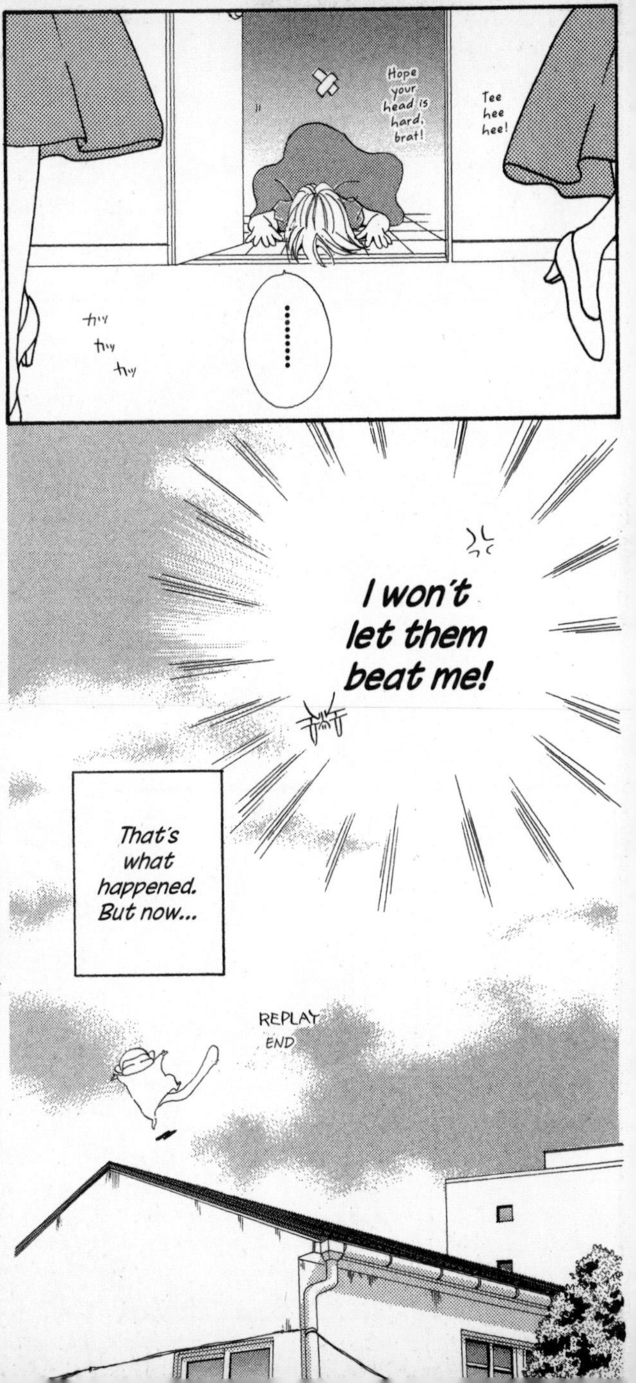
Tee hee hee!
Hope your head is hard, brat!
....
I won't let them beat me!
That's what happened. But now...
REPLAY END

DRAMA CD

Not only did I get to do a Dramatic CD for my previous manga, Omukae Desu, but now they're asking me to do one for Pearl Pink, too!

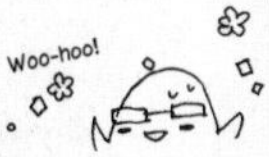
Woo-hoo!

Right now, as I'm writing these words, I have yet to decide on the story, which characters will be involved or, well, anything at all!

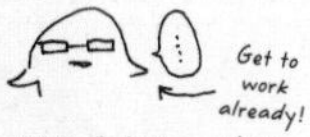
Get to work already!

Well, I do know that I'd like to do something different from what I've already written in the manga. In fact, if possible, I'd really, really love to do something with the bonus comic strip, "Idol P.I. Momoko." It's already set up as something fun and a little edgy, so I want to see how far I can push things. Heh heh. Anyone who is curious, please feel free to pick up the CD and have a listen.

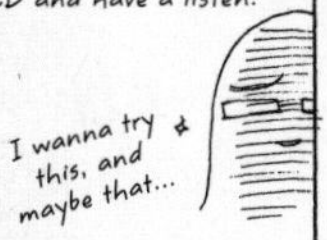
I wanna try this, and maybe that...

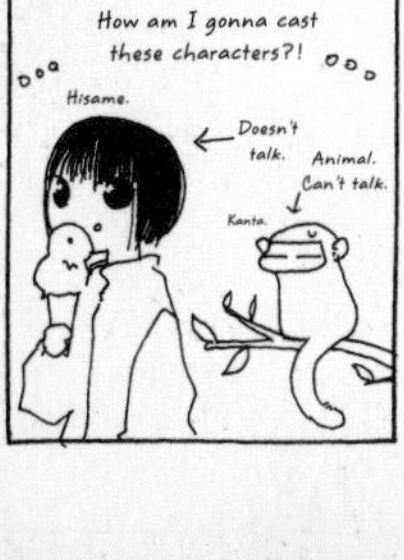
How am I gonna cast these characters?!
Hisame.
Doesn't talk.
Animal. Can't talk.
Kanta.

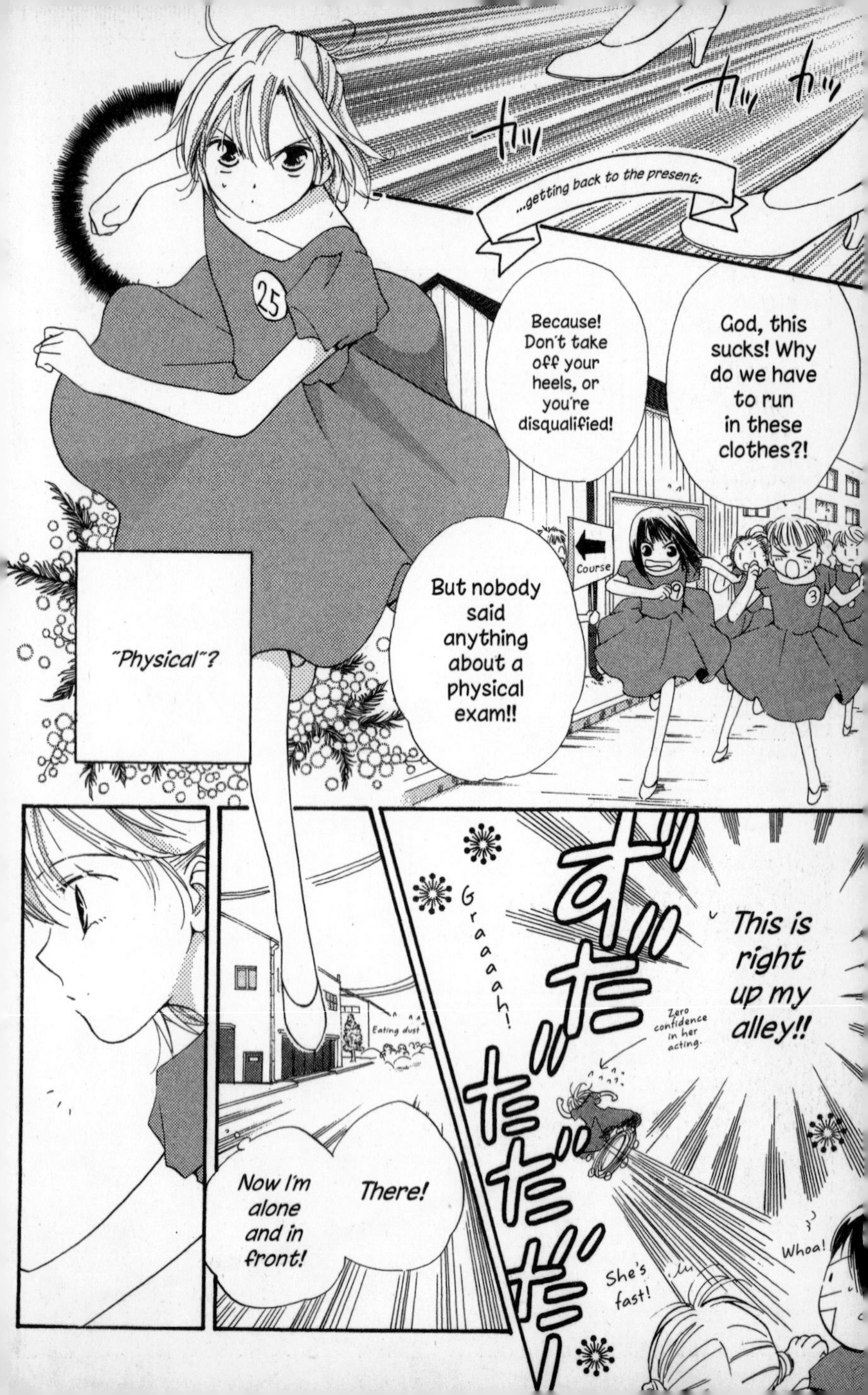

カッ カッ カッ
...getting back to the present:
God, this sucks! Why do we have to run in these clothes?!
Because! Don't take off your heels, or you're disqualified!
Course
But nobody said anything about a physical exam!!
"Physical"?
This is right up my alley!!
Graaaah!
Zero confidence in her acting.
Whoa!
She's fast!
Eating dust
There!
Now I'm alone and in front!

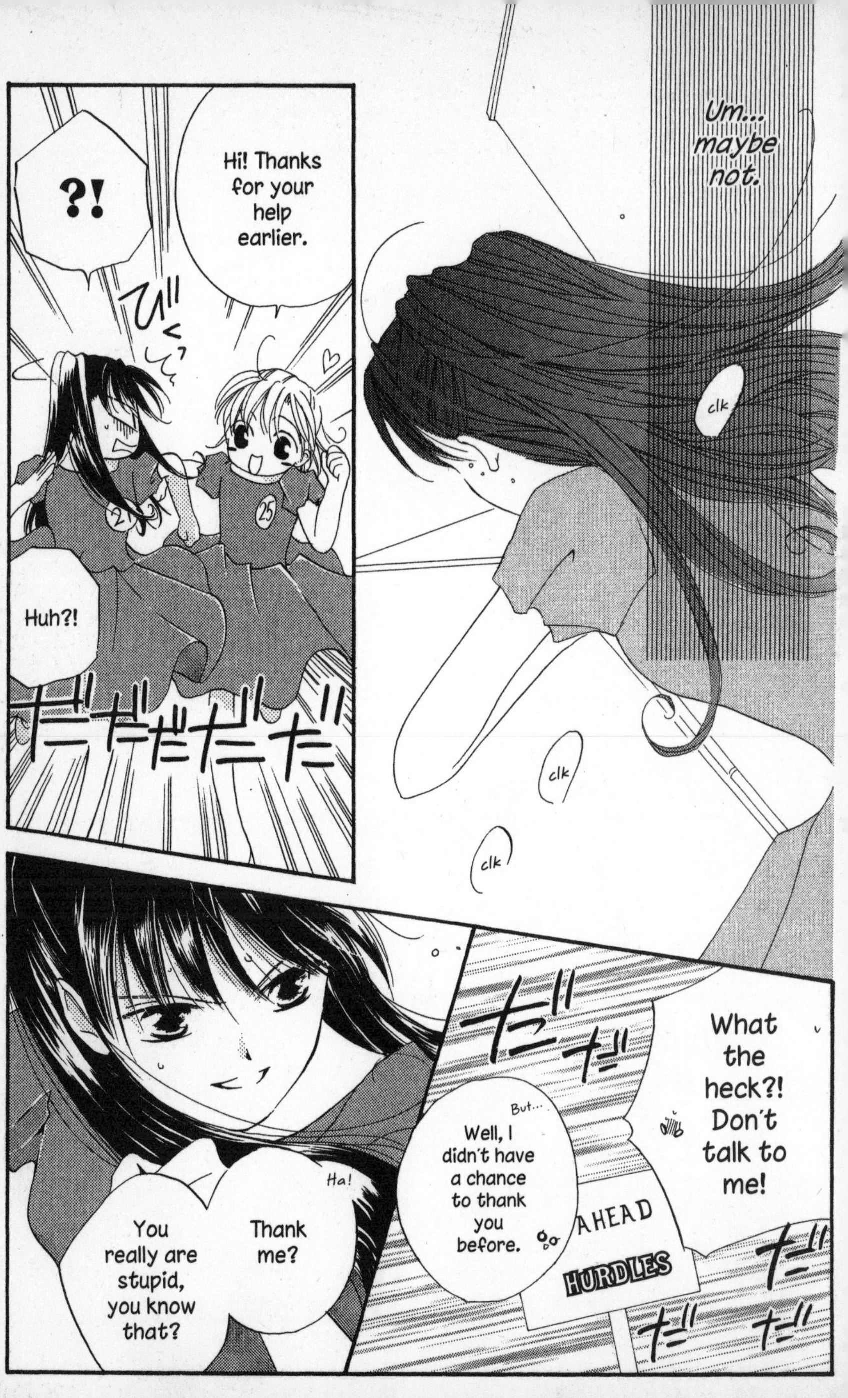
Um... maybe not.
clk
clk
clk
Hi! Thanks for your help earlier.
?!
Huh?!
What the heck?! Don't talk to me!
But...
Well, I didn't have a chance to thank you before.
AHEAD
HURDLES
Thank me?
Ha!
You really are stupid, you know that?

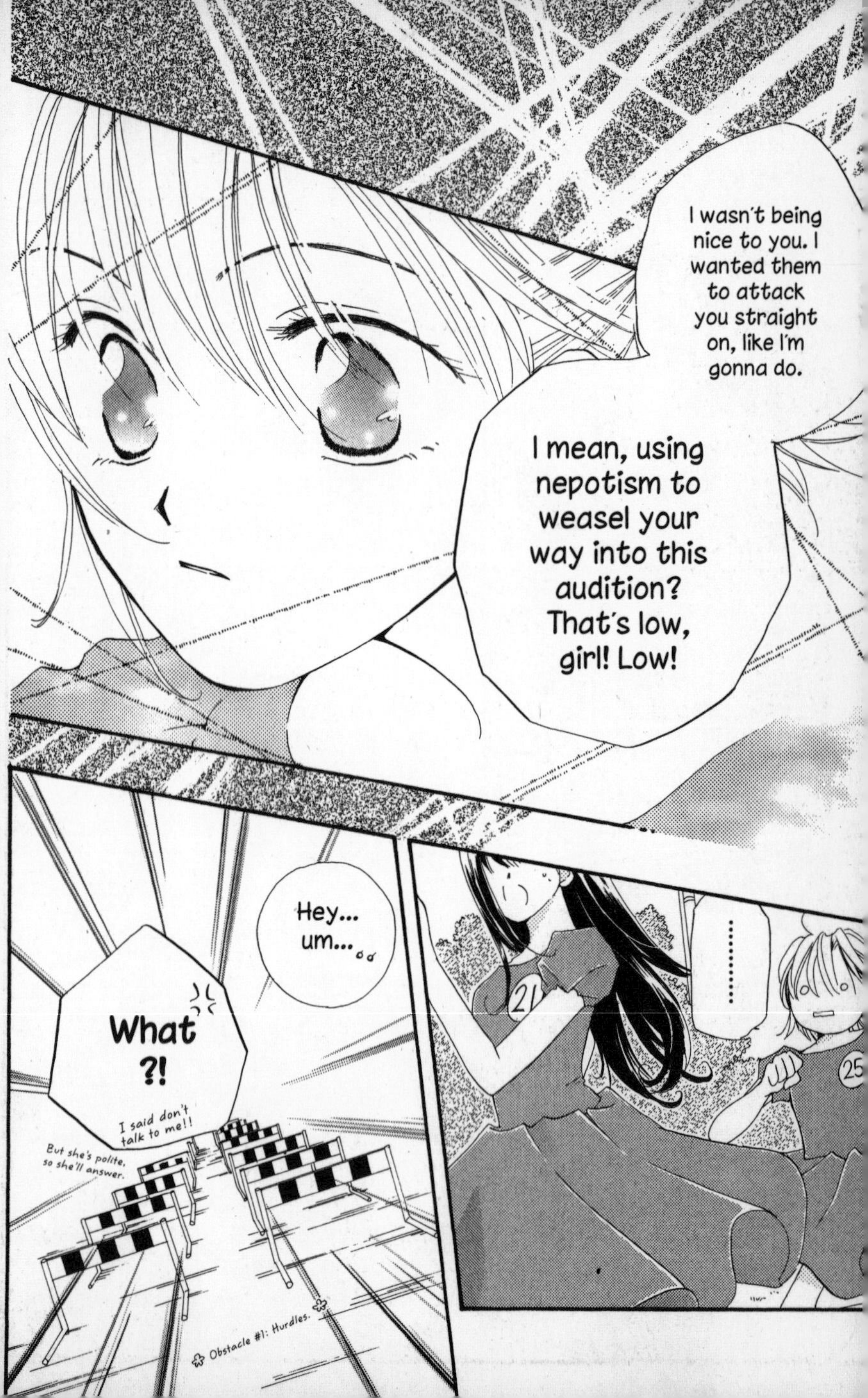
I wasn't being nice to you. I wanted them to attack you straight on, like I'm gonna do.
I mean, using nepotism to weasel your way into this audition? That's low, girl! Low!
......
21
25
Hey... um...
What?!
I said don't talk to me!!
But she's polite, so she'll answer.
Obstacle #1: Hurdles.

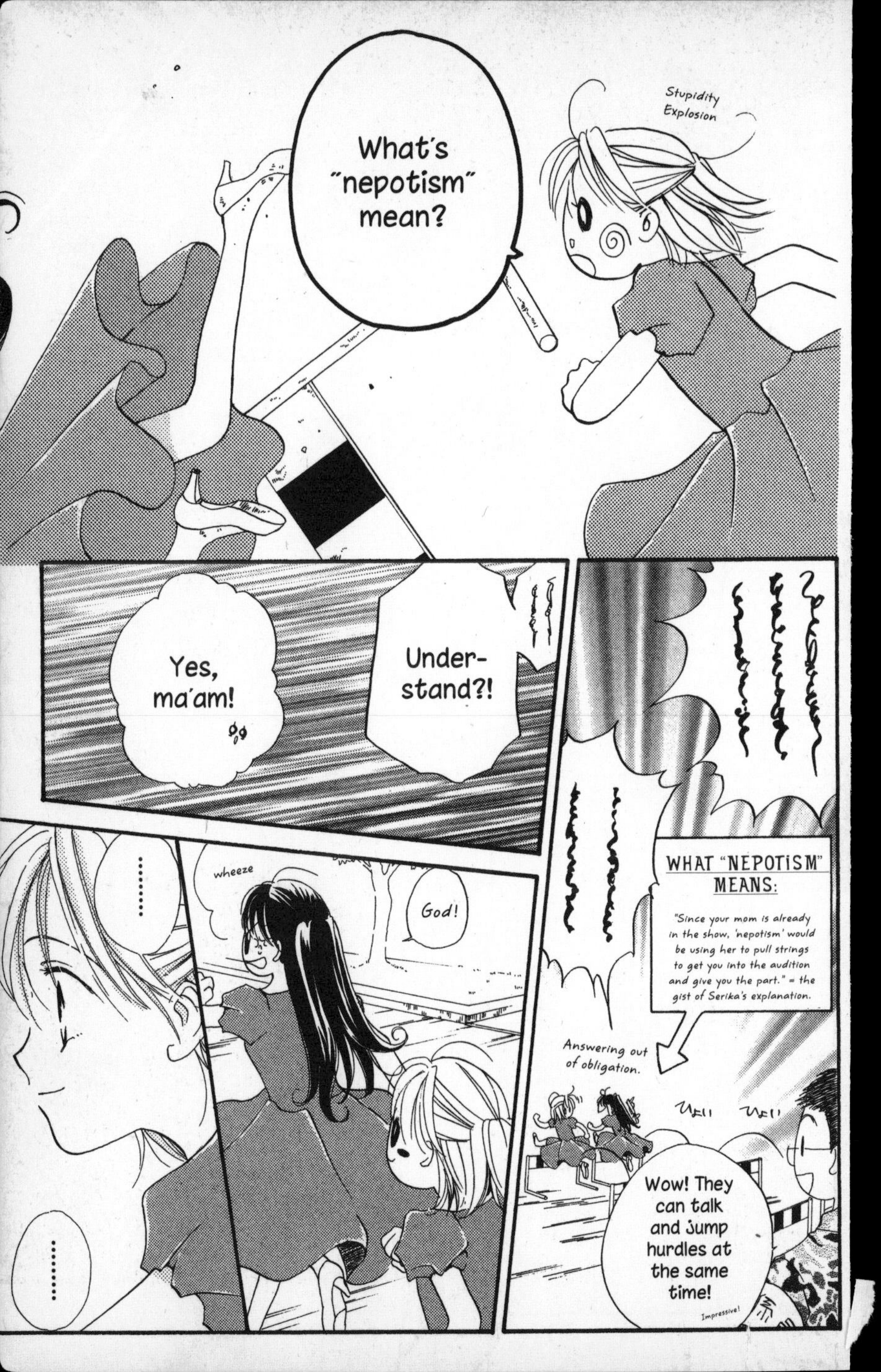
Stupidity Explosion
What's "nepotism" mean?
WHAT "NEPOTISM" MEANS:
"Since your mom is already in the show, 'nepotism' would be using her to pull strings to get you into the audition and give you the part." = the gist of Serika's explanation.
Answering out of obligation.
Wow! They can talk and jump hurdles at the same time!
Impressive!
Under-stand?!
Yes, ma'am!
wheeze
God!
......
......

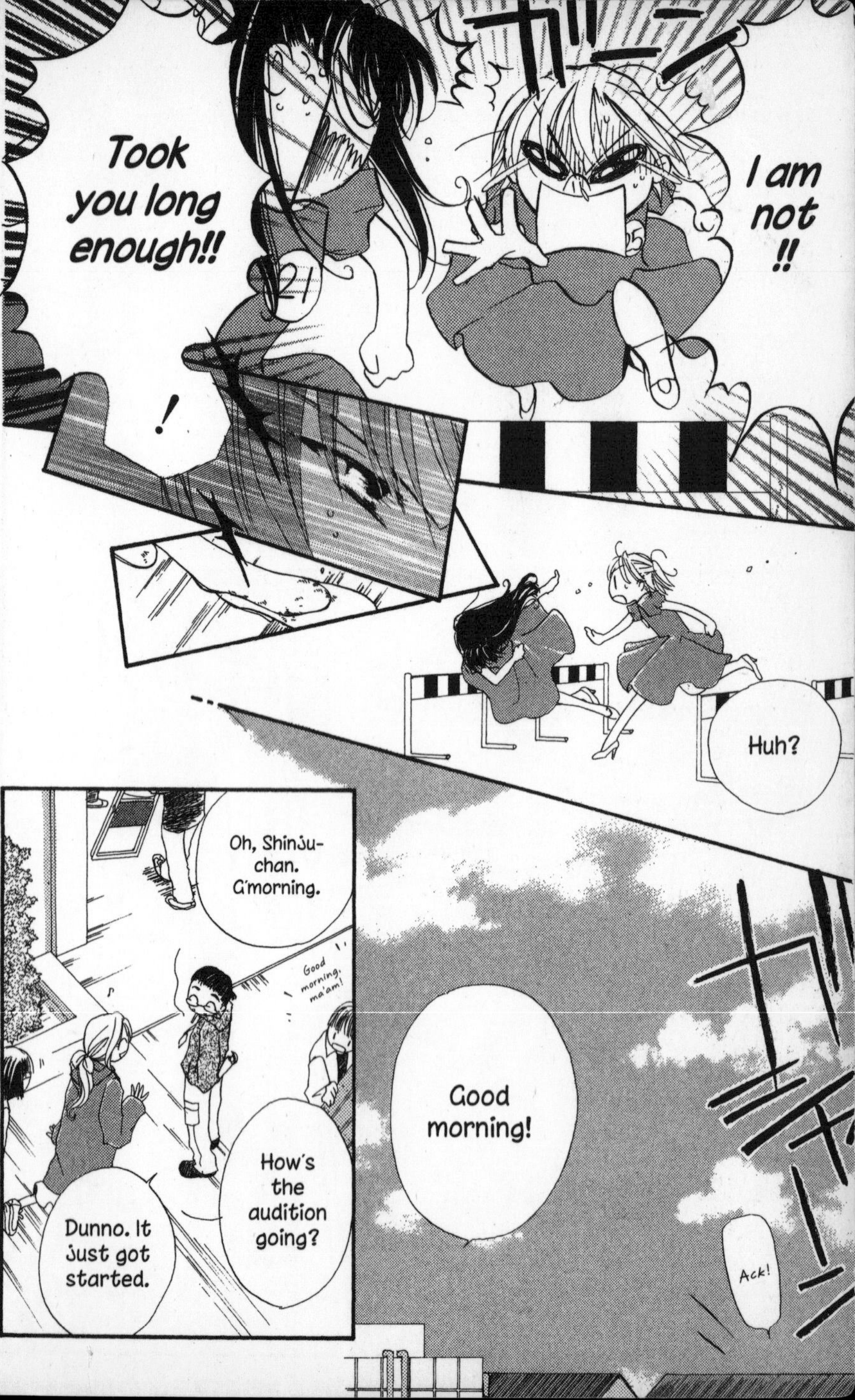
I am not !!
Took you long enough!!
!
Huh?
Good morning!
Ack!
Oh, Shinju-chan. G'morning.
Good morning, ma'am!
How's the audition going?
Dunno. It just got started.

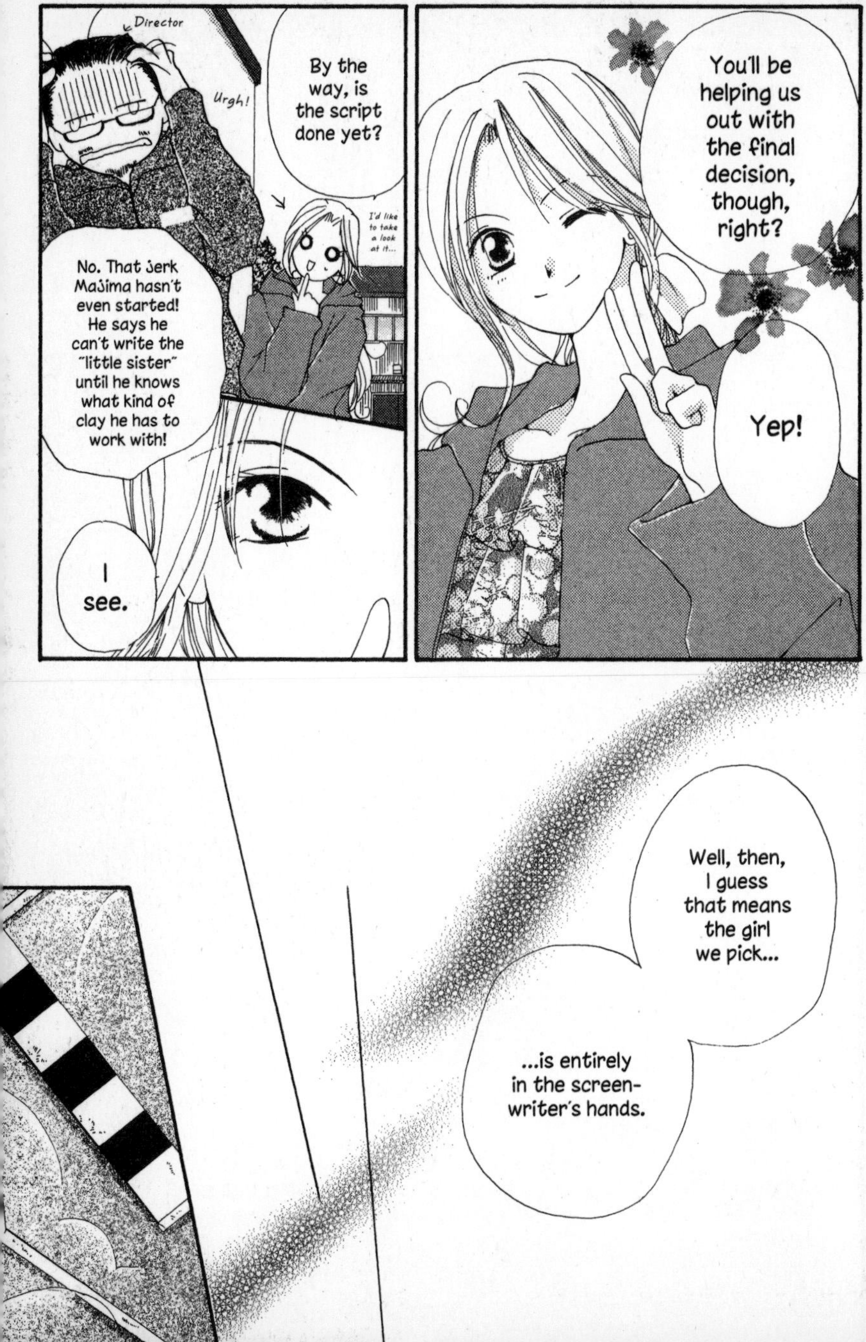
You'll be helping us out with the final decision, though, right?
Yep!
By the way, is the script done yet?
I'd like to take a look at it...
Urgh!
Director
No. That jerk Majima hasn't even started! He says he can't write the "little sister" until he knows what kind of clay he has to work with!
I see.
Well, then, I guess that means the girl we pick...
...is entirely in the screen-writer's hands.

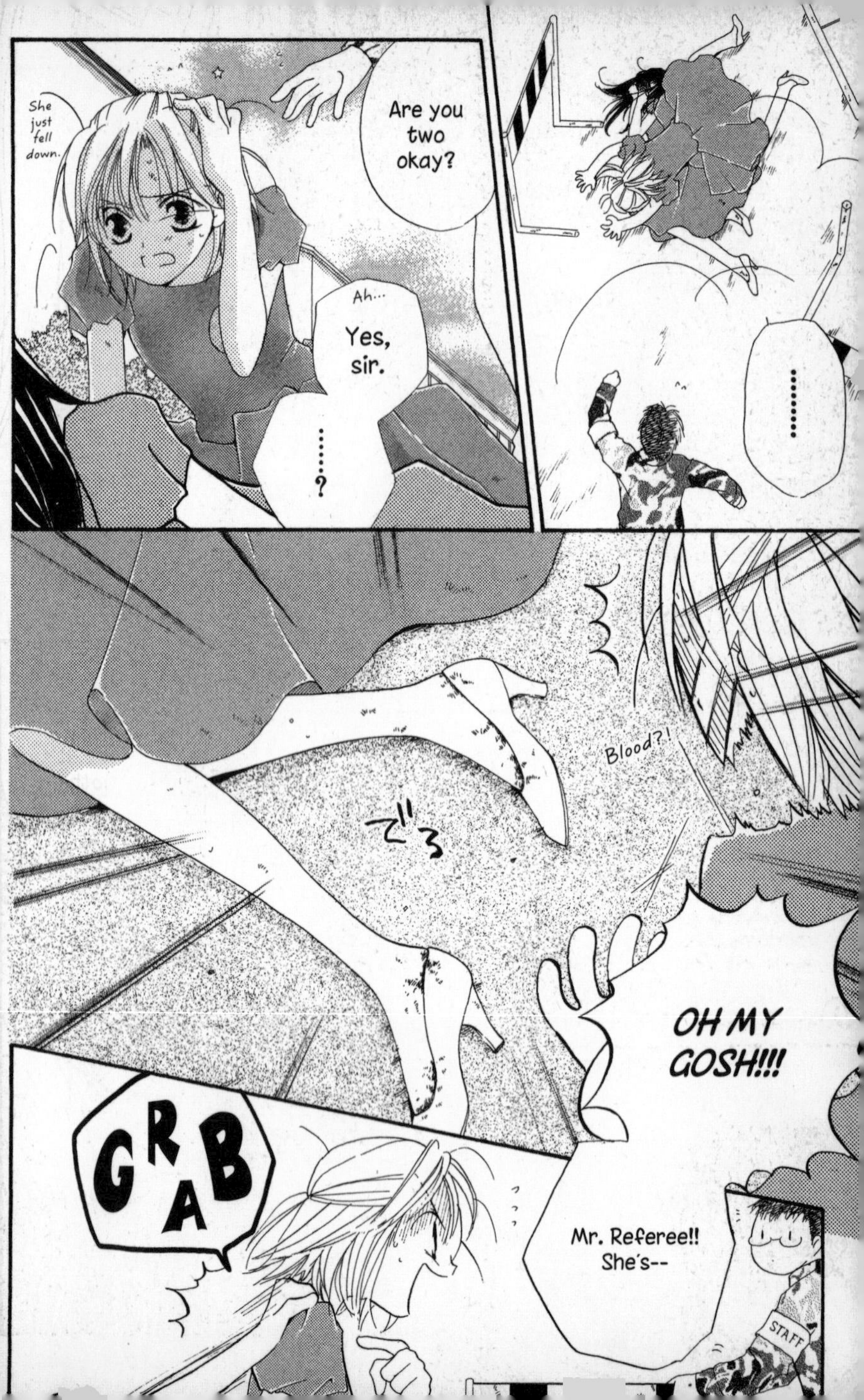
....
Are you two okay?
She just fell down.
Ah...
Yes, sir.
......?
Blood?!
でろ
OH MY GOSH!!!
Mr. Referee!! She's--
GRAB

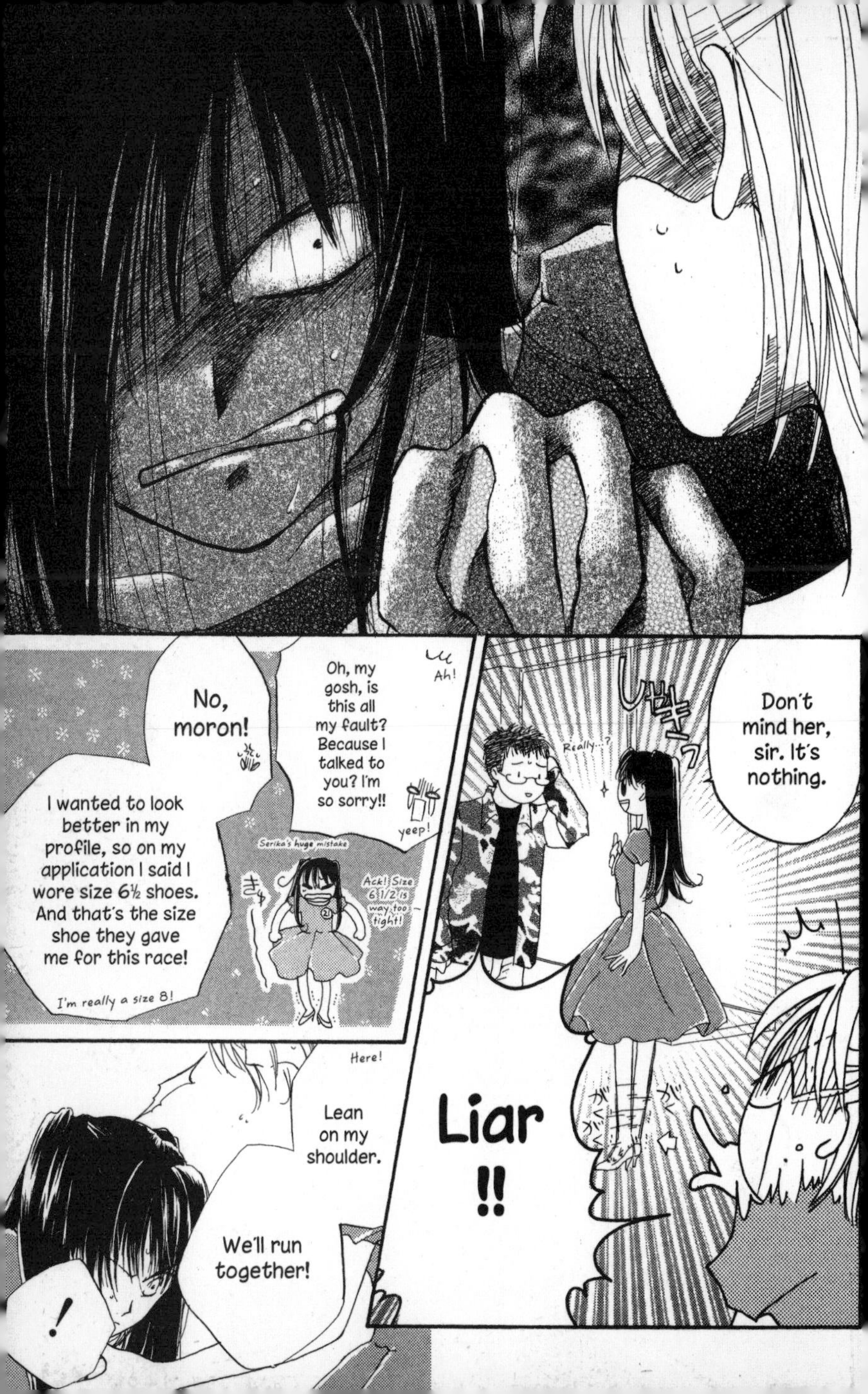
Don't mind her, sir. It's nothing.
Really...?
Ah!
Oh, my gosh, is this all my fault? Because I talked to you? I'm so sorry!!
yeep!
No, moron!
I wanted to look better in my profile, so on my application I said I wore size 6½ shoes. And that's the size shoe they gave me for this race!
Serika's huge mistake
Ack! Size 6 1/2 is way too tight!
I'm really a size 8!
Liar !!
Here!
Lean on my shoulder.
We'll run together!
!

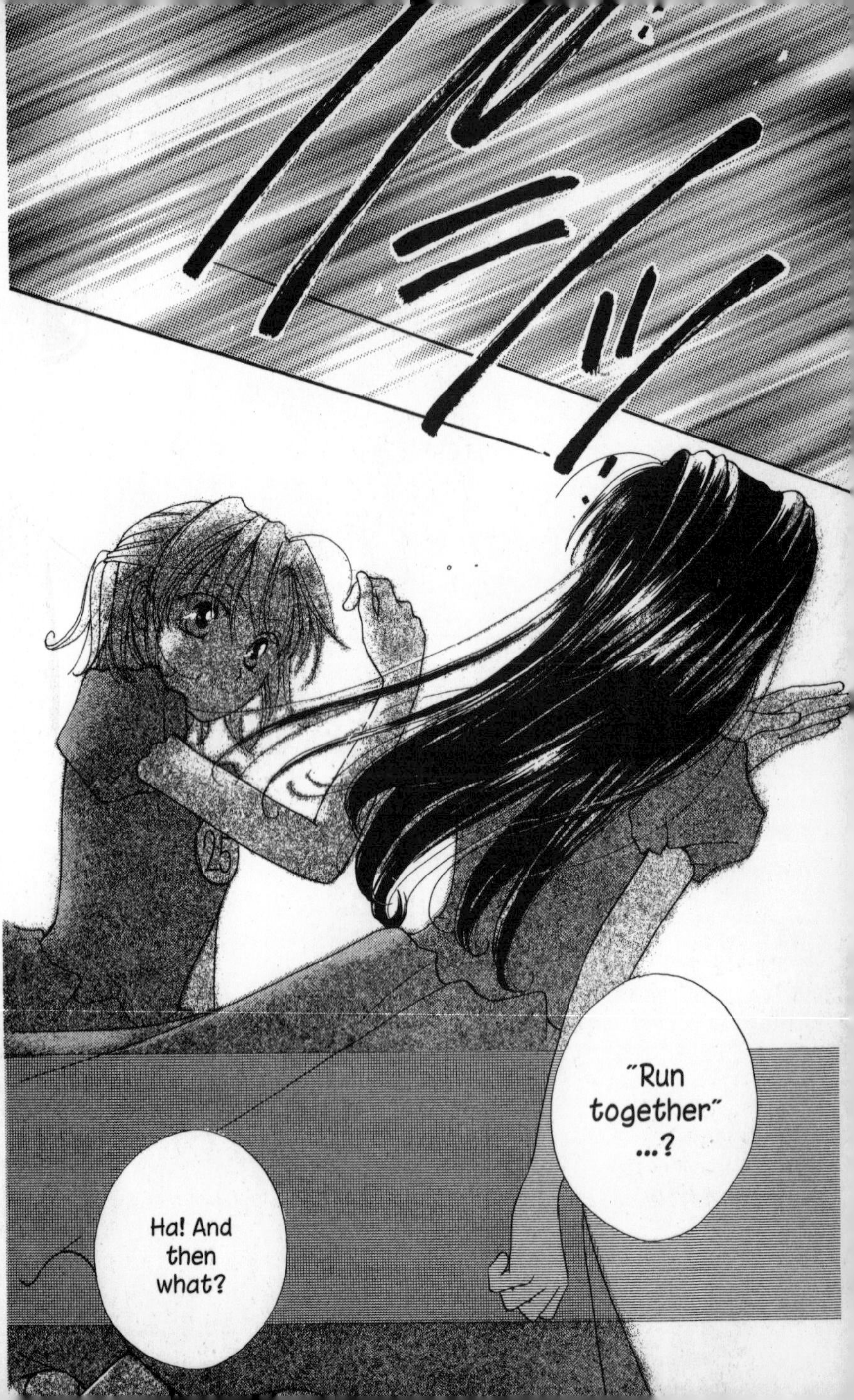
"Run together" ...?
Ha! And then what?

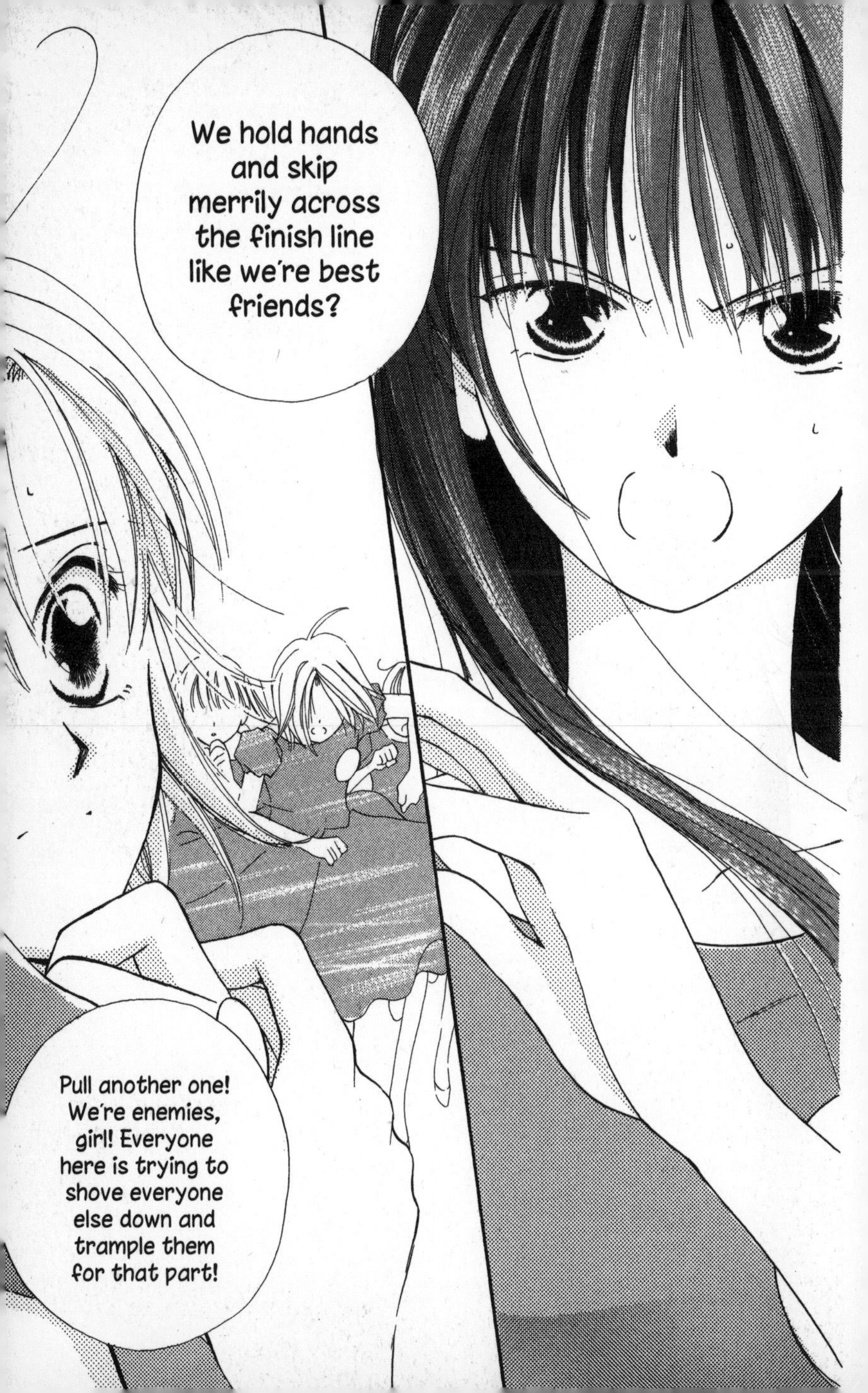
We hold hands and skip merrily across the finish line like we're best friends?
Pull another one! We're enemies, girl! Everyone here is trying to shove everyone else down and trample them for that part!

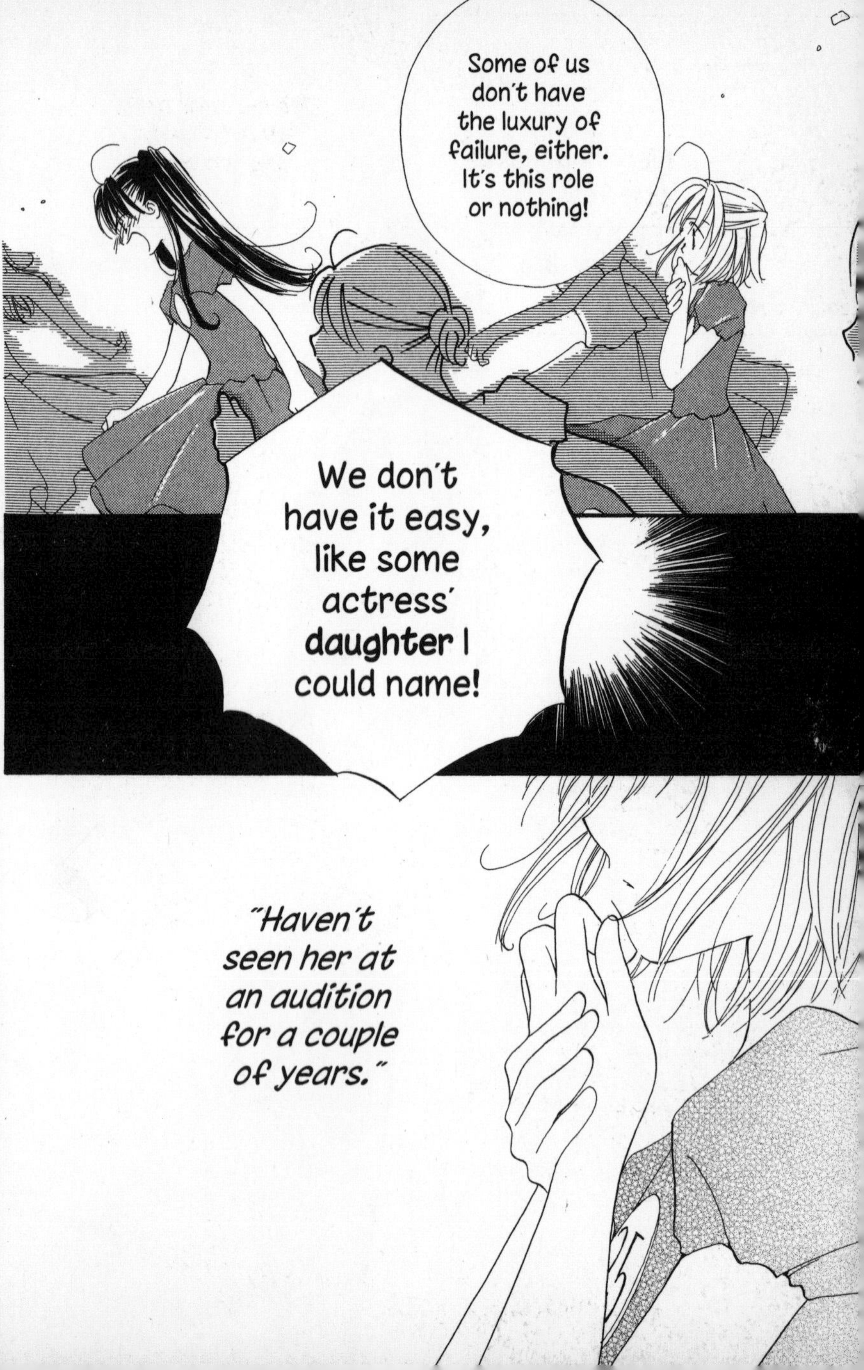

Some of us don't have the luxury of failure, either. It's this role or nothing!
We don't have it easy, like some actress' **daughter** I could name!
"Haven't seen her at an audition for a couple of years."

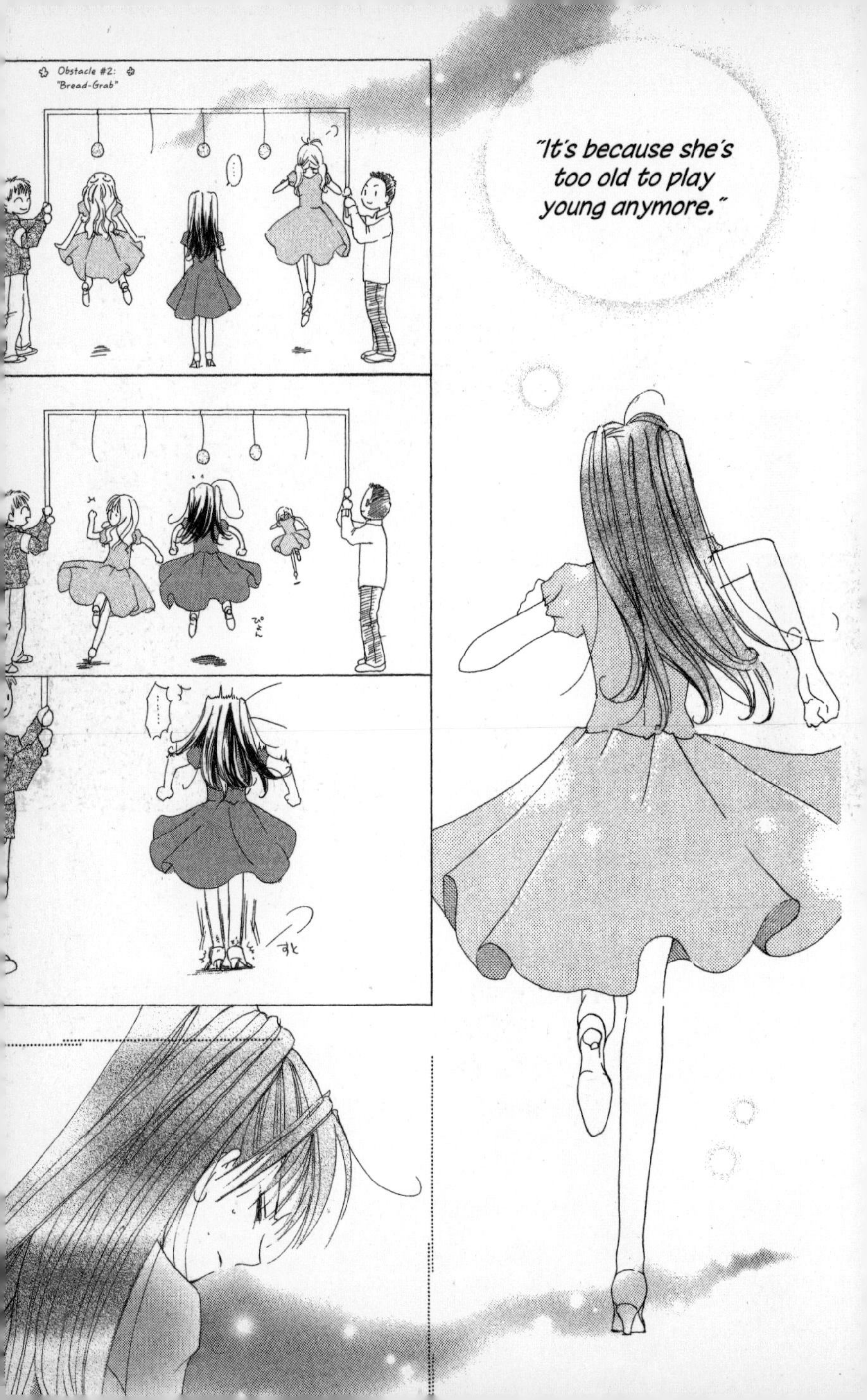
"It's because she's too old to play young anymore."
Obstacle #2: "Bread-Grab"

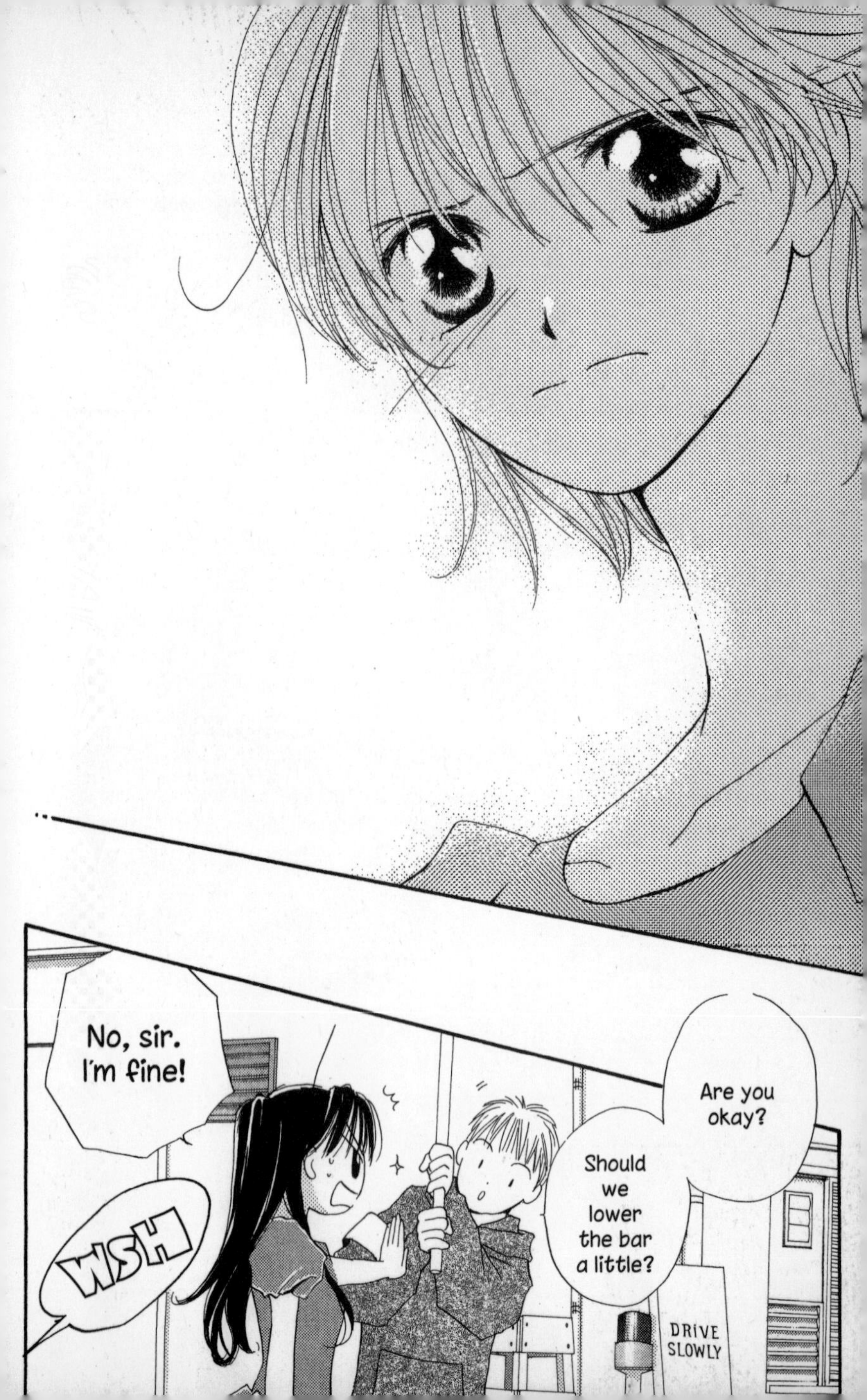
Are you okay?
Should we lower the bar a little?
No, sir. I'm fine!
WSH
DRIVE SLOWLY

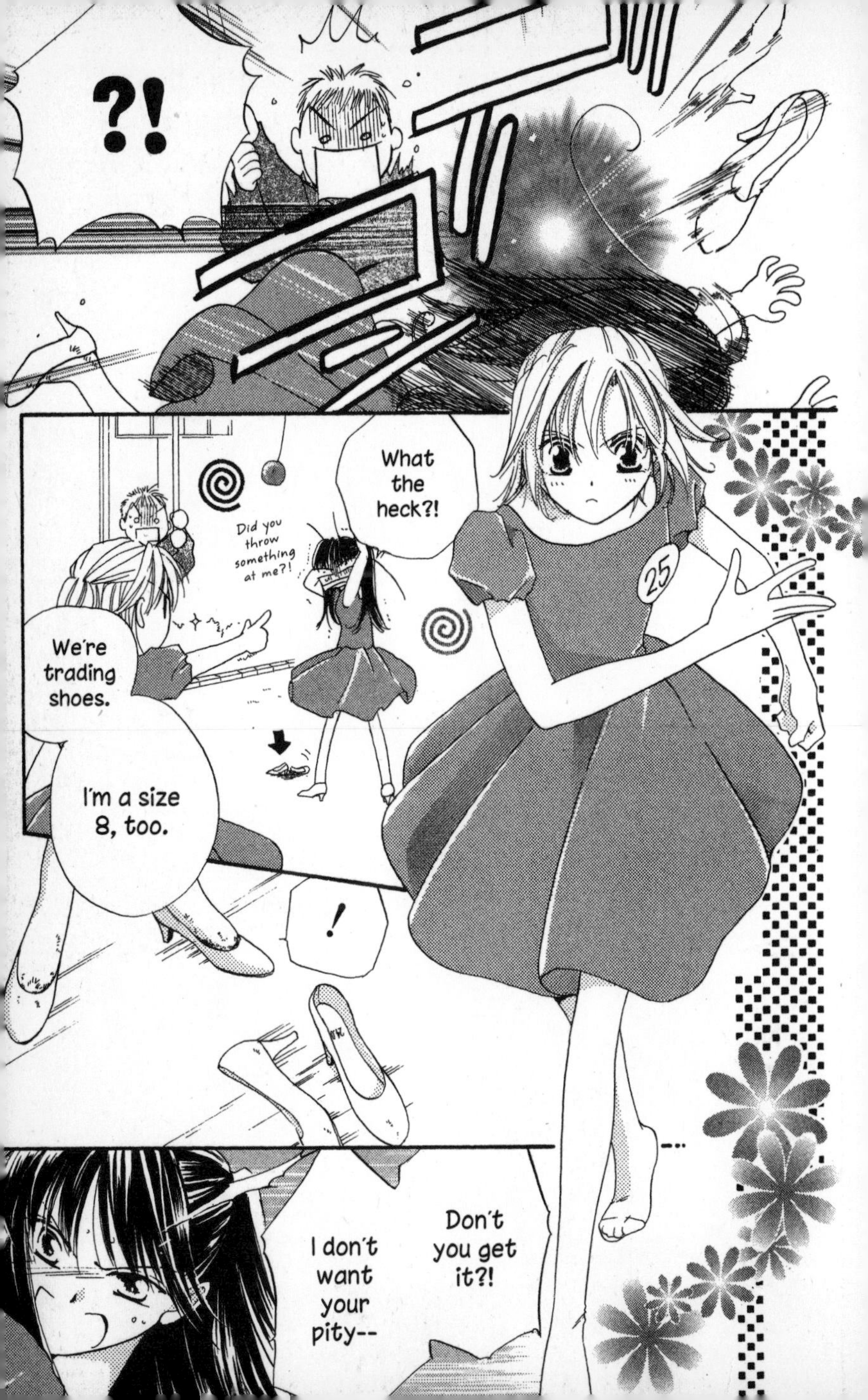
?!
What the heck?!
Did you throw something at me?!
We're trading shoes.
I'm a size 8, too.
!
...
Don't you get it?!
I don't want your pity--

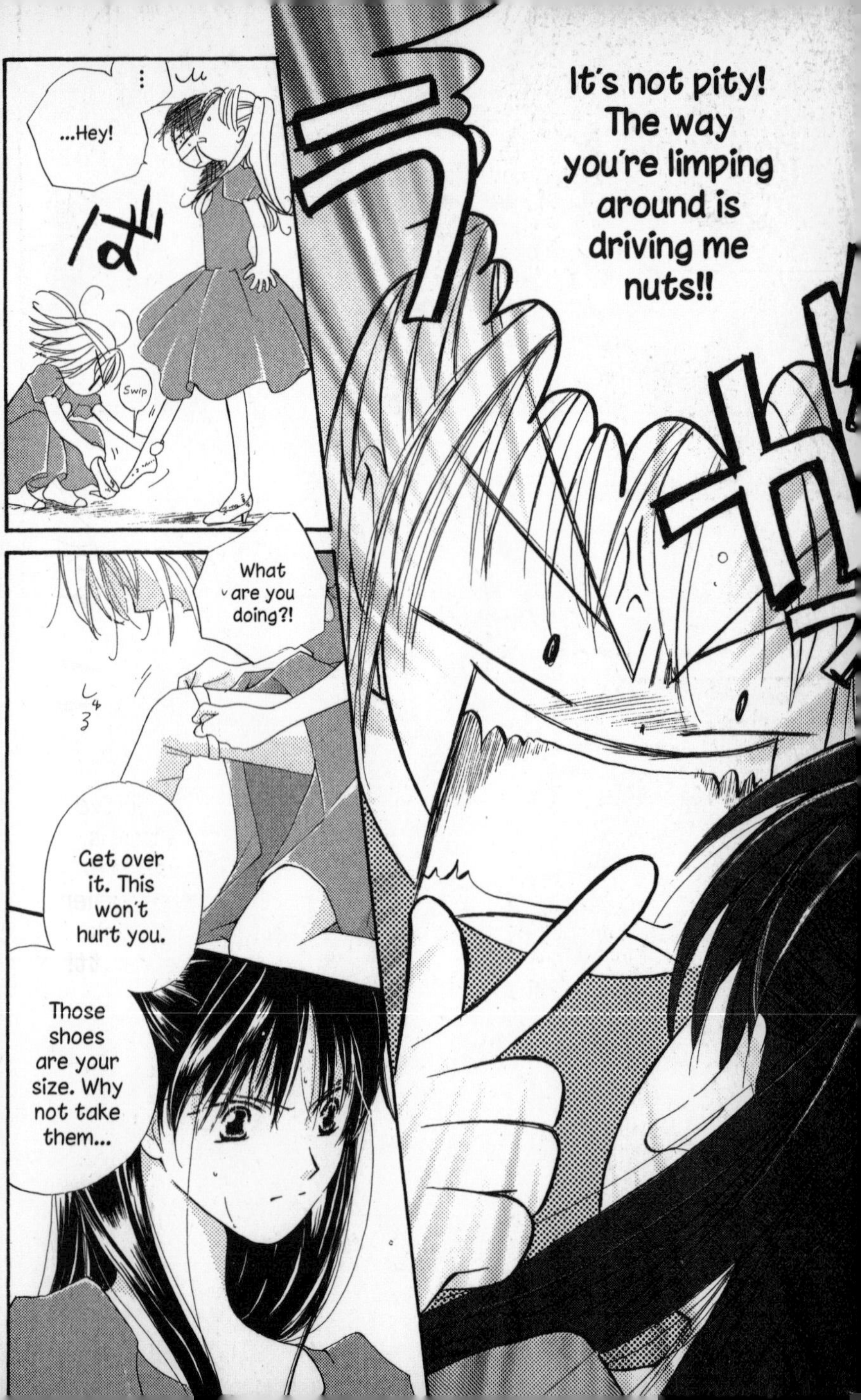

It's not pity! The way you're limping around is driving me nuts!!
...Hey!
Swip
What are you doing?!
Get over it. This won't hurt you.
Those shoes are your size. Why not take them...

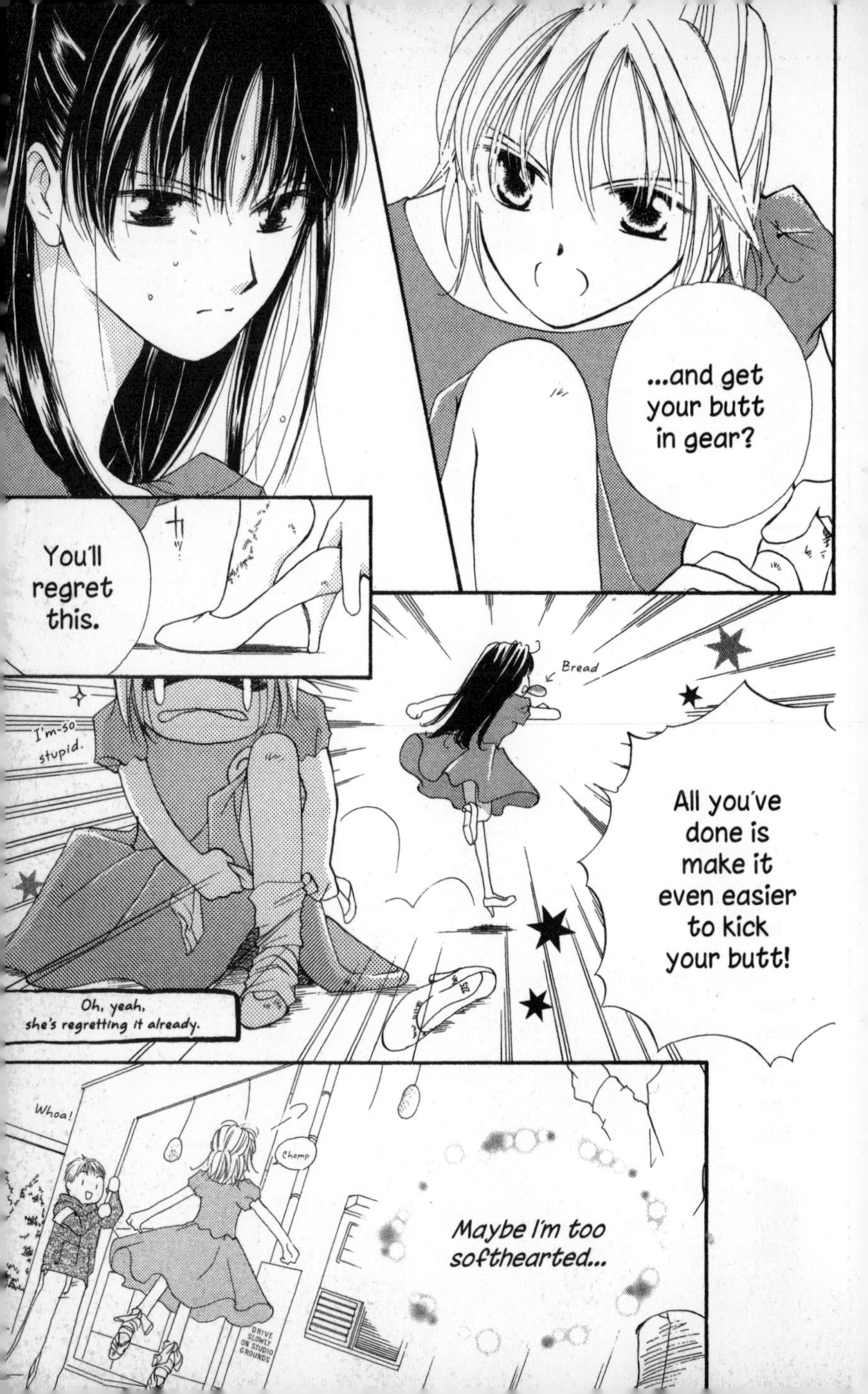
...and get your butt in gear?
You'll regret this.
Bread
All you've done is make it even easier to kick your butt!
I'm-so stupid.
Oh, yeah, she's regretting it already.
Maybe I'm too softhearted...
Chomp
Whoa!
DRIVE SLOWLY ON STUDIO GROUNDS

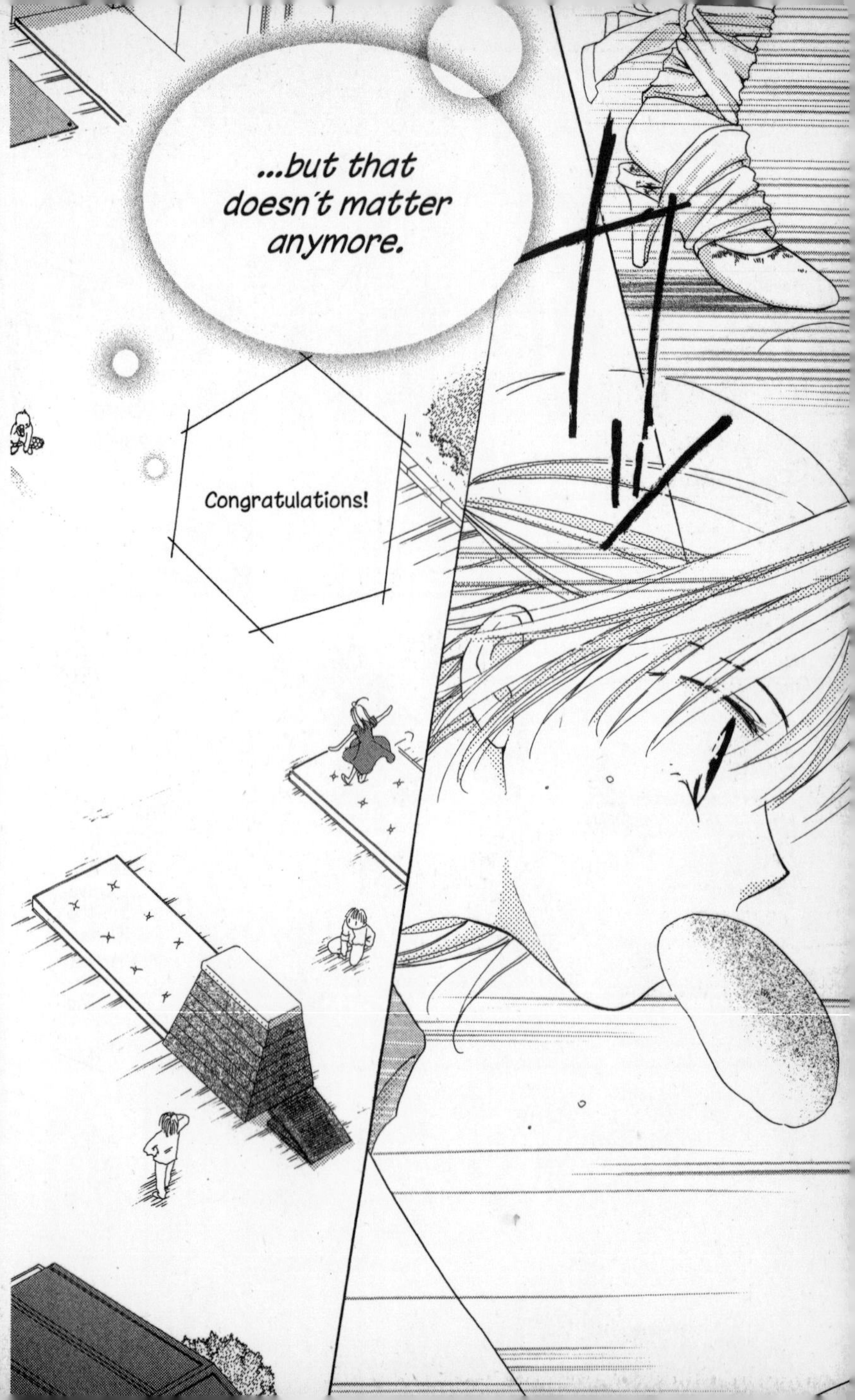
...but that doesn't matter anymore.
Congratulations!

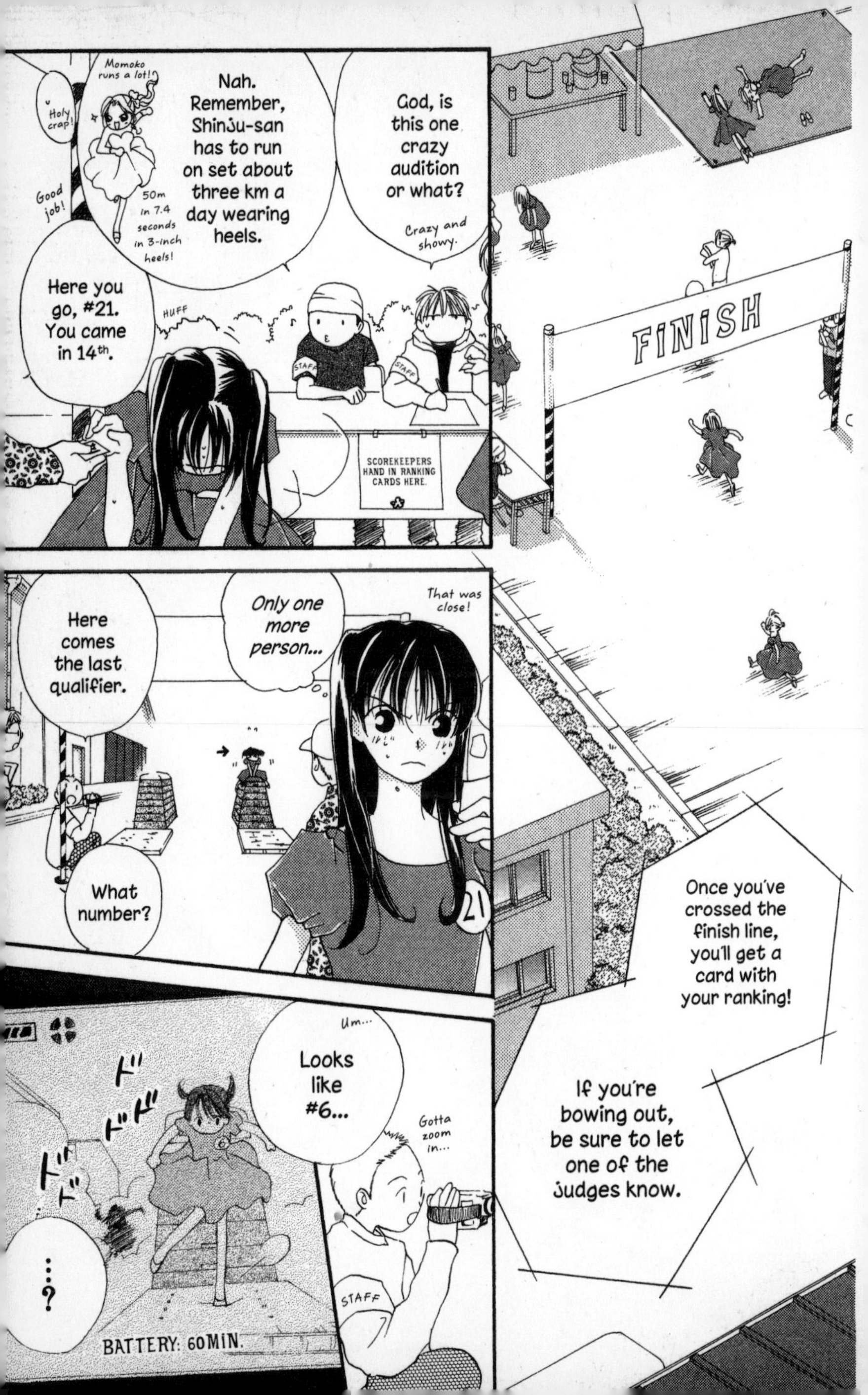
FINISH
Once you've crossed the finish line, you'll get a card with your ranking!
If you're bowing out, be sure to let one of the judges know.
God, is this one crazy audition or what?
Crazy and showy.
Nah. Remember, Shinju-san has to run on set about three km a day wearing heels.
Momoko runs a lot!
Holy crap!
50m in 7.4 seconds in 3-inch heels!
Good job!
HUFF
STAFF
STAFF
SCOREKEEPERS HAND IN RANKING CARDS HERE.
Here you go, #21. You came in 14th.
That was close!
Only one more person...
Here comes the last qualifier.
What number?
Um...
Looks like #6...
Gotta zoom in...
STAFF
ドドド
ドド
...?
BATTERY: 60MIN.

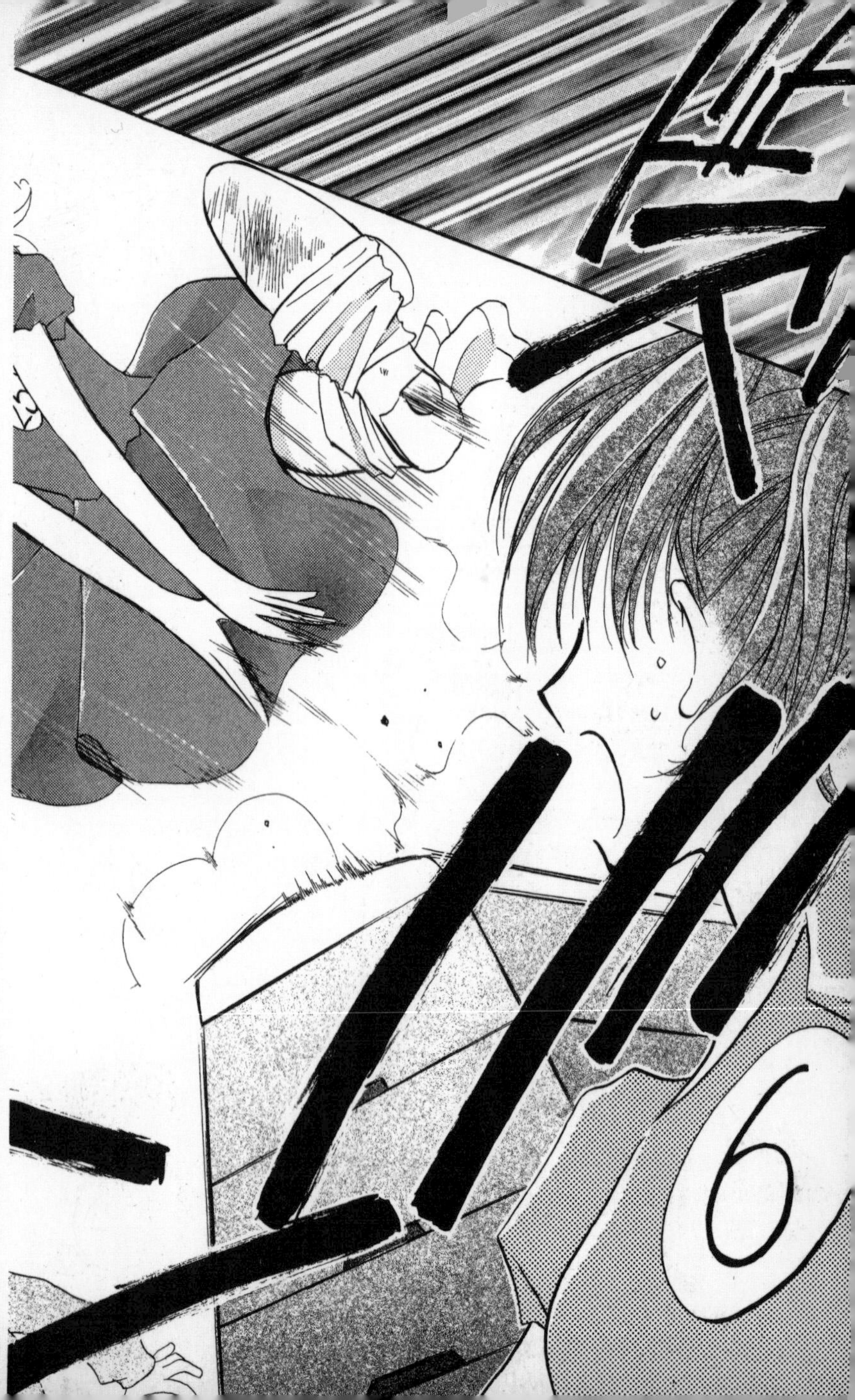

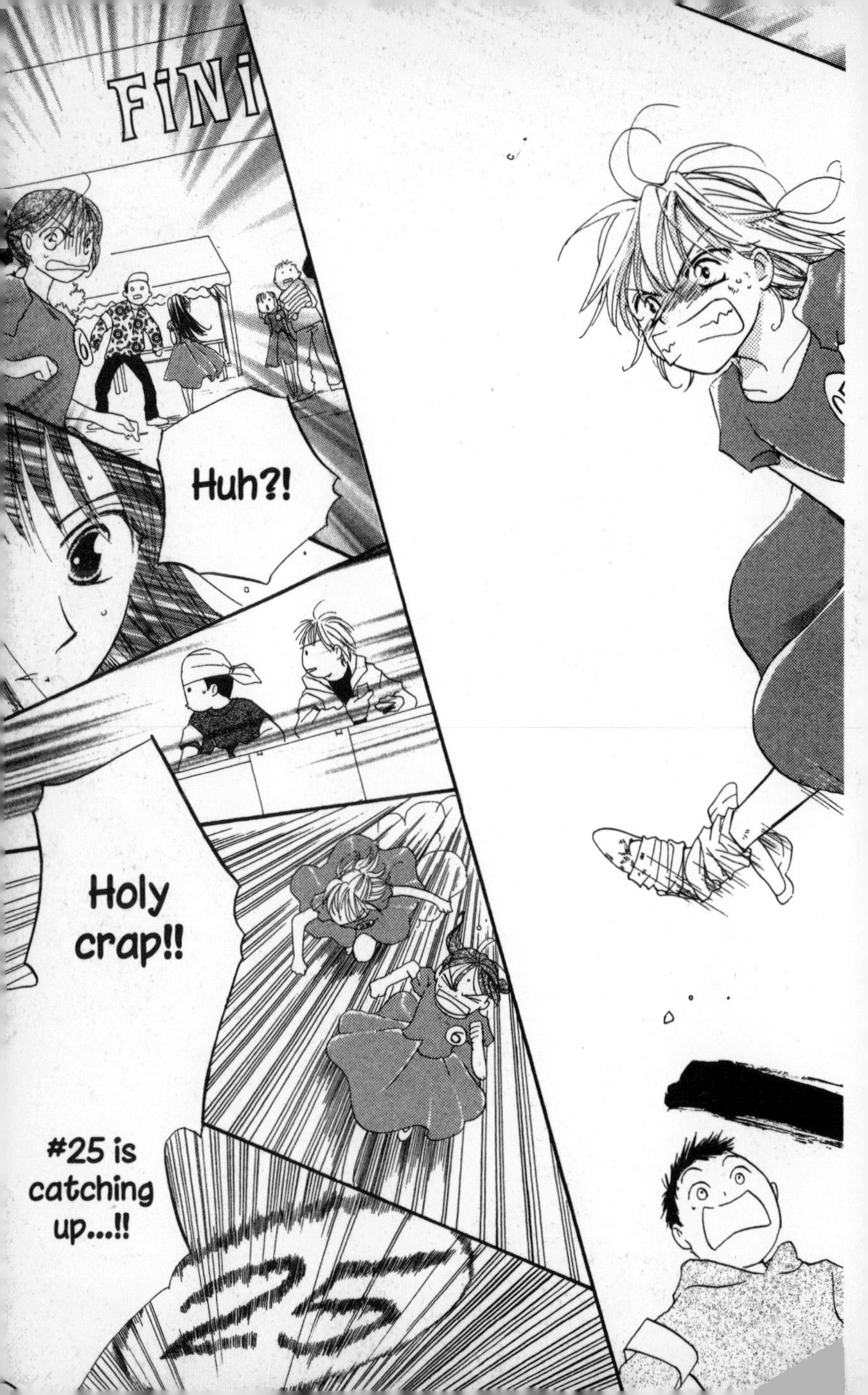
FiNi
Huh?!
Holy crap!!
#25 is catching up...!!
25

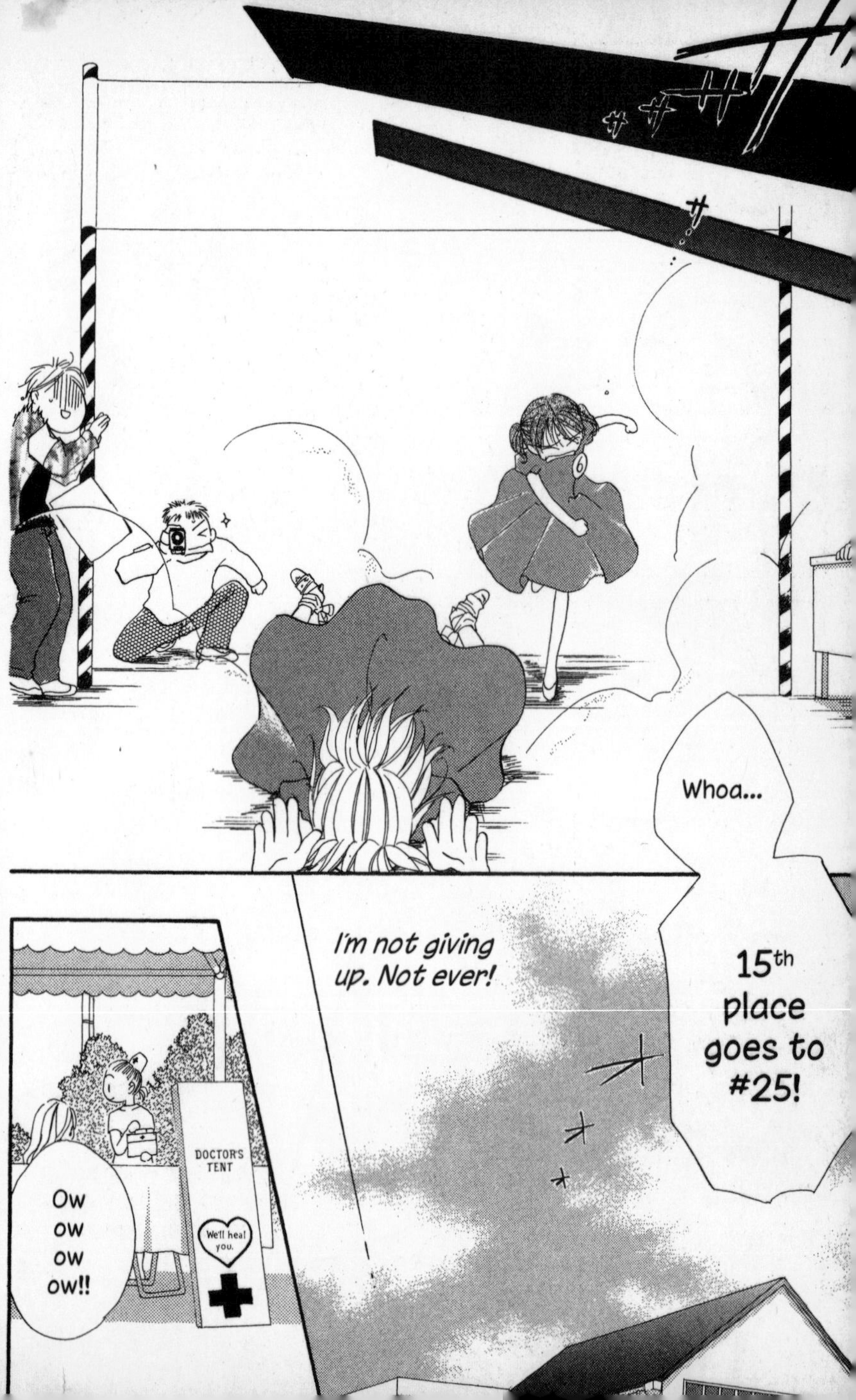
Whoa...
15th place goes to #25!
I'm not giving up. Not ever!
DOCTOR'S TENT
We'll heal you.
Ow ow ow ow!!

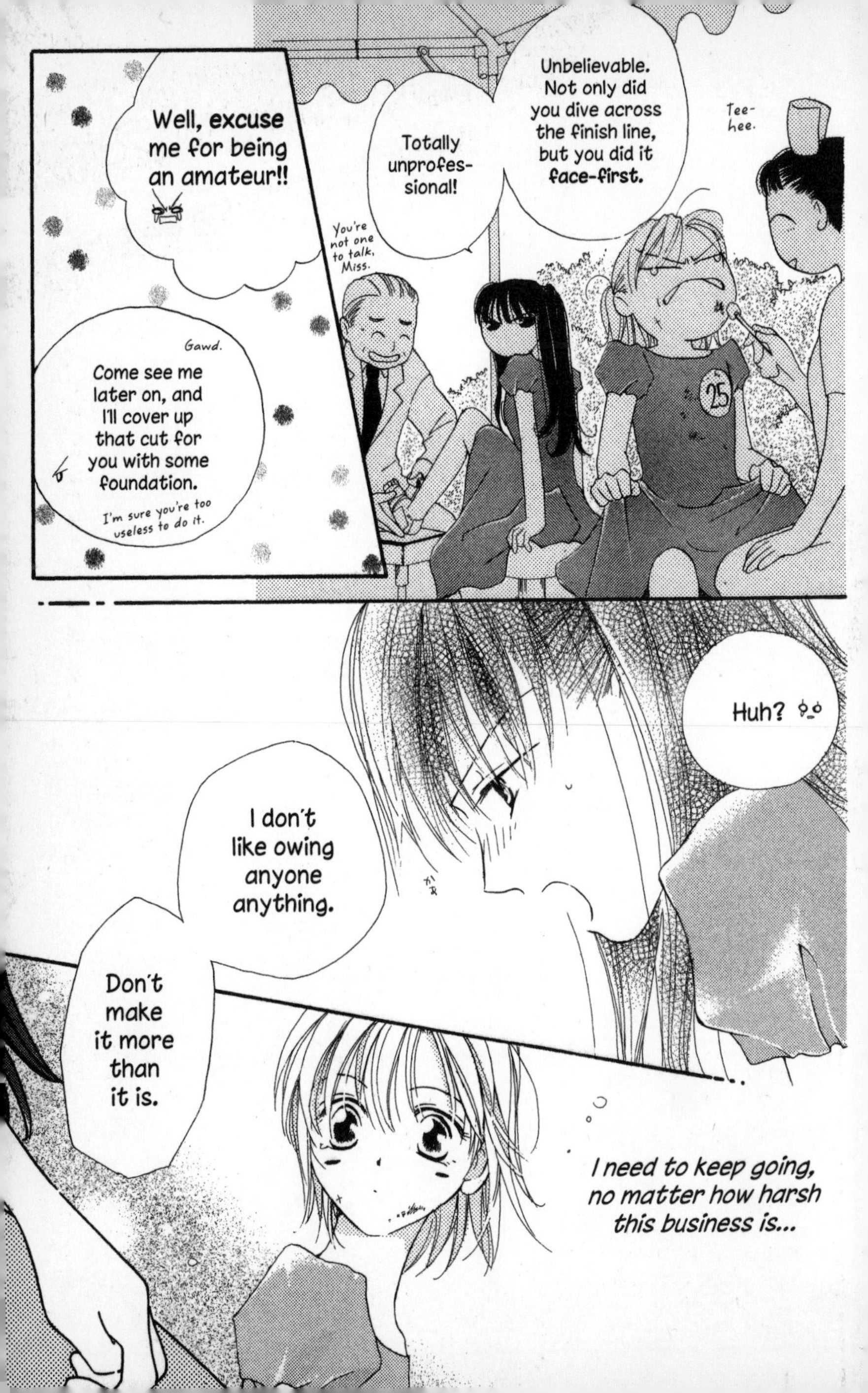
Unbelievable. Not only did you dive across the finish line, but you did it face-first.
Tee-hee.
Totally unprofes-sional!
You're not one to talk, Miss.
Well, excuse me for being an amateur!!
Gawd.
Come see me later on, and I'll cover up that cut for you with some foundation.
I'm sure you're too useless to do it.
Huh?
I don't like owing anyone anything.
Don't make it more than it is.
I need to keep going, no matter how harsh this business is...

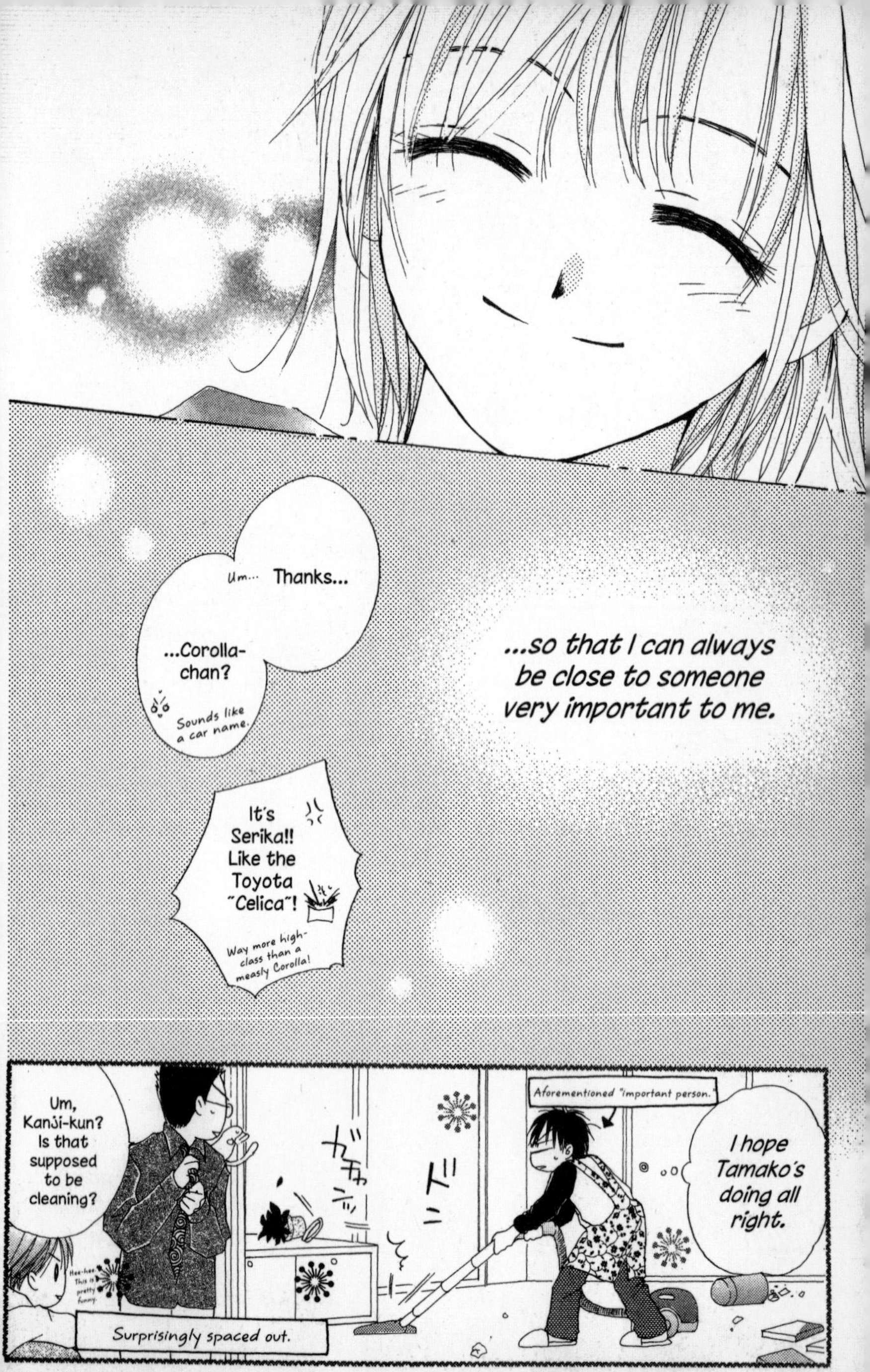
...so that I can always be close to someone very important to me.
Um... Thanks...
...Corolla-chan?
Sounds like a car name.
It's Serika!! Like the Toyota "Celica"!
Way more high-class than a measly Corolla!
Aforementioned "important person."
I hope Tamako's doing all right.
Um, Kanji-kun? Is that supposed to be cleaning?
Hee-hee. This is pretty funny.
Surprisingly spaced out.

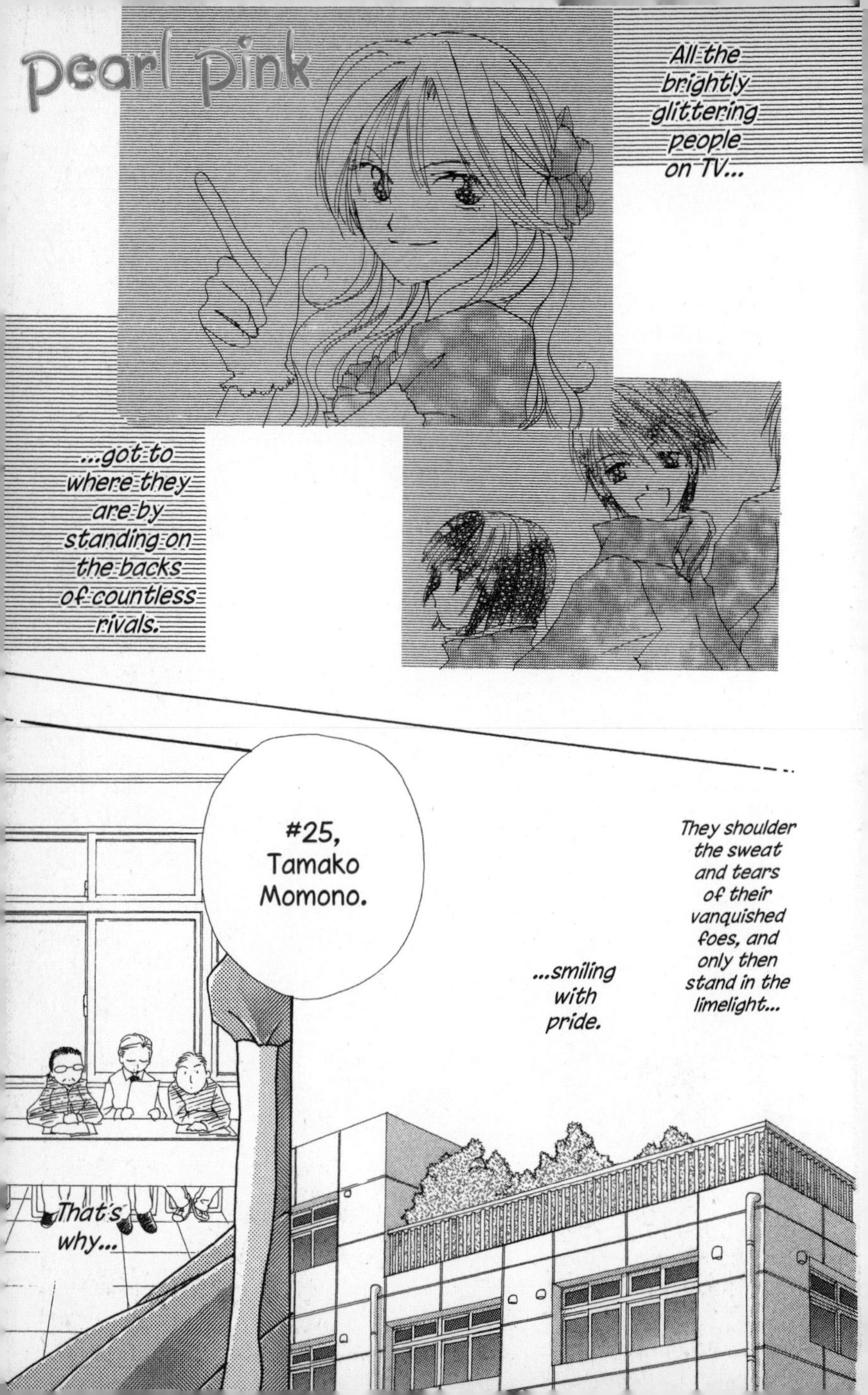
pearl pink
All the brightly glittering people on TV...
...got to where they are by standing on the backs of countless rivals.
They shoulder the sweat and tears of their vanquished foes, and only then stand in the limelight...
...smiling with pride.
#25, Tamako Momono.
That's why...

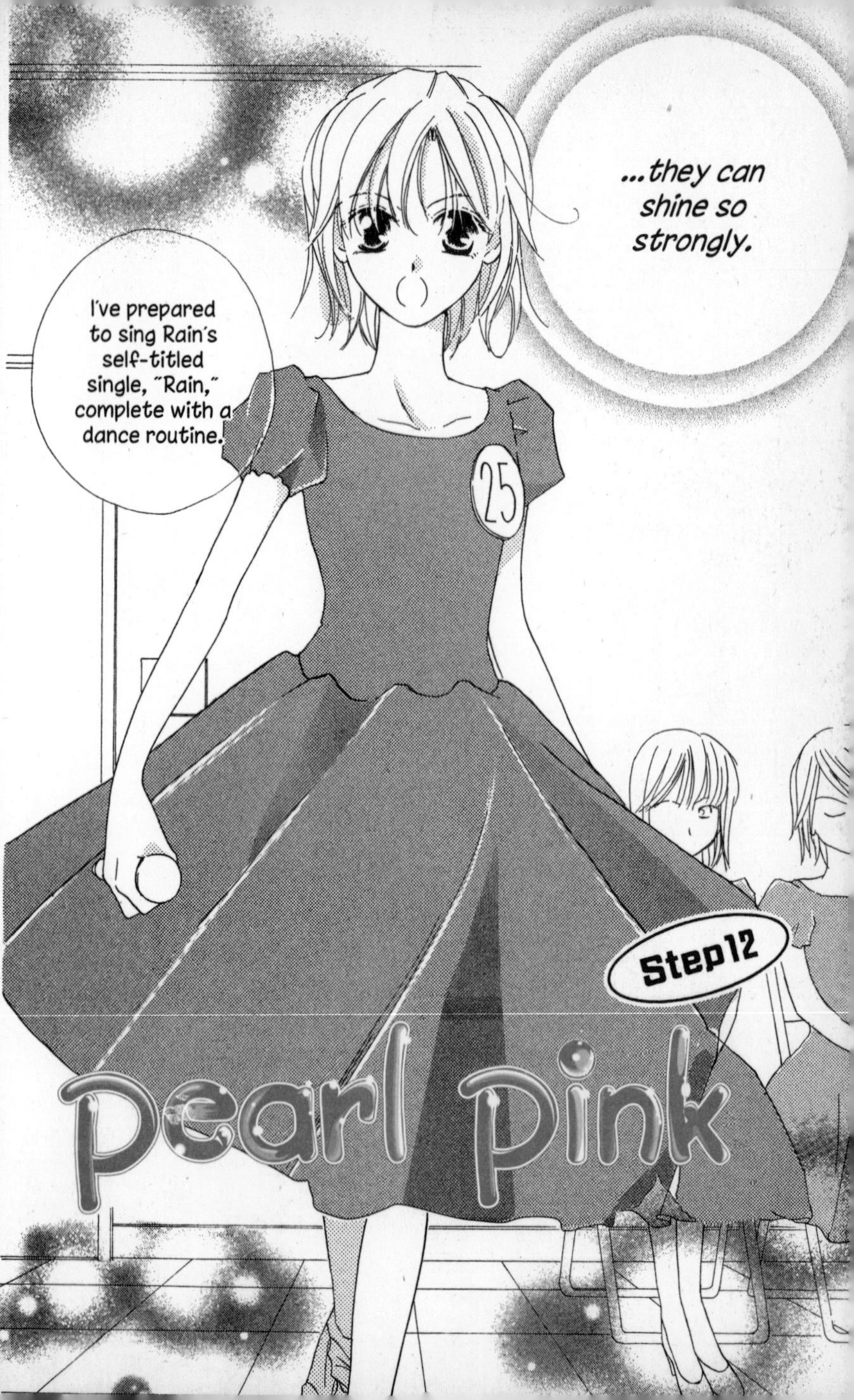
...they can shine so strongly.
I've prepared to sing Rain's self-titled single, "Rain," complete with a dance routine.
Step 12
Pearl Pink

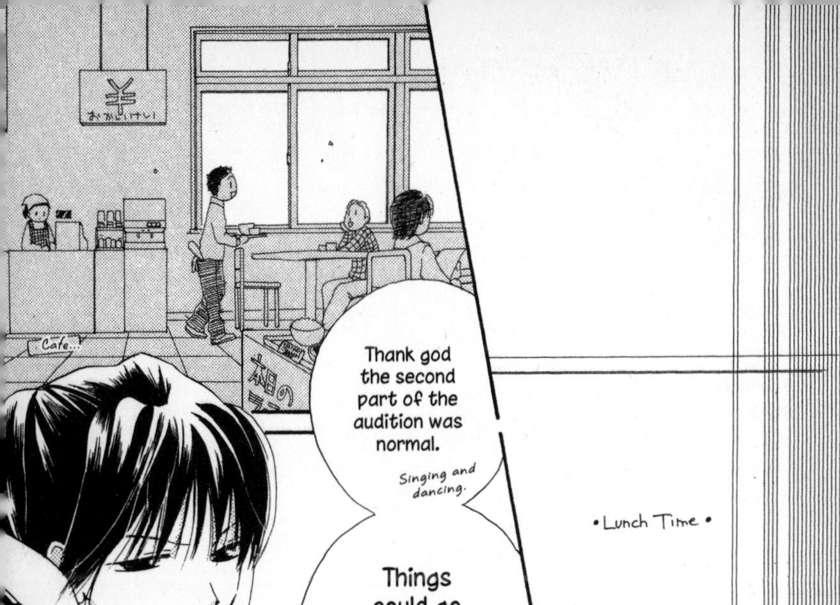

•Lunch Time•
Cafe...
Thank god the second part of the audition was normal.
Singing and dancing.
Things could go all crazy again for round 3, though.
By the way...

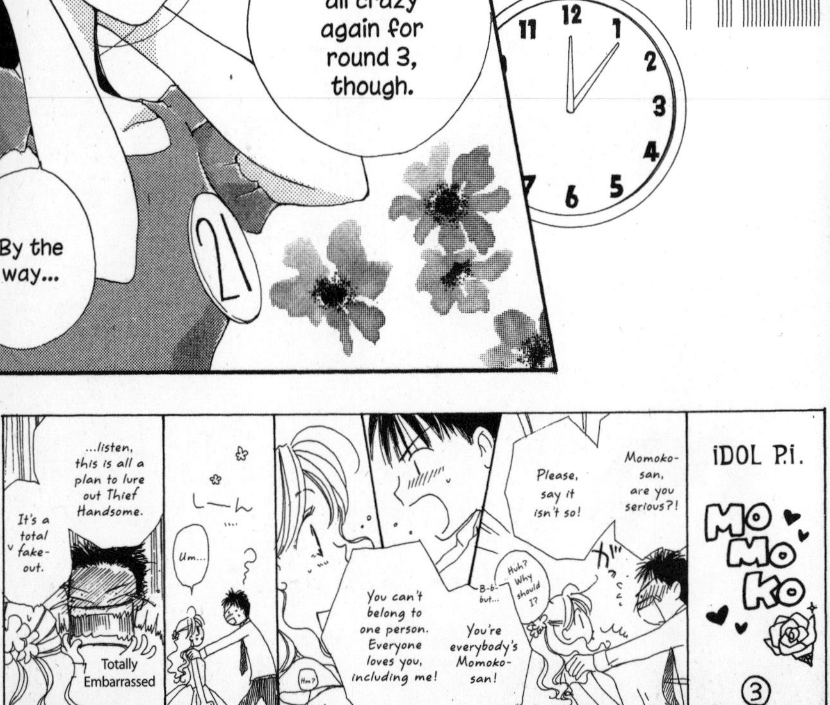

iDOL P.i.
MOMOKO
③
Momoko-san, are you serious?!
Please, say it isn't so!
Huh? Why should I?
B-b-but...
You're everybody's Momoko-san!
You can't belong to one person. Everyone loves you, including me!
Hm?
しーん
Um...
...listen, this is all a plan to lure out Thief Handsome.
It's a total fake-out.
Totally Embarrassed

←Cont. on pg 98...

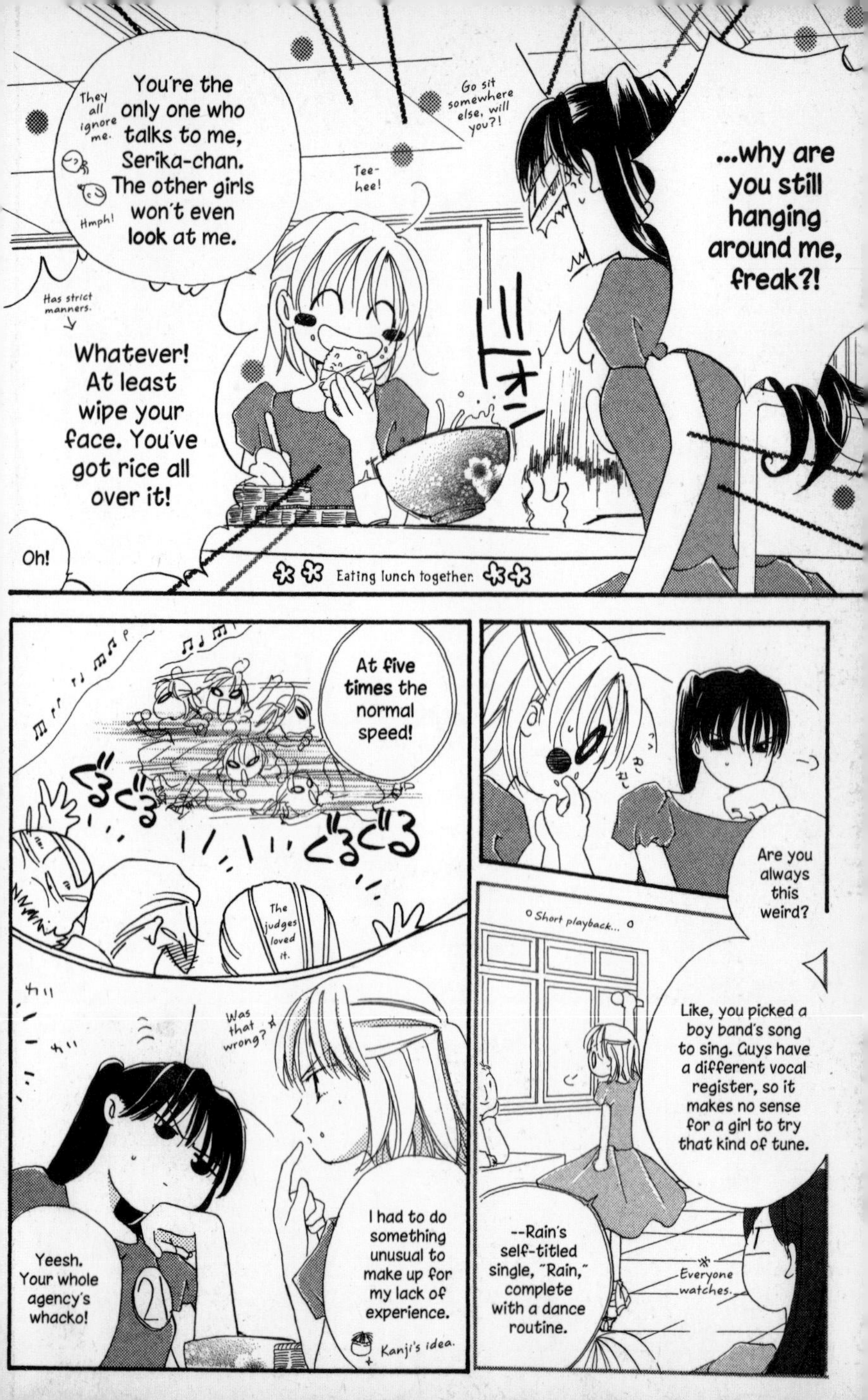
...why are you still hanging around me, freak?!
Go sit somewhere else, will you?!
Tee-hee!
You're the only one who talks to me, Serika-chan. The other girls won't even look at me.
They all ignore me.
Hmph!
Has strict manners.
Whatever! At least wipe your face. You've got rice all over it!
Oh!
Eating lunch together.
Are you always this weird?
Like, you picked a boy band's song to sing. Guys have a different vocal register, so it makes no sense for a girl to try that kind of tune.
Short playback...
--Rain's self-titled single, "Rain," complete with a dance routine.
Everyone watches.
At five times the normal speed!
ぐるぐる
ぐるぐる
The judges loved it.
Was that wrong?
I had to do something unusual to make up for my lack of experience.
Kanji's idea.
Yeesh. Your whole agency's whacko!

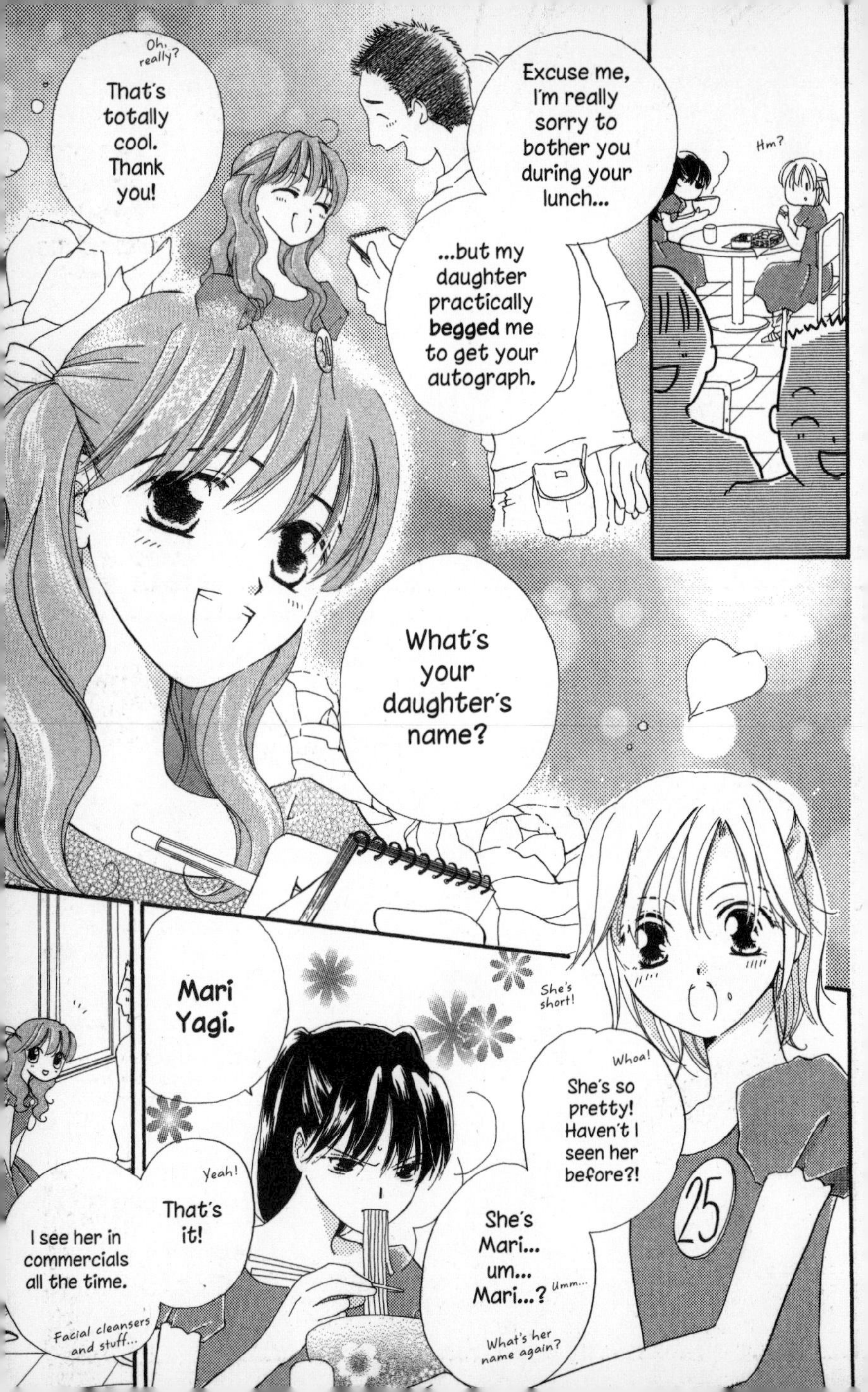

Hm?
Excuse me, I'm really sorry to bother you during your lunch...
...but my daughter practically **begged** me to get your autograph.
Oh, really?
That's totally cool. Thank you!
What's your daughter's name?
Mari Yagi.
She's short!
Whoa!
She's so pretty! Haven't I seen her before?!
She's Mari... um... Mari...?
Umm...
What's her name again?
Yeah!
That's it!
I see her in commercials all the time.
Facial cleansers and stuff...

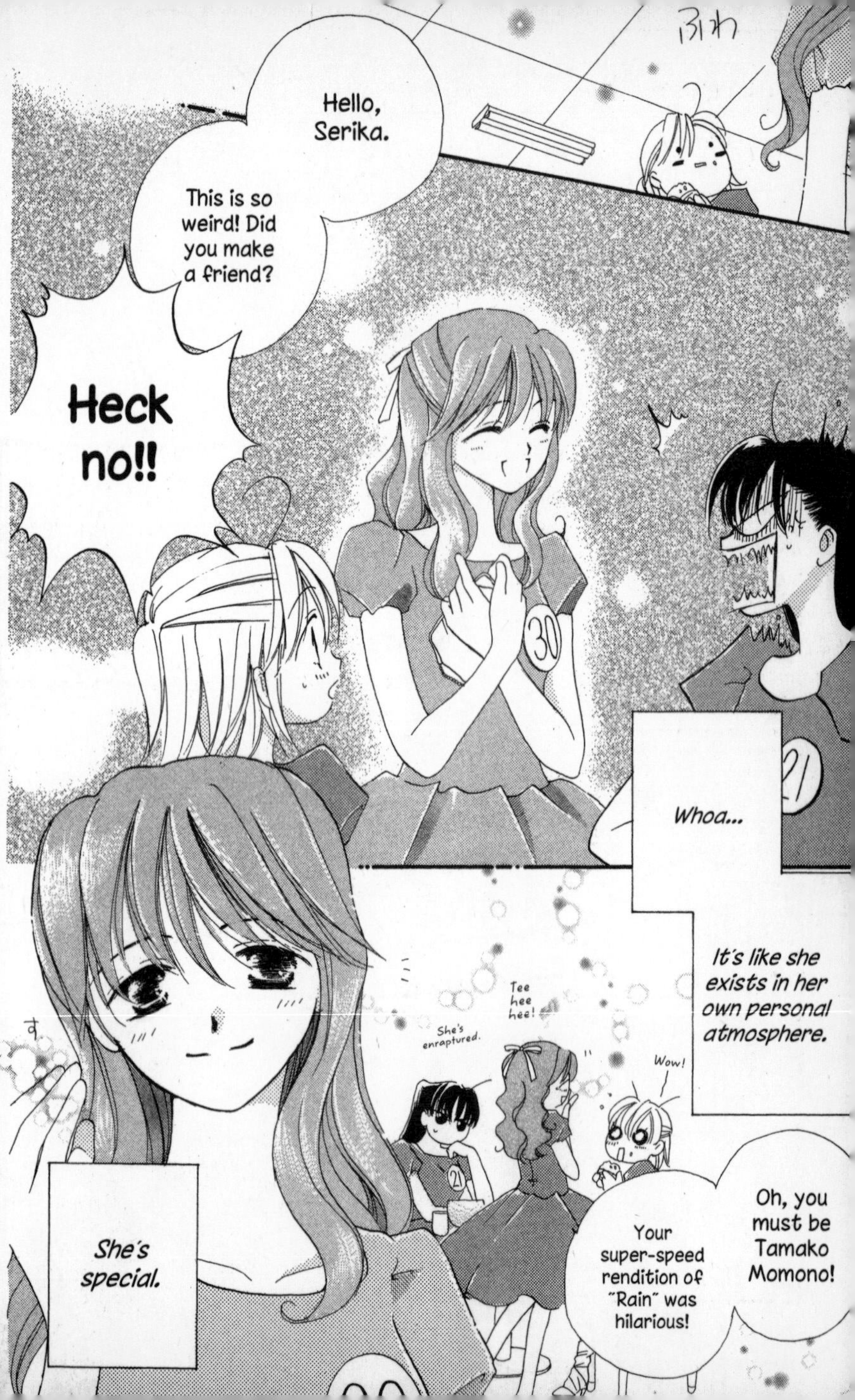
ふわ
Hello, Serika.
This is so weird! Did you make a friend?
Heck no!!
Whoa...
It's like she exists in her own personal atmosphere.
Oh, you must be Tamako Momono!
Your super-speed rendition of "Rain" was hilarious!
Wow!
Tee hee hee!
She's enraptured.
す
She's special.

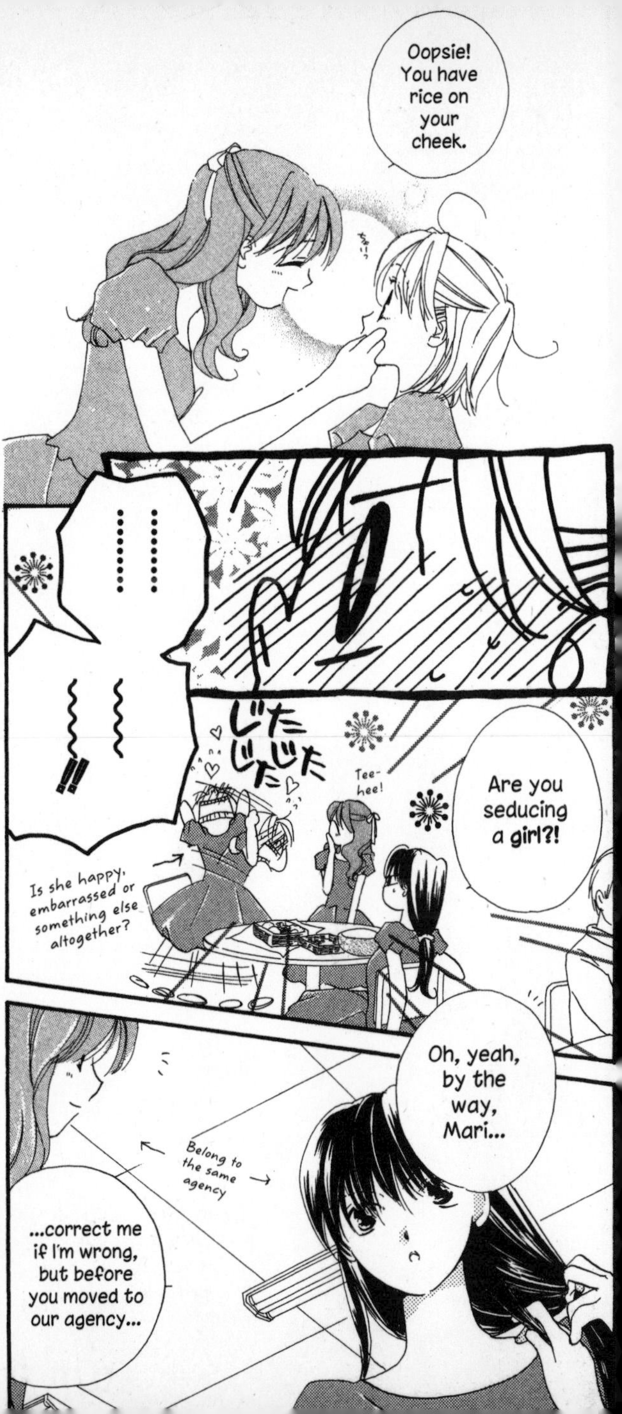
Oopsie! You have rice on your cheek.
......
~~ ~~ !!
じたじた じたじた
Tee-hee!
Are you seducing a girl?!
Is she happy, embarrassed or something else altogether?
Oh, yeah, by the way, Mari...
Belong to the same agency
...correct me if I'm wrong, but before you moved to our agency...

Dieting

Oink

Yes, I'm on a diet. I was surprised to find out that, since my debut as a manga artist, I'd managed to pack on an extra 10-12 pounds. And I wasn't really skinny to begin with, either...

I am quite, quite sure that work, stress, and bad habits are the main cause of the extra me now hanging around my middle, so I've been changing my routine bit by bit. And, happy surprise, three months after seriously getting started, I lost eight pounds!

Woo! Awesome!

But, I'm not giving up! I'm going to try to lose a couple more pounds. Here are a few tricks I've learned that help me stick to my diet:

- Don't take the whole "I'm on a diet!!" idea too far.
- Don't start any habit you don't think you'll be able to continue faithfully.
- Keep your stomach and intestines in good health. ← very important

And that's about it.

To all you other dieters out there, let's keep up the good work!

OiNK OiNK!!

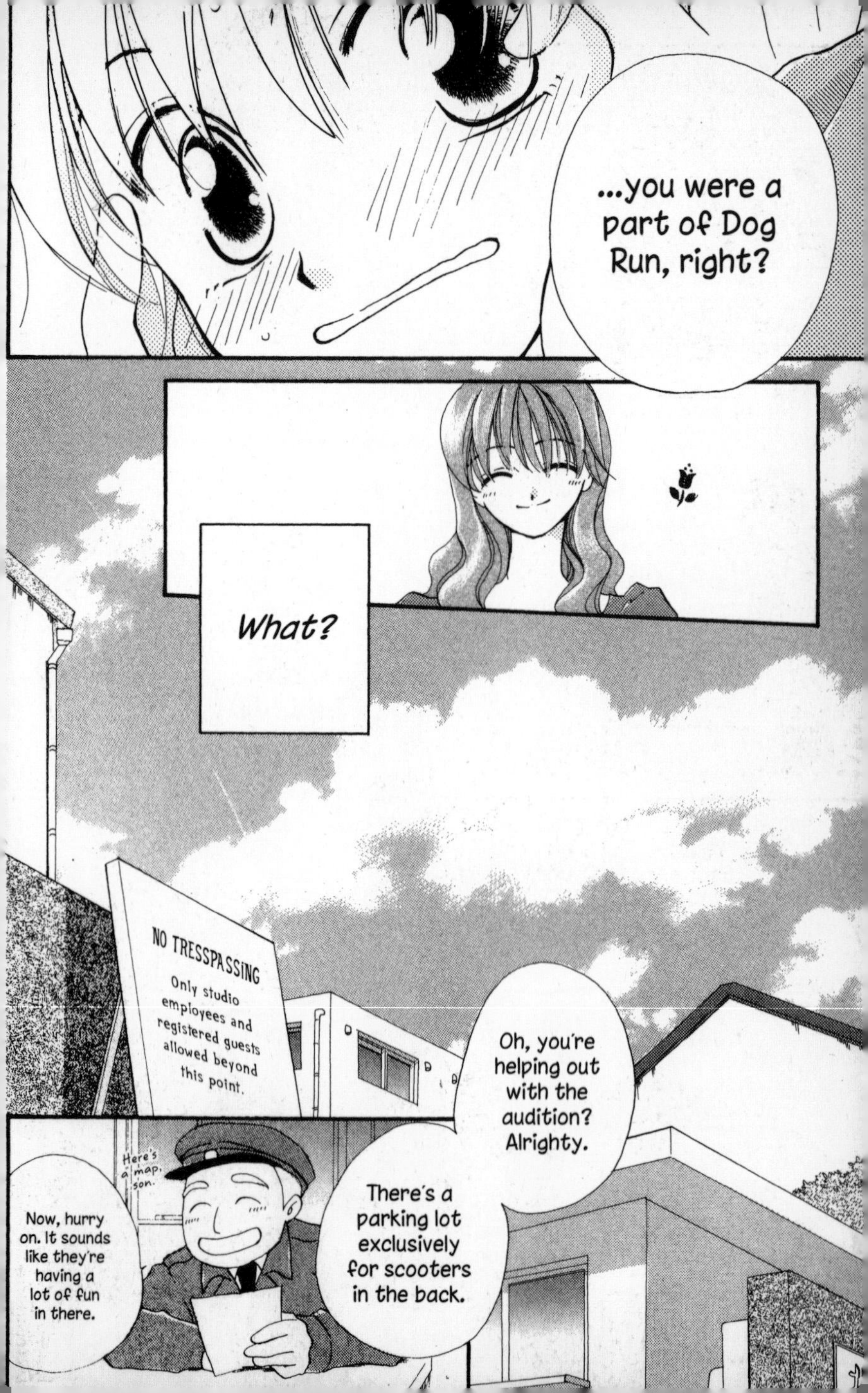
...you were a part of Dog Run, right?
What?
NO TRESSPASSING
Only studio employees and registered guests allowed beyond this point.
Oh, you're helping out with the audition? Alrighty.
There's a parking lot exclusively for scooters in the back.
Here's a map, son.
Now, hurry on. It sounds like they're having a lot of fun in there.

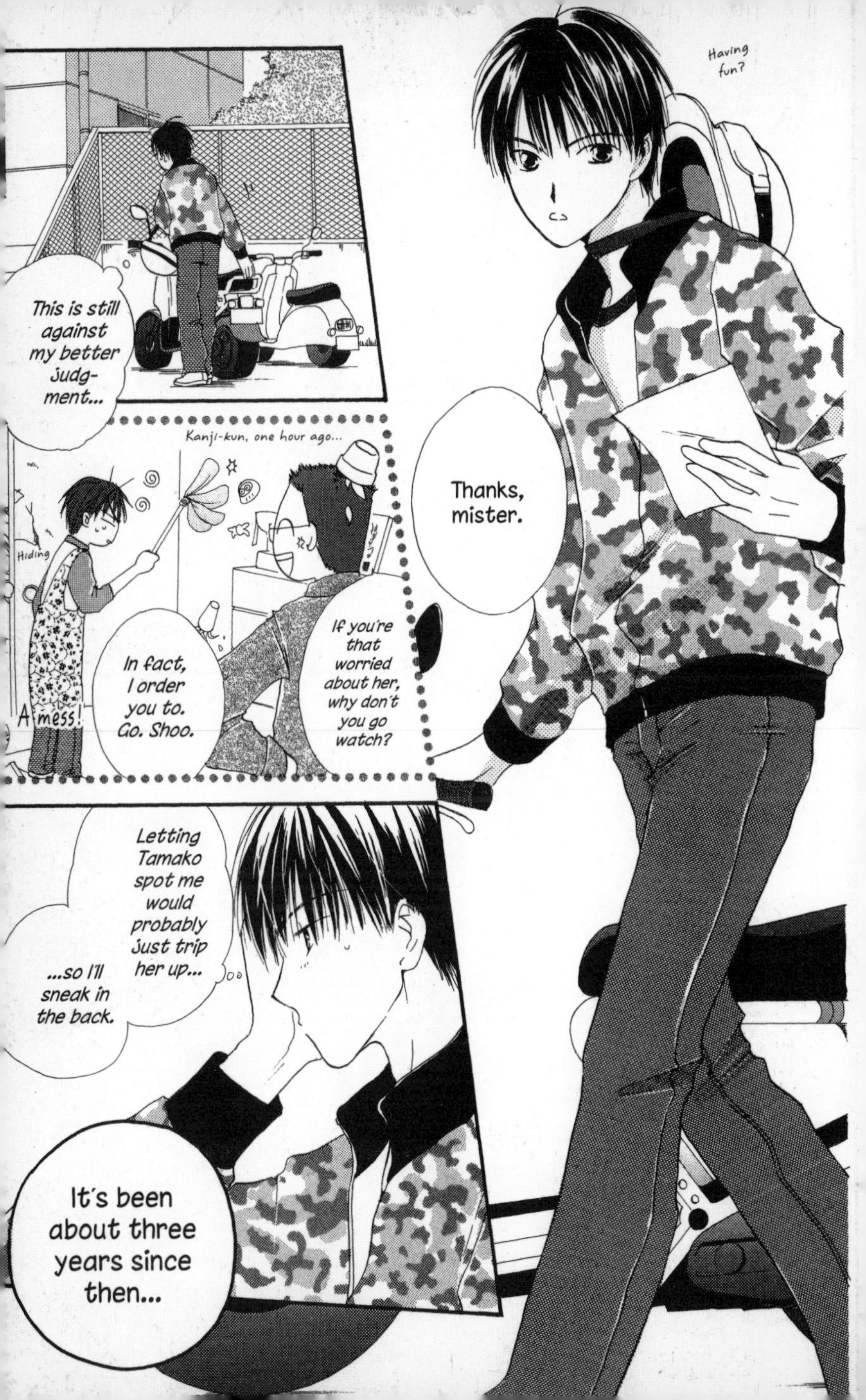
Having fun?
Thanks, mister.
This is still against my better judg-ment...
Kanji-kun, one hour ago...
If you're that worried about her, why don't you go watch?
In fact, I order you to. Go. Shoo.
Hiding
A mess!
Letting Tamako spot me would probably just trip her up...
...so I'll sneak in the back.
It's been about three years since then...

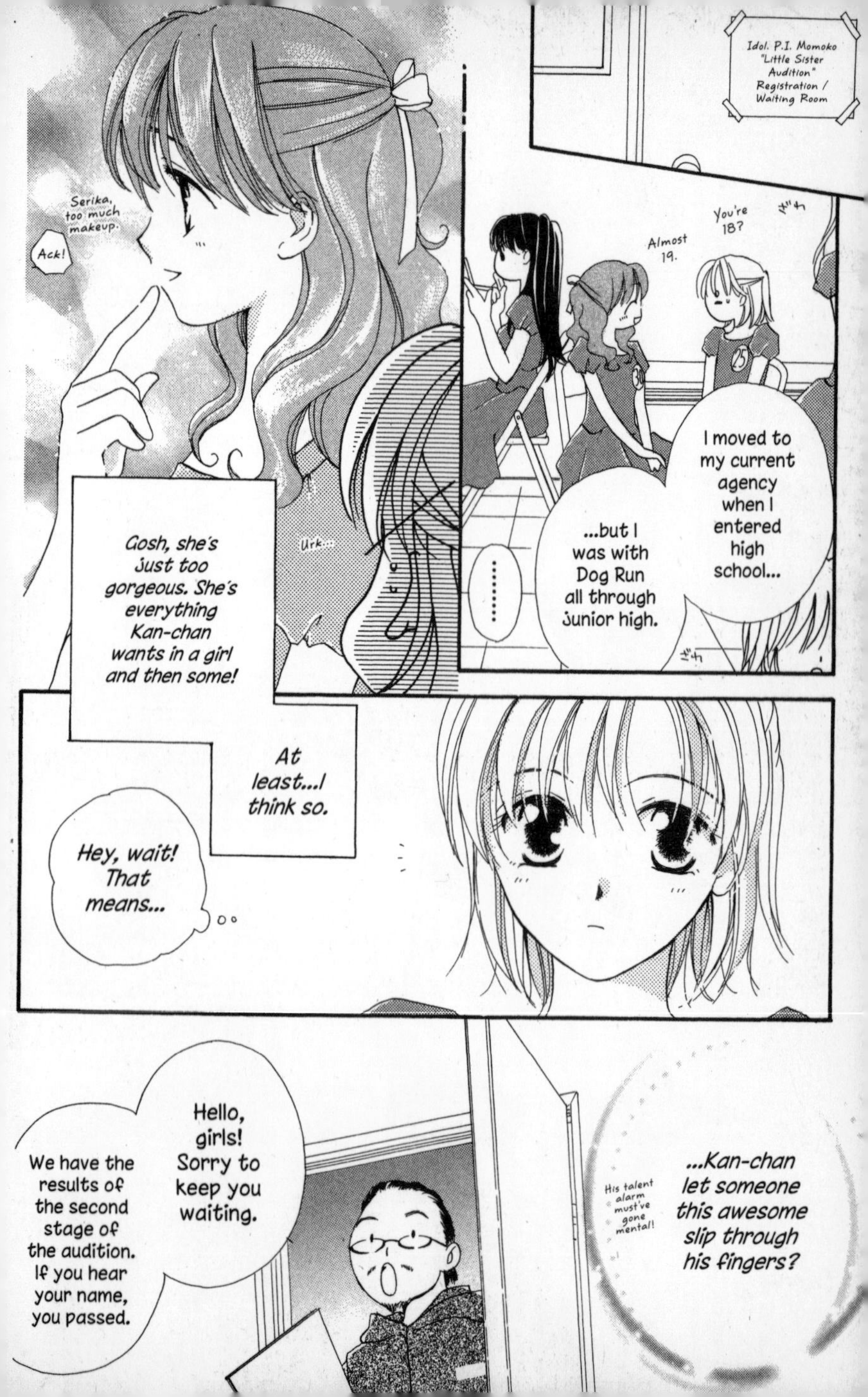
Idol. P.I. Momoko "Little Sister Audition" Registration / Waiting Room
You're 18?
Almost 19.
I moved to my current agency when I entered high school...
...but I was with Dog Run all through junior high.
......
Urk...
Serika, too much makeup.
Ack!
Gosh, she's just too gorgeous. She's everything Kan-chan wants in a girl and then some!
At least...I think so.
Hey, wait! That means...
...Kan-chan let someone this awesome slip through his fingers?
His talent alarm must've gone mental!
Hello, girls! Sorry to keep you waiting.
We have the results of the second stage of the audition. If you hear your name, you passed.

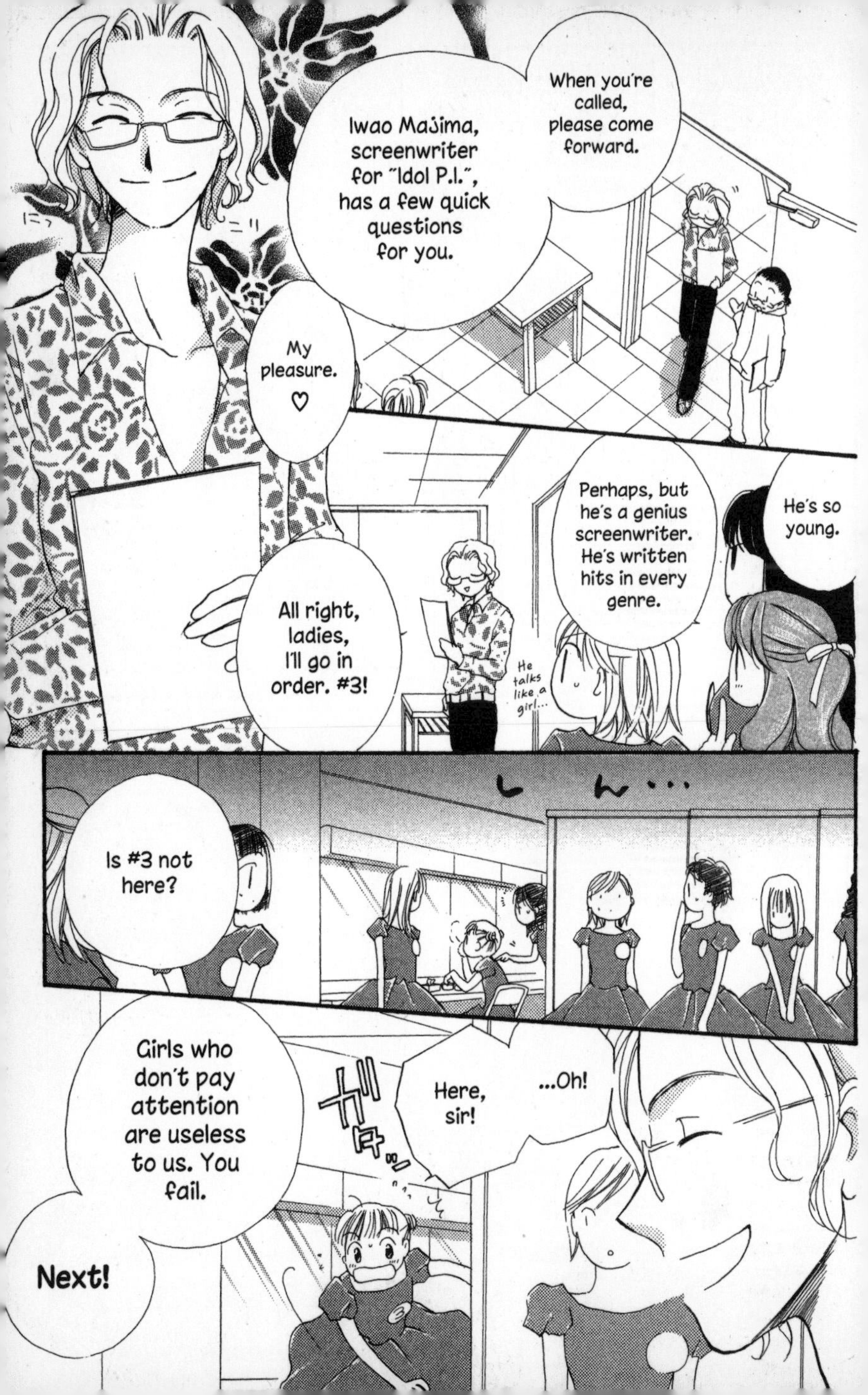
When you're called, please come forward.
Iwao Majima, screenwriter for "Idol P.I.", has a few quick questions for you.
My pleasure. ♡
He's so young.
Perhaps, but he's a genius screenwriter. He's written hits in every genre.
He talks like a girl...
All right, ladies, I'll go in order. #3!
しん…
Is #3 not here?
...Oh!
Here, sir!
ガタッ
Girls who don't pay attention are useless to us. You fail.
Next!

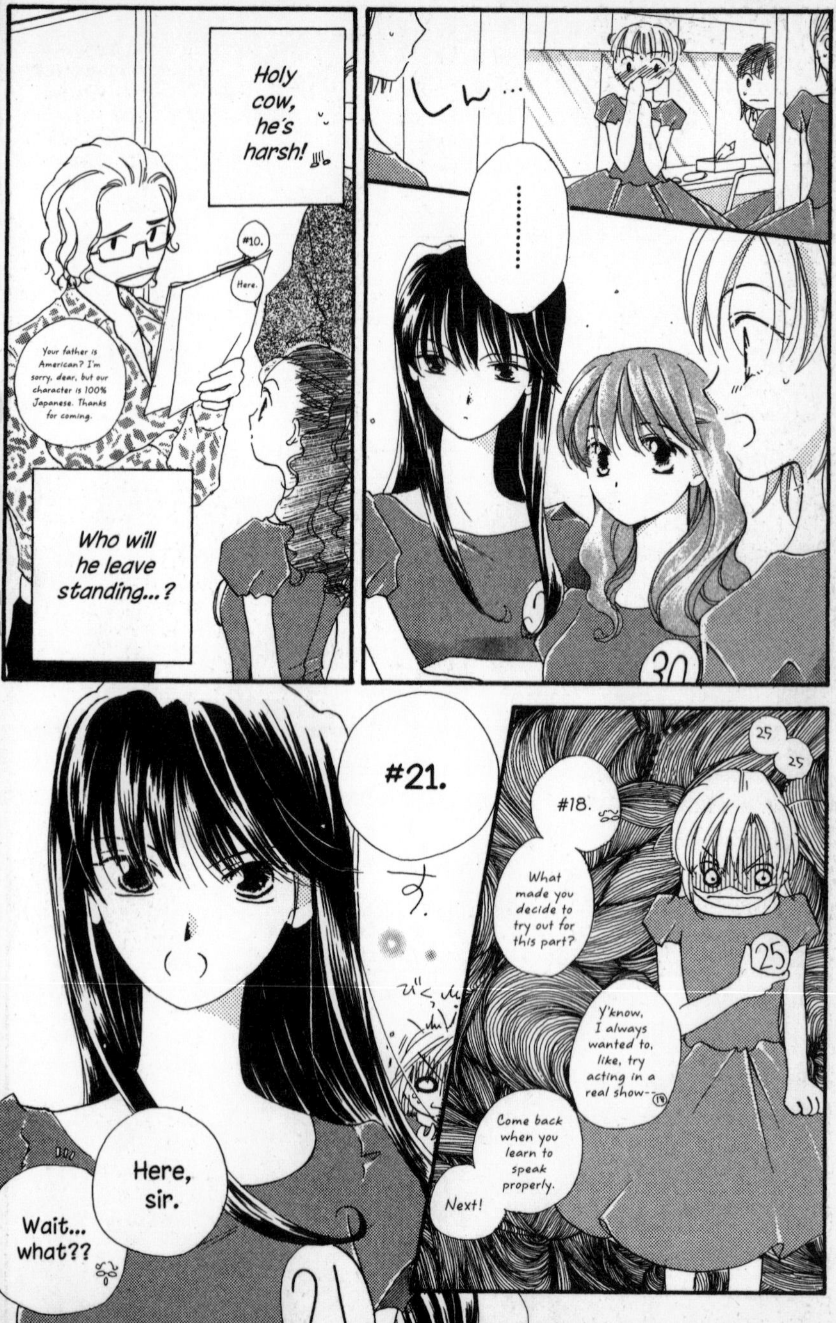
しん…
……
Holy cow, he's harsh!
#10.
Here.
Your father is American? I'm sorry, dear, but our character is 100% Japanese. Thanks for coming.
Who will he leave standing...?
25
25
#18.
What made you decide to try out for this part?
Y'know, I always wanted to, like, try acting in a real show--
Come back when you learn to speak properly.
Next!
#21.
す.
Here, sir.
Wait... what??

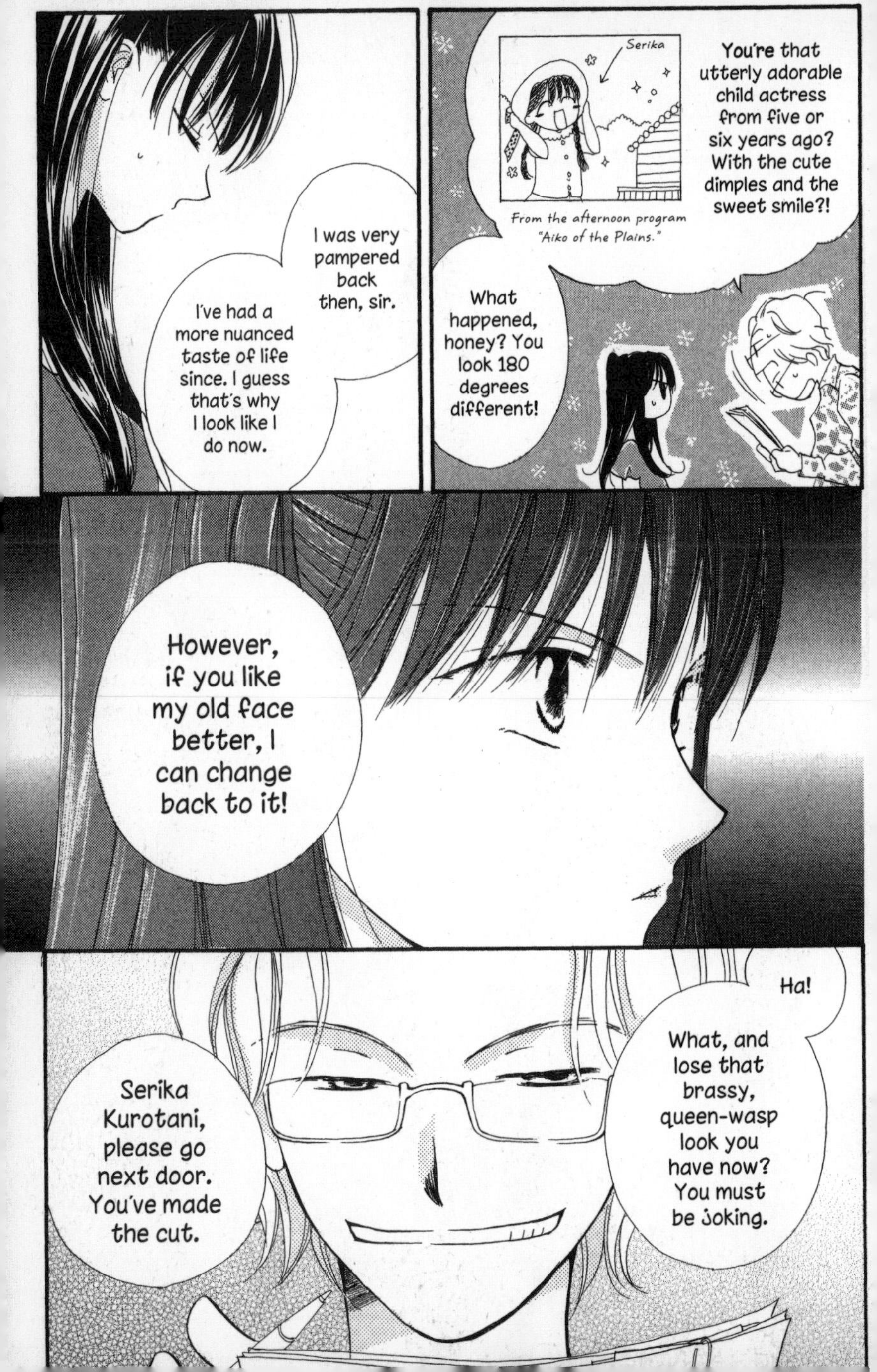
You're that utterly adorable child actress from five or six years ago? With the cute dimples and the sweet smile?!
Serika
From the afternoon program "Aiko of the Plains."
What happened, honey? You look 180 degrees different!
I was very pampered back then, sir.
I've had a more nuanced taste of life since. I guess that's why I look like I do now.
However, if you like my old face better, I can change back to it!
Ha!
What, and lose that brassy, queen-wasp look you have now? You must be joking.
Serika Kurotani, please go next door. You've made the cut.

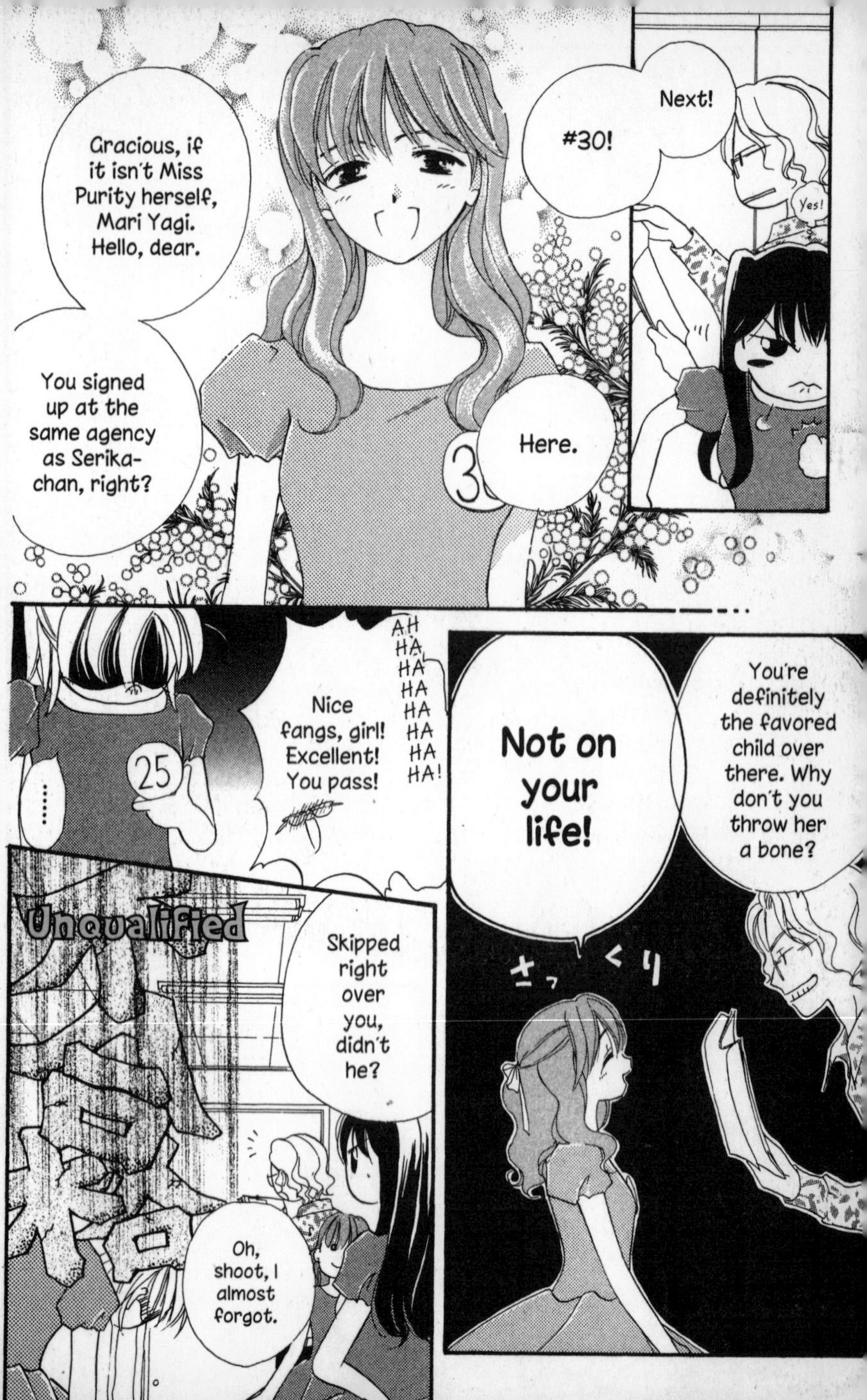
Next!
#30!
Yes!
Here.
Gracious, if it isn't Miss Purity herself, Mari Yagi. Hello, dear.
You signed up at the same agency as Serika-chan, right?
You're definitely the favored child over there. Why don't you throw her a bone?
Not on your life!
さっ くり
AH HA HA HA HA HA HA HA!
Nice fangs, girl! Excellent! You pass!
......
Skipped right over you, didn't he?
Unqualified
Oh, shoot, I almost forgot.

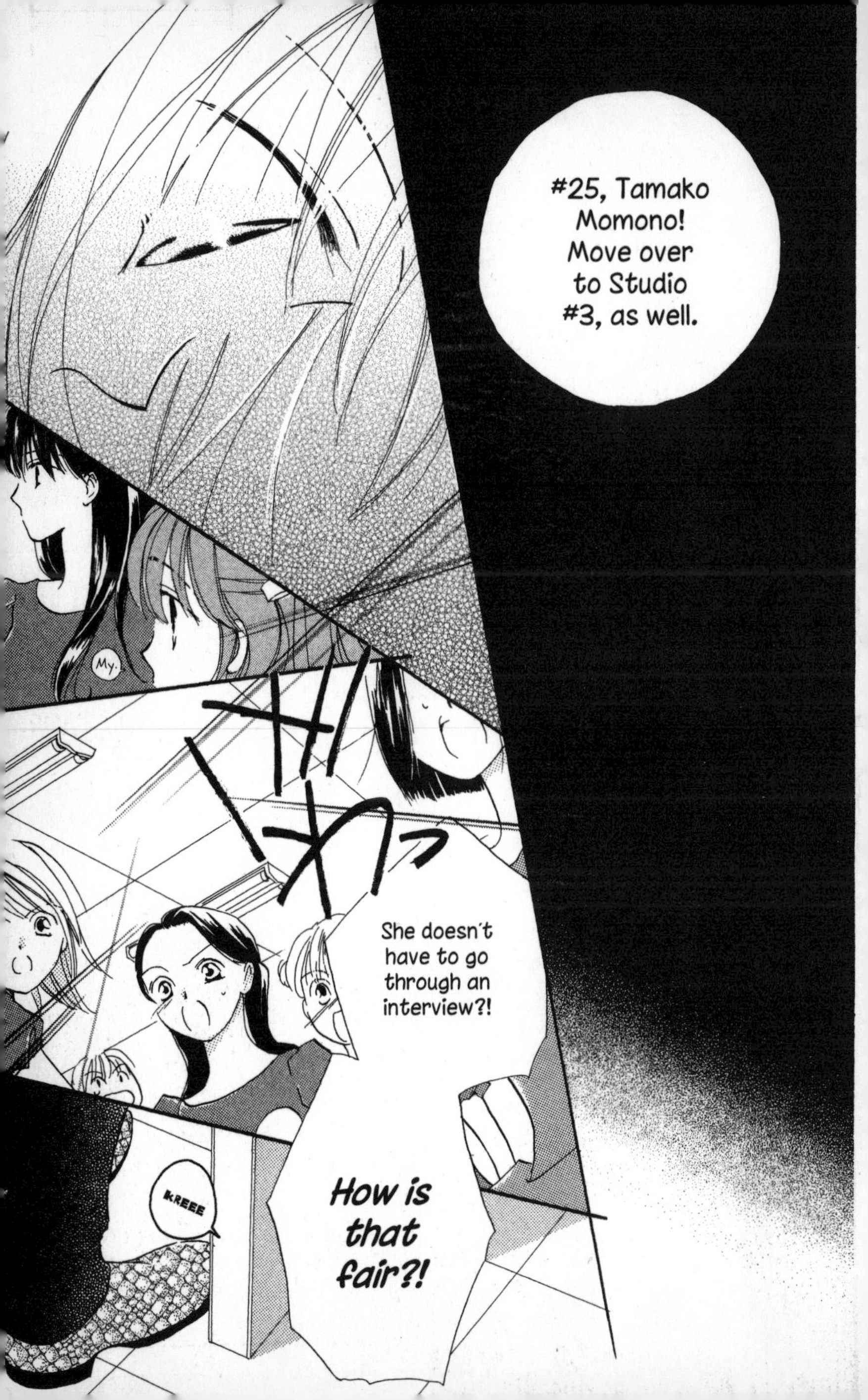
#25, Tamako Momono! Move over to Studio #3, as well.
My.
She doesn't have to go through an interview?!
KREEE
How is that fair?!

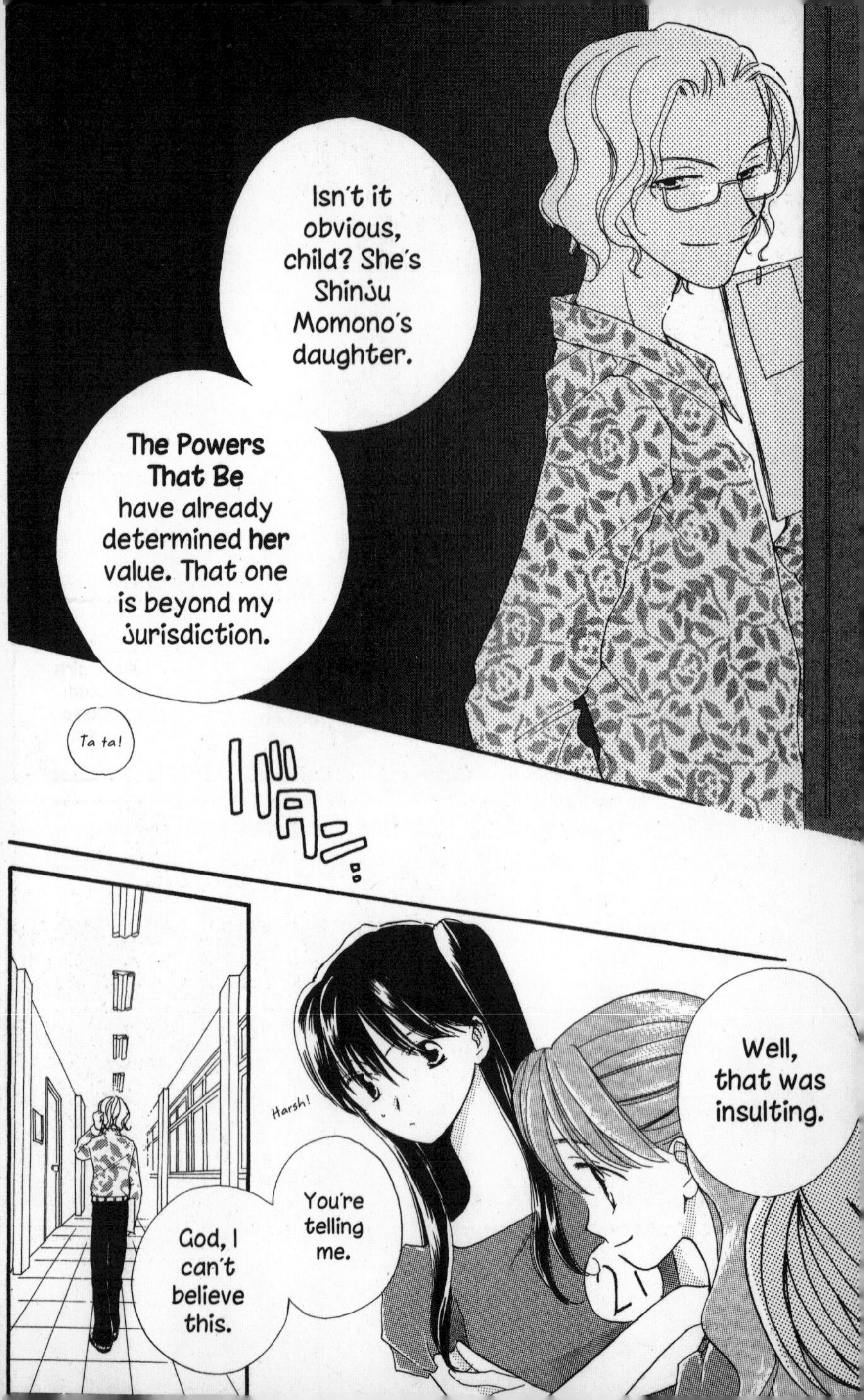
Isn't it obvious, child? She's Shinju Momono's daughter.
The Powers That Be have already determined her value. That one is beyond my jurisdiction.
Ta ta!
Well, that was insulting.
Harsh!
You're telling me.
God, I can't believe this.

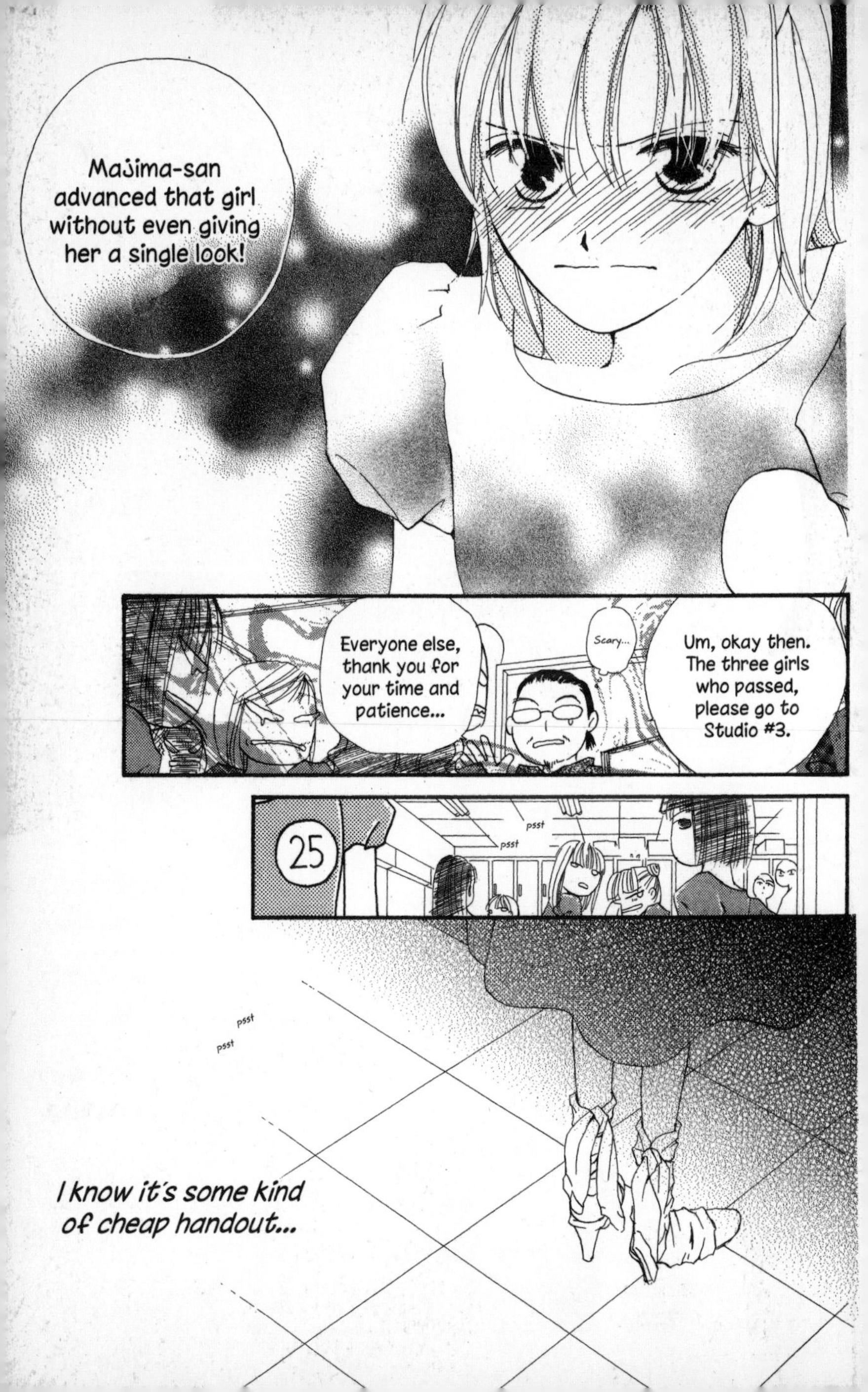
Majima-san advanced that girl without even giving her a single look!
Um, okay then. The three girls who passed, please go to Studio #3.
Scary...
Everyone else, thank you for your time and patience...
psst
psst
25
psst
psst
I know it's some kind of cheap handout...

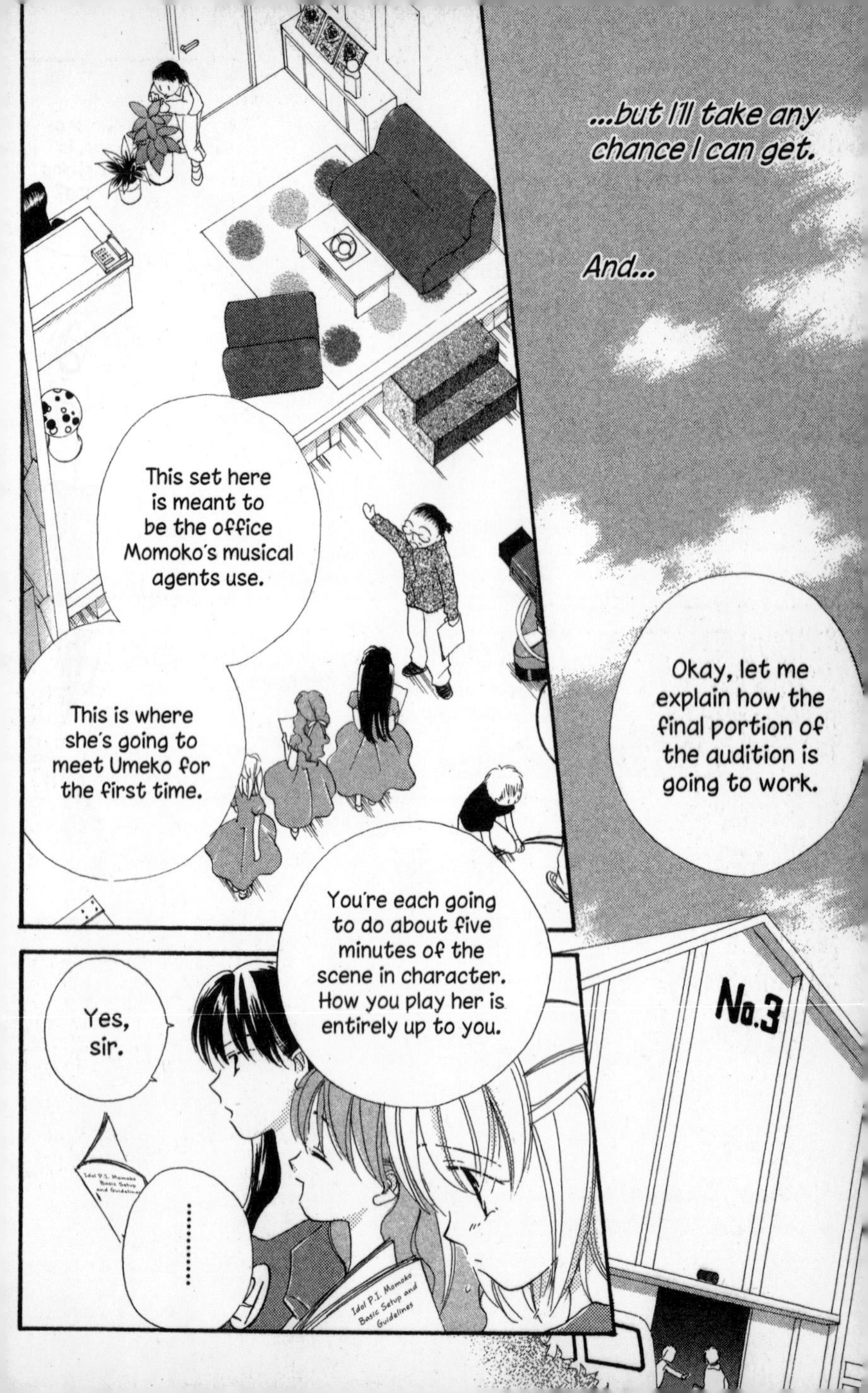
...but I'll take any chance I can get.
And...
Okay, let me explain how the final portion of the audition is going to work.
No.3
This set here is meant to be the office Momoko's musical agents use.
This is where she's going to meet Umeko for the first time.
You're each going to do about five minutes of the scene in character. How you play her is entirely up to you.
Yes, sir.
....
Idol P.I. Momoko Basic Setup and Guidelines
Idol P.I. Momoko Basic Setup and Guidelines

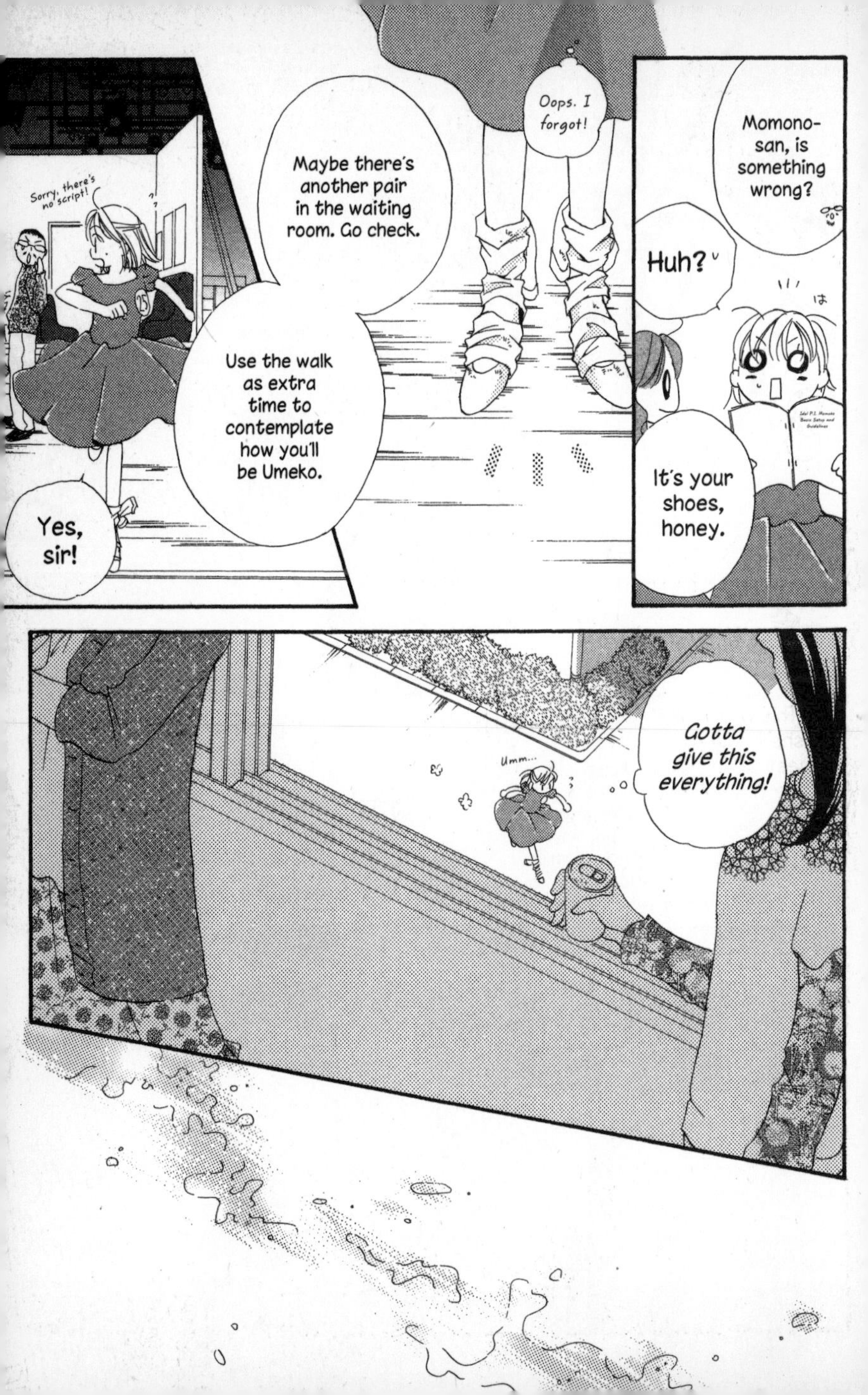
Momono-san, is something wrong?
Huh?
は
It's your shoes, honey.
Oops. I forgot!
Maybe there's another pair in the waiting room. Go check.
Use the walk as extra time to contemplate how you'll be Umeko.
Sorry, there's no script!
Yes, sir!
Gotta give this everything!
Umm...

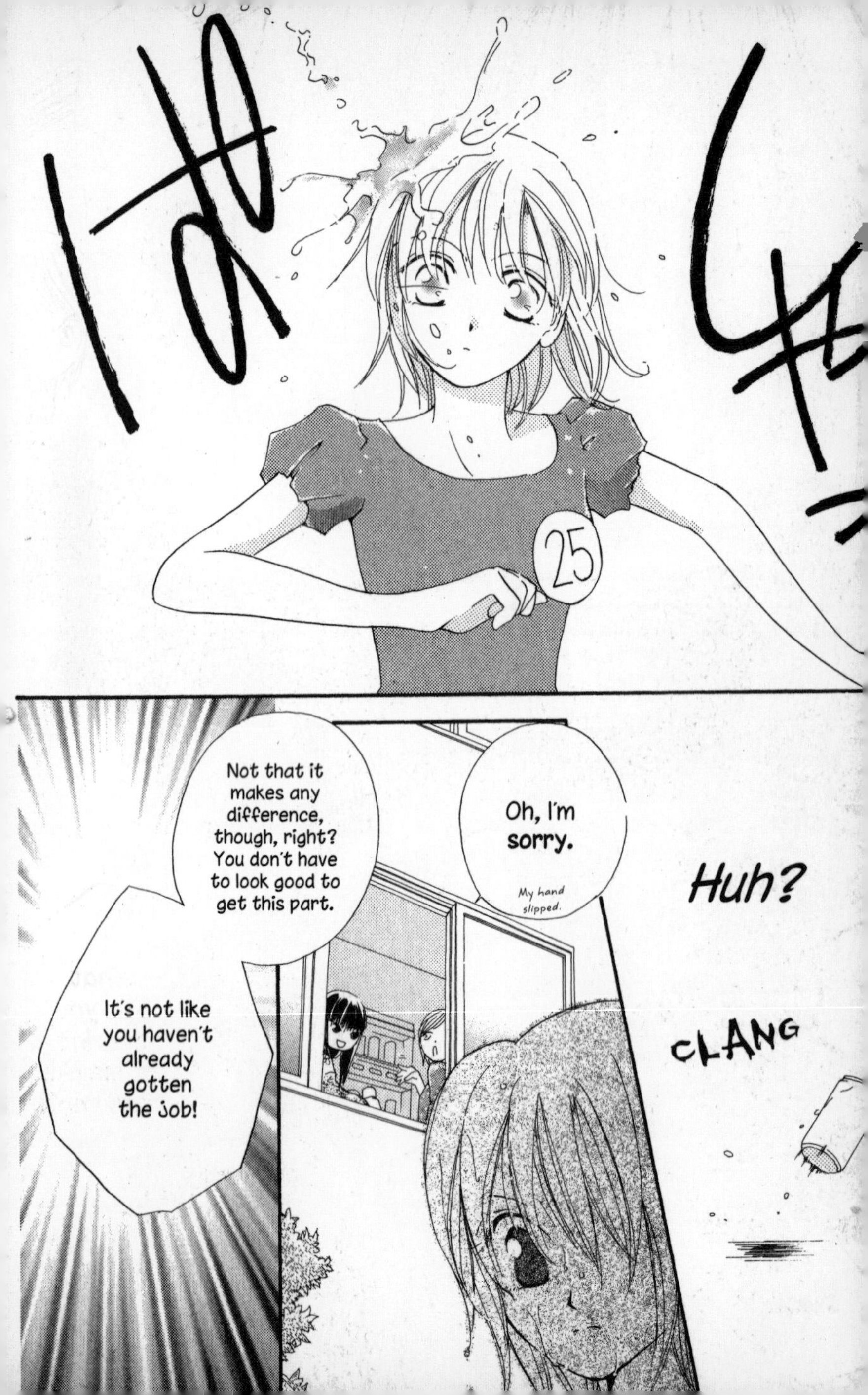
25
Huh?
Oh, I'm sorry.
My hand slipped.
Not that it makes any difference, though, right? You don't have to look good to get this part.
CLANG
It's not like you haven't already gotten the job!

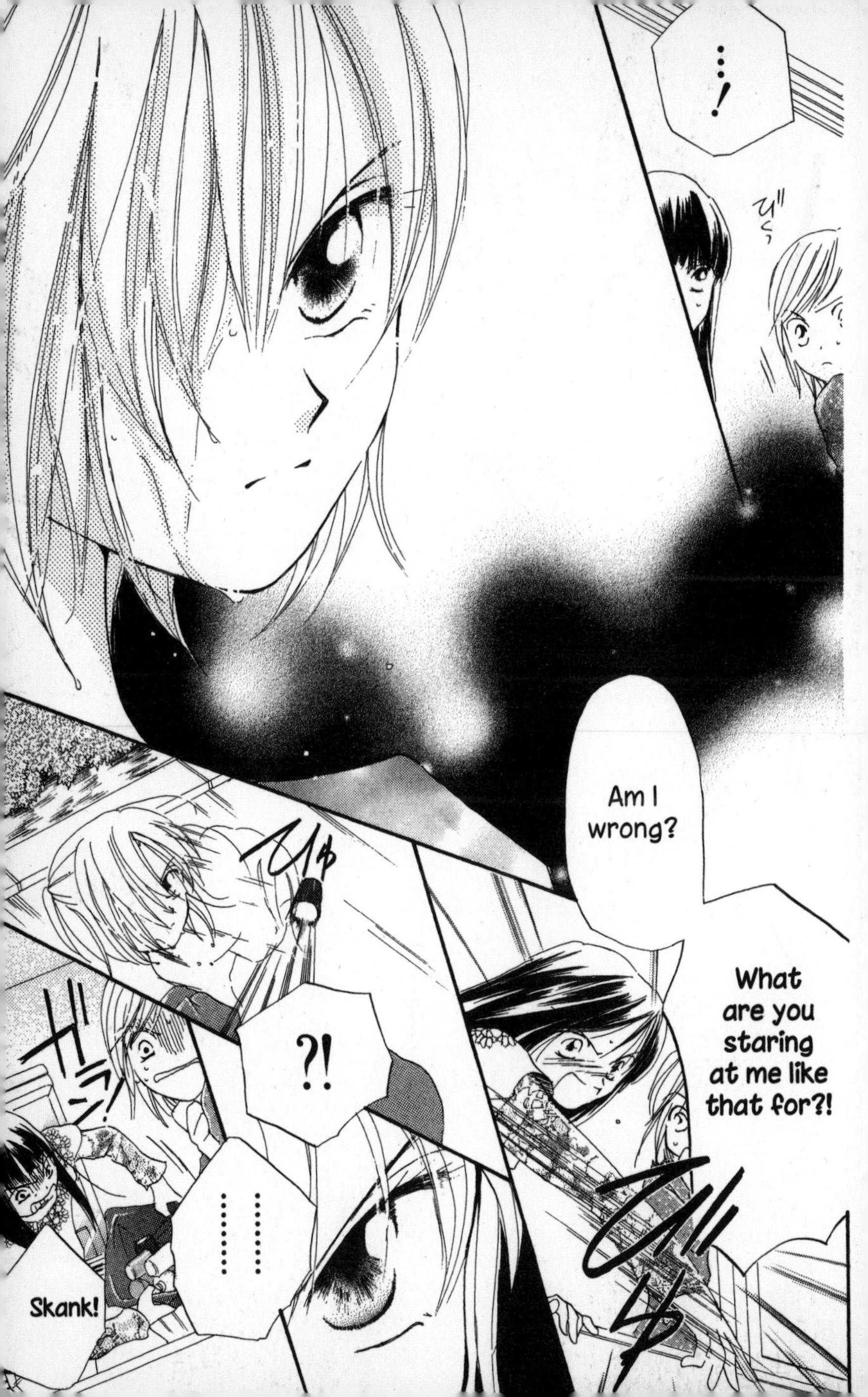
...!
Am I wrong?
What are you staring at me like that for?!
?!
......
Skank!

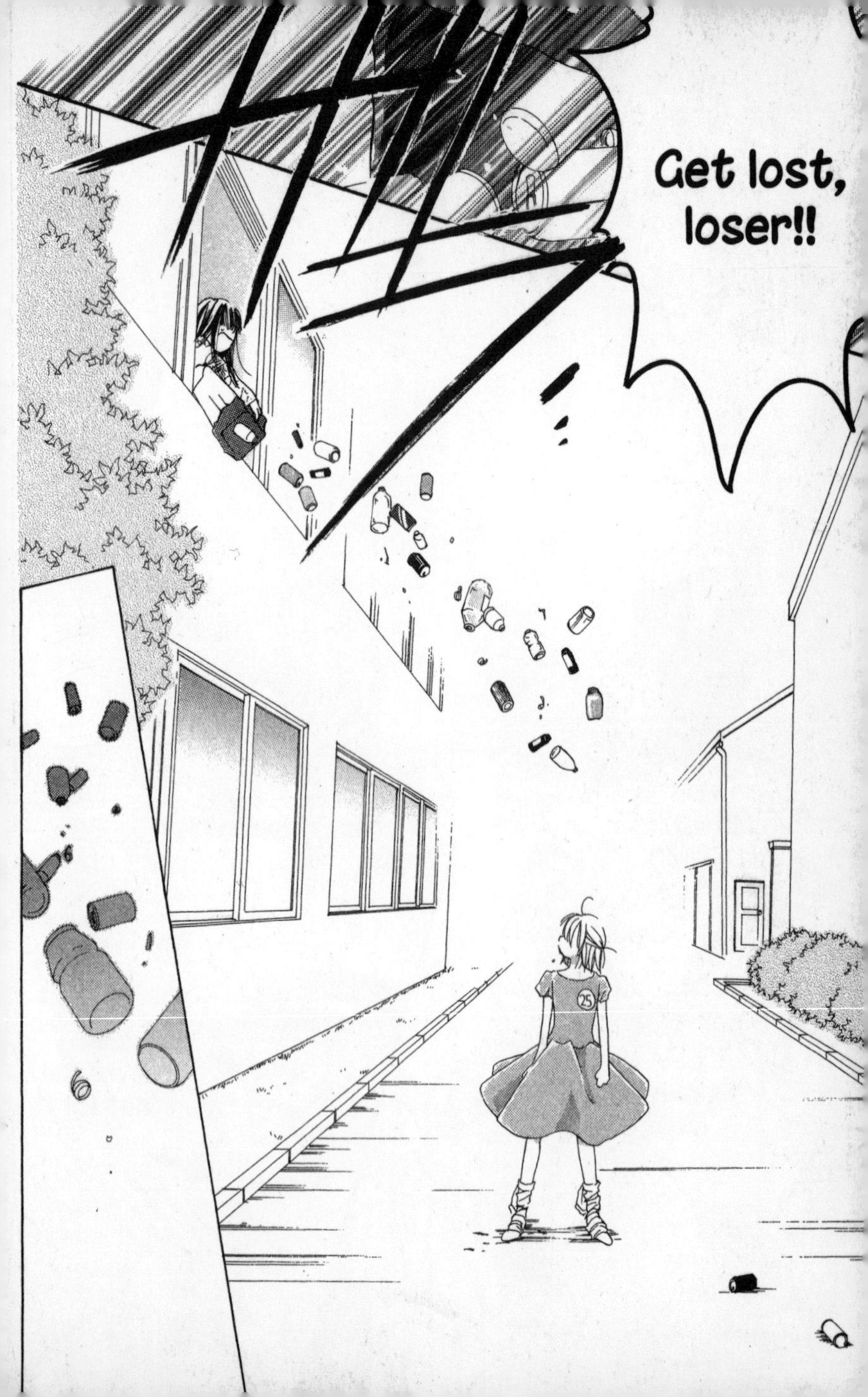
Get lost, loser!!

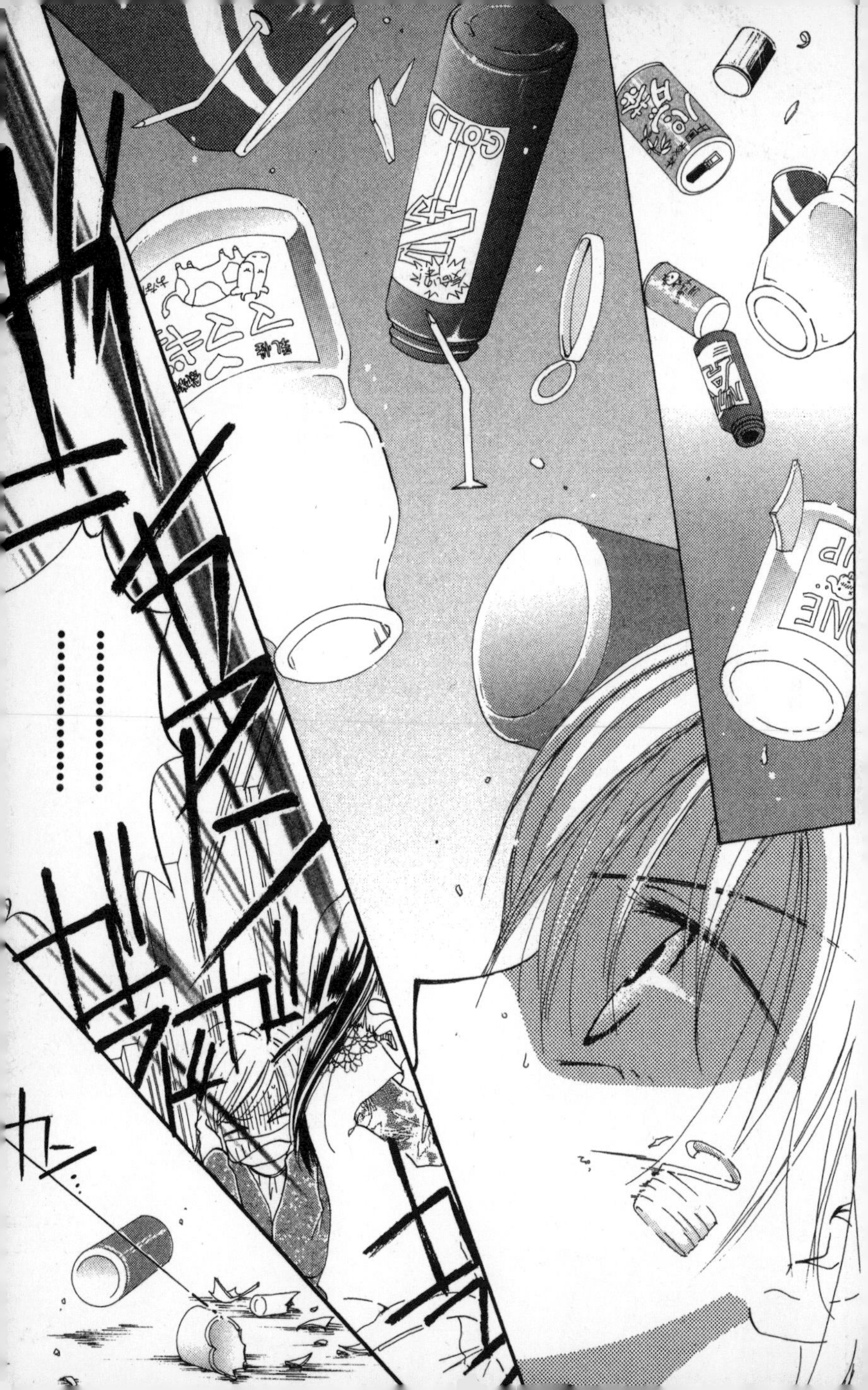

……
……
カーン…

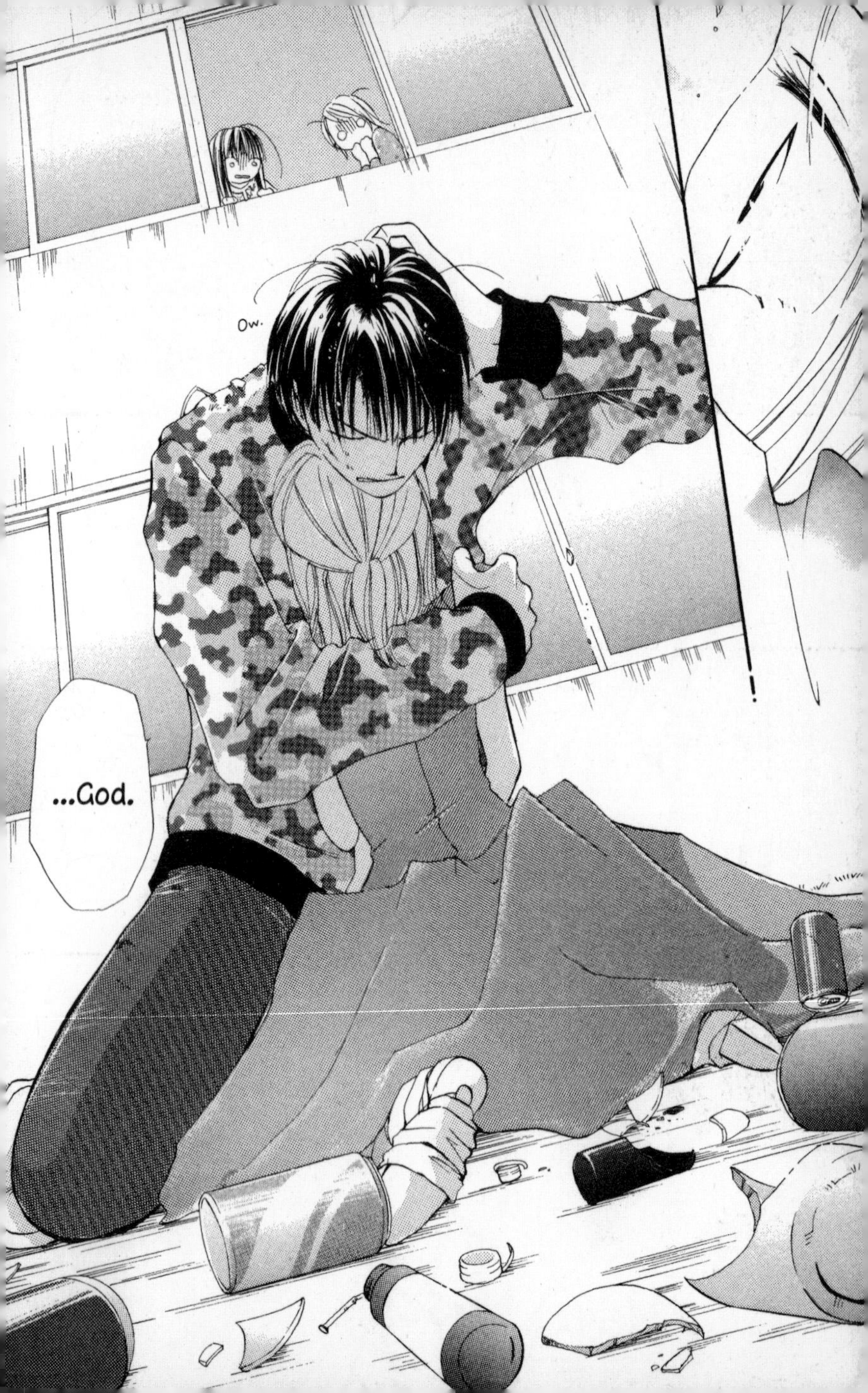
Ow.
...God.

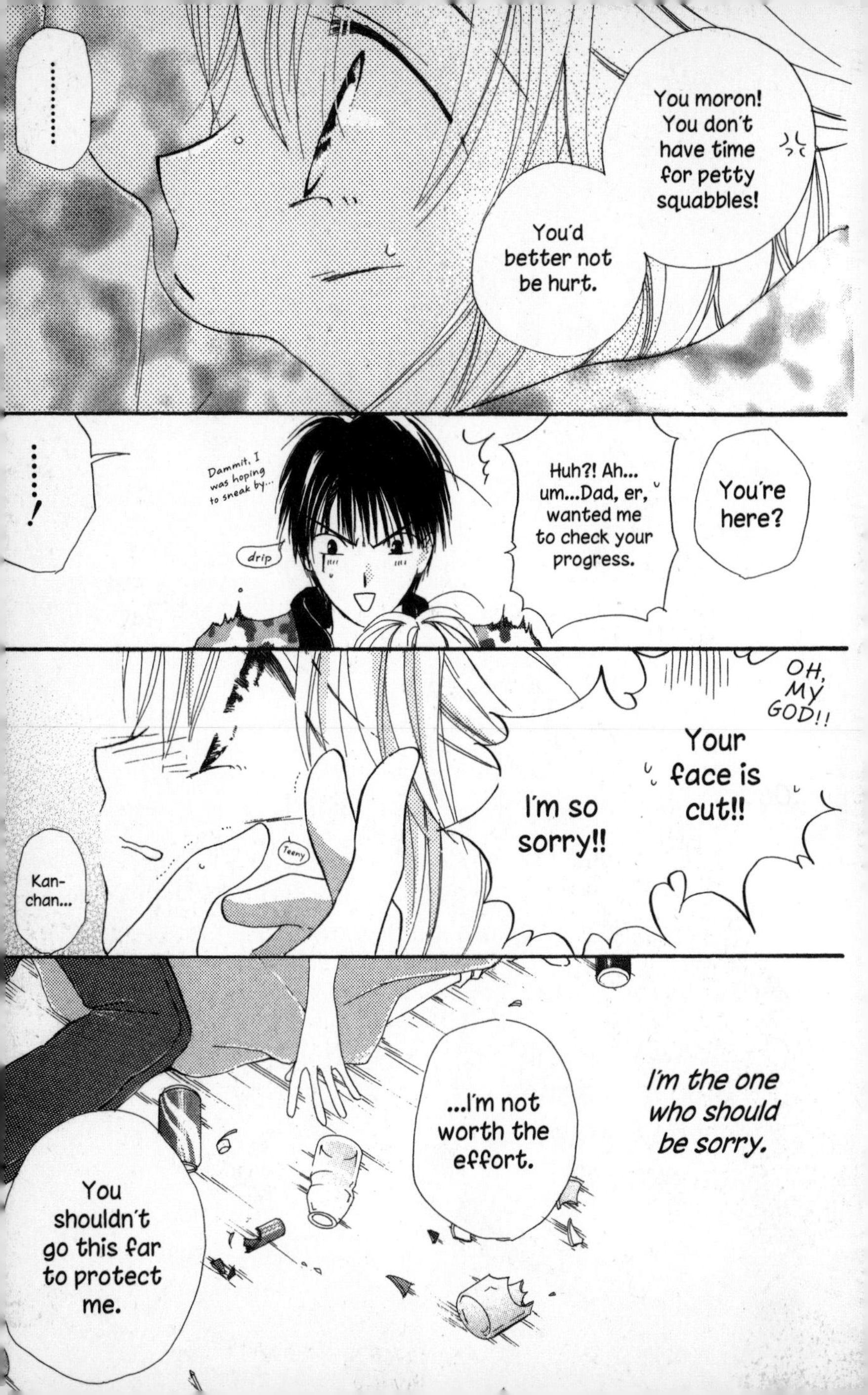
You moron! You don't have time for petty squabbles!
You'd better not be hurt.
......
You're here?
Huh?! Ah... um...Dad, er, wanted me to check your progress.
Dammit, I was hoping to sneak by...
drip
......!
OH, MY GOD!!
Your face is cut!!
I'm so sorry!!
Teeny
Kan-chan...
I'm the one who should be sorry.
...I'm not worth the effort.
You shouldn't go this far to protect me.

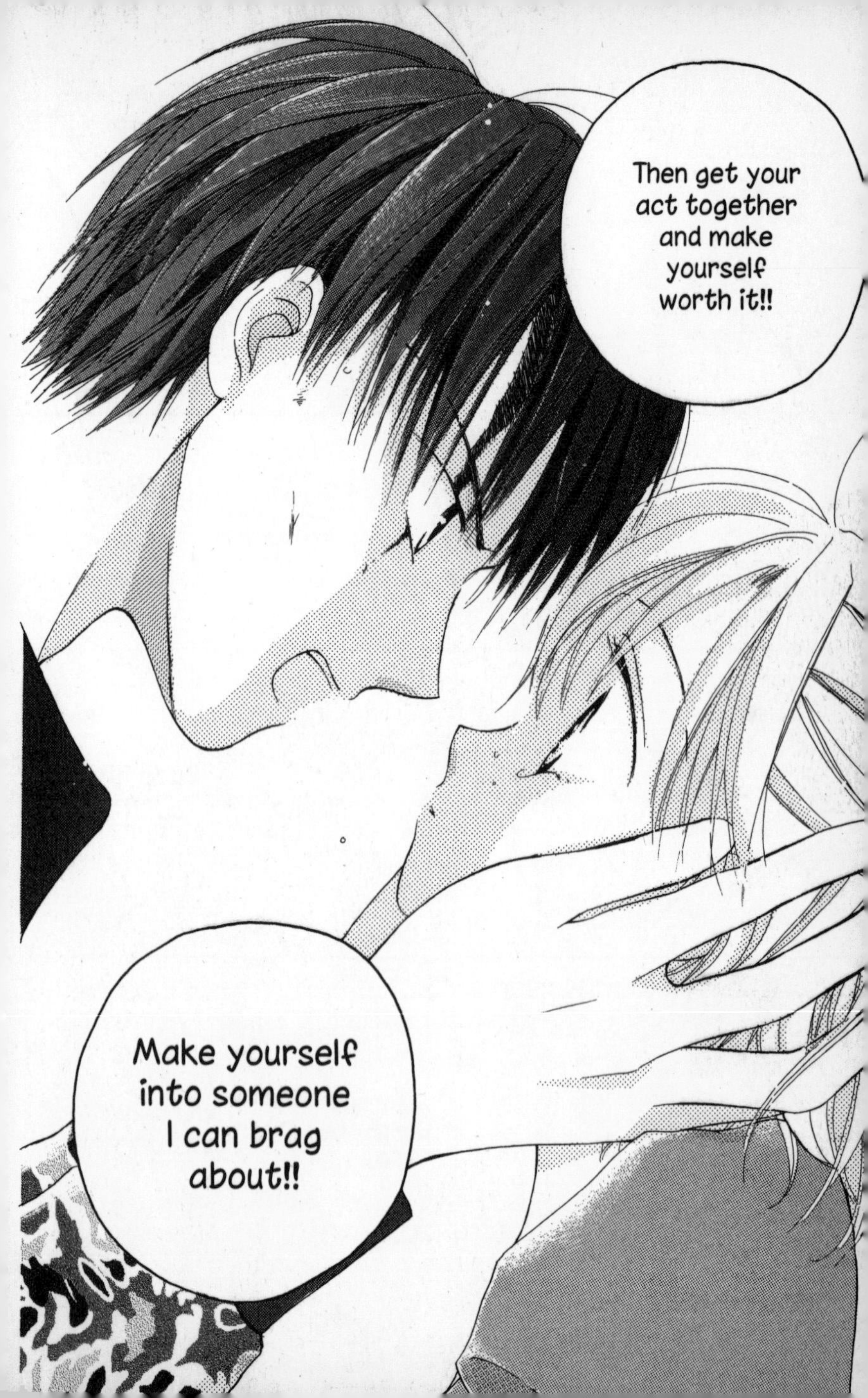
Then get your act together and make yourself worth it!!
Make yourself into someone I can brag about!!

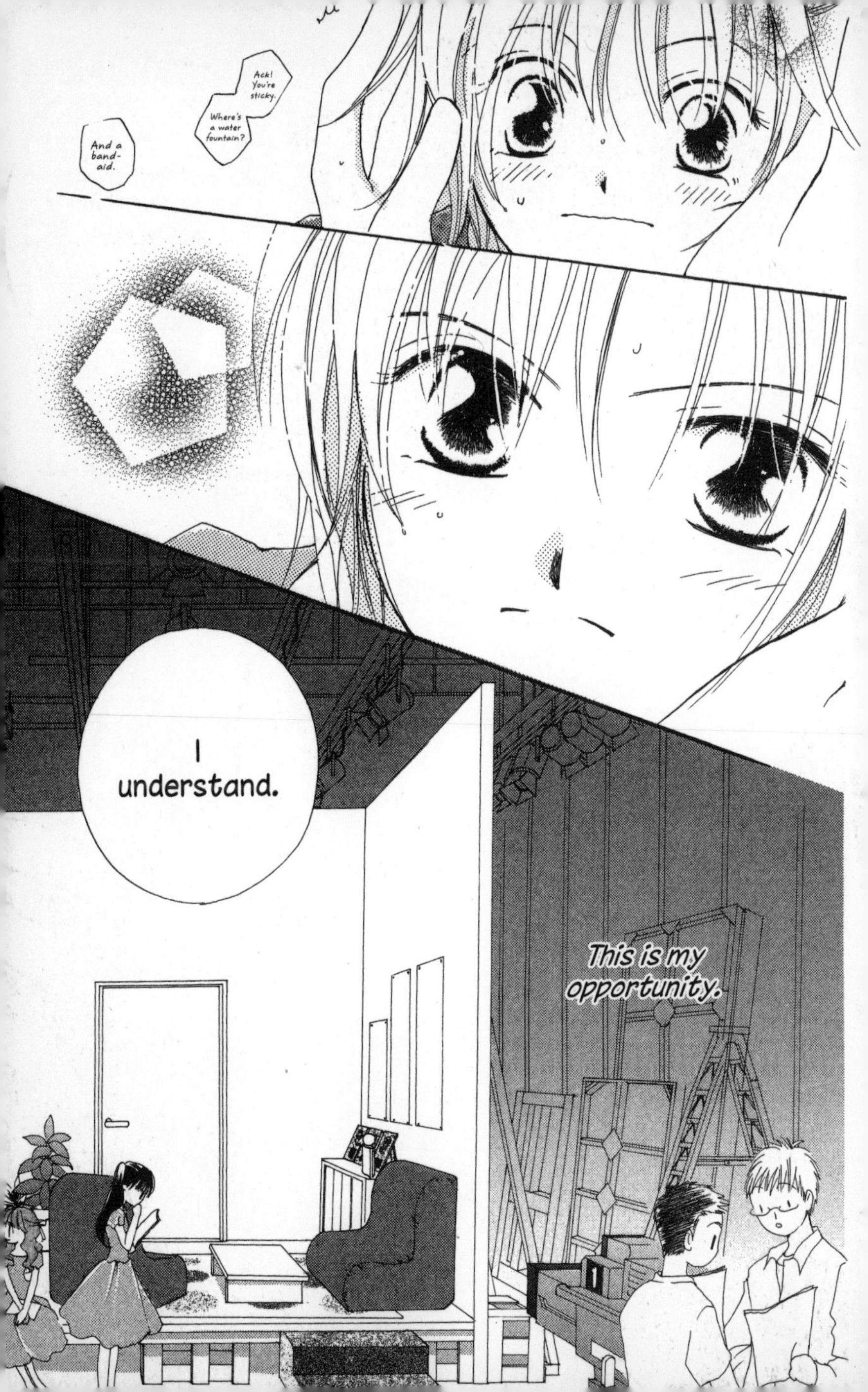
Ack! You're sticky.
Where's a water fountain?
And a band-aid.
I understand.
This is my opportunity.

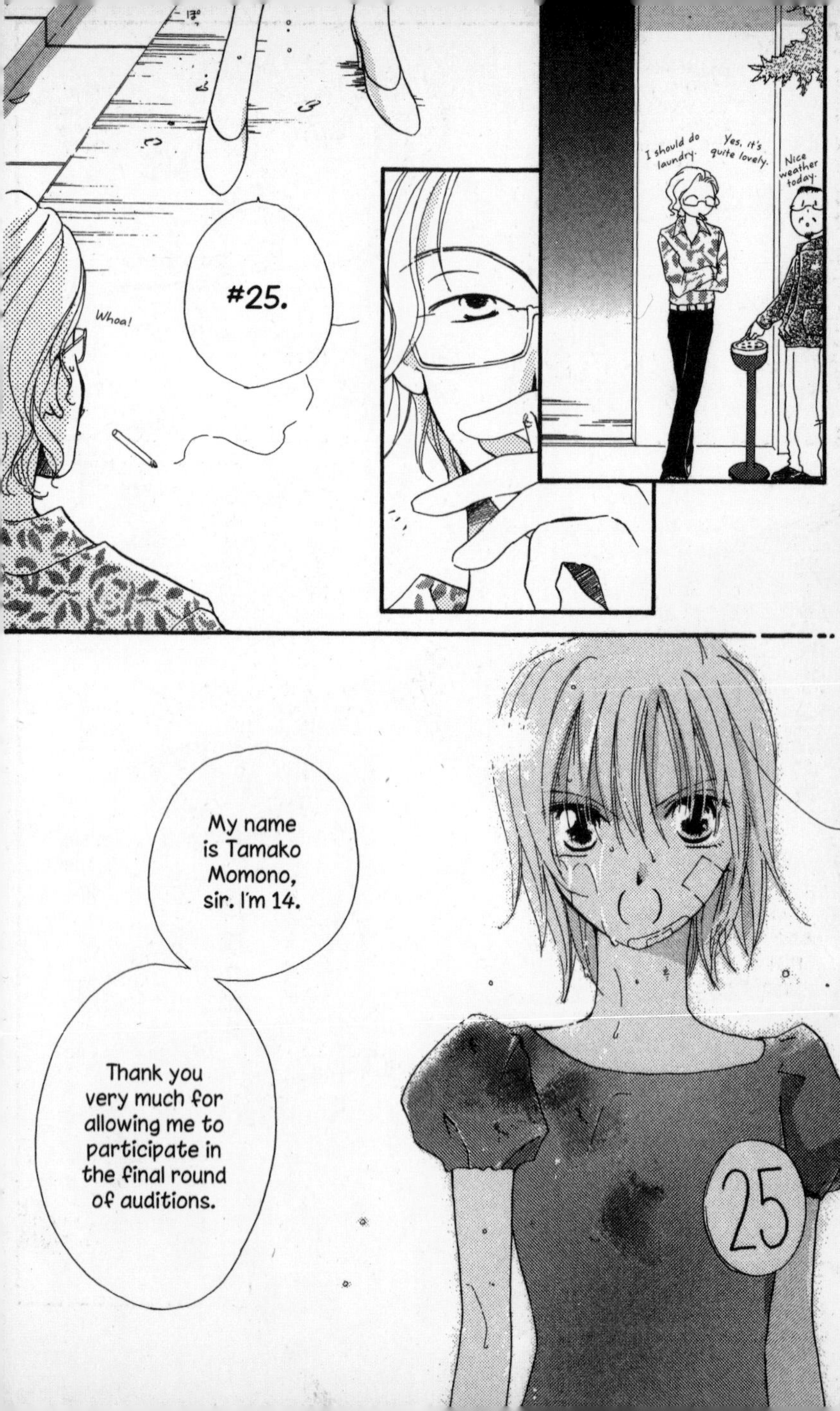
Nice weather today.
Yes, it's quite lovely.
I should do laundry.
#25.
Whoa!
My name is Tamako Momono, sir. I'm 14.
Thank you very much for allowing me to participate in the final round of auditions.

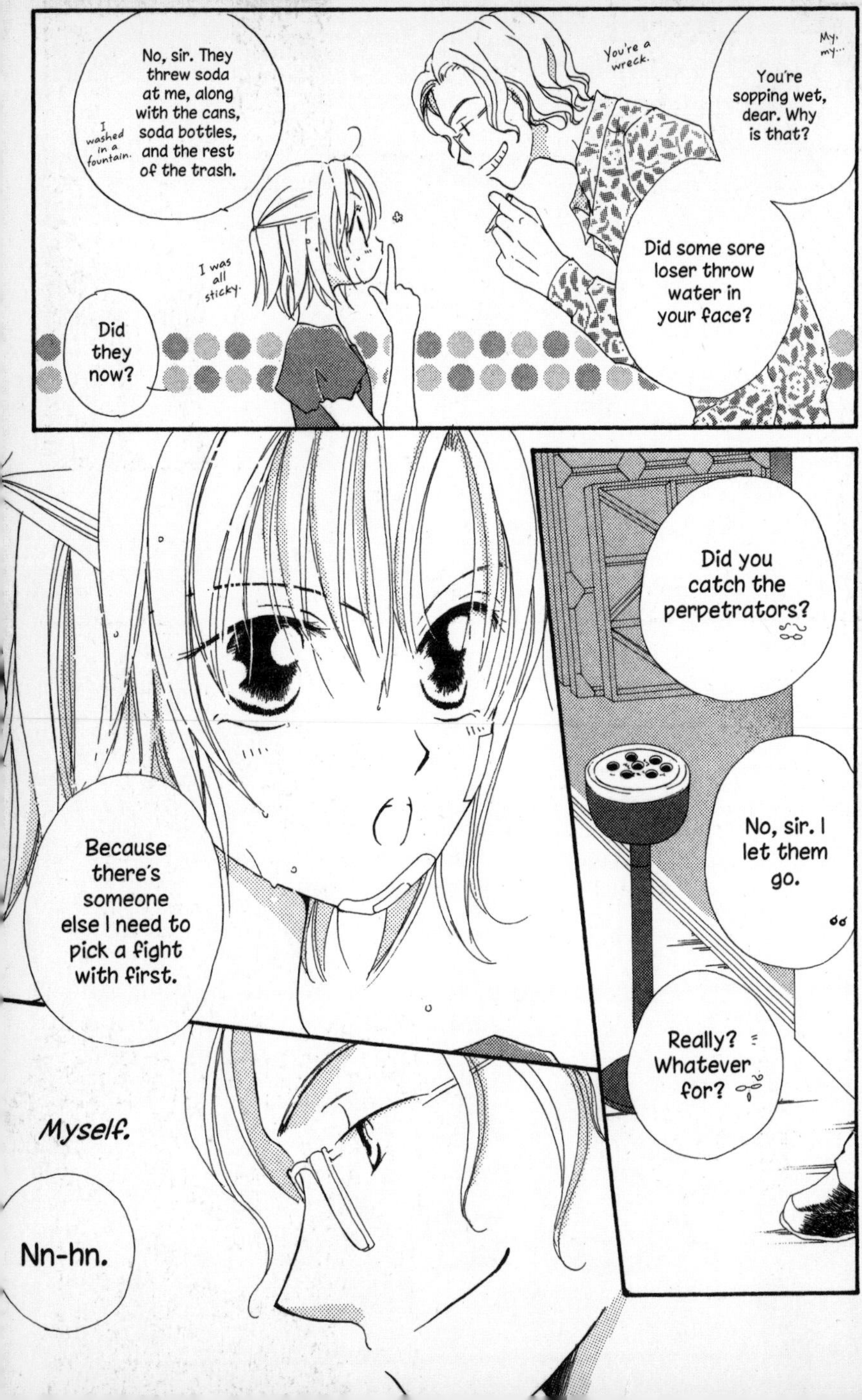
My, my...
You're a wreck.
You're sopping wet, dear. Why is that?
Did some sore loser throw water in your face?
No, sir. They threw soda at me, along with the cans, soda bottles, and the rest of the trash.
I washed in a fountain.
I was all sticky.
Did they now?
Did you catch the perpetrators?
No, sir. I let them go.
Really? Whatever for?
Because there's someone else I need to pick a fight with first.
Myself.
Nn-hn.

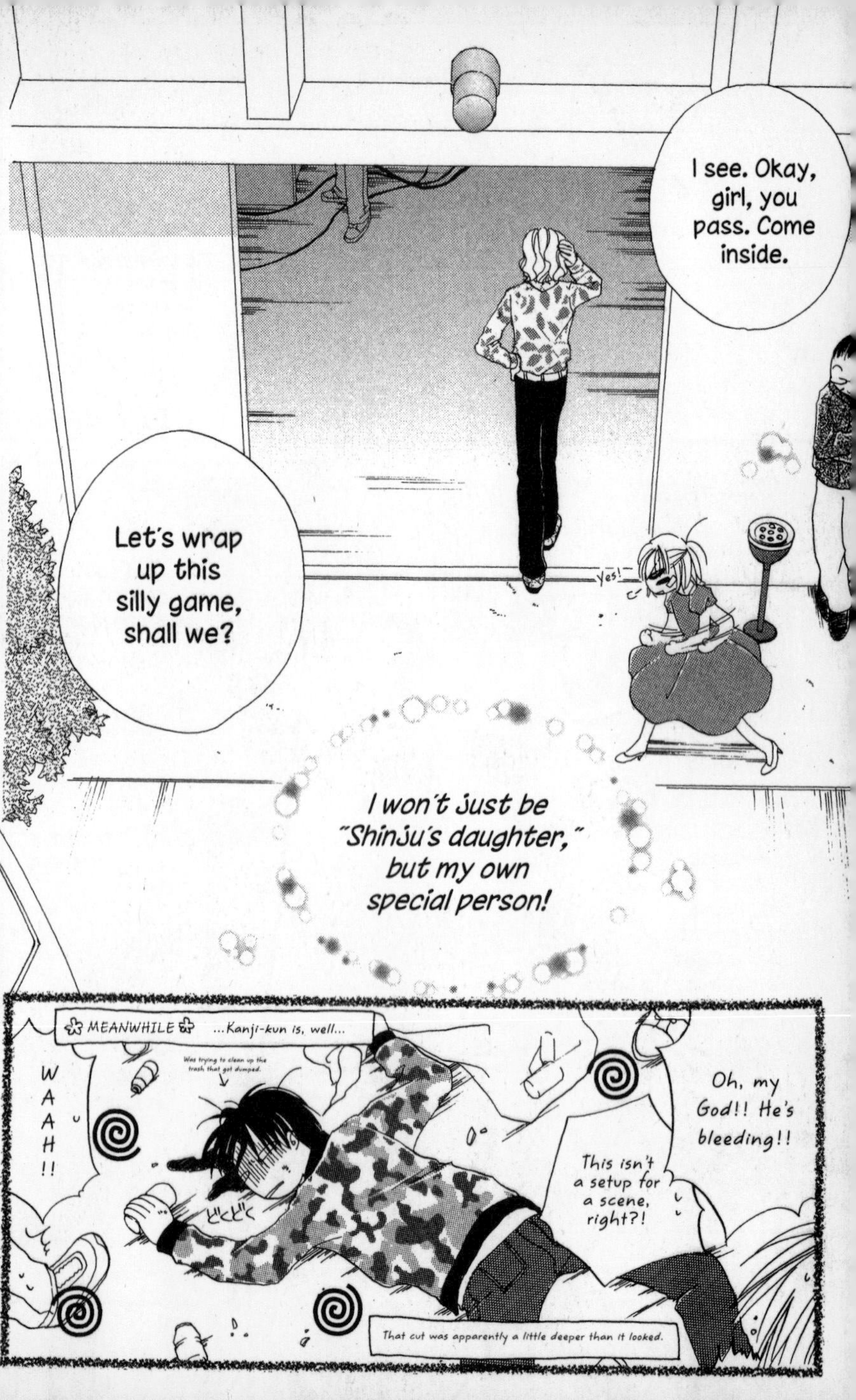
I see. Okay, girl, you pass. Come inside.
Yes!
Let's wrap up this silly game, shall we?
I won't just be "Shinju's daughter," but my own special person!
MEANWHILE ...Kanji-kun is, well...
Oh, my God!! He's bleeding!!
This isn't a setup for a scene, right?!
Was trying to clean up the trash that got dumped.
WAAAH!!
どくどく
That cut was apparently a little deeper than it looked.

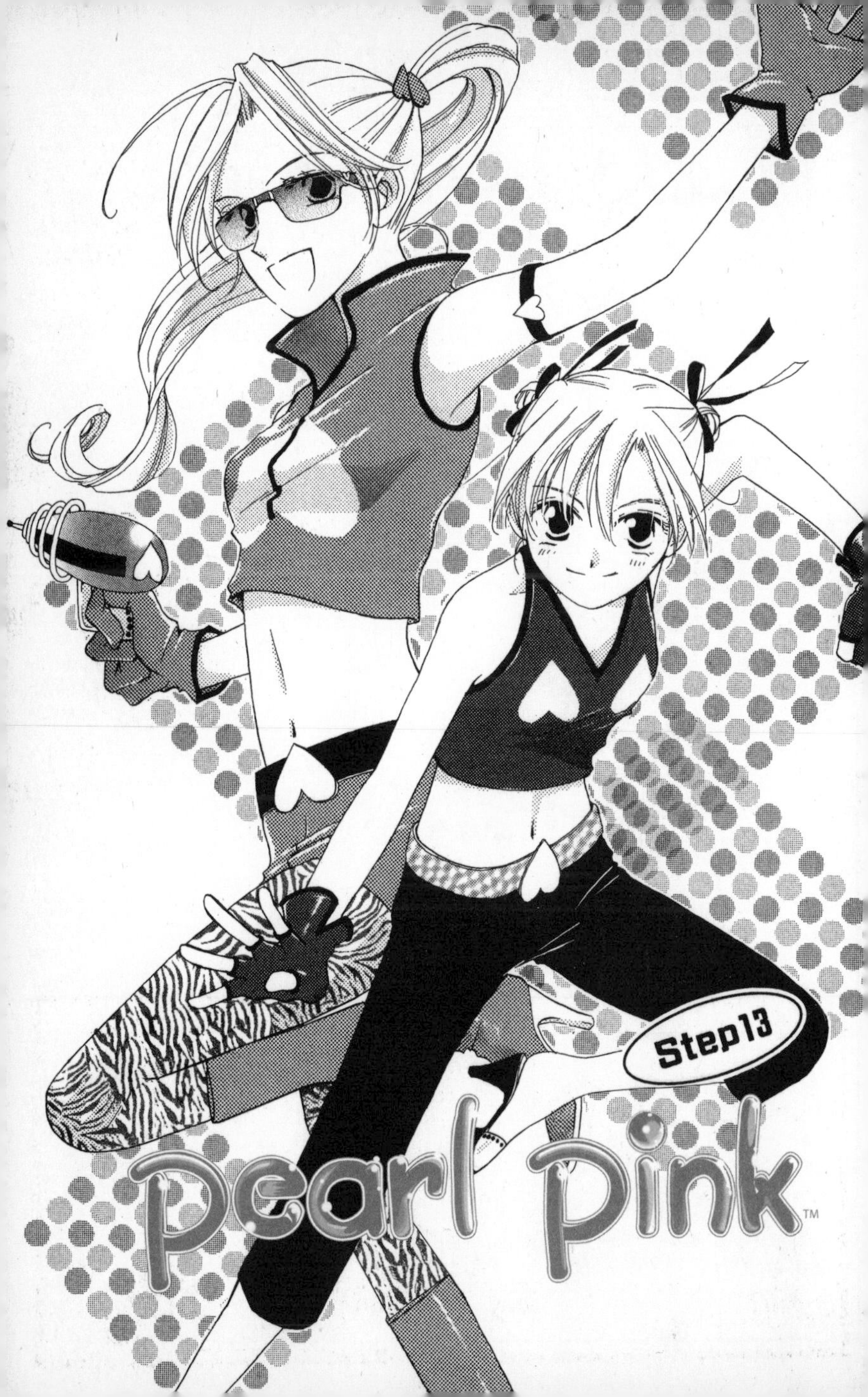
Step 13
Pearl Pink™

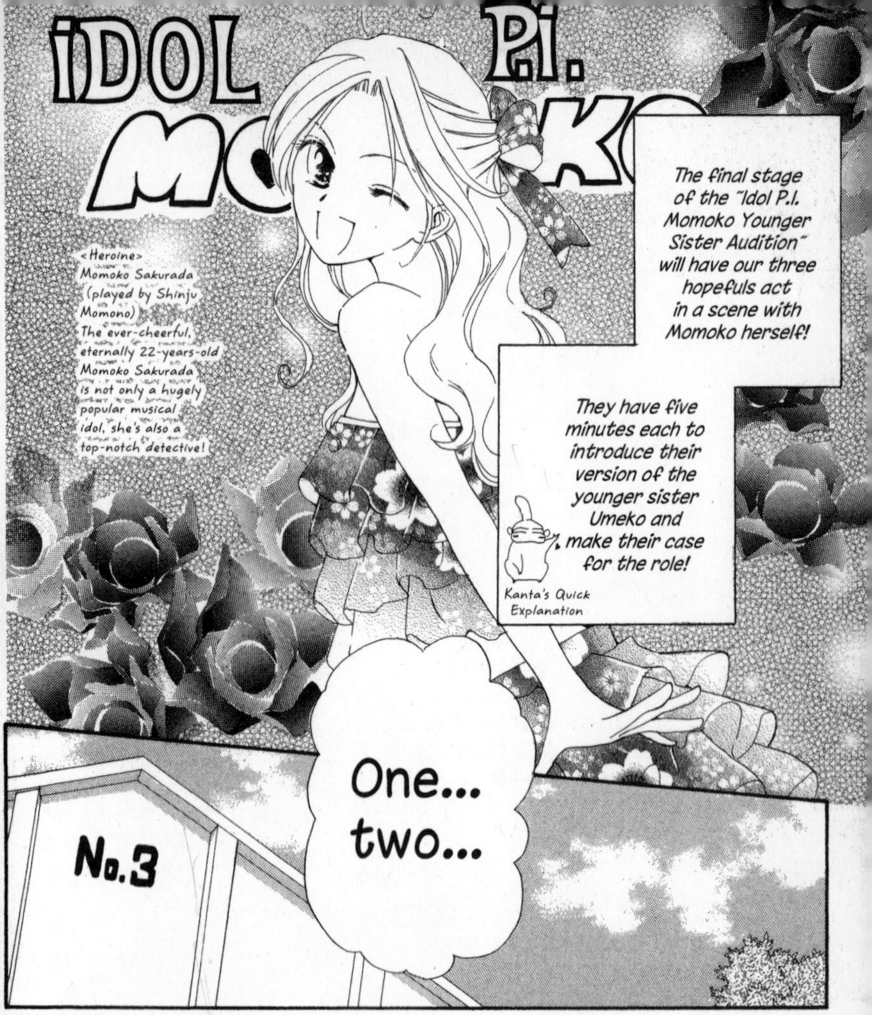
iDOL P.I. MOMOKO
The final stage of the "Idol P.I. Momoko Younger Sister Audition" will have our three hopefuls act in a scene with Momoko herself!
They have five minutes each to introduce their version of the younger sister Umeko and make their case for the role!
Kanta's Quick Explanation
<Heroine> Momoko Sakurada (played by Shinju Momono) The ever-cheerful, eternally 22-years-old Momoko Sakurada is not only a hugely popular musical idol, she's also a top-notch detective!
One... two...
No.3

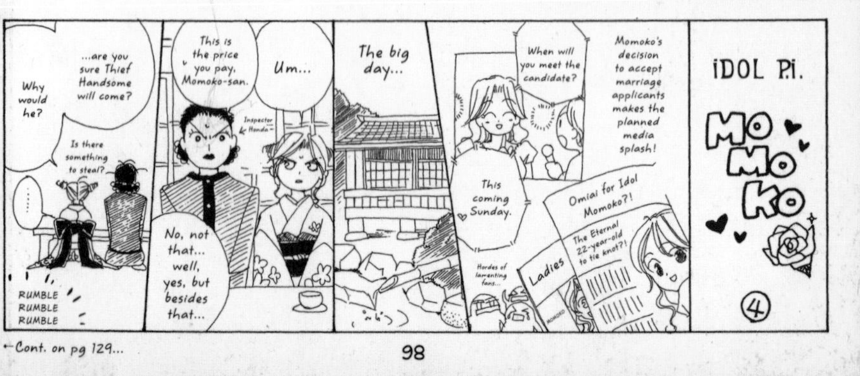
iDOL P.I. MOMOKO
4
Momoko's decision to accept marriage applicants makes the planned media splash!
When will you meet the candidate?
This coming Sunday.
Omiai for Idol Momoko?!
The Eternal 22-year-old to tie knot?!
Ladies
Hordes of lamenting fans...
The big day...
This is the price you pay, Momoko-san.
Um...
Inspector Honda
No, not that... well, yes, but besides that...
...are you sure Thief Handsome will come?
Why would he?
Is there something to steal?
......
RUMBLE RUMBLE RUMBLE

←Cont. on pg 129...

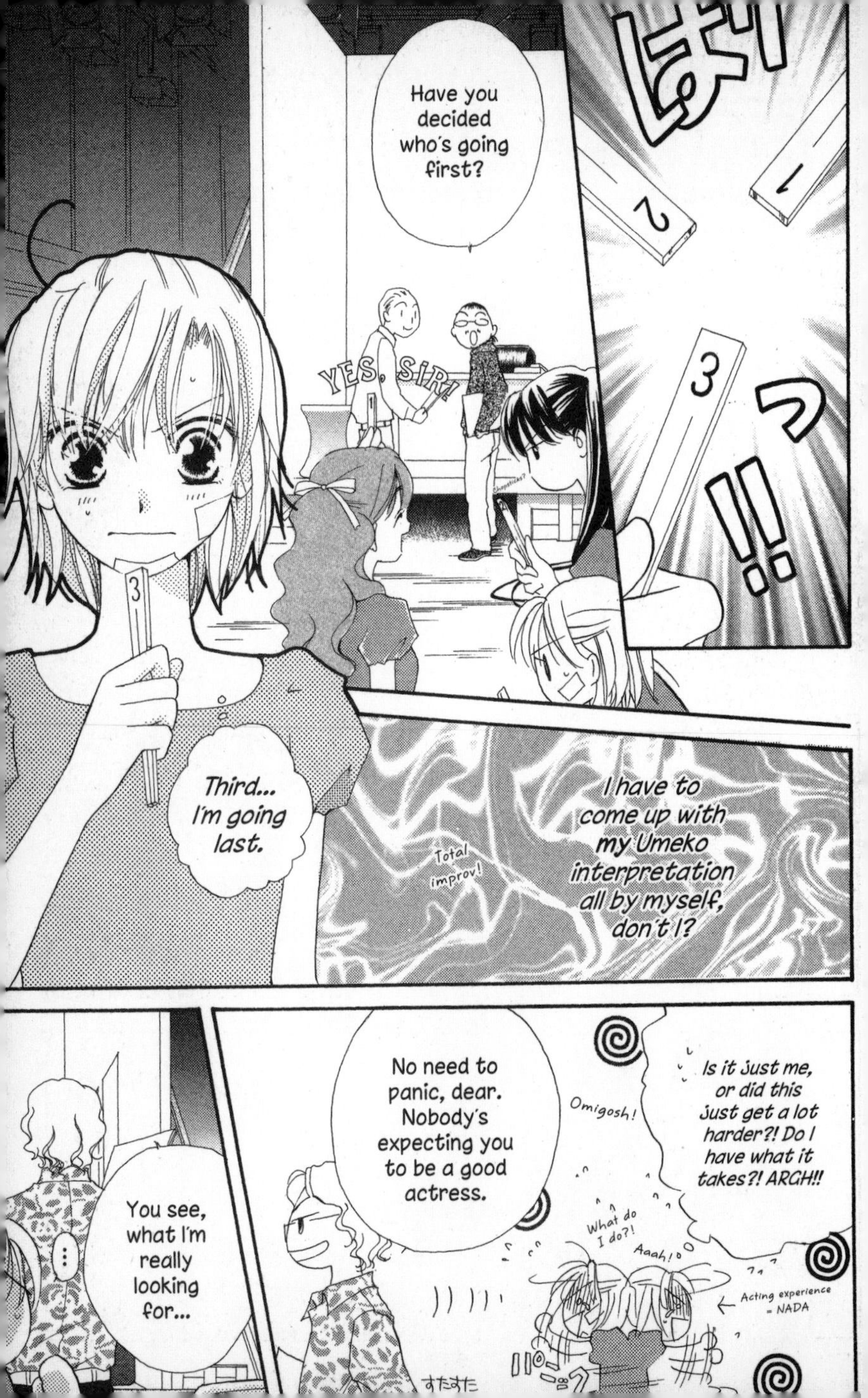
ぽ
っ!!
Have you decided who's going first?
YES, SIR!
I have to come up with my Umeko interpretation all by myself, don't I?
Total improv!
Third... I'm going last.
Is it just me, or did this just get a lot harder?! Do I have what it takes?! ARGH!!
Omigosh!
What do I do?!
Aaah!
Acting experience = NADA
No need to panic, dear. Nobody's expecting you to be a good actress.
すたすた
...
You see, what I'm really looking for...

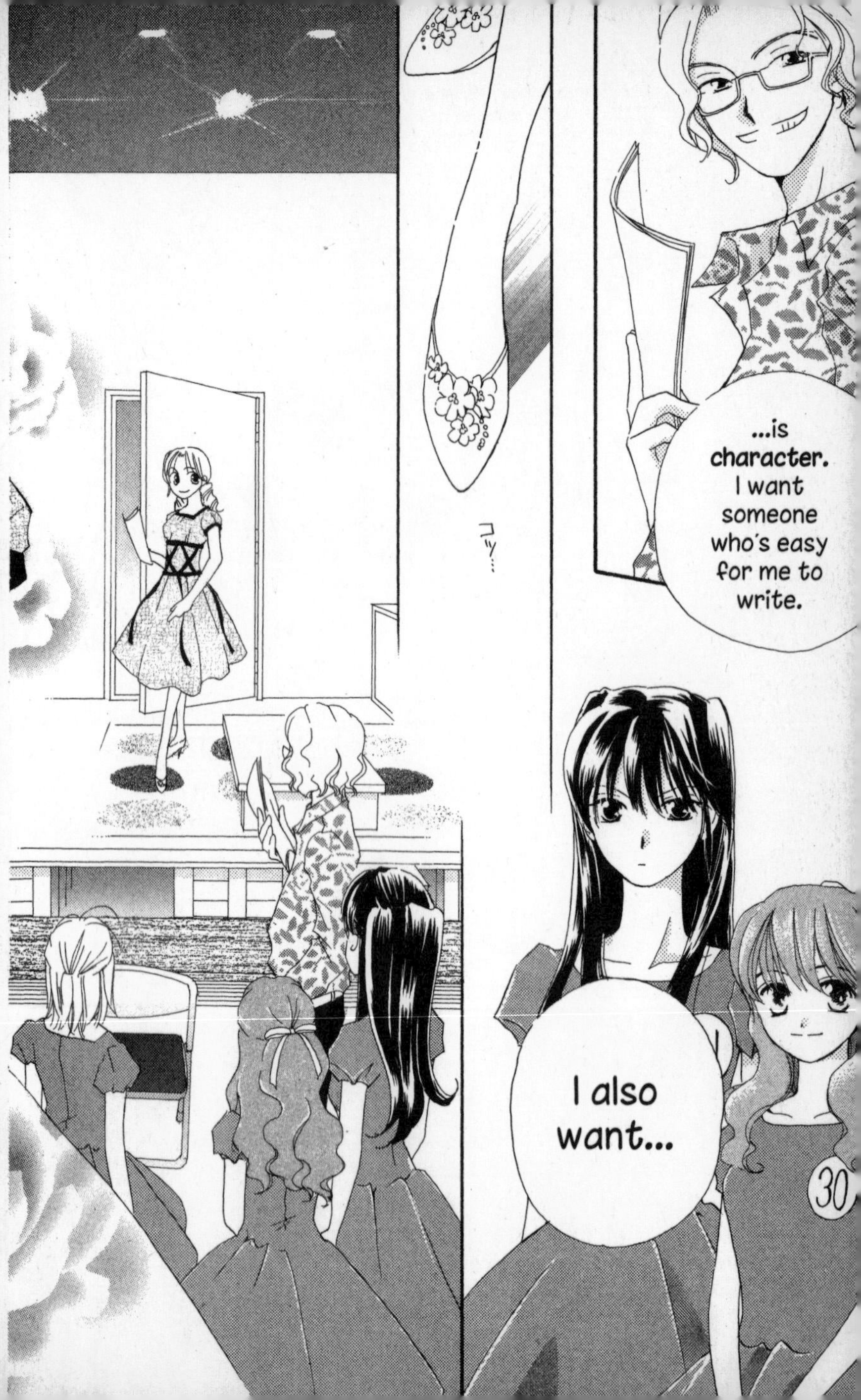
...is character. I want someone who's easy for me to write.
コツ…
I also want...

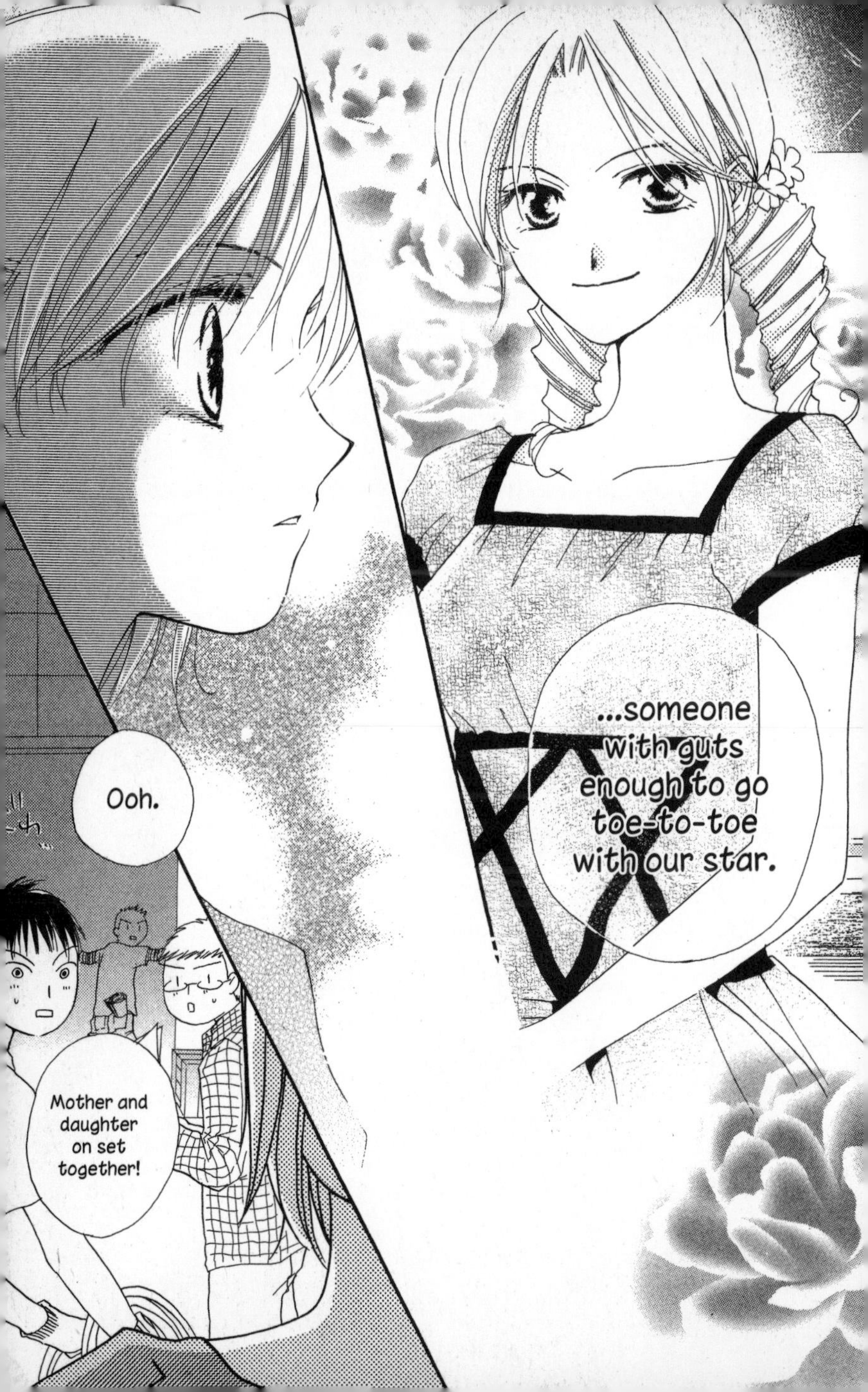
...someone with guts enough to go toe-to-toe with our star.
Ooh.
Mother and daughter on set together!

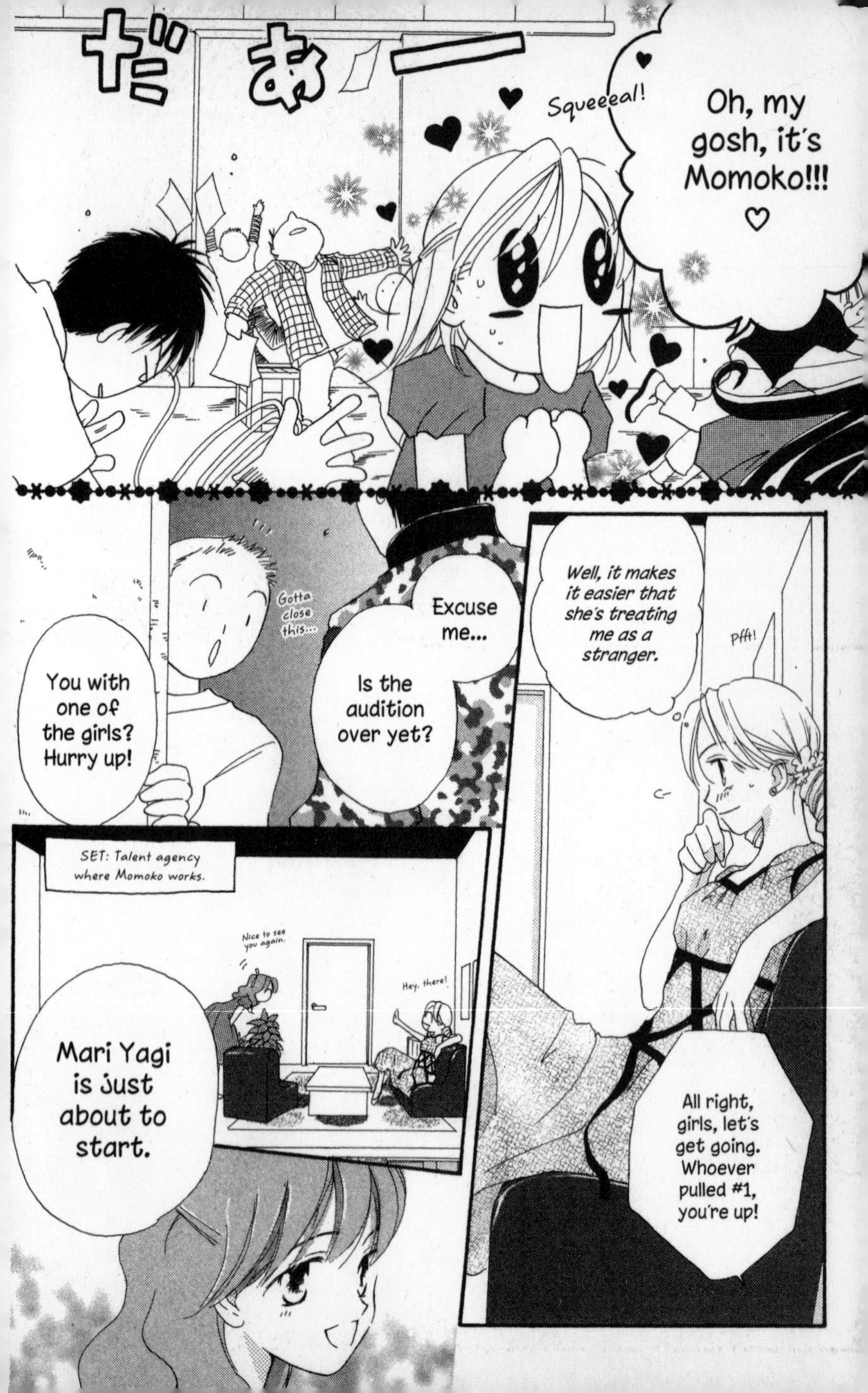
Oh, my gosh, it's Momoko!!! ♡
Squeeeal!
だぁー
Well, it makes it easier that she's treating me as a stranger.
Pfft!
All right, girls, let's get going. Whoever pulled #1, you're up!
Excuse me...
Gotta close this...
Is the audition over yet?
You with one of the girls? Hurry up!
SET: Talent agency where Momoko works.
Hey, there!
Nice to see you again.
Mari Yagi is just about to start.

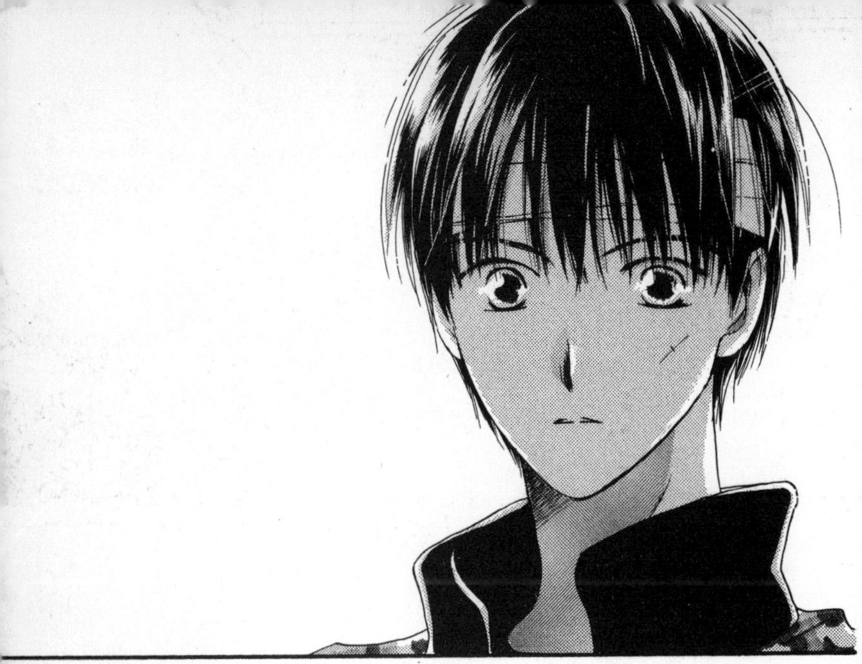
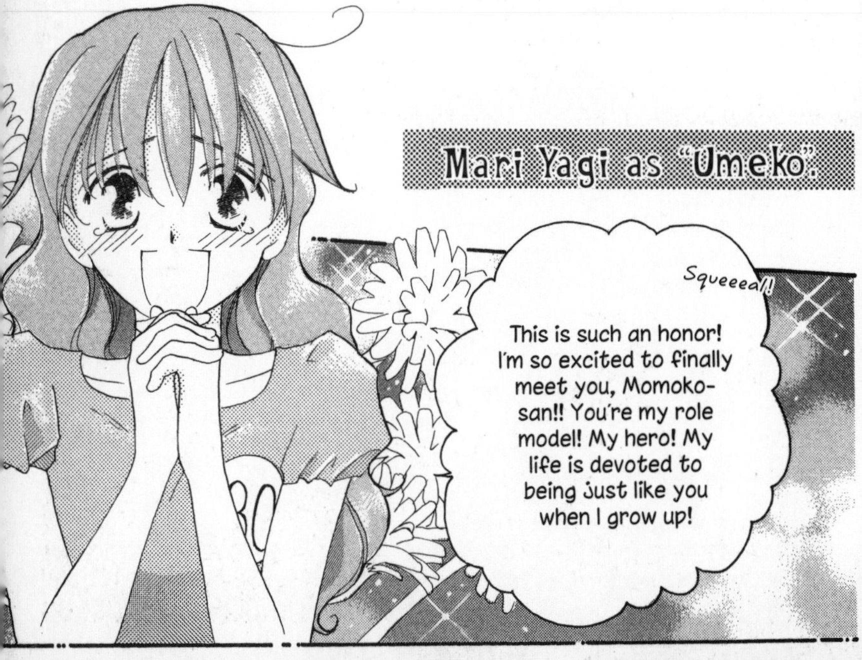
Mari Yagi as "Umeko".
Squeeeal!
This is such an honor! I'm so excited to finally meet you, Momoko-san!! You're my role model! My hero! My life is devoted to being just like you when I grow up!

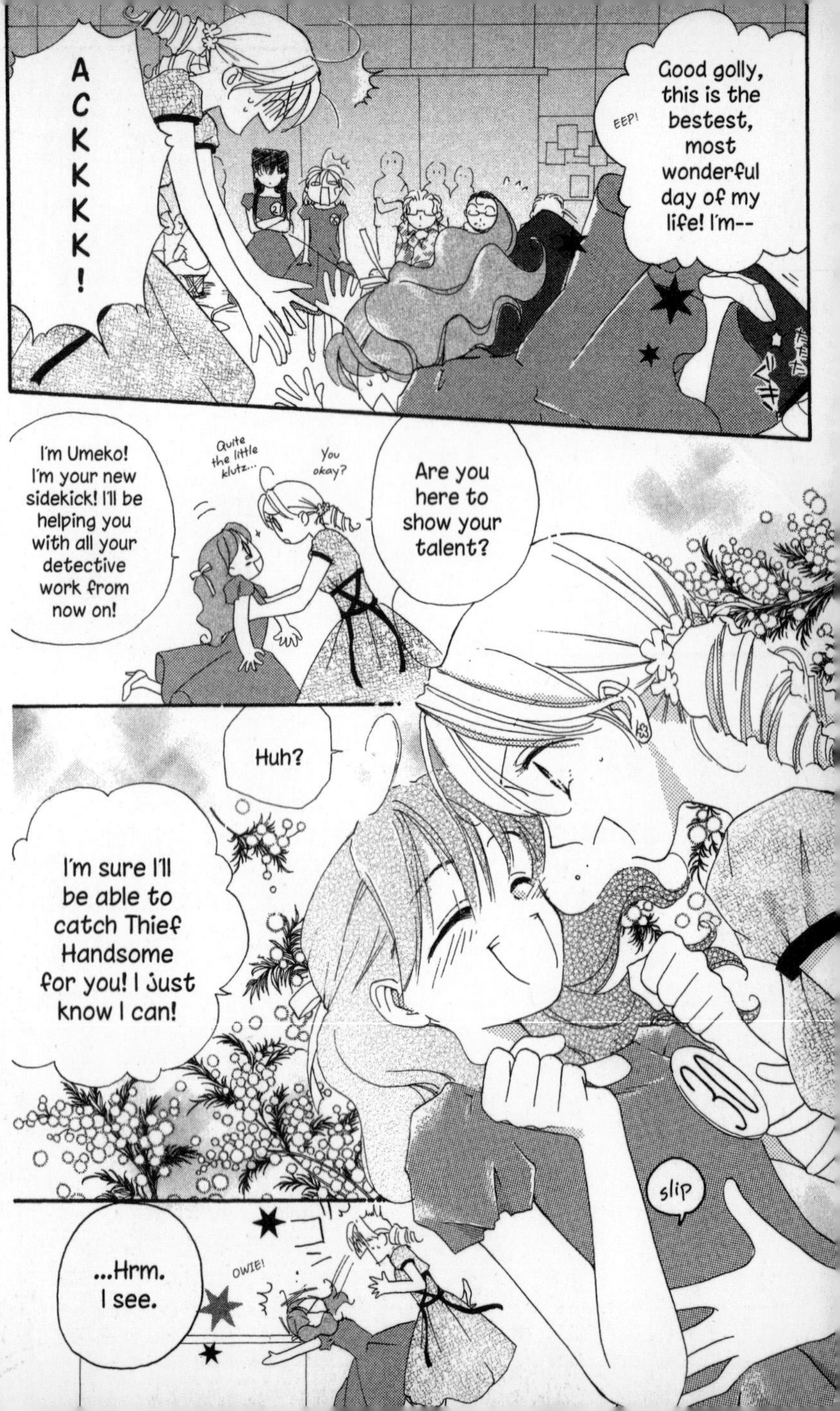

Good golly, this is the bestest, most wonderful day of my life! I'm--
EEP!
ACKKKKK!
Are you here to show your talent?
You okay?
Quite the little klutz...
I'm Umeko! I'm your new sidekick! I'll be helping you with all your detective work from now on!
Huh?
I'm sure I'll be able to catch Thief Handsome for you! I just know I can!
slip
...Hrm. I see.
OWIE!

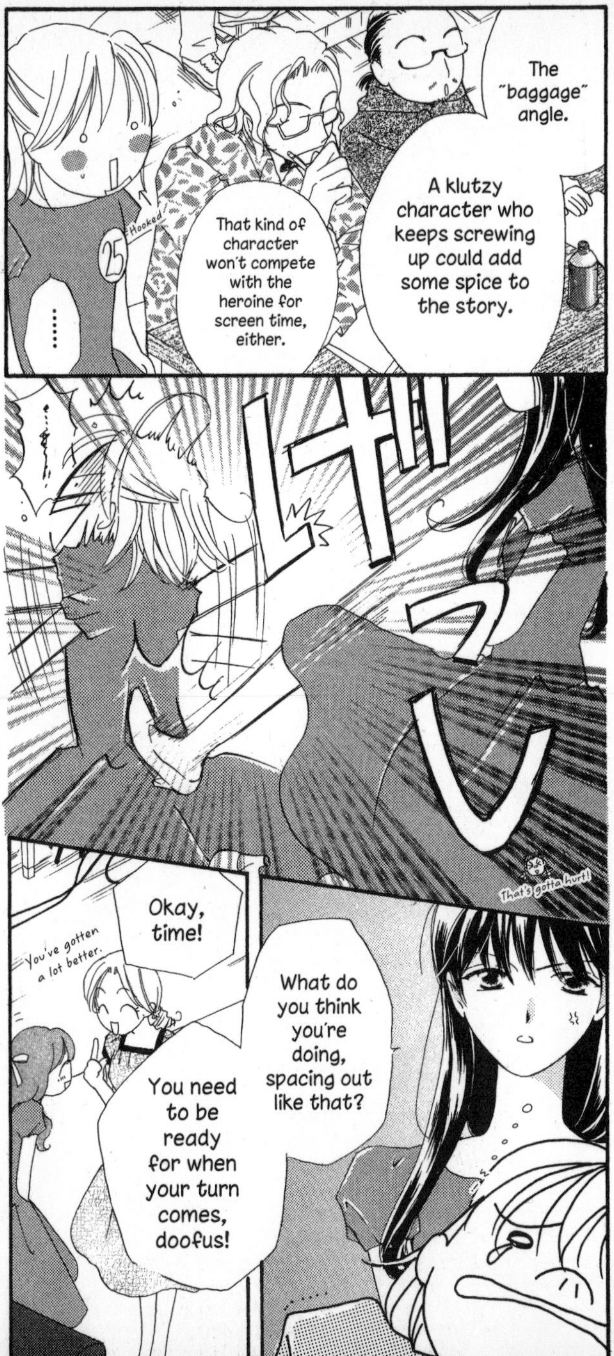
The "baggage" angle.
A klutzy character who keeps screwing up could add some spice to the story.
That kind of character won't compete with the heroine for screen time, either.
Hooked
......
That's gotta hurt!
What do you think you're doing, spacing out like that?
You need to be ready for when your turn comes, doofus!
Okay, time!
You've gotten a lot better.

BOXiNG.

This year, I've had more and more chances to go watch K-1 and boxing matches. It's great.

I've always loved watching matches designed purely for entertainment, like pro wrestling and stuff, but getting to see everything that goes on in a serious fight is something else entirely. K-1 is a lot more showbiz-y than boxing, but with boxing, you get to watch all those gorgeously muscled men...Aaah...

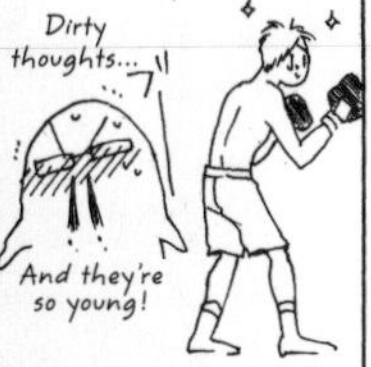
Dirty thoughts...
And they're so young!

One of the best things about getting to see a live match is being so close to the boxers. You can see them breathe and feel every last ounce of tension in the air. Even though I've only ever seen live bouts at a smaller, local hall, it's still great!

Recommending this to all the young lady readers out there might not be the best idea, but, well, I will anyway. Live boxing is best. You can really get caught up in the action.

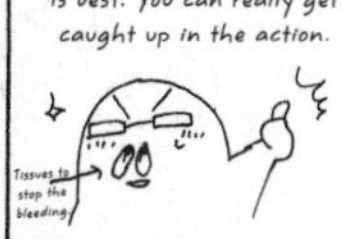
Tissues to stop the bleeding

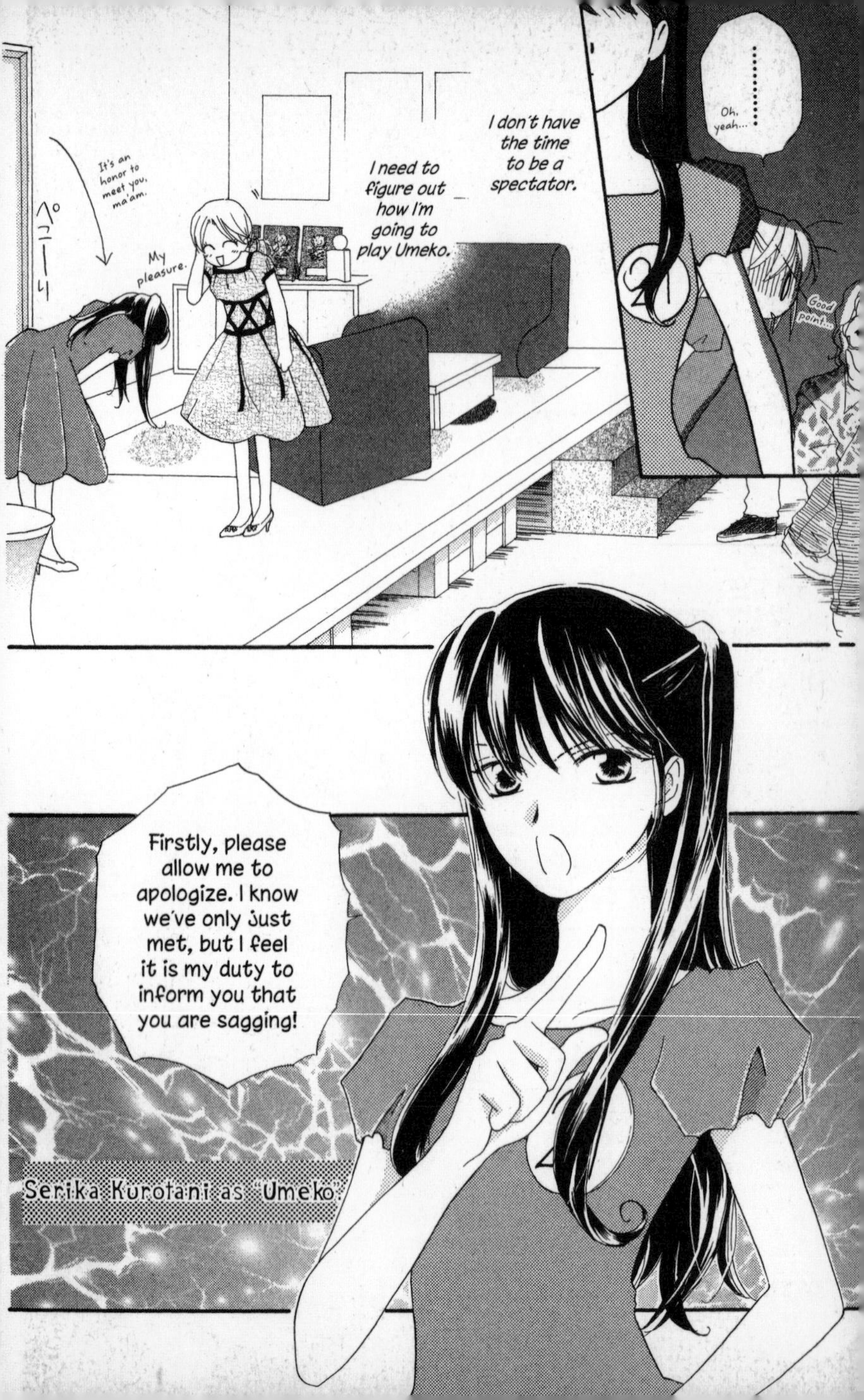
Oh, yeah......
Good point...
I don't have the time to be a spectator.
I need to figure out how I'm going to play Umeko.
It's an honor to meet you, ma'am.
My pleasure.
Firstly, please allow me to apologize. I know we've only just met, but I feel it is my duty to inform you that you are sagging!
Serika Kurotani as "Umeko"

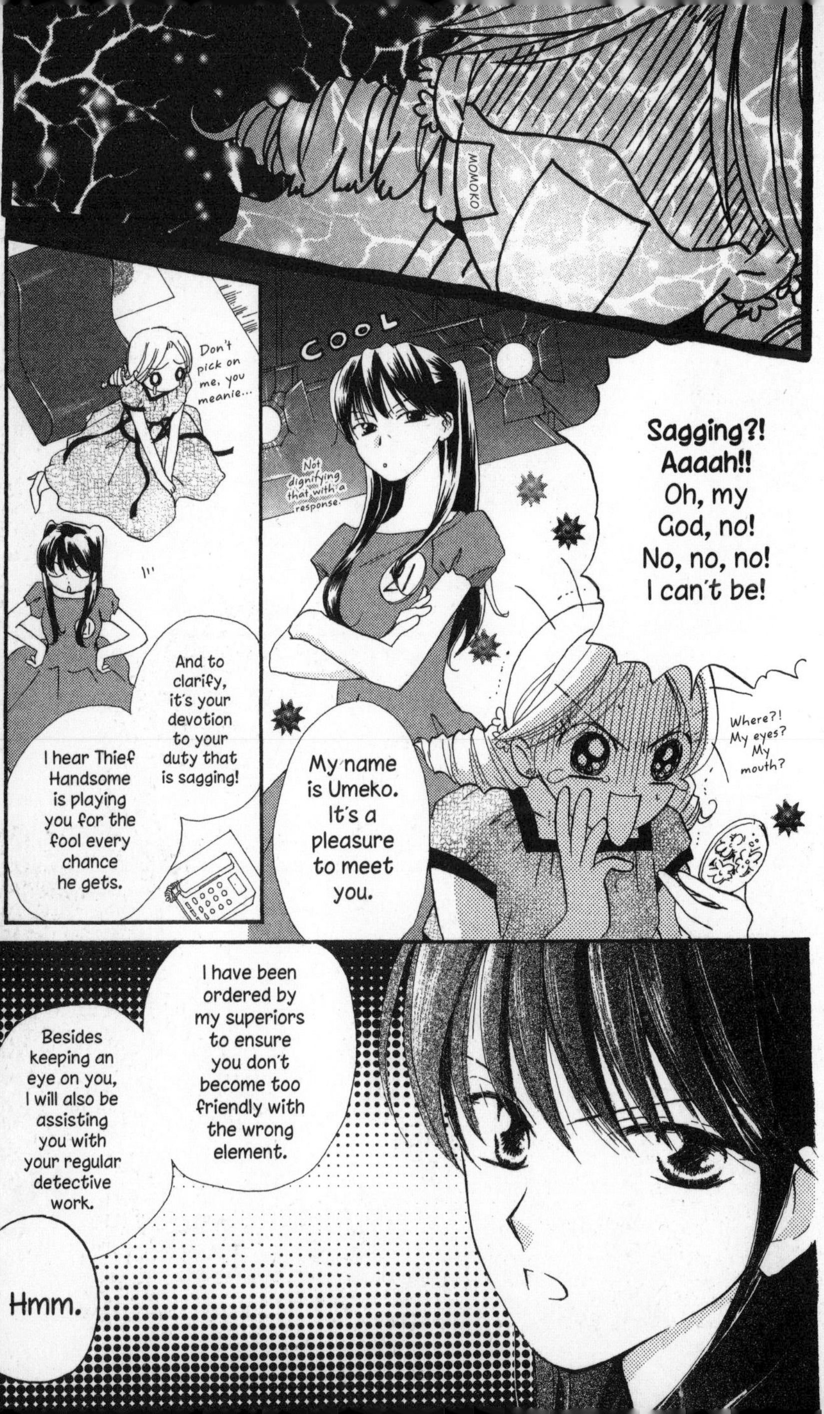
MOMOKO
Sagging?! Aaaah!! Oh, my God, no! No, no, no! I can't be!
COOL
Not dignifying that with a response.
Where?! My eyes? My mouth?
My name is Umeko. It's a pleasure to meet you.
Don't pick on me, you meanie...
And to clarify, it's your devotion to your duty that is sagging!
I hear Thief Handsome is playing you for the fool every chance he gets.
I have been ordered by my superiors to ensure you don't become too friendly with the wrong element.
Besides keeping an eye on you, I will also be assisting you with your regular detective work.
Hmm.

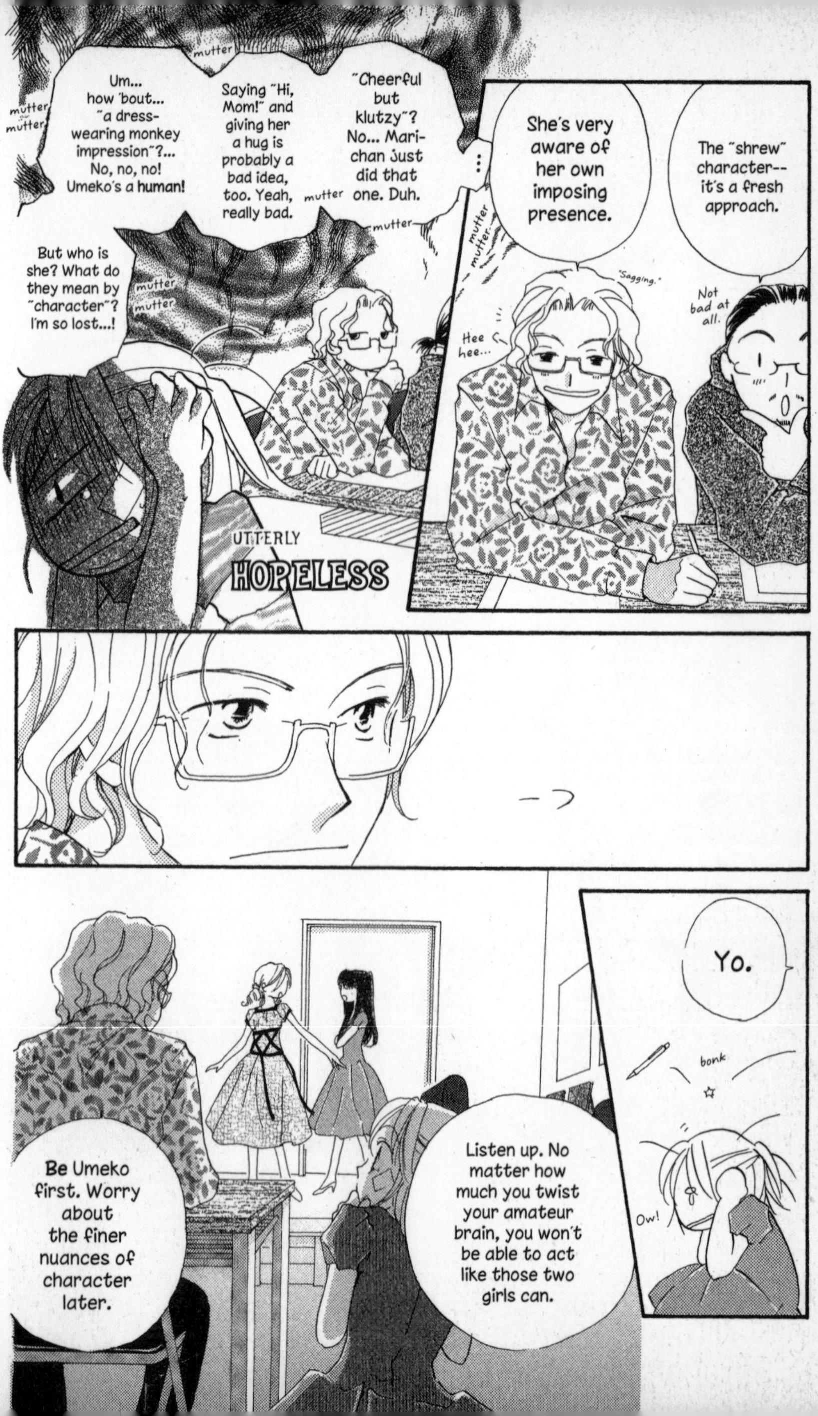
The "shrew" character-- it's a fresh approach.
She's very aware of her own imposing presence.
Not bad at all.
"Sagging."
Hee hee...
mutter mutter
mutter
"Cheerful but klutzy"? No... Mari-chan just did that one. Duh.
mutter
Saying "Hi, Mom!" and giving her a hug is probably a bad idea, too. Yeah, really bad.
Um... how 'bout... "a dress-wearing monkey impression"?... No, no, no! Umeko's a human!
mutter mutter
mutter
mutter mutter
But who is she? What do they mean by "character"? I'm so lost...!
UTTERLY HOPELESS
Yo.
bonk
Ow!
Listen up. No matter how much you twist your amateur brain, you won't be able to act like those two girls can.
Be Umeko first. Worry about the finer nuances of character later.

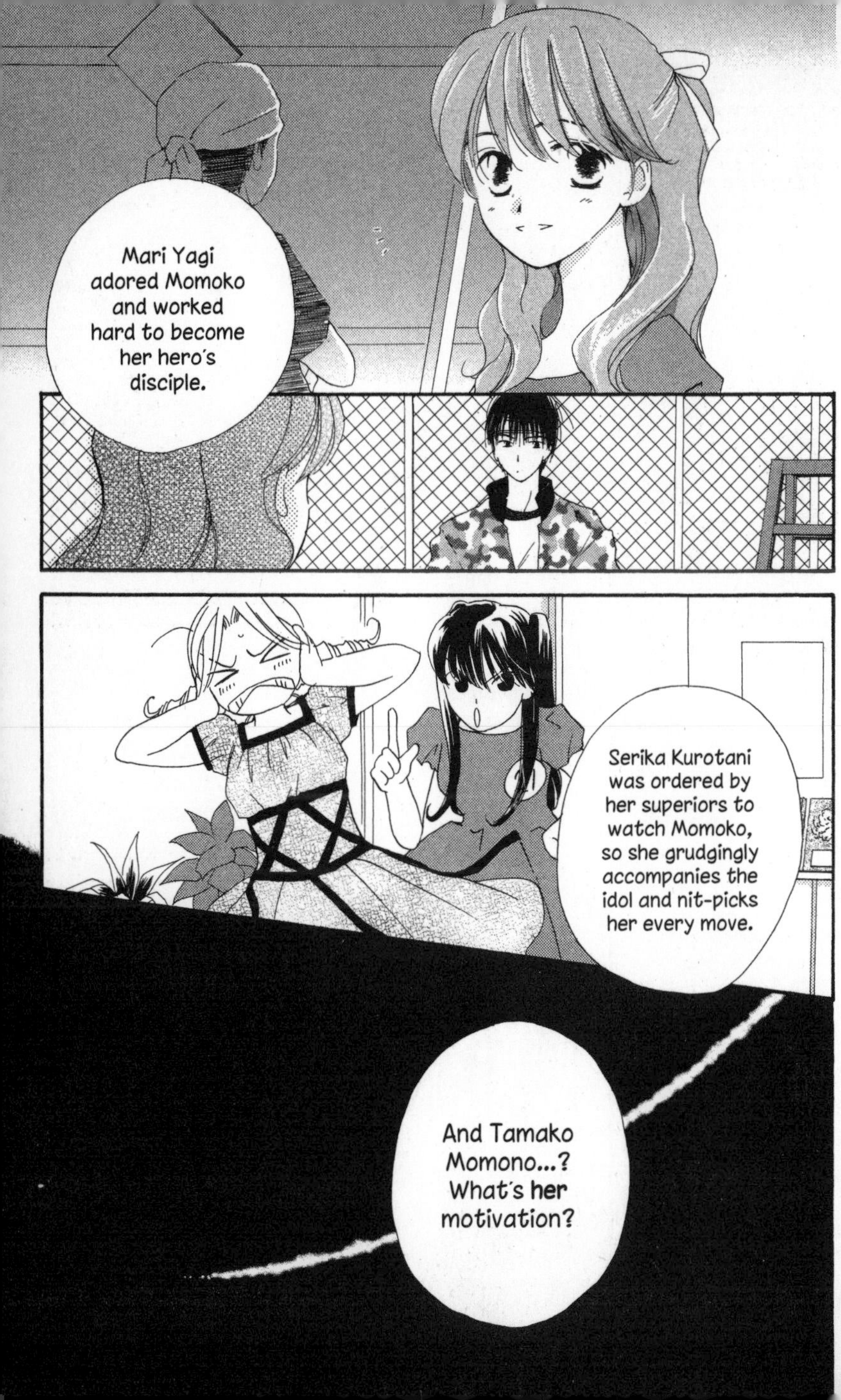
Mari Yagi adored Momoko and worked hard to become her hero's disciple.
Serika Kurotani was ordered by her superiors to watch Momoko, so she grudgingly accompanies the idol and nit-picks her every move.
And Tamako Momono...? What's **her** motivation?

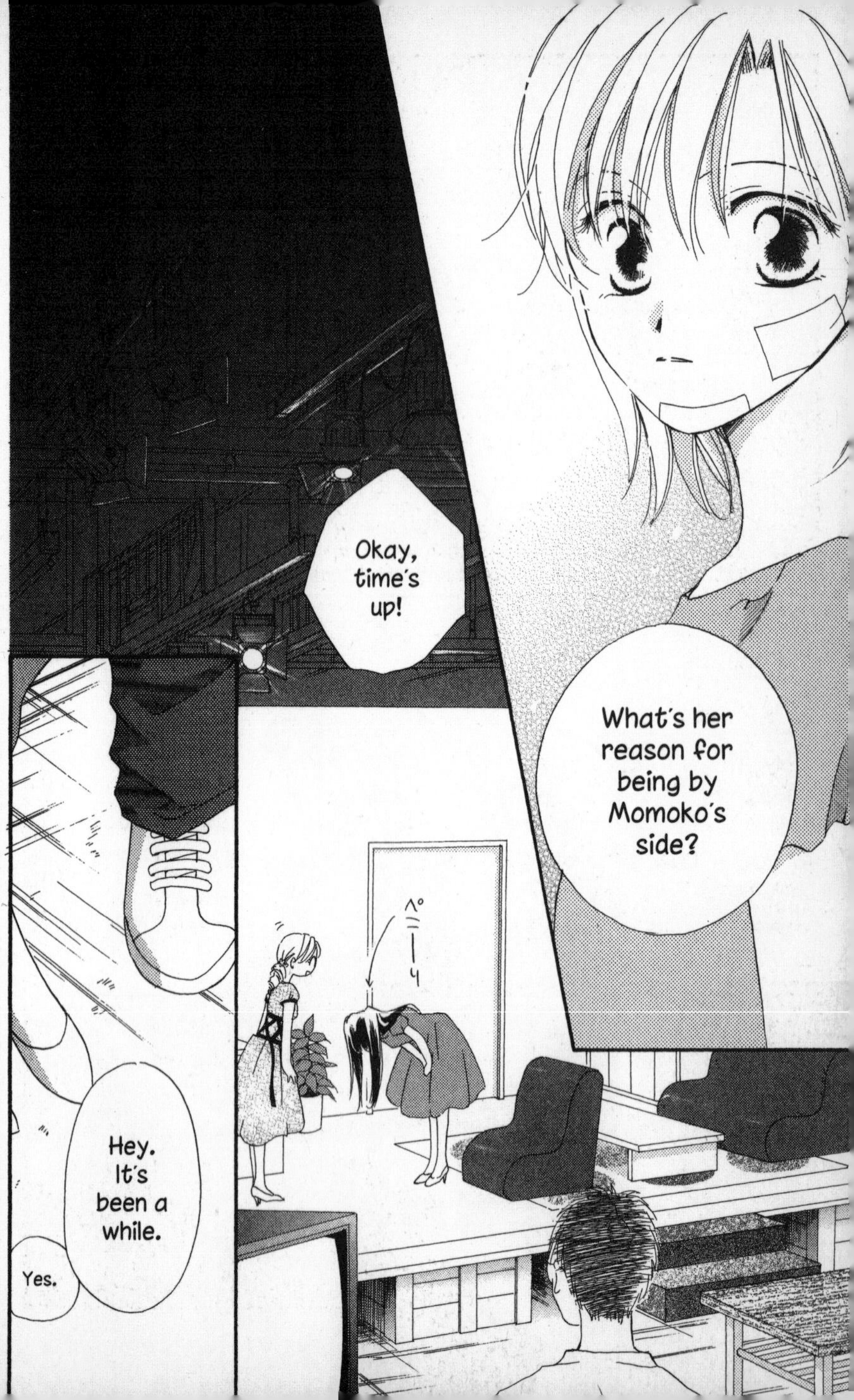
What's her reason for being by Momoko's side?
Okay, time's up!
Hey. It's been a while.
Yes.

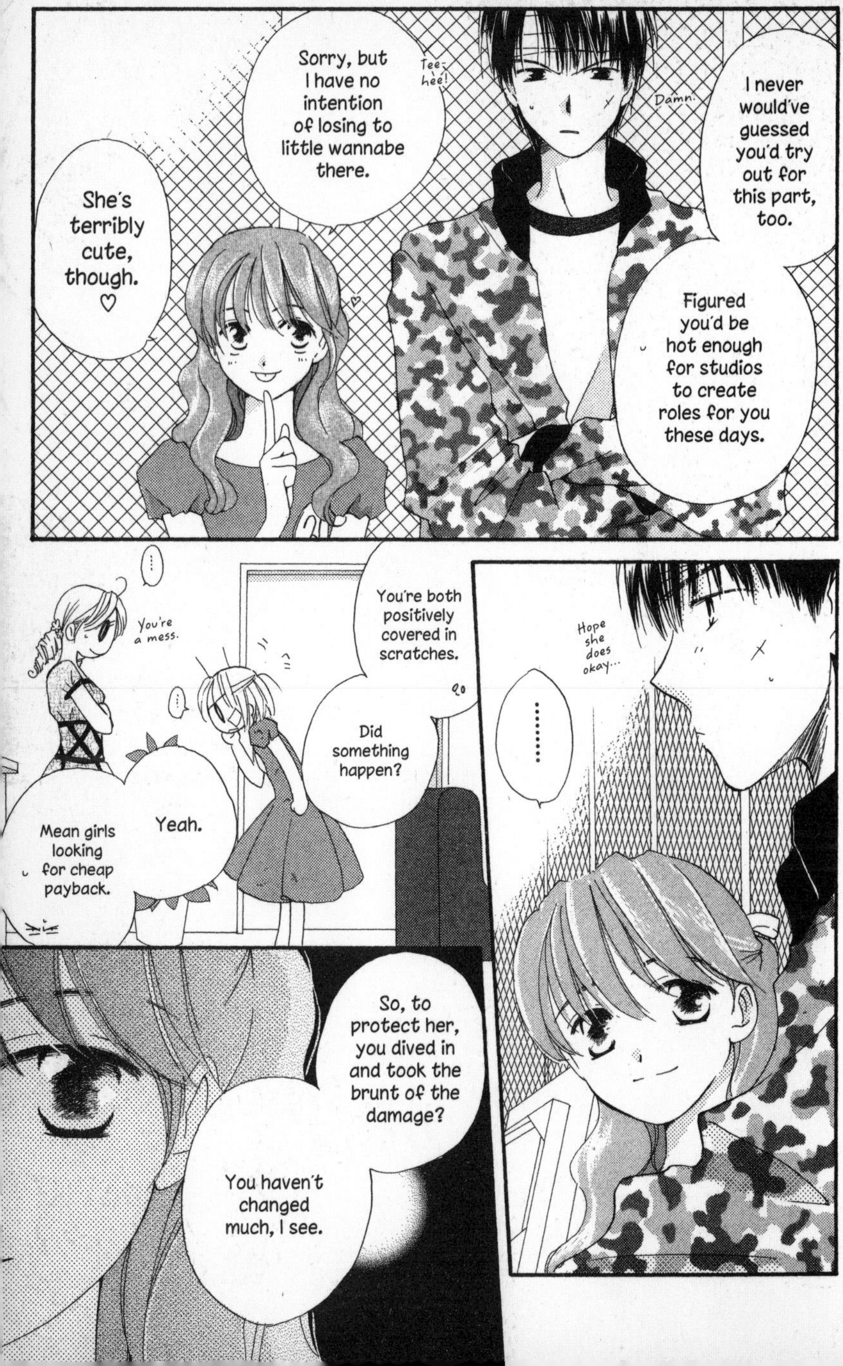
Damn.
I never would've guessed you'd try out for this part, too.
Figured you'd be hot enough for studios to create roles for you these days.
Tee-hee!
Sorry, but I have no intention of losing to little wannabe there.
She's terribly cute, though. ♡
Hope she does okay...
....
You're both positively covered in scratches.
Did something happen?
Yeah.
Mean girls looking for cheap payback.
...
You're a mess.
...
So, to protect her, you dived in and took the brunt of the damage?
You haven't changed much, I see.

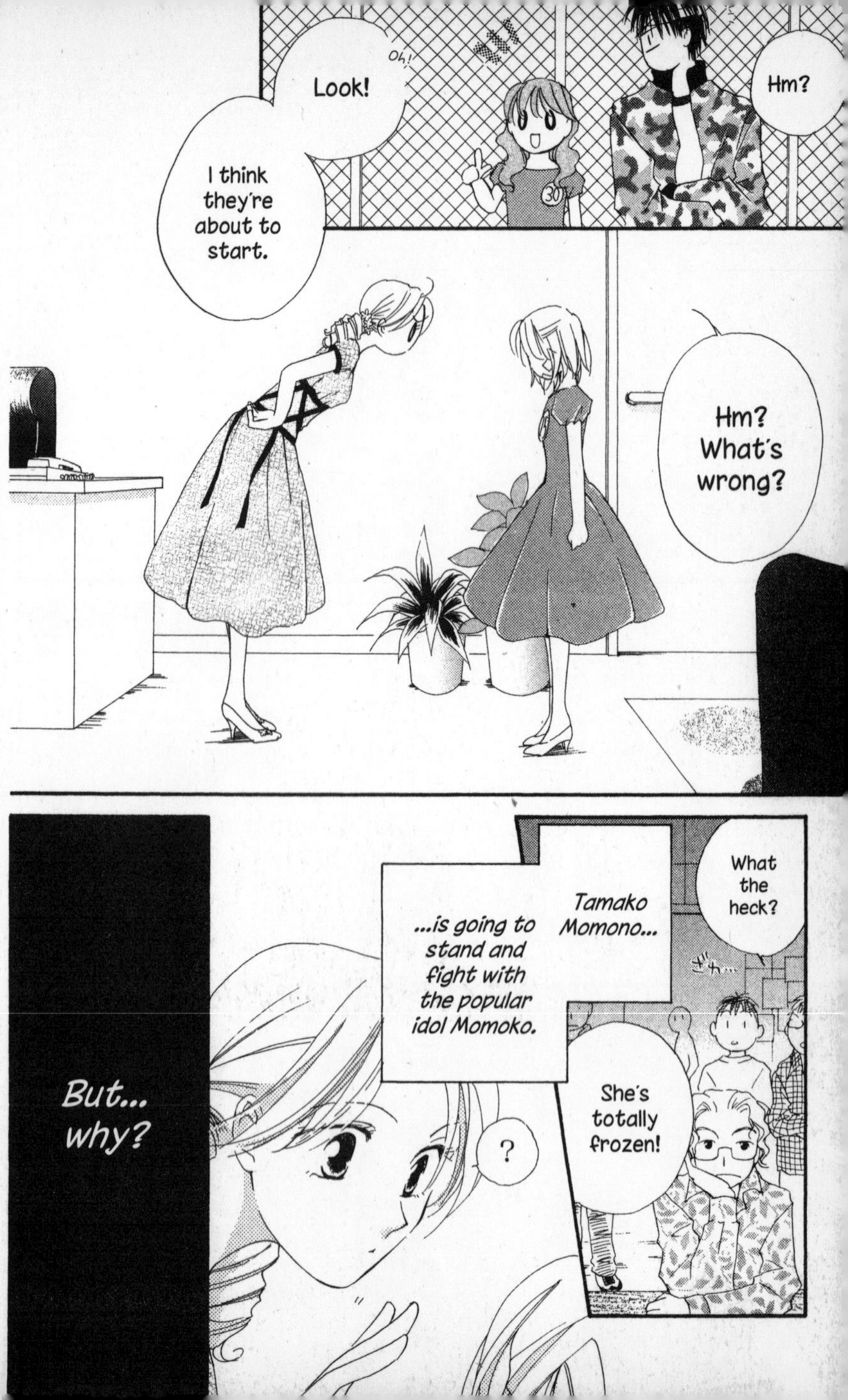
Hm?
Oh!
Look!
I think they're about to start.
Hm? What's wrong?
What the heck?
Tamako Momono...
...is going to stand and fight with the popular idol Momoko.
She's totally frozen!
?
But... why?

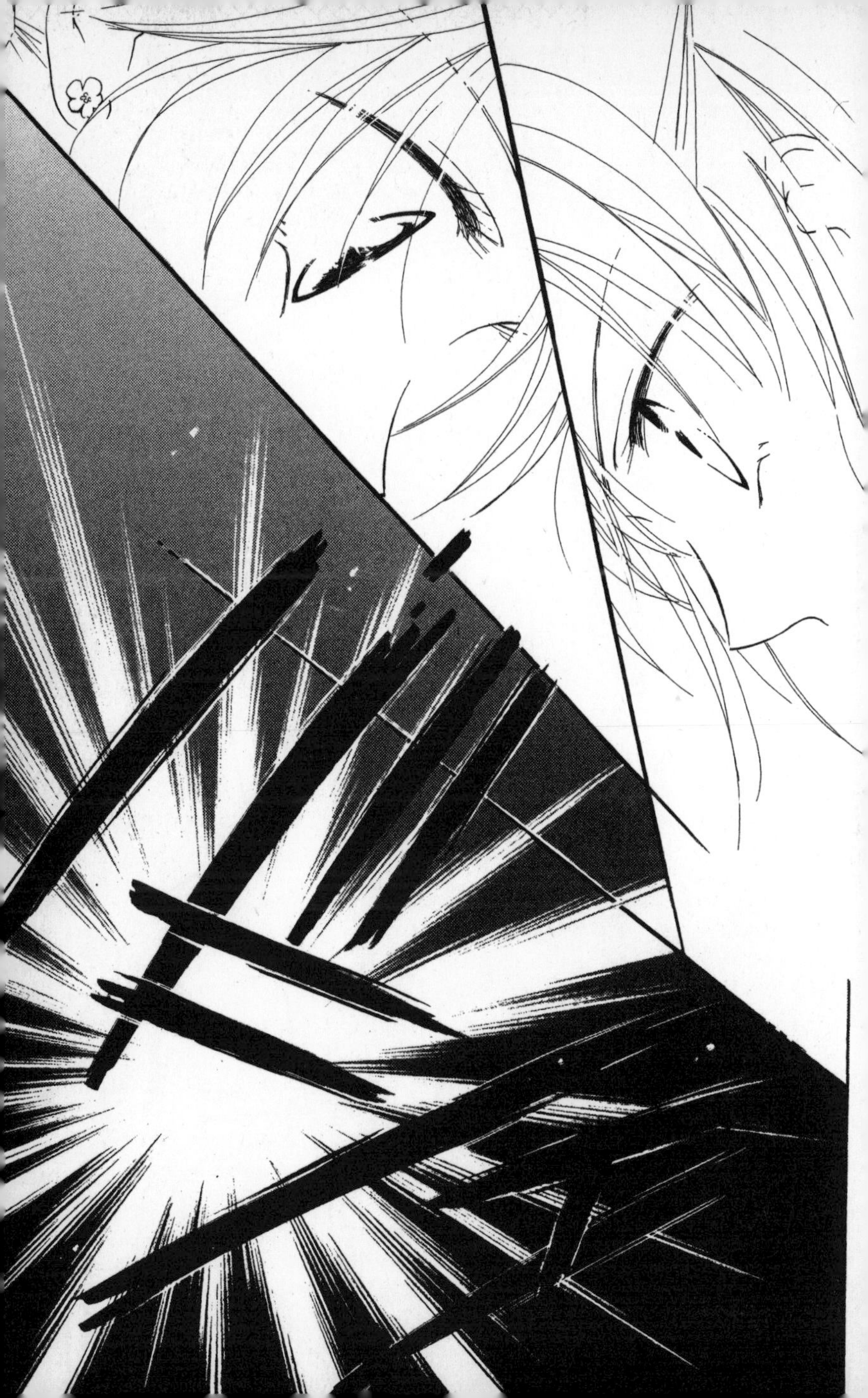

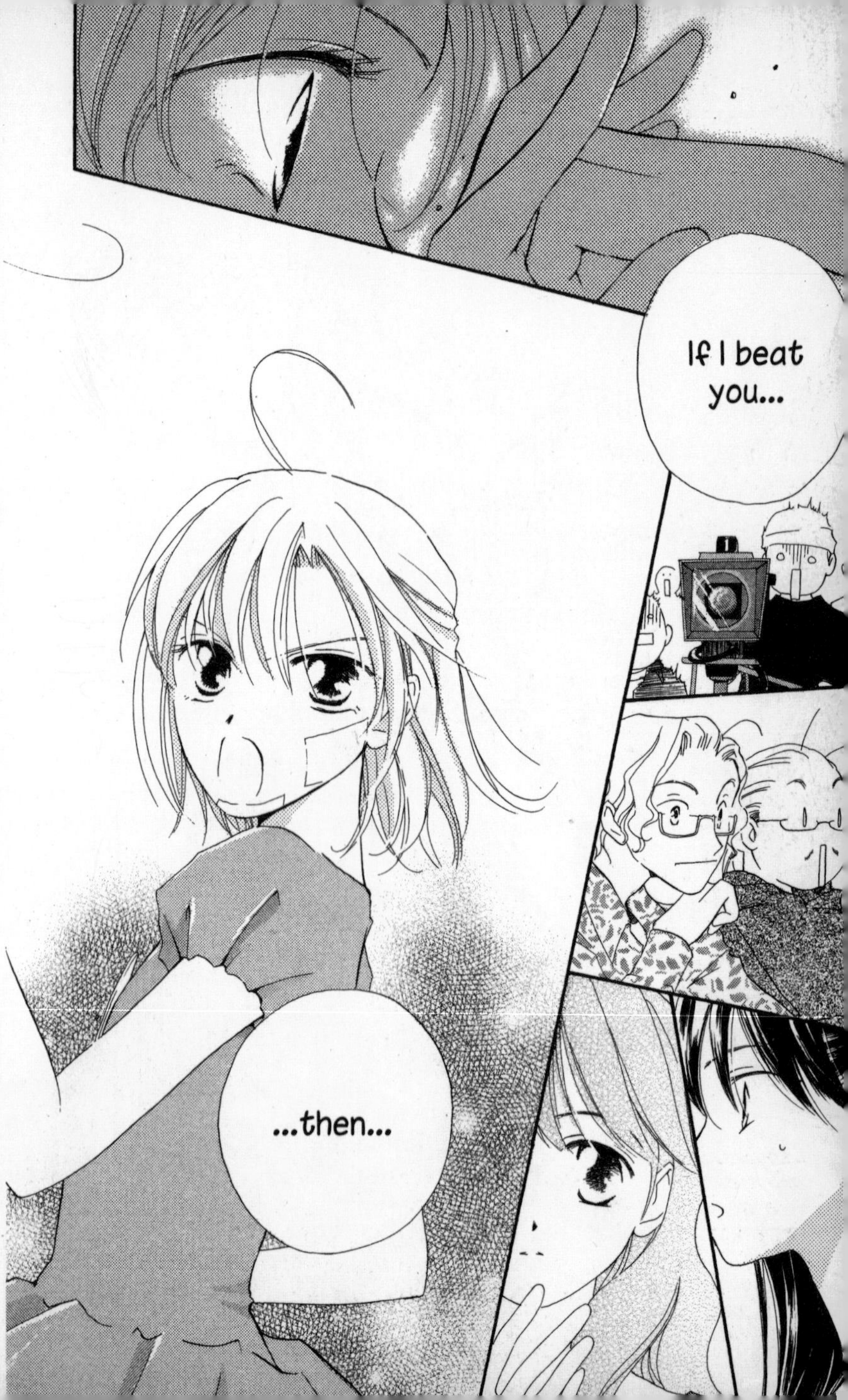
If I beat you...
...then...

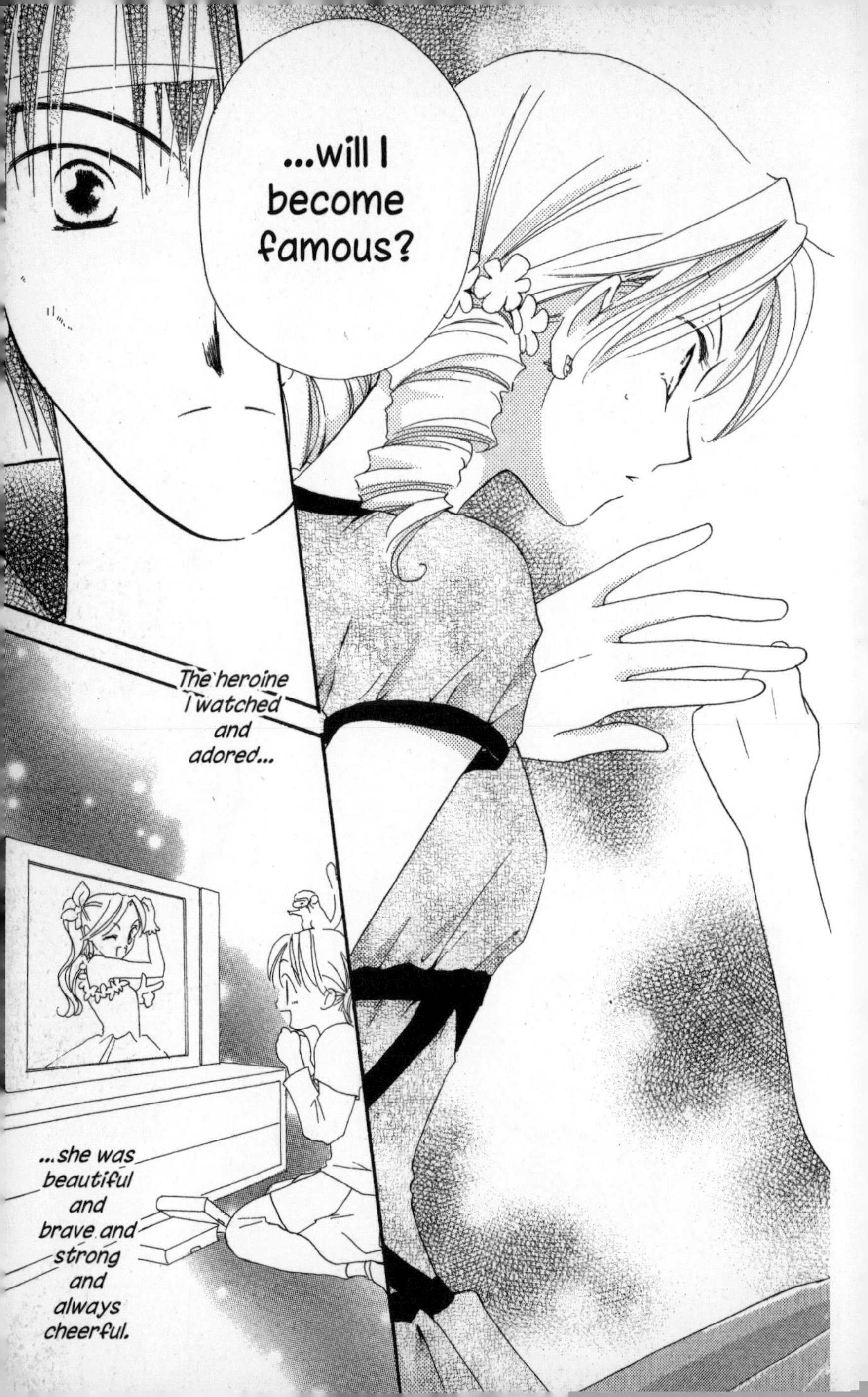
...will I become famous?
The heroine I watched and adored...
...she was beautiful and brave and strong and always cheerful.

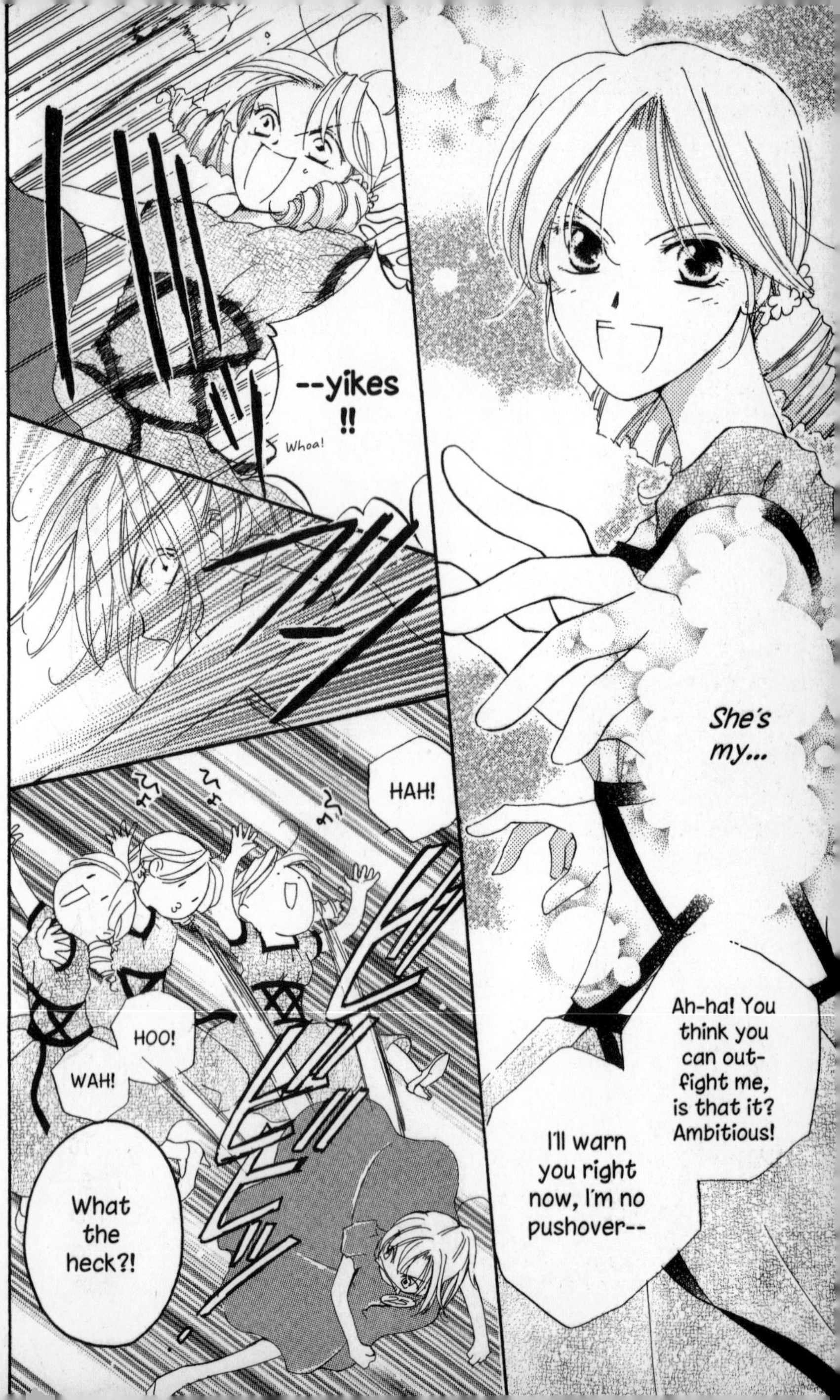
She's my...
Ah-ha! You think you can out-fight me, is that it? Ambitious!
I'll warn you right now, I'm no pushover--
--yikes !!
Whoa!
HAH!
HOO!
WAH!
What the heck?!

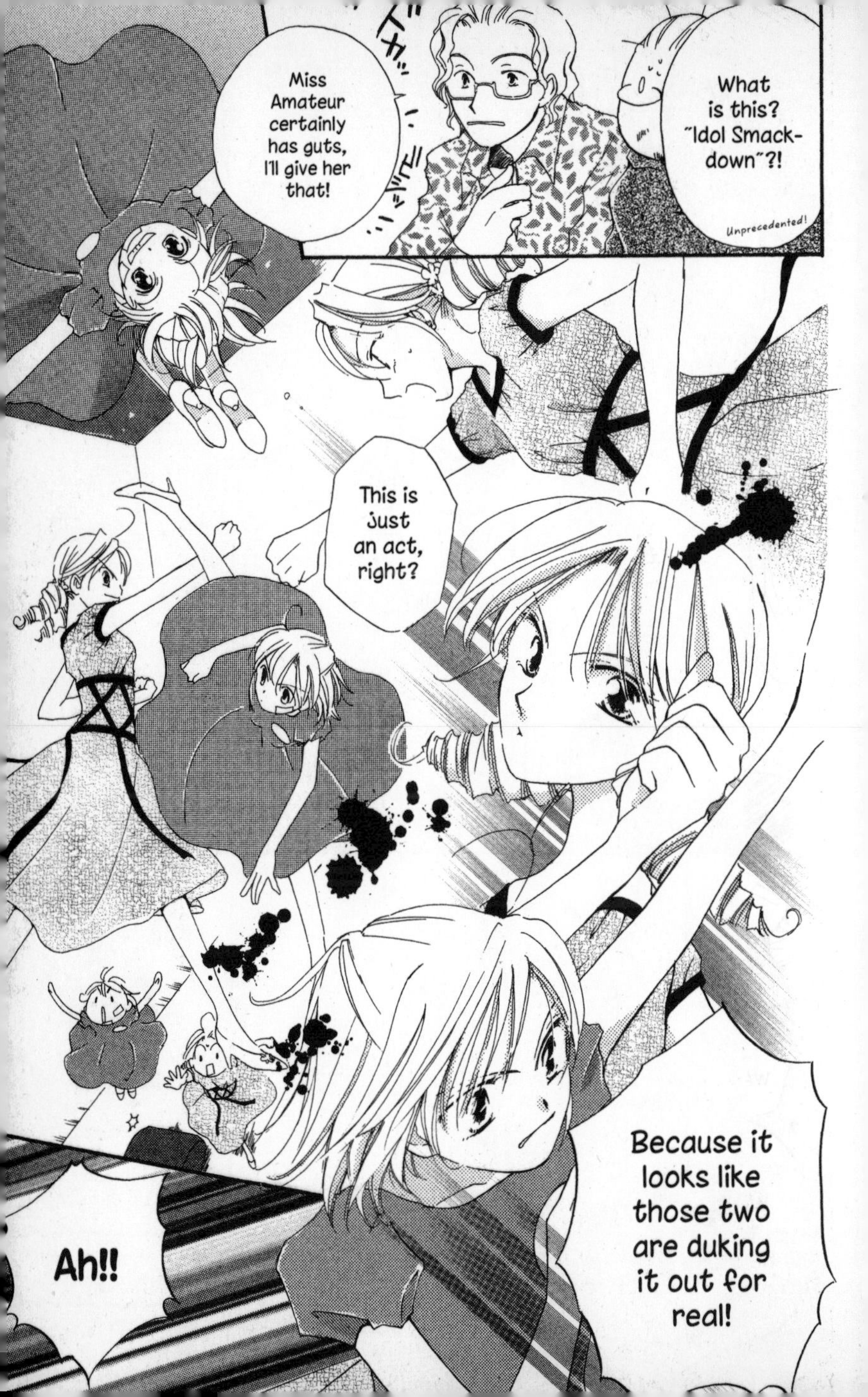

What is this? "Idol Smack-down"?!
Unprecedented!
Miss Amateur certainly has guts, I'll give her that!
This is just an act, right?
Because it looks like those two are duking it out for real!
Ah!!

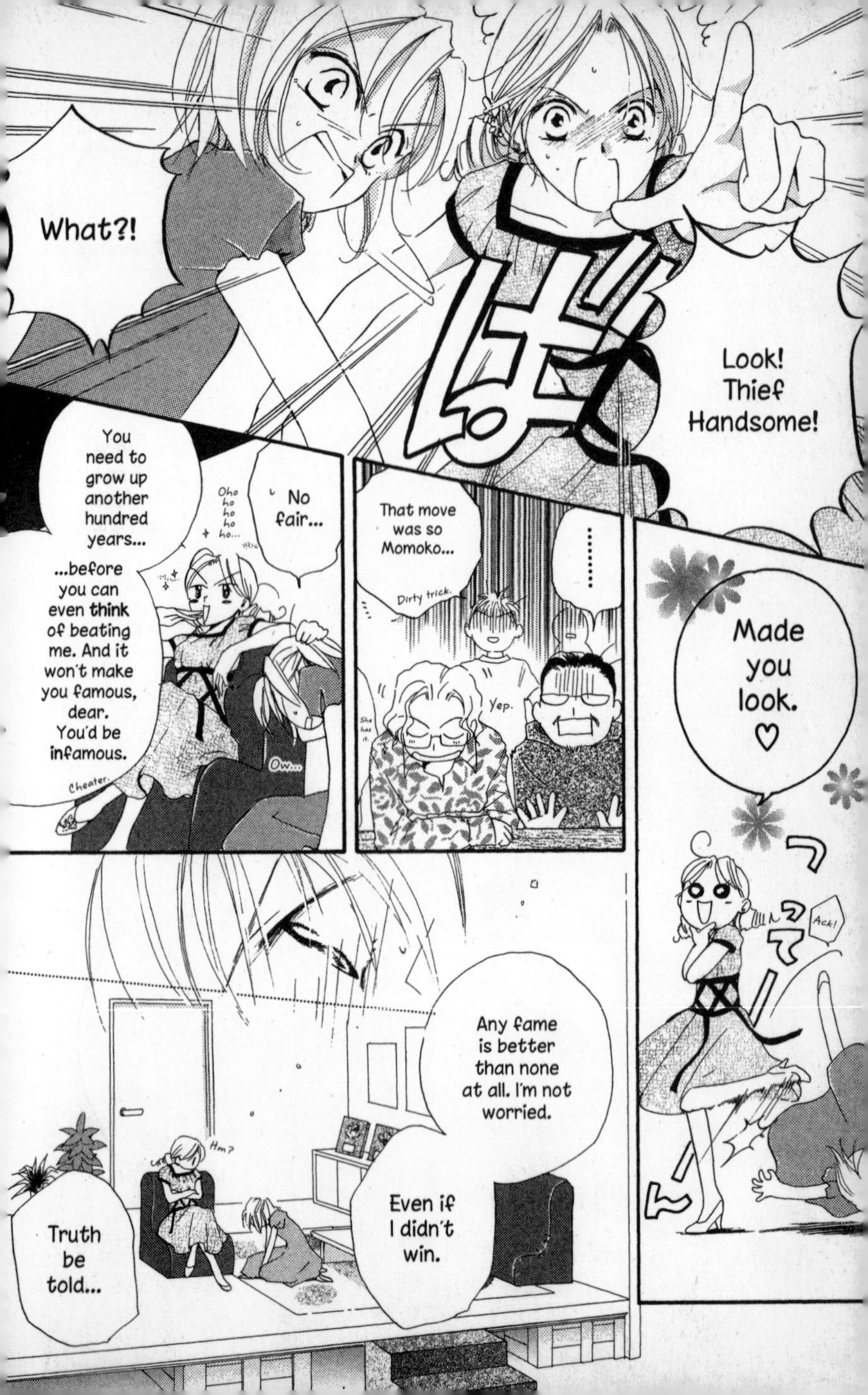
Look! Thief Handsome!
What?!
Made you look. ♡
Ack!
......
That move was so Momoko...
Dirty trick.
Yep.
She has it.
No fair...
You need to grow up another hundred years...
...before you can even **think** of beating me. And it won't make you famous, dear. You'd be **infamous**.
Oho ho ho ho ho...
Ow...
Cheater.
Any fame is better than none at all. I'm not worried.
Even if I didn't win.
Hm?
Truth be told...

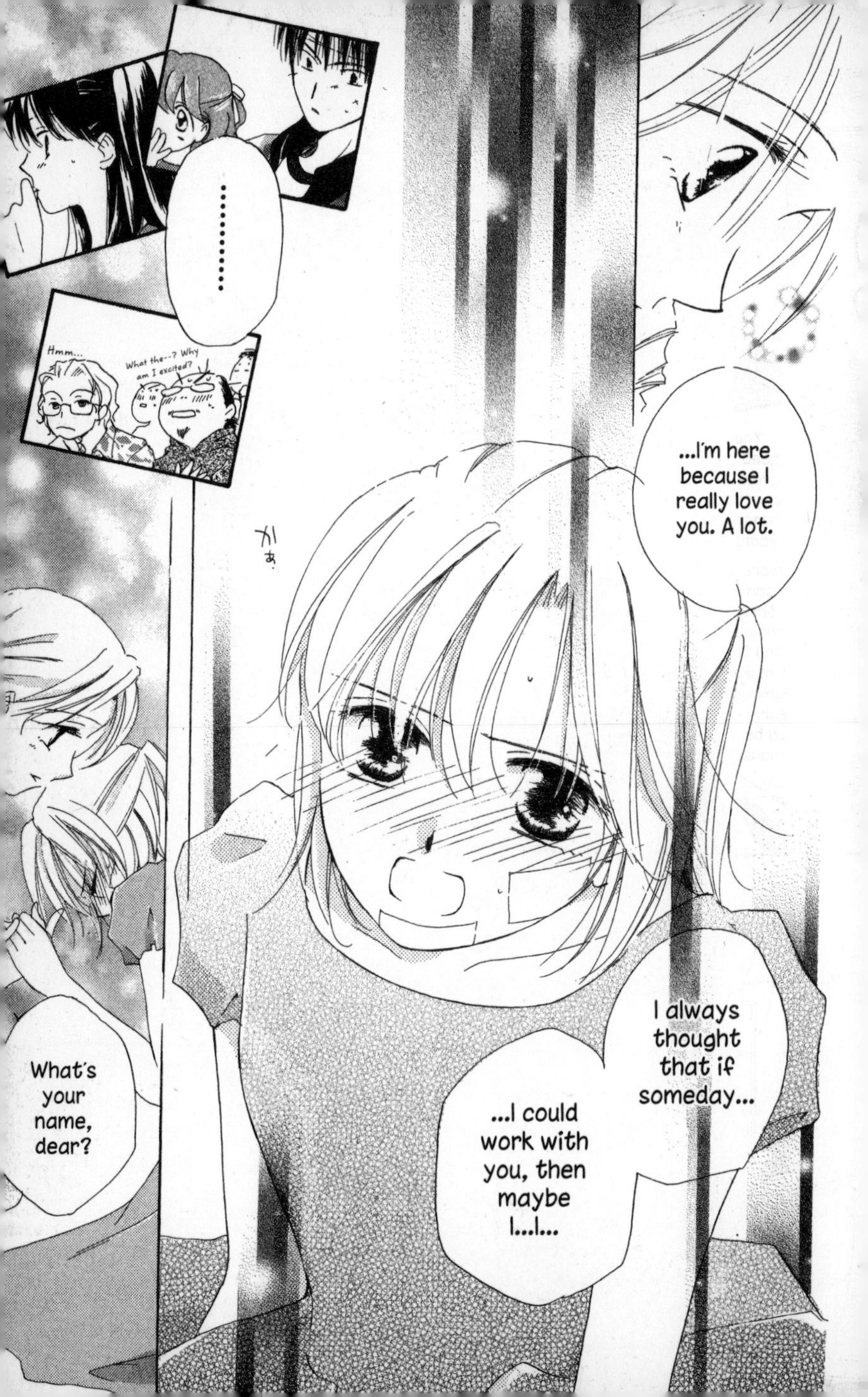

...I'm here because I really love you. A lot.
かあ
I always thought that if someday...
...I could work with you, then maybe I...I...
......
Hmm...
What the--? Why am I excited?
What's your name, dear?

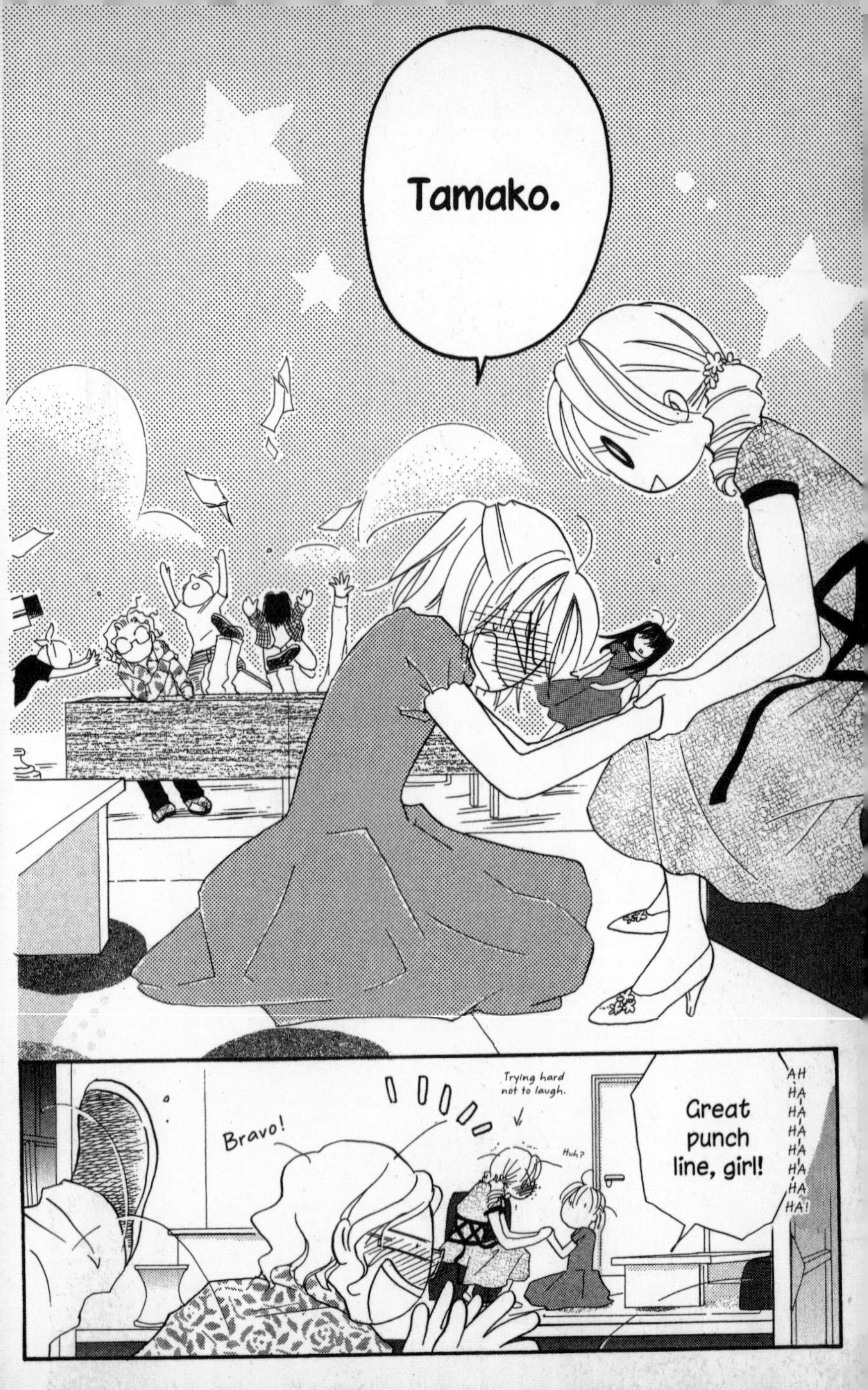
Tamako.
AH HA HA HA HA HA HA HA HA!
Great punch line, girl!
Trying hard not to laugh.
Huh?
Bravo!

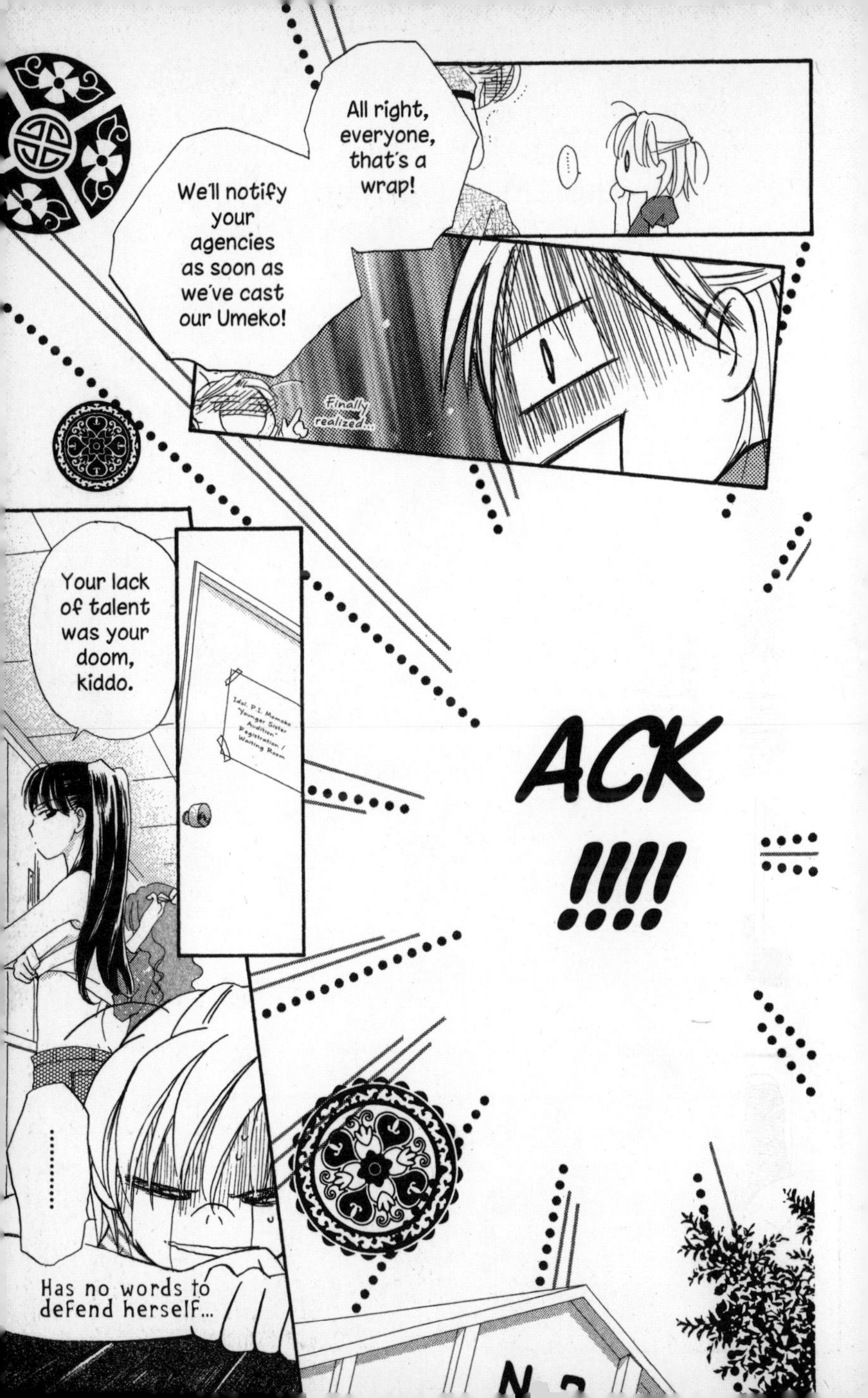
......
All right, everyone, that's a wrap!
We'll notify your agencies as soon as we've cast our Umeko!
Finally realized...
ACK!!!!
Your lack of talent was your doom, kiddo.
Idol: P.I. Momoko "Younger Sister Audition" Registration / Waiting Room
....
Has no words to defend herself...

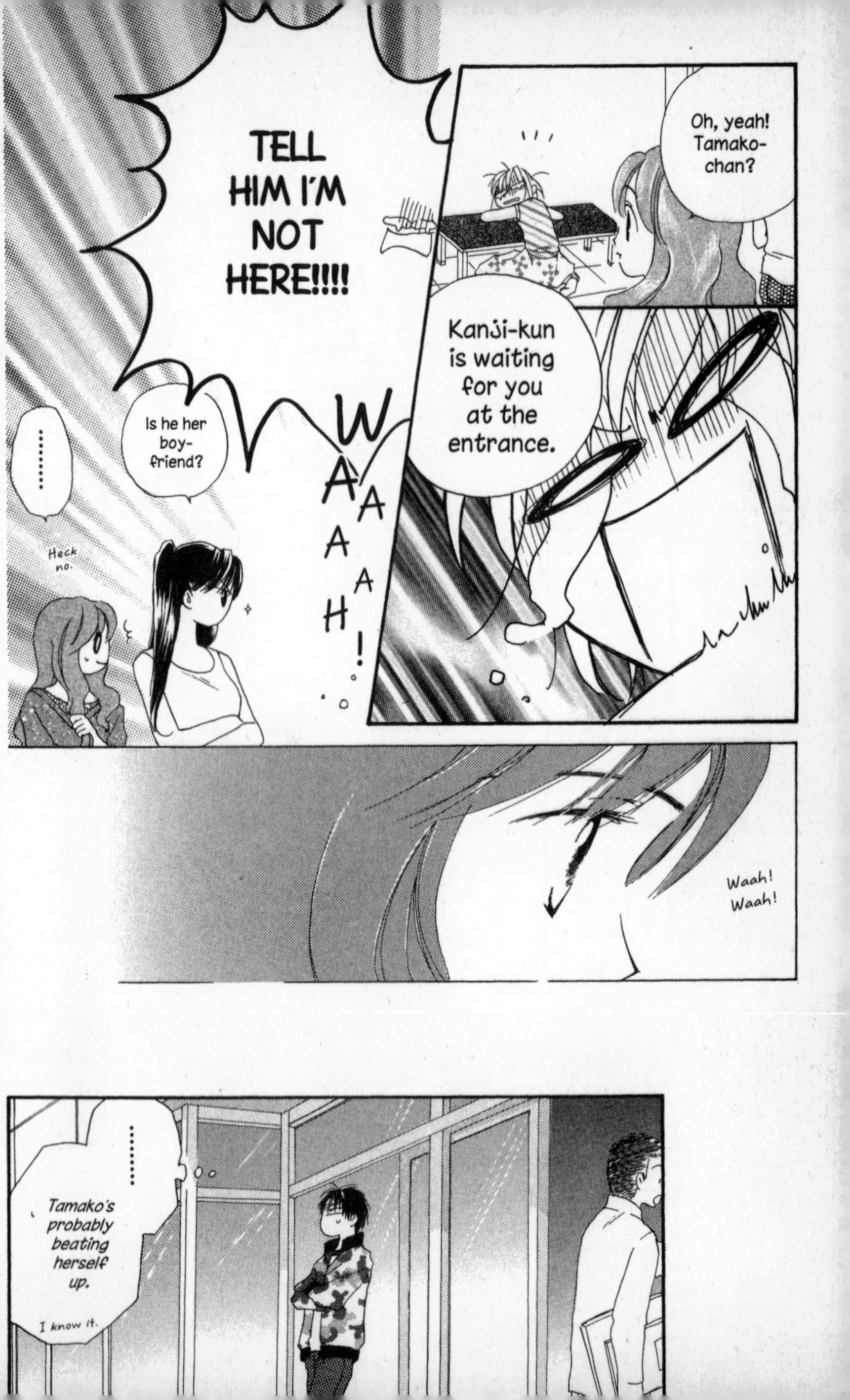

Oh, yeah! Tamako-chan?
Kanji-kun is waiting for you at the entrance.
TELL HIM I'M NOT HERE!!!!
WAAAAH!
Is he her boy-friend?
......
Heck no.
Waah! Waah!
......
Tamako's probably beating herself up.
I know it.

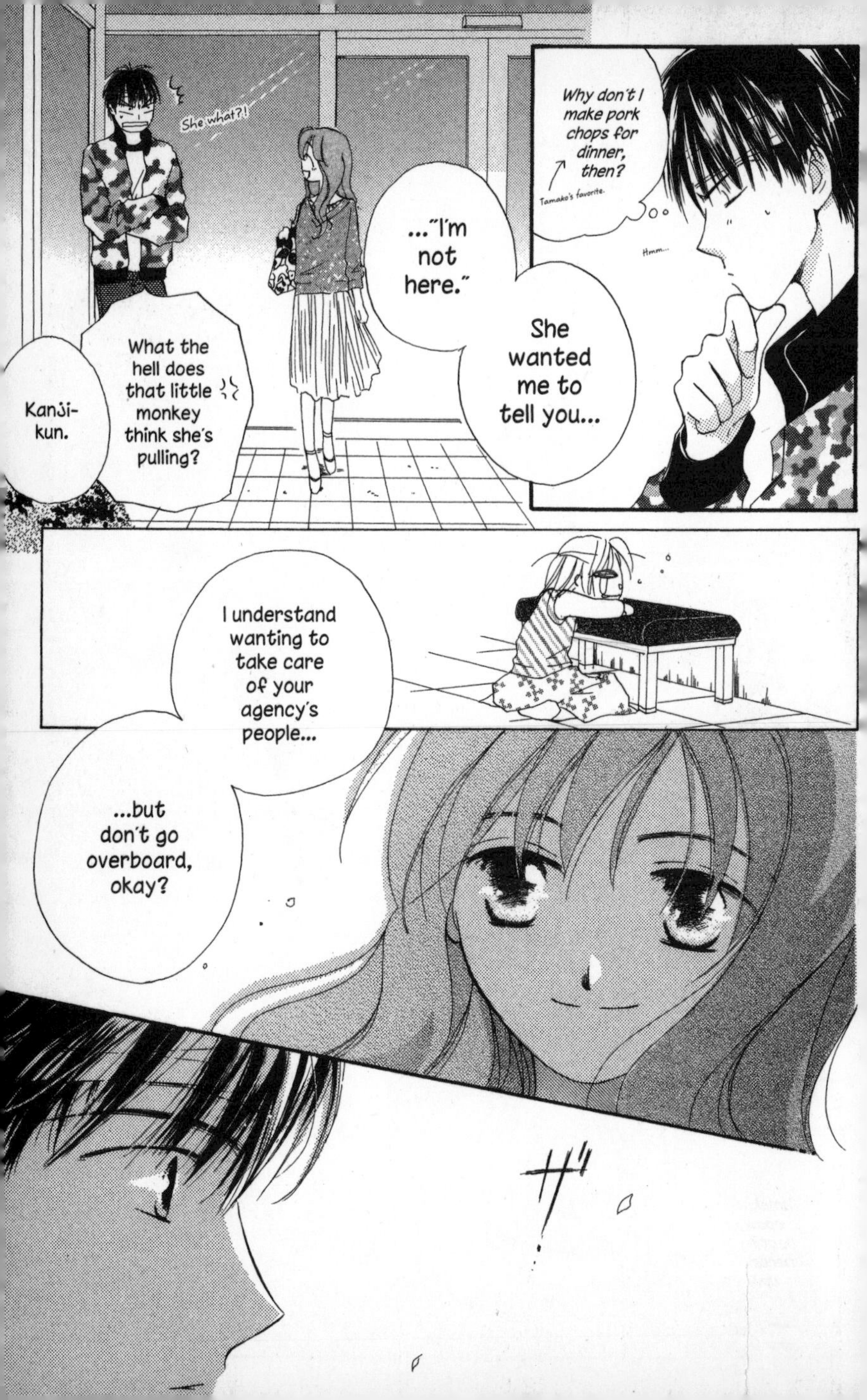
Why don't I make pork chops for dinner, then?
Tamako's favorite.
Hmm...
She wanted me to tell you...
..."I'm not here."
She what?!
What the hell does that little monkey think she's pulling?
Kanji-kun.
I understand wanting to take care of your agency's people...
...but don't go overboard, okay?

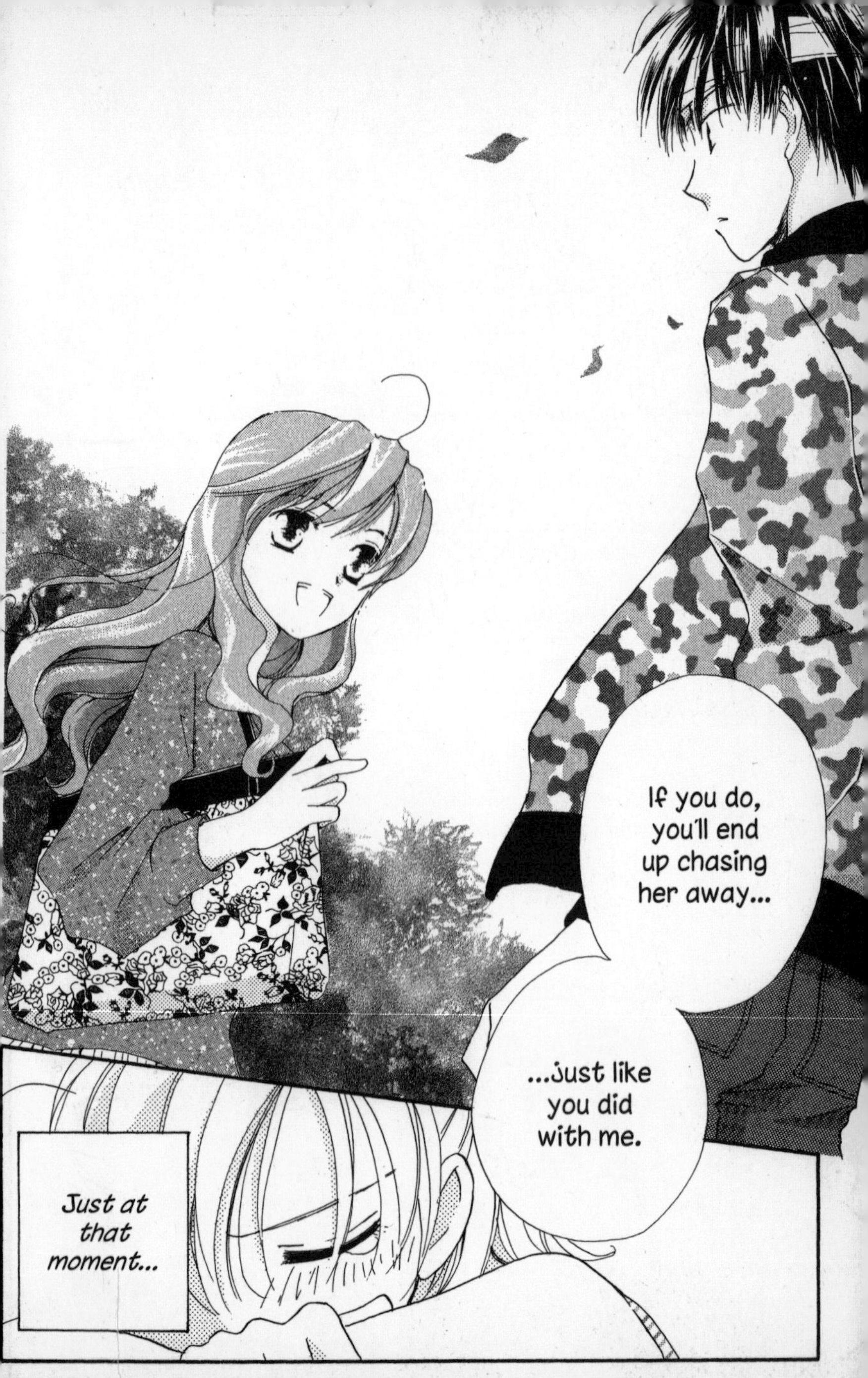
If you do, you'll end up chasing her away...
...Just like you did with me.
Just at that moment...

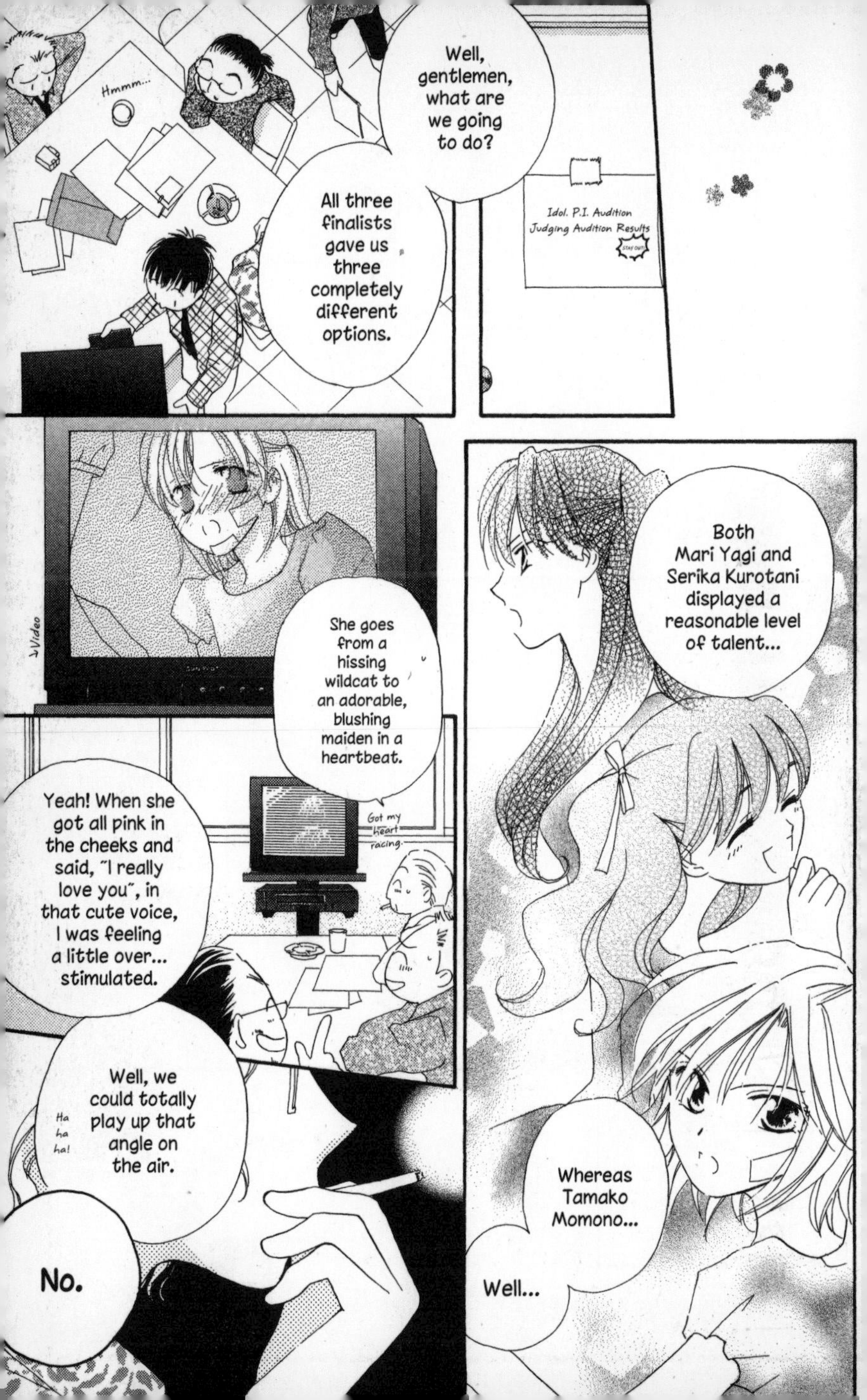

Idol. P.I. Audition
Judging Audition Results
STAY OUT!
Well, gentlemen, what are we going to do?
All three finalists gave us three completely different options.
Hmmm...
Both Mari Yagi and Serika Kurotani displayed a reasonable level of talent...
Whereas Tamako Momono...
Well...
Video
She goes from a hissing wildcat to an adorable, blushing maiden in a heartbeat.
Got my heart racing.
Yeah! When she got all pink in the cheeks and said, "I really love you", in that cute voice, I was feeling a little over... stimulated.
Well, we could totally play up that angle on the air.
Ha ha ha!
No.

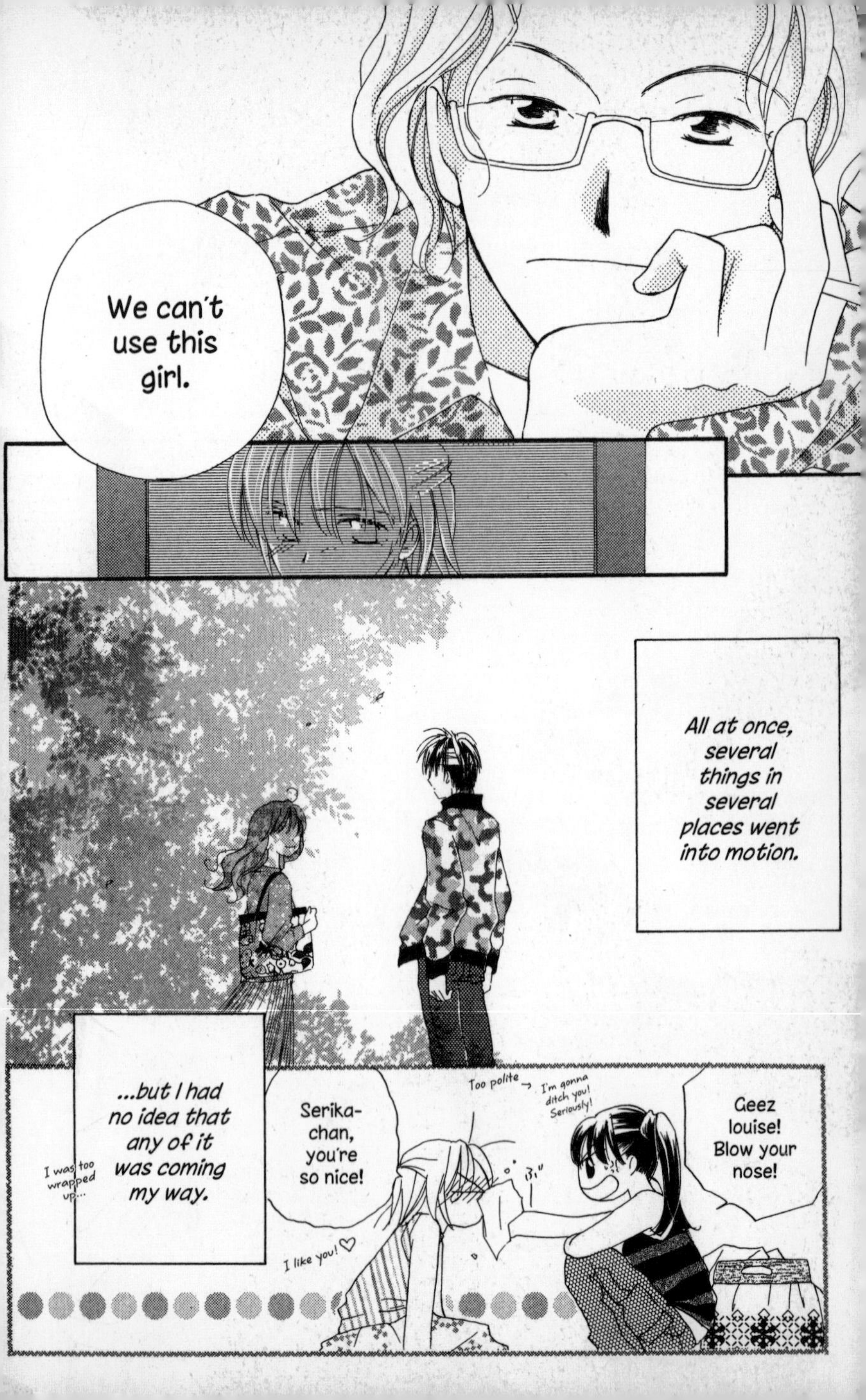

We can't use this girl.
All at once, several things in several places went into motion.
Geez louise! Blow your nose!
Too polite →
I'm gonna ditch you! Seriously!
Serika-chan, you're so nice!
I like you! ♡
...but I had no idea that any of it was coming my way.
I was too wrapped up...

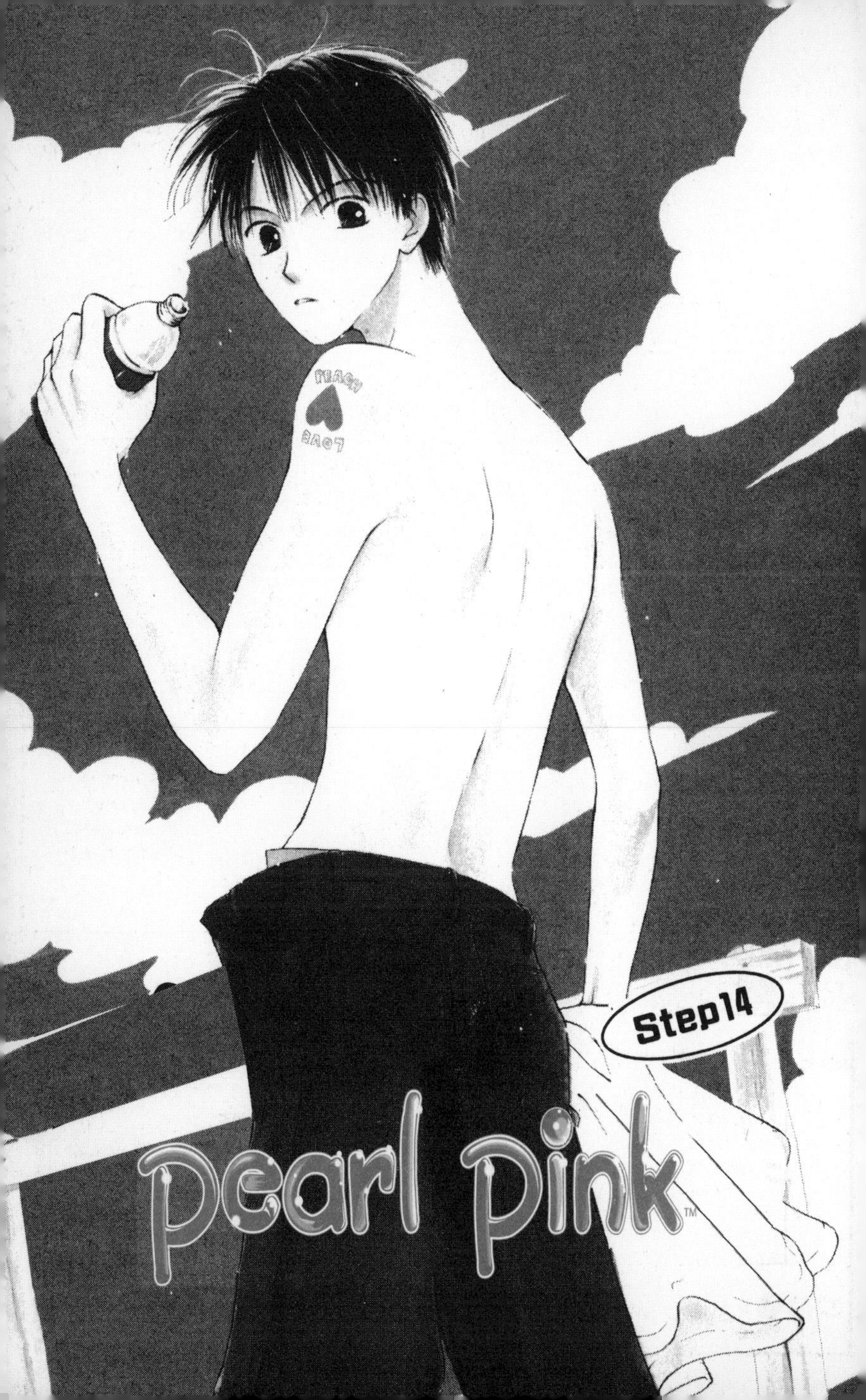
Step 14
pearl pink™

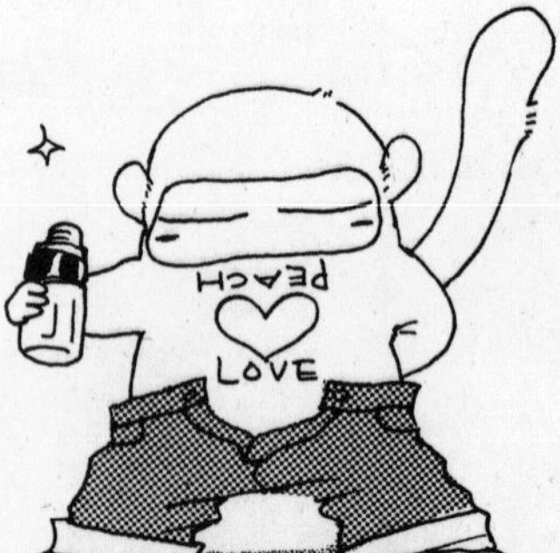
LOVE

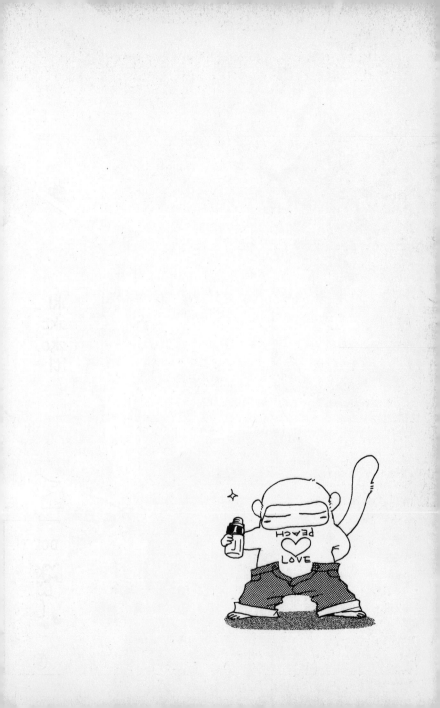

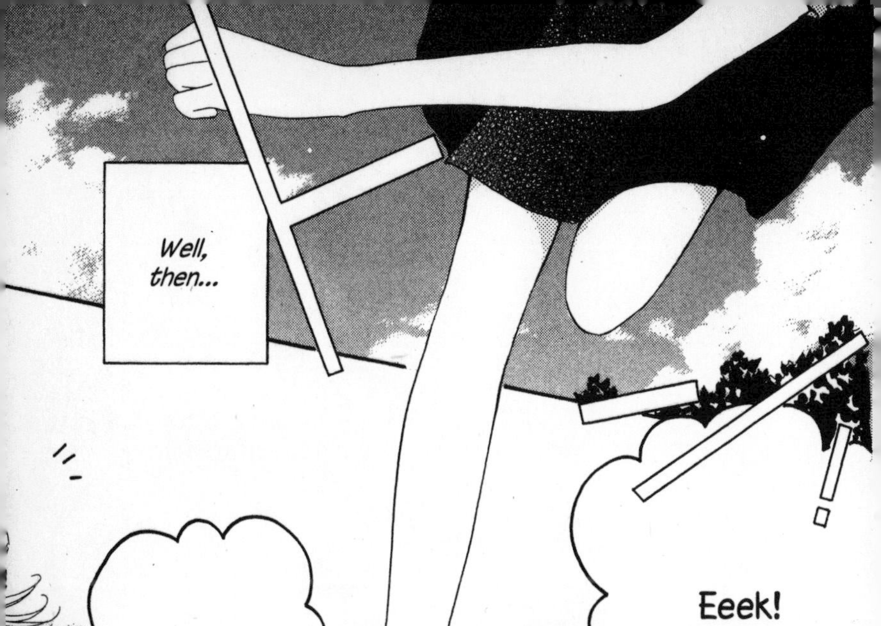
Well, then...
Eeek! Tamako! Tamako, wait!
Be "Umeko" for us again! Pleeaase?

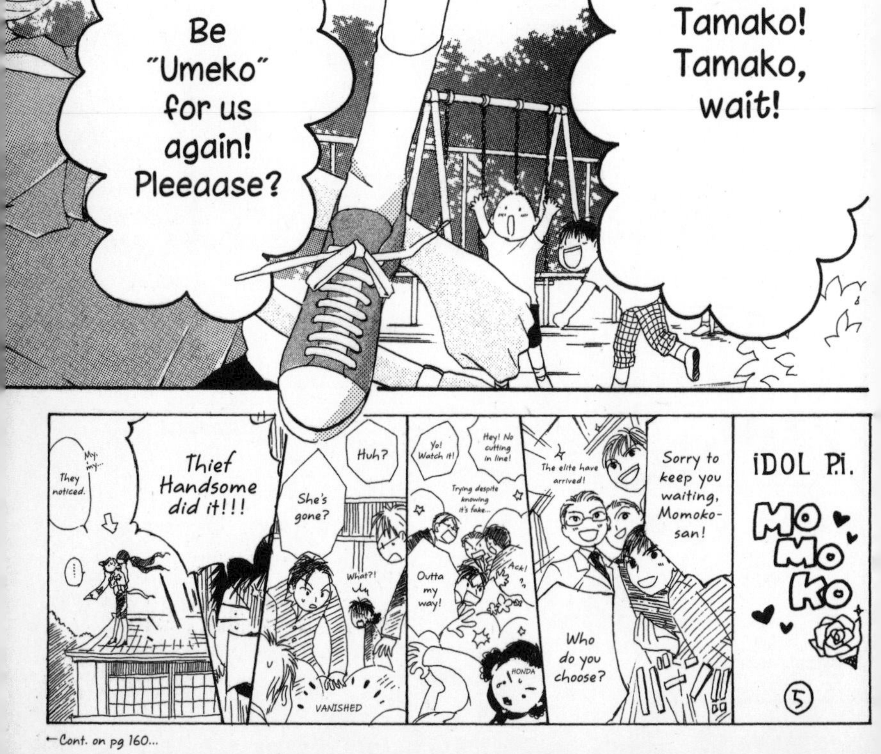
IDOL P.I.
MOMOKO
5
Sorry to keep you waiting, Momoko-san!
The elite have arrived!
Who do you choose?
Hey! No cutting in line!
Yo! Watch it!
Trying despite knowing it's fake...
Ack!
Outta my way!
HONDA
Huh?
She's gone?
What?!
VANISHED
Thief Handsome did it!!!
My, my...
They noticed.
...

←Cont. on pg 160...

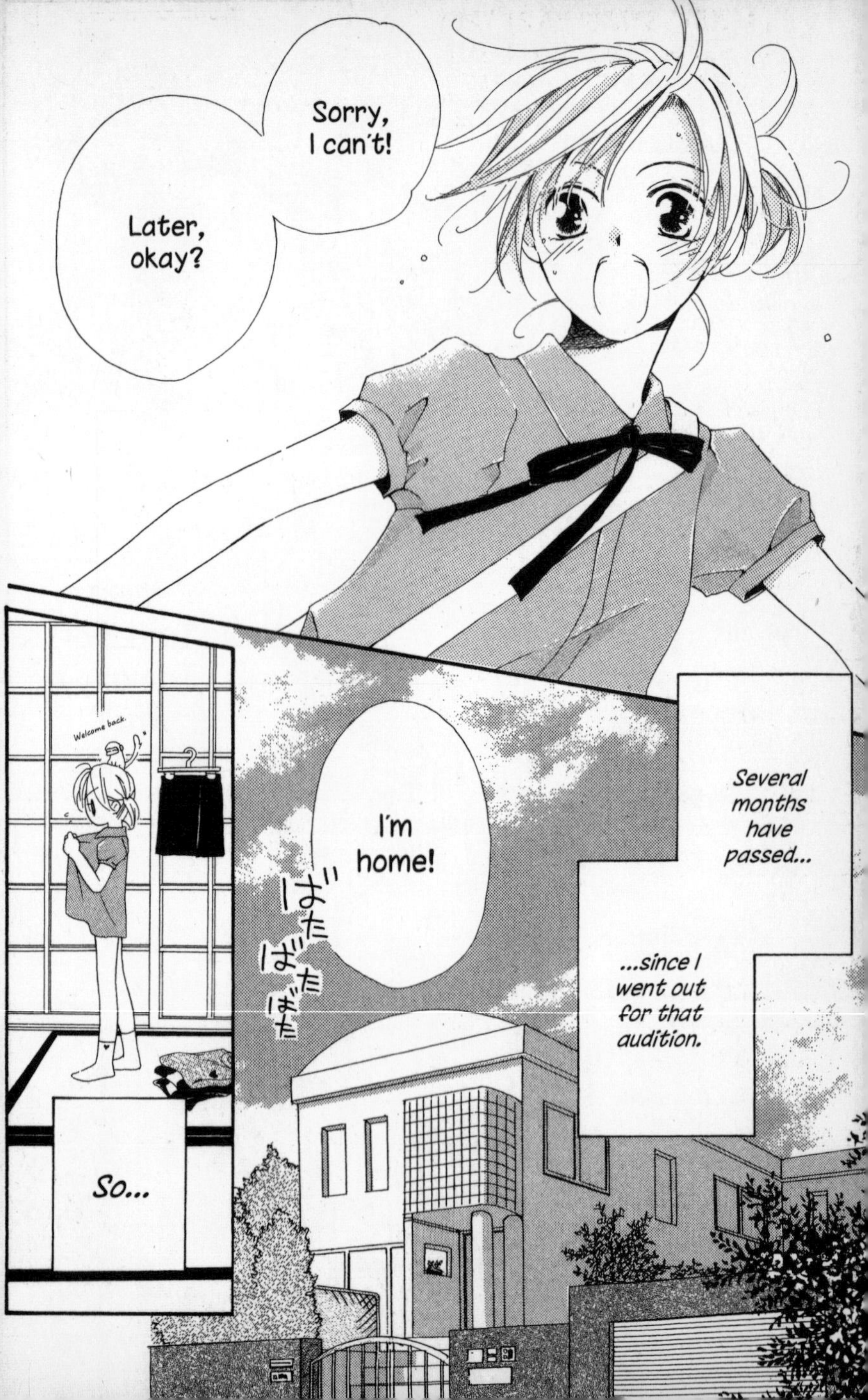

Sorry, I can't!
Later, okay?
Several months have passed...
...since I went out for that audition.
I'm home!
ばたばたばた
Welcome back.
So...

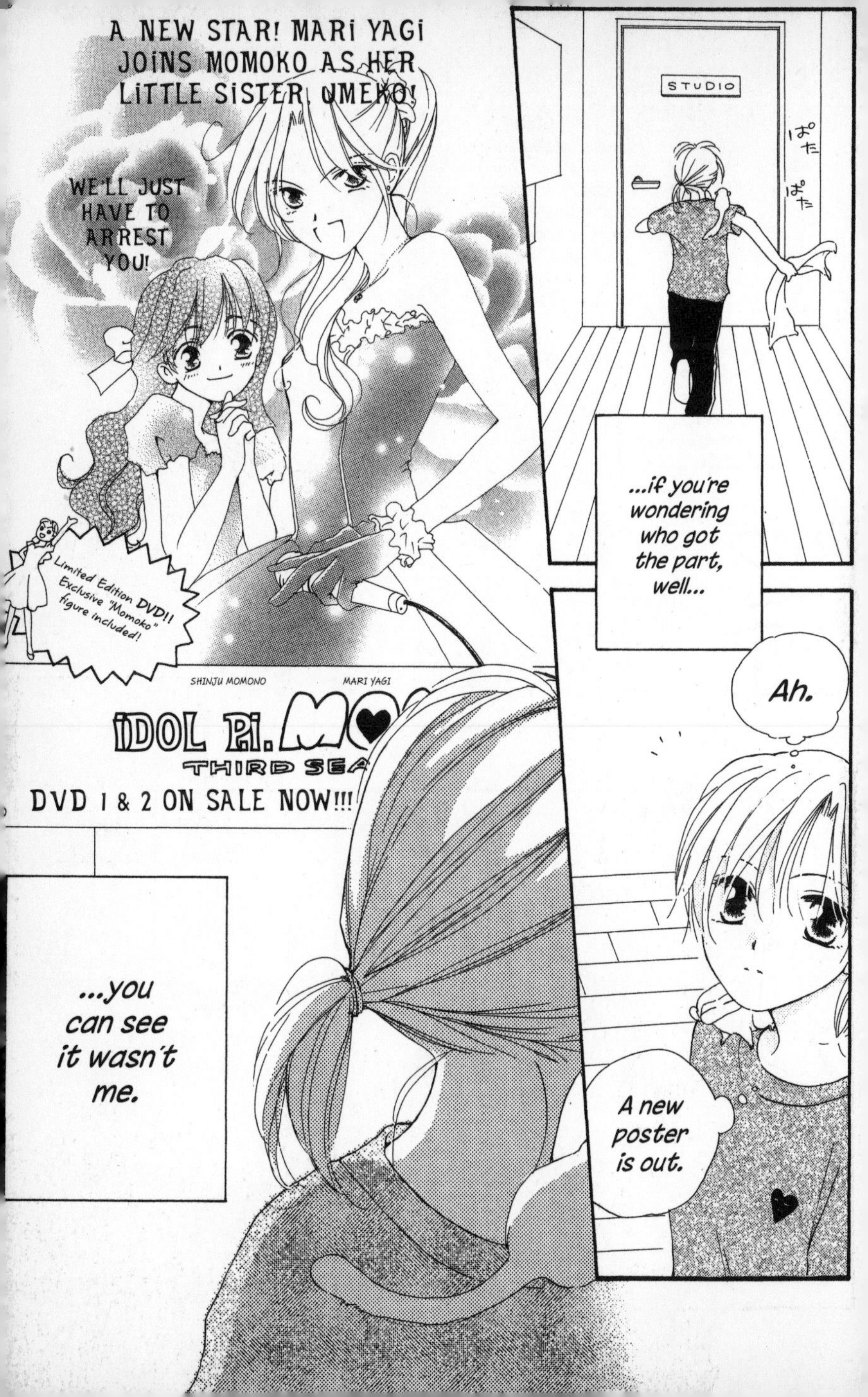
STUDIO
ぱた
ぱた
...if you're wondering who got the part, well...
Ah.
A new poster is out.
A NEW STAR! MARI YAGI JOINS MOMOKO AS HER LITTLE SISTER, UMEKO!
WE'LL JUST HAVE TO ARREST YOU!
Limited Edition DVD!! Exclusive "Momoko" figure included!
SHINJU MOMONO
MARI YAGI
iDOL Pi.
DVD 1 & 2 ON SALE NOW!!!
...you can see it wasn't me.

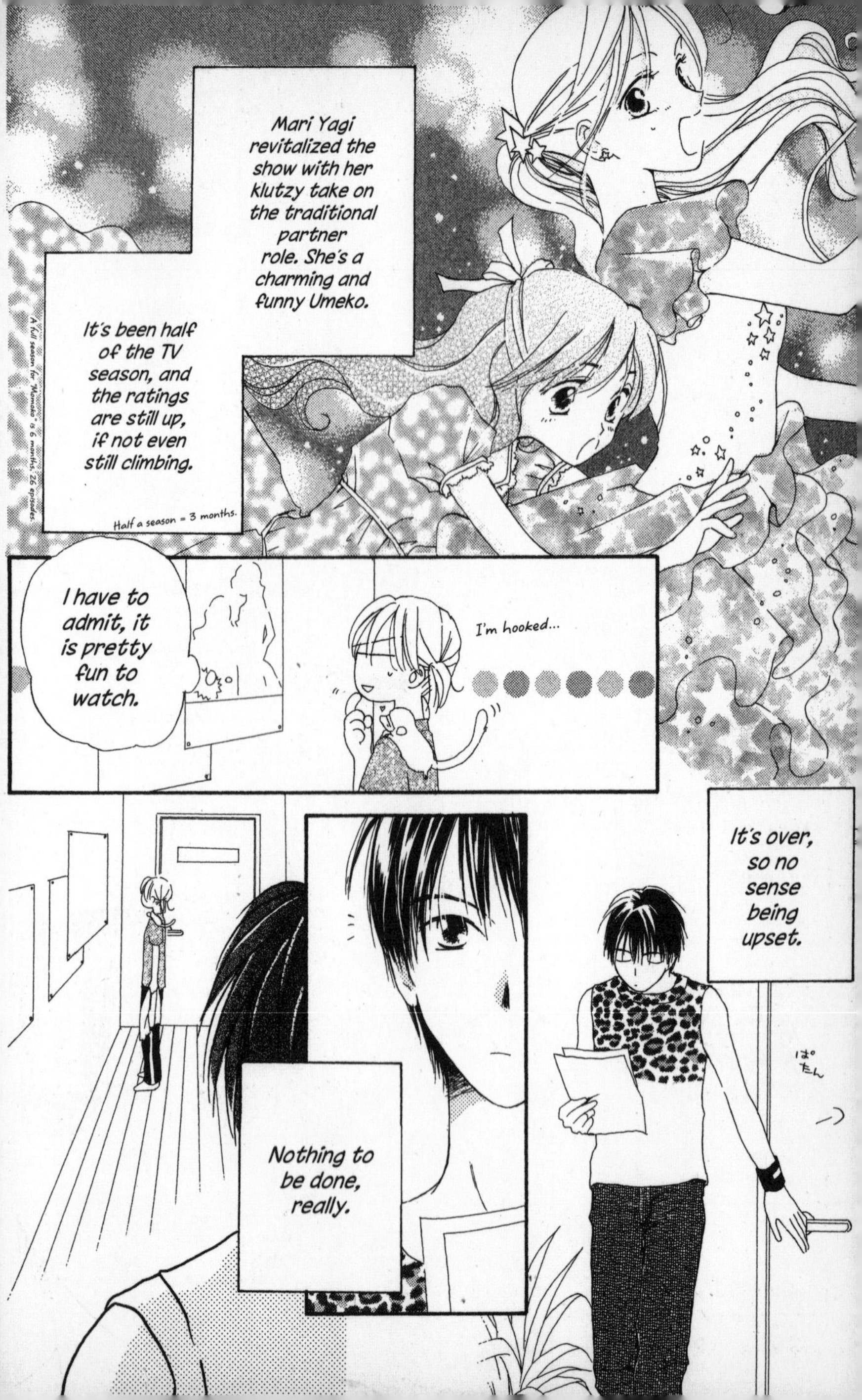
Mari Yagi revitalized the show with her klutzy take on the traditional partner role. She's a charming and funny Umeko.
It's been half of the TV season, and the ratings are still up, if not even still climbing.
Half a season = 3 months.
A full season for "Momoko" is 6 months, 26 episodes.
I have to admit, it is pretty fun to watch.
I'm hooked...
It's over, so no sense being upset.
ぱたん
Nothing to be done, really.

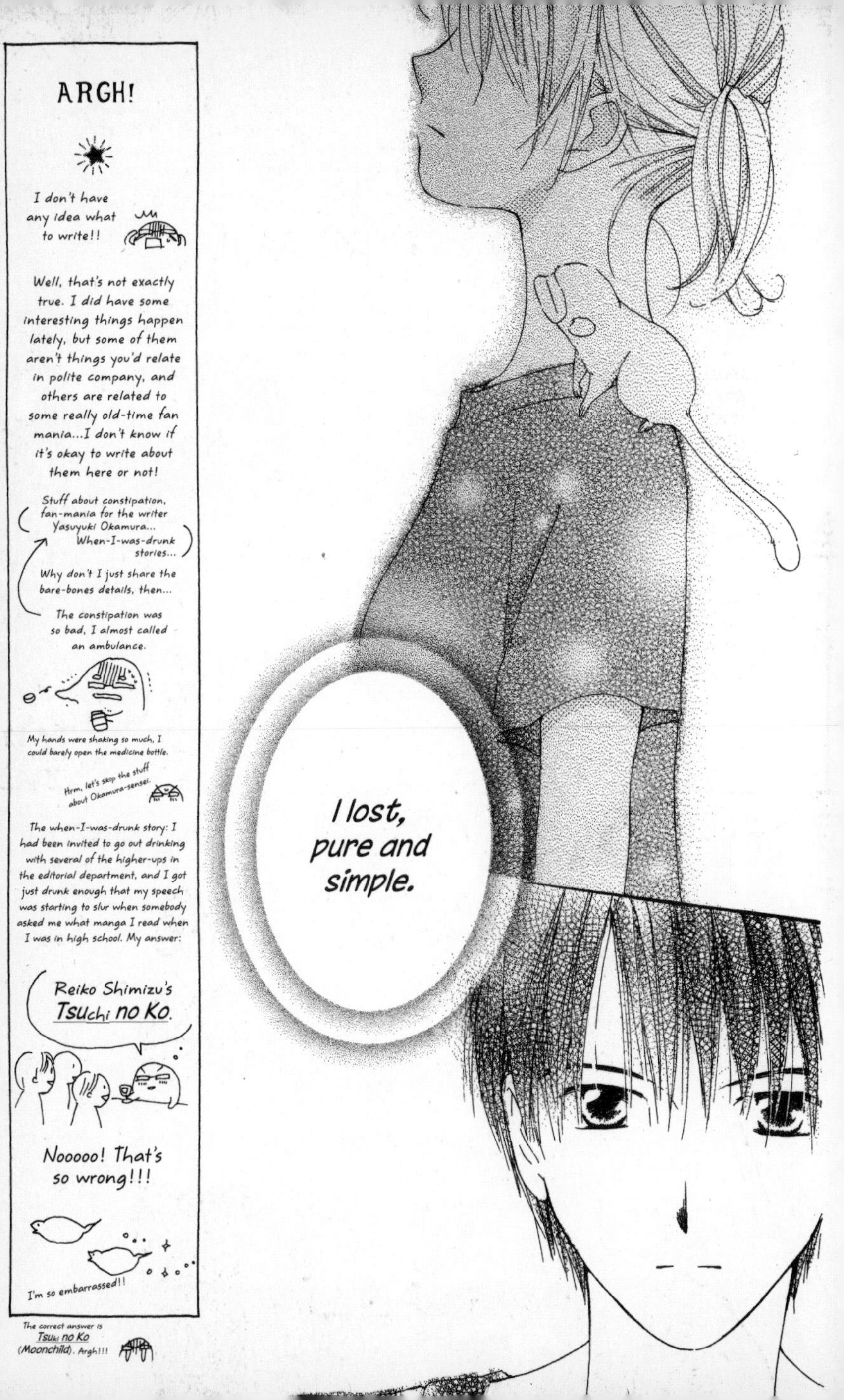
I lost, pure and simple.

ARGH!

I don't have any idea what to write!!

Well, that's not exactly true. I did have some interesting things happen lately, but some of them aren't things you'd relate in polite company, and others are related to some really old-time fan mania...I don't know if it's okay to write about them here or not!

(Stuff about constipation, fan-mania for the writer Yasuyuki Okamura... When-I-was-drunk stories...)

Why don't I just share the bare-bones details, then...

The constipation was so bad, I almost called an ambulance.

My hands were shaking so much, I could barely open the medicine bottle.

Hrm, let's skip the stuff about Okamura-sensei.

The when-I-was-drunk story: I had been invited to go out drinking with several of the higher-ups in the editorial department, and I got just drunk enough that my speech was starting to slur when somebody asked me what manga I read when I was in high school. My answer:

Reiko Shimizu's Tsuchi no Ko.

Nooooo! That's so wrong!!!

I'm so embarrassed!!

The correct answer is Tsuki no Ko (Moonchild). Argh!!!

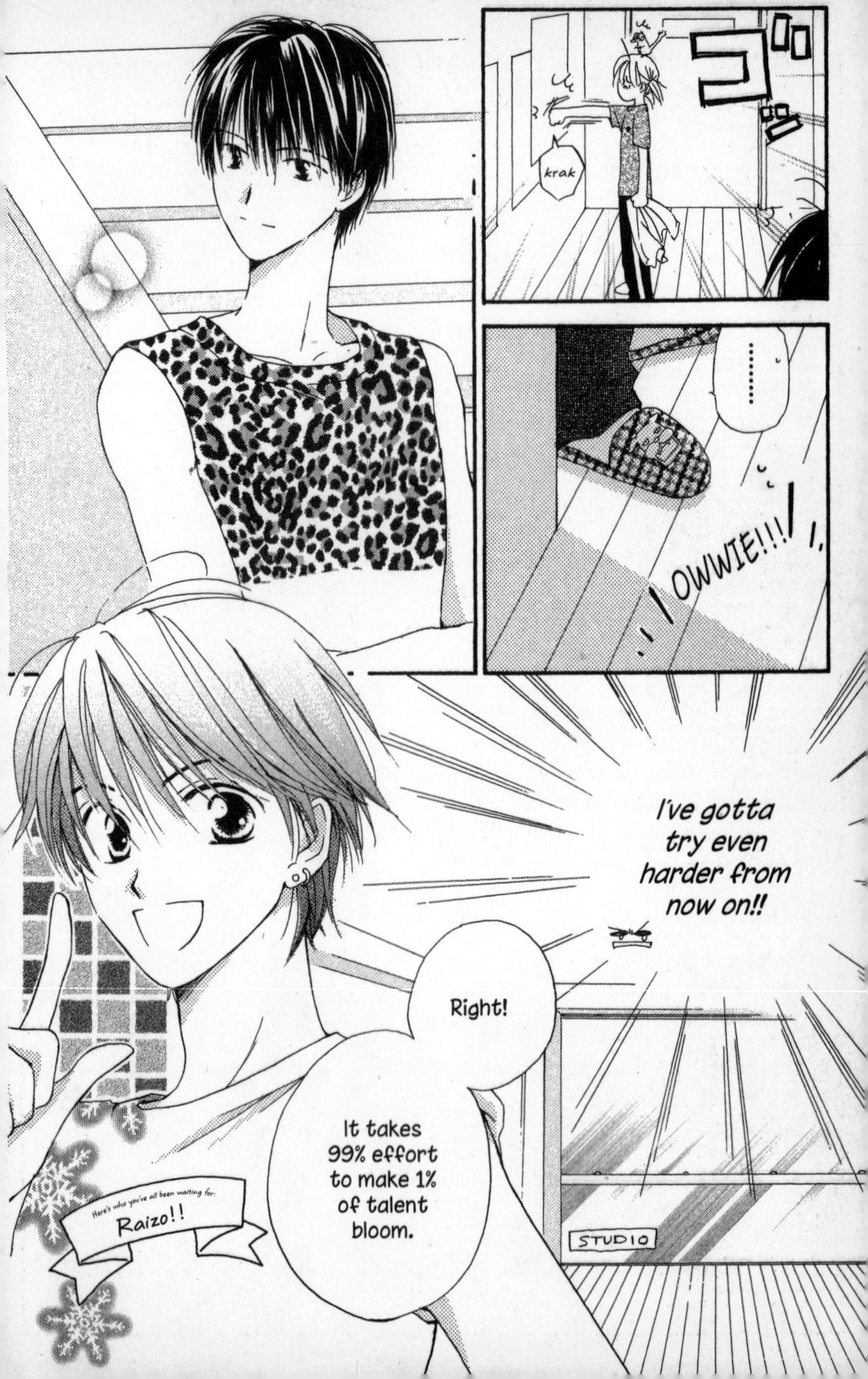
krak
......
OWWIE!!!
I've gotta try even harder from now on!!
Right!
It takes 99% effort to make 1% of talent bloom.
STUDIO
Here's who you've all been waiting for:
Raizo!!

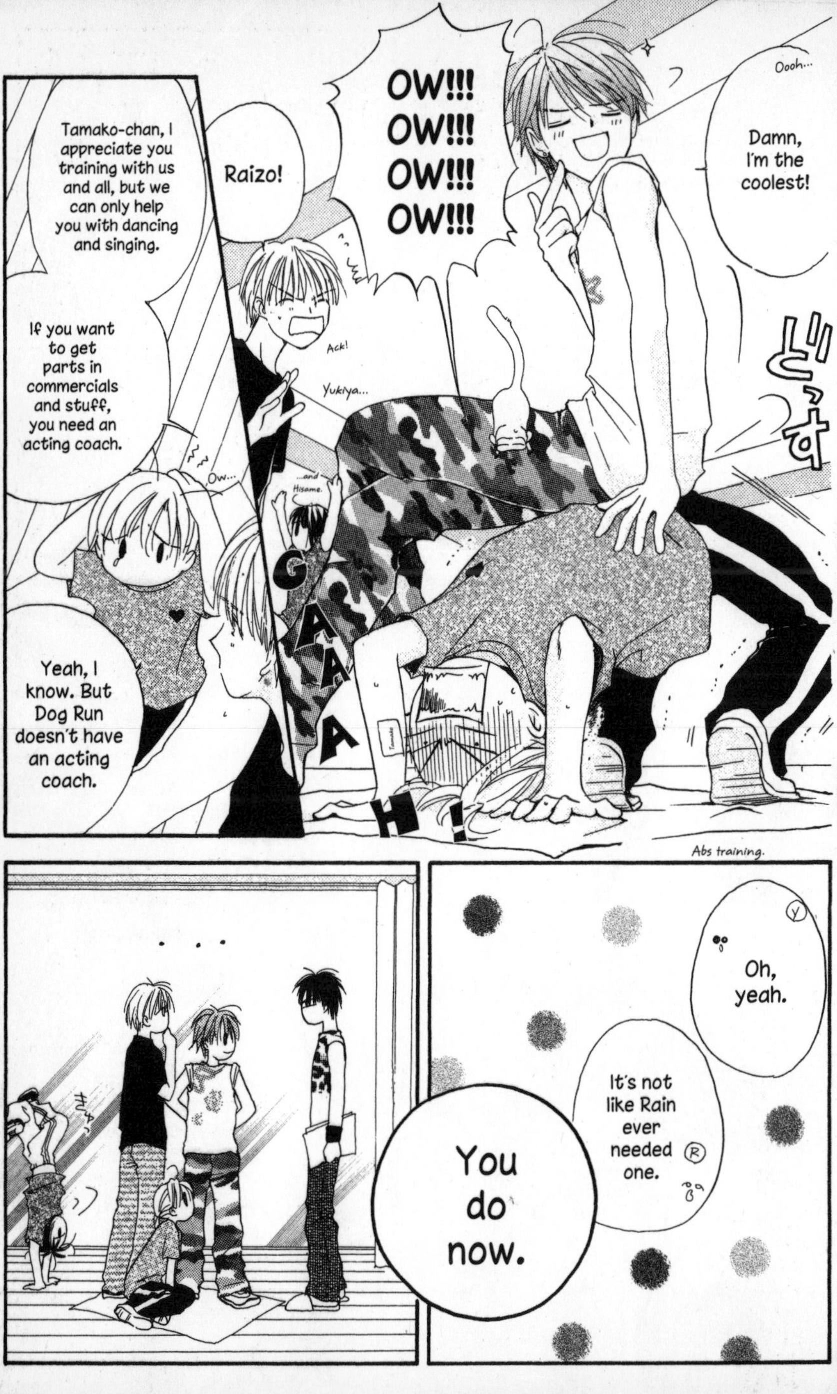
Oooh...
Damn, I'm the coolest!
どすっ
OW!!! OW!!! OW!!! OW!!!
Ack!
Yukiya...
...and Hisame.
GAAAH!
Ow...
Raizo!
Tamako-chan, I appreciate you training with us and all, but we can only help you with dancing and singing.
If you want to get parts in commercials and stuff, you need an acting coach.
Yeah, I know. But Dog Run doesn't have an acting coach.
Abs training.
Oh, yeah.
It's not like Rain ever needed one.
You do now.
• • •

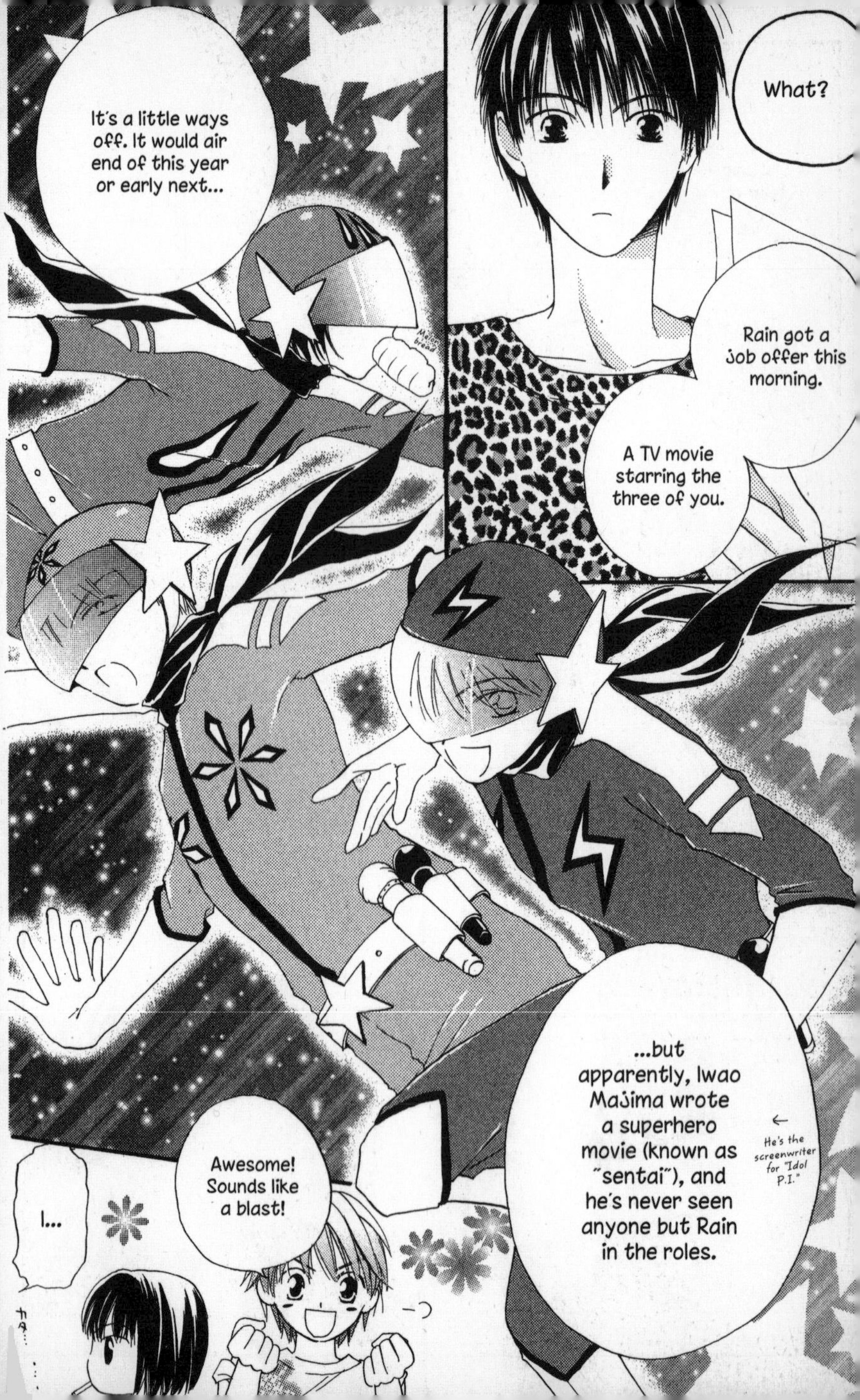
What?
Rain got a job offer this morning.
A TV movie starring the three of you.
It's a little ways off. It would air end of this year or early next...
Melon bread
...but apparently, Iwao Majima wrote a superhero movie (known as "sentai"), and he's never seen anyone but Rain in the roles.
He's the screenwriter for "Idol P.I."
Awesome! Sounds like a blast!
I...

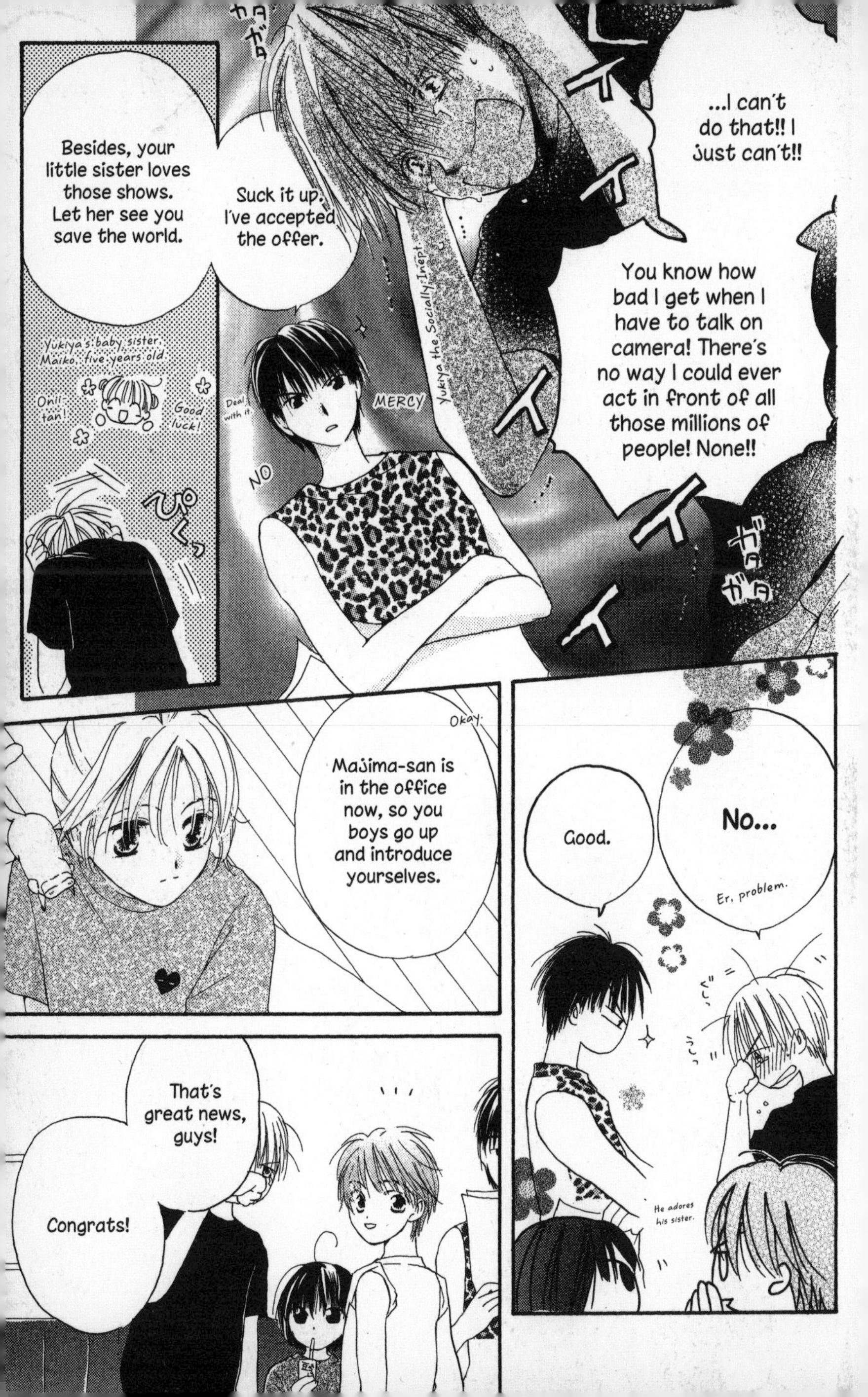
...I can't do that!! I just can't!!
You know how bad I get when I have to talk on camera! There's no way I could ever act in front of all those millions of people! None!!
Yukiya the Socially Inept.
Suck it up. I've accepted the offer.
MERCY
Deal with it.
NO
Besides, your little sister loves those shows. Let her see you save the world.
Yukiya's baby sister, Maiko, five years old
Good luck!
Onii-tan!
No...
Er, problem.
Good.
He adores his sister.
Okay.
Majima-san is in the office now, so you boys go up and introduce yourselves.
That's great news, guys!
Congrats!

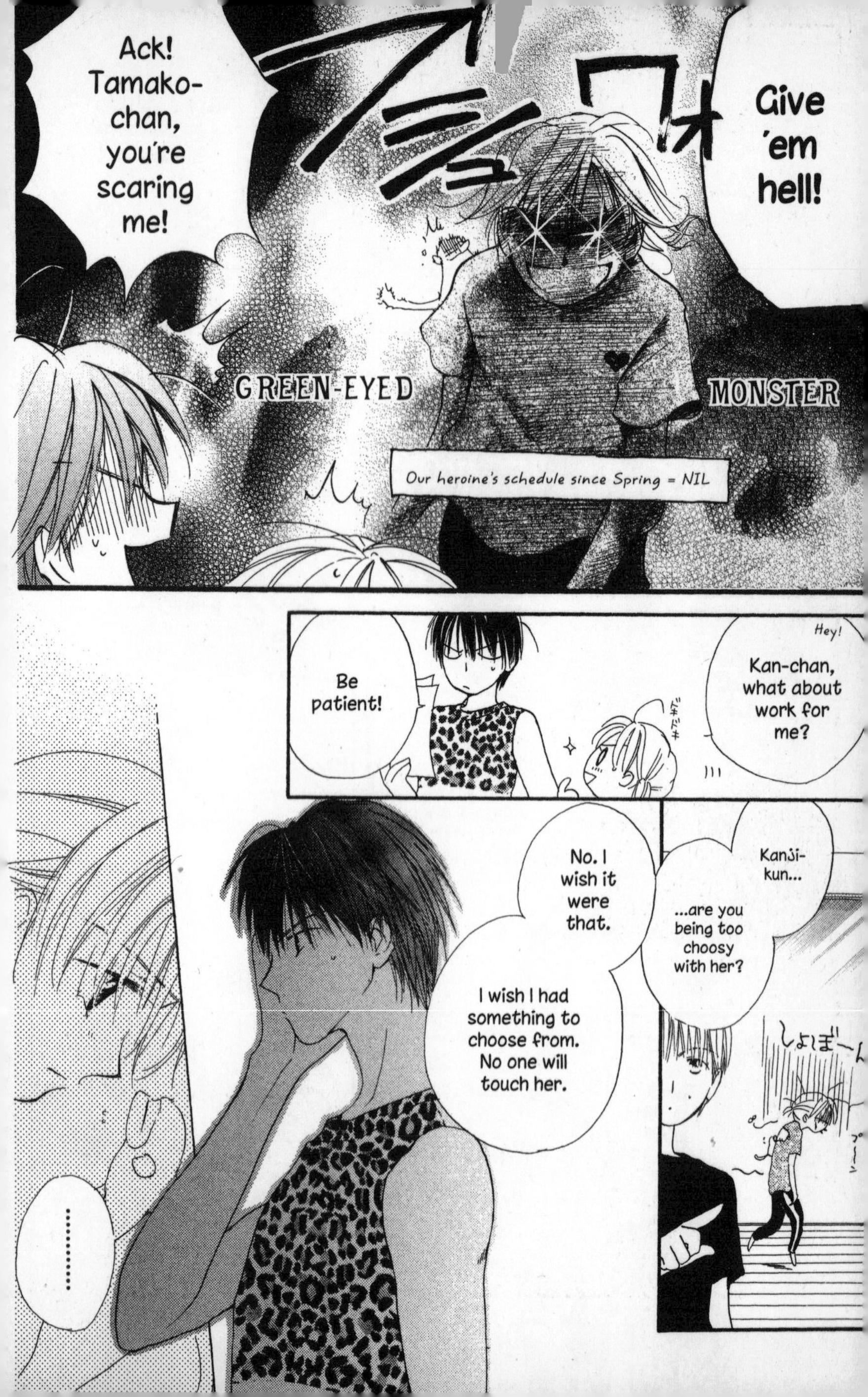
Give 'em hell!
Ack! Tamako-chan, you're scaring me!
GREEN-EYED MONSTER
Our heroine's schedule since Spring = NIL
Hey! Kan-chan, what about work for me?
Be patient!
Kanji-kun...
...are you being too choosy with her?
しょぼ〜ん
No. I wish it were that.
I wish I had something to choose from. No one will touch her.
....

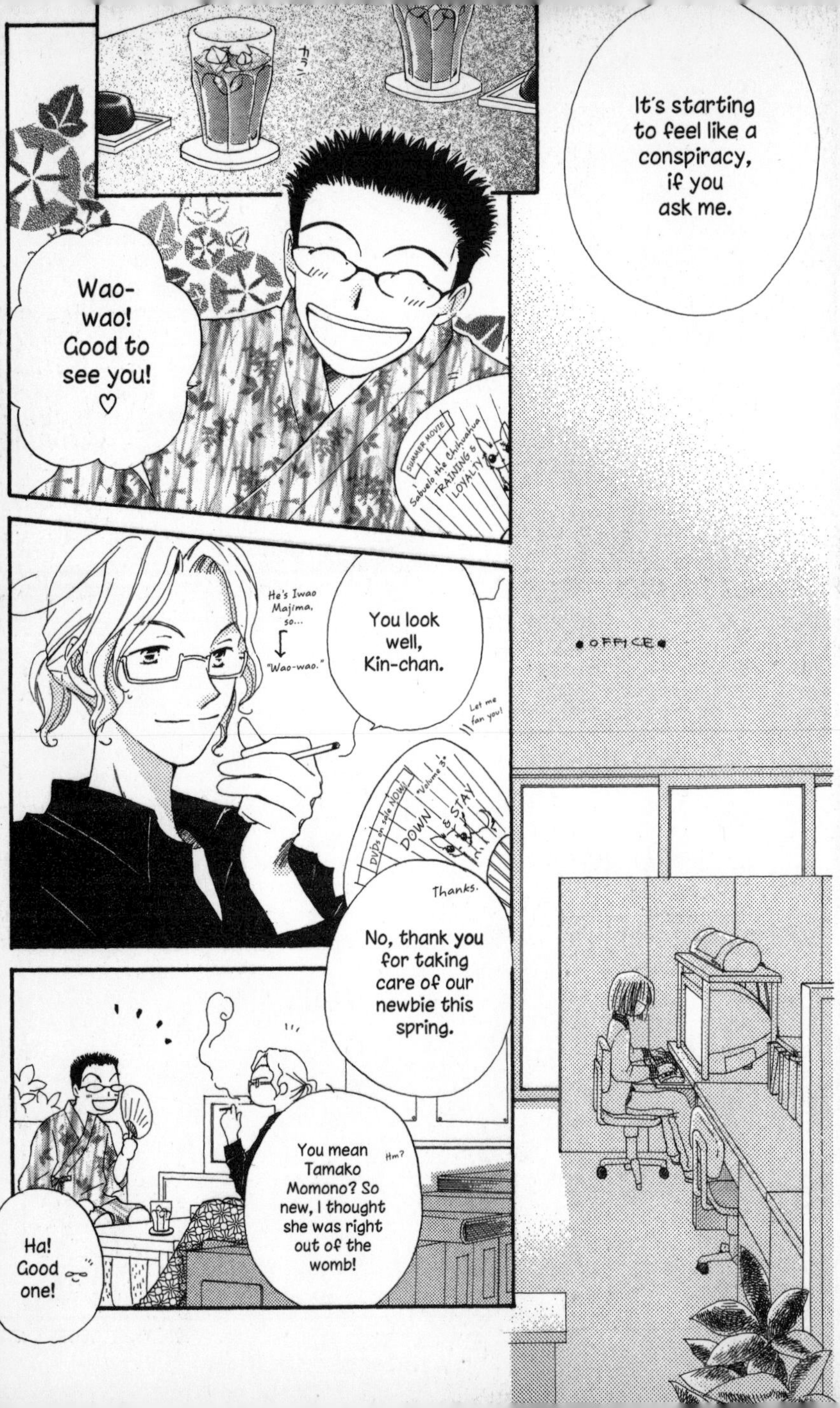

It's starting to feel like a conspiracy, if you ask me.
•OFFICE•
カラン
Wao-wao! Good to see you! ♡
SUMMER MOVIE
Sabuelo the Chihuahua
TRAINING & LOYALTY
You look well, Kin-chan.
He's Iwao Majima, so... "Wao-wao."
Let me fan you!
DVDs on sale NOW!
"Volume 3"
DOWN & STAY
Thanks.
No, thank you for taking care of our newbie this spring.
Hm?
You mean Tamako Momono? So new, I thought she was right out of the womb!
Ha! Good one!

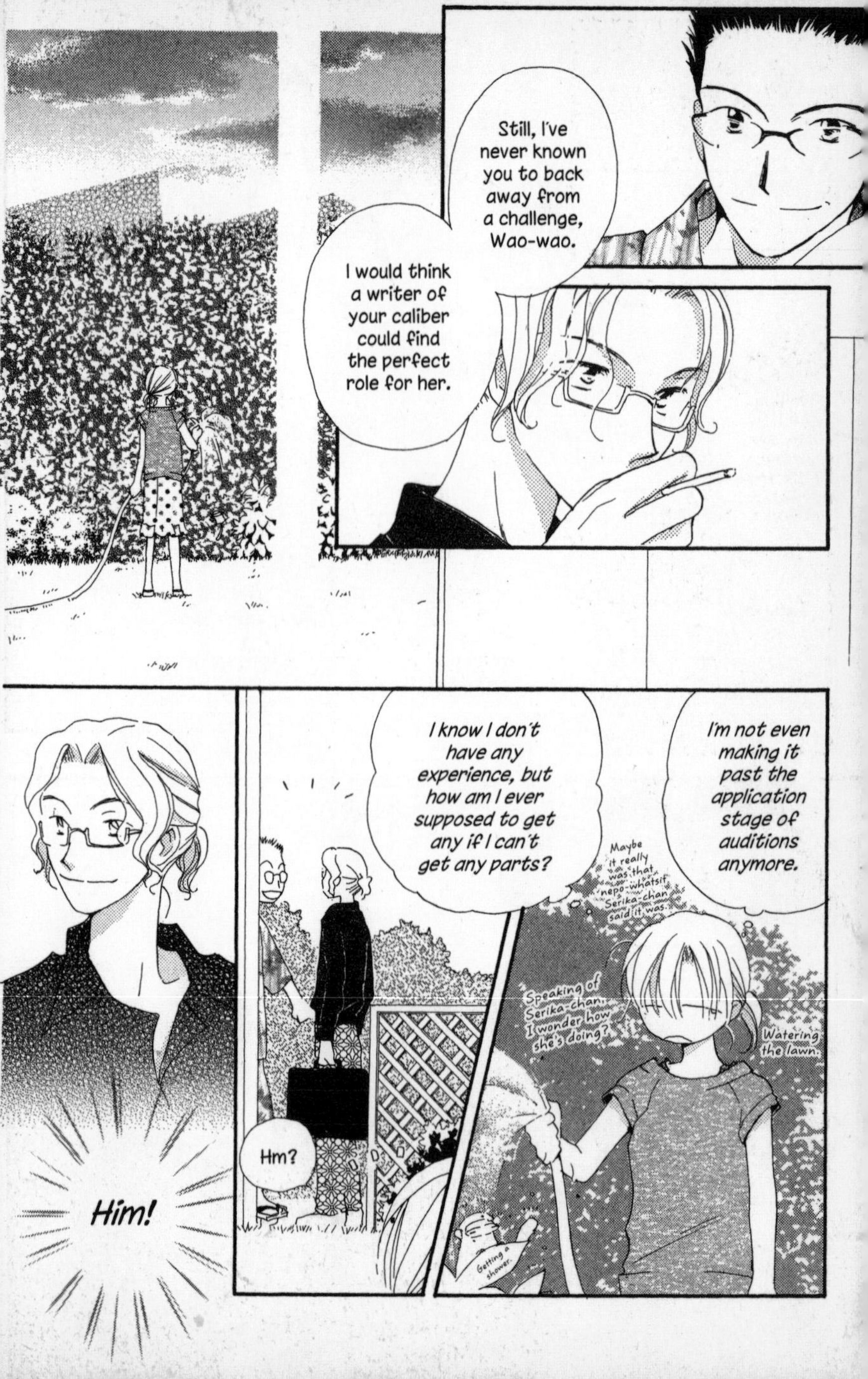
Still, I've never known you to back away from a challenge, Wao-wao.
I would think a writer of your caliber could find the perfect role for her.
I'm not even making it past the application stage of auditions anymore.
I know I don't have any experience, but how am I ever supposed to get any if I can't get any parts?
Maybe it really was that nepo-whatsit Serika-chan said it was.
Watering the lawn.
Speaking of Serika-chan. I wonder how she's doing?
Getting a shower.
Hm?
Him!

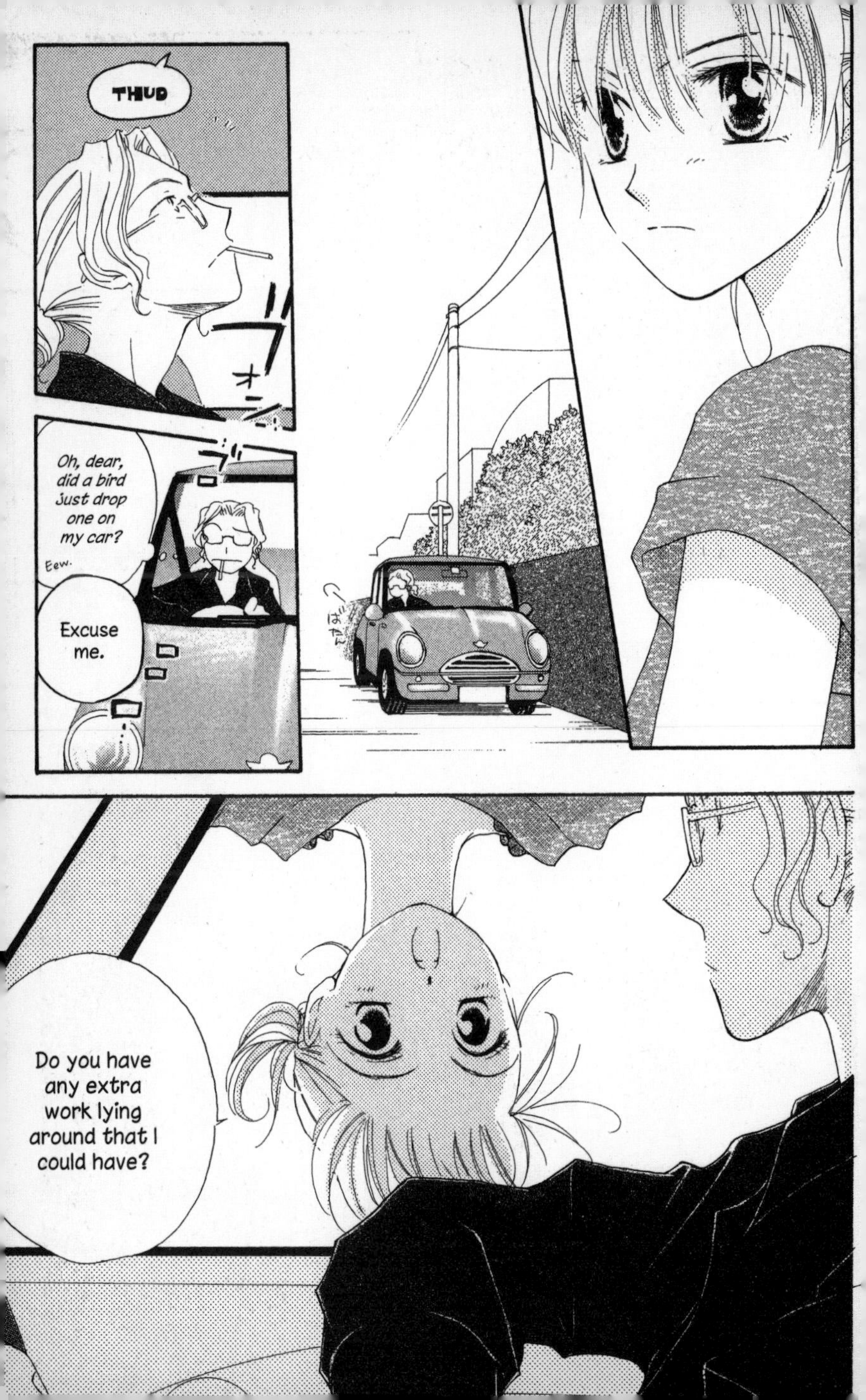
THUD
Oh, dear, did a bird just drop one on my car?
Eew.
Excuse me.
Do you have any extra work lying around that I could have?

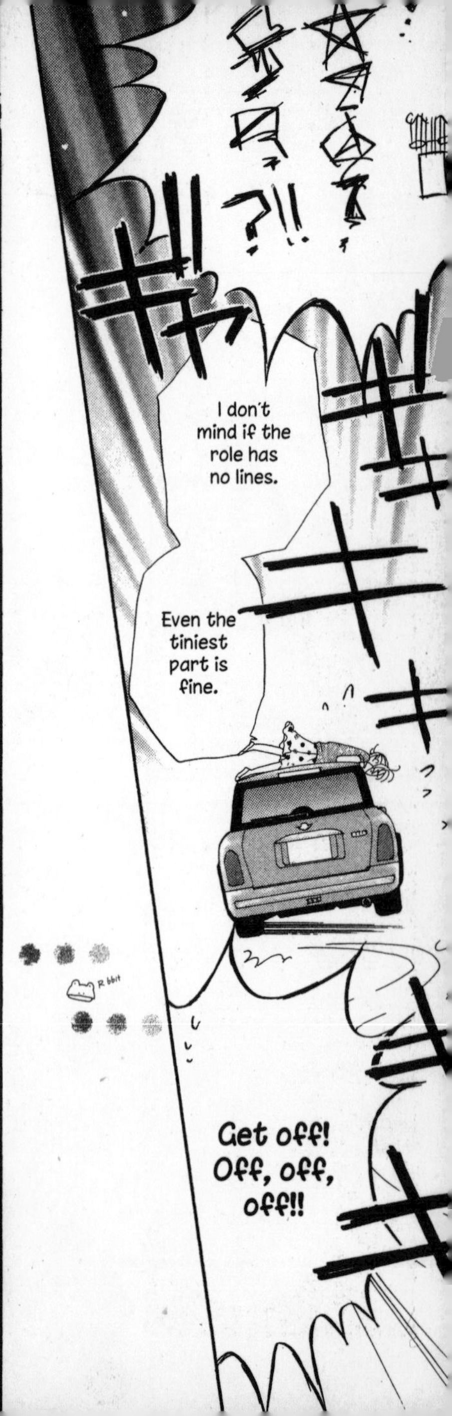
I don't mind if the role has no lines.
Even the tiniest part is fine.
Get off! Off, off, off!!

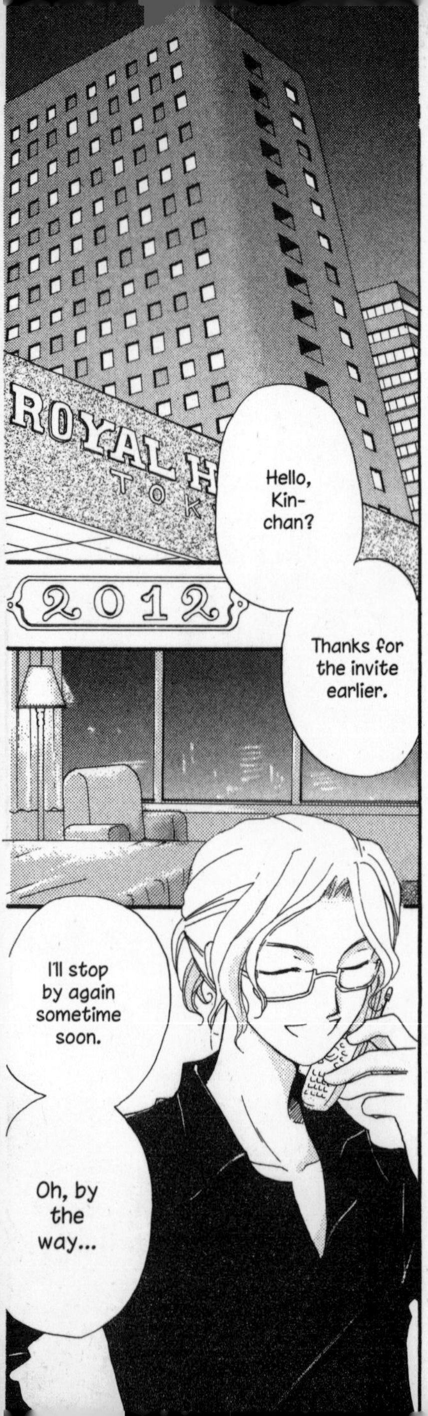
ROYAL H
TOK
2012
Hello, Kin-chan?
Thanks for the invite earlier.
I'll stop by again sometime soon.
Oh, by the way...

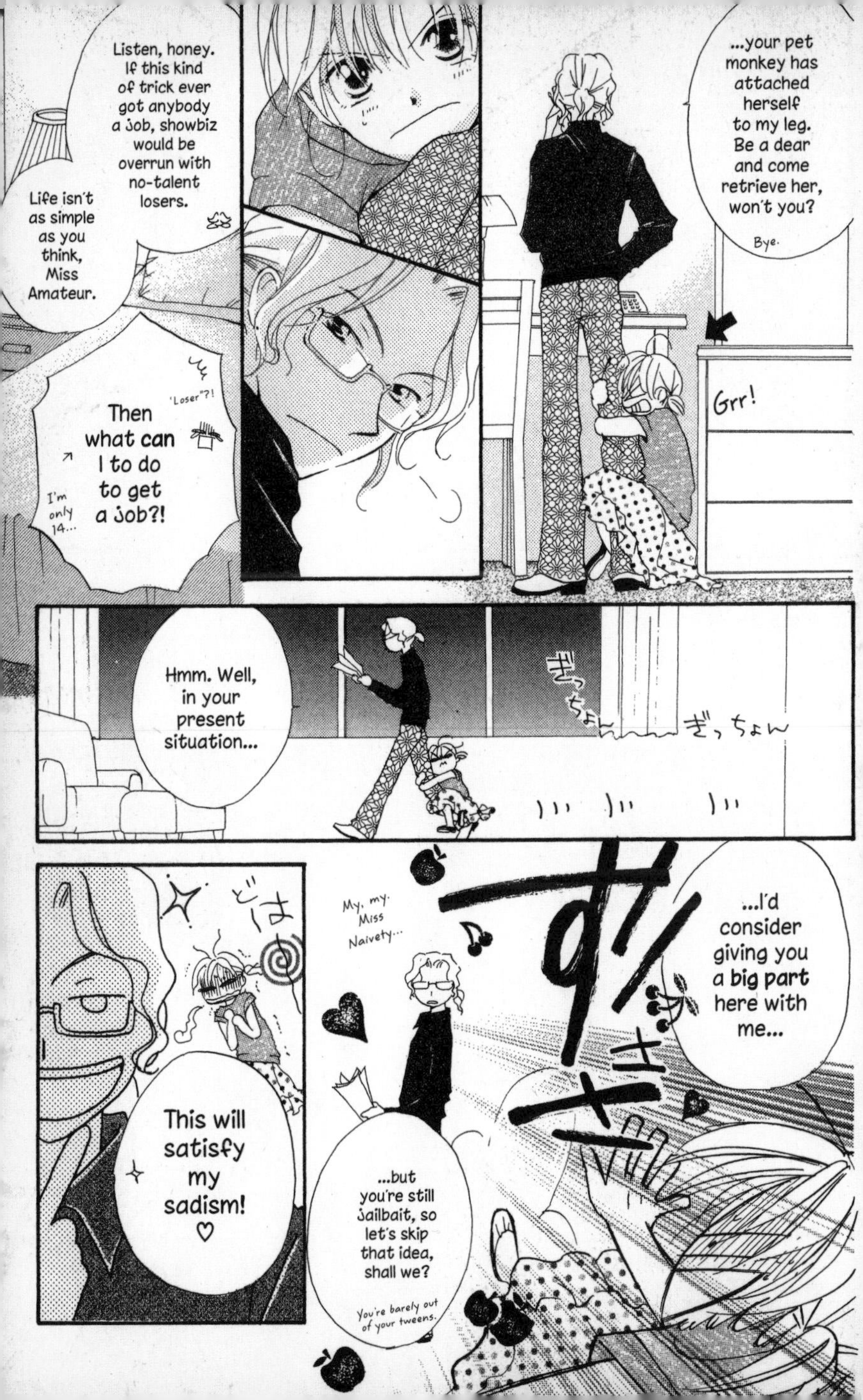
...your pet monkey has attached herself to my leg. Be a dear and come retrieve her, won't you?
Bye.
Grr!
Listen, honey. If this kind of trick ever got anybody a job, showbiz would be overrun with no-talent losers.
Life isn't as simple as you think, Miss Amateur.
'Loser'?!
Then what can I to do to get a job?!
I'm only 14...
Hmm. Well, in your present situation...
ぎっちょん
ぎっちょん
...I'd consider giving you a **big part** here with me...
My, my. Miss Naivety...
...but you're still jailbait, so let's skip that idea, shall we?
You're barely out of your tweens.
This will satisfy my sadism! ♡

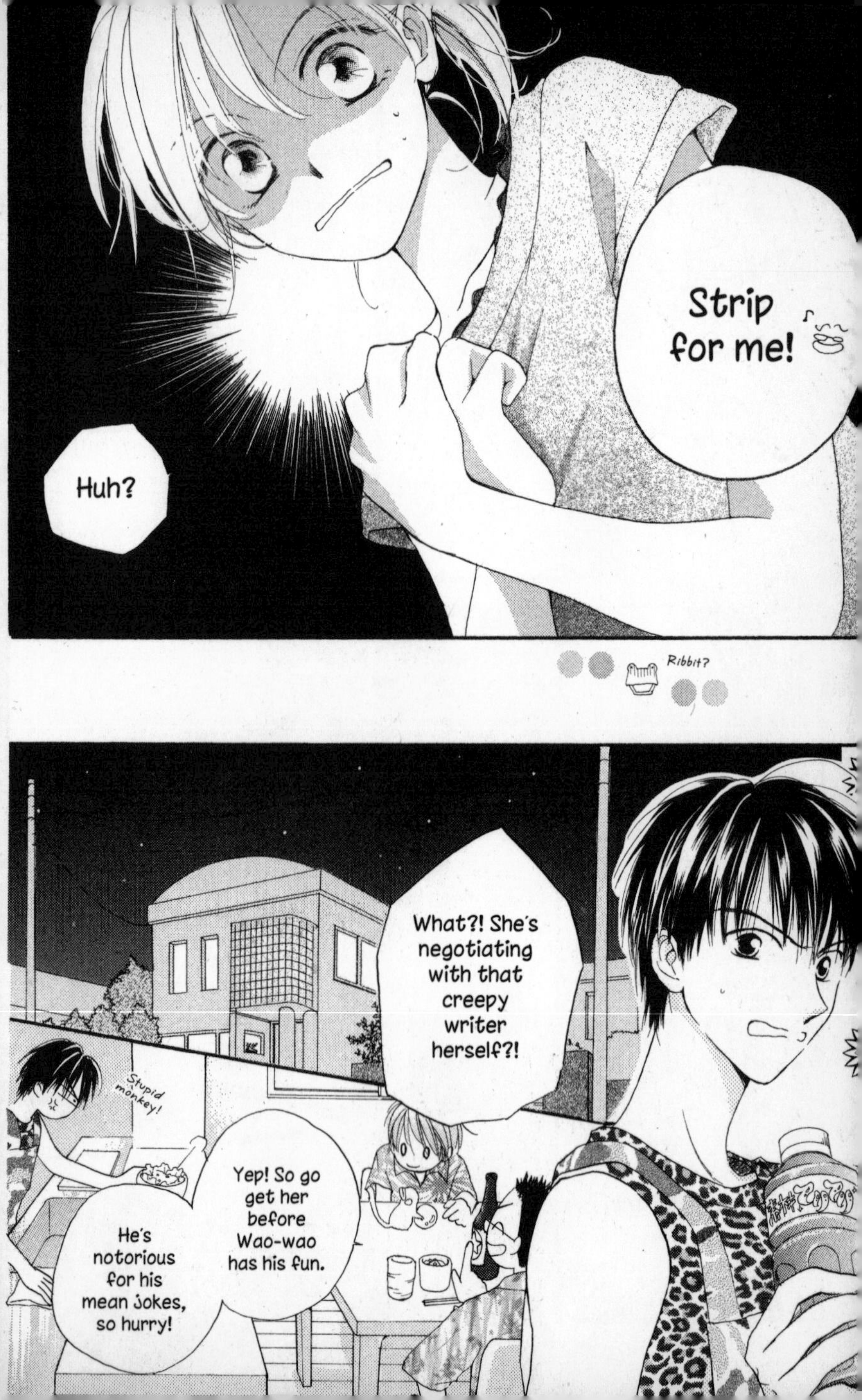
Strip for me!
Huh?
Ribbit?
What?! She's negotiating with that creepy writer herself?!
Yep! So go get her before Wao-wao has his fun.
He's notorious for his mean jokes, so hurry!
Stupid monkey!

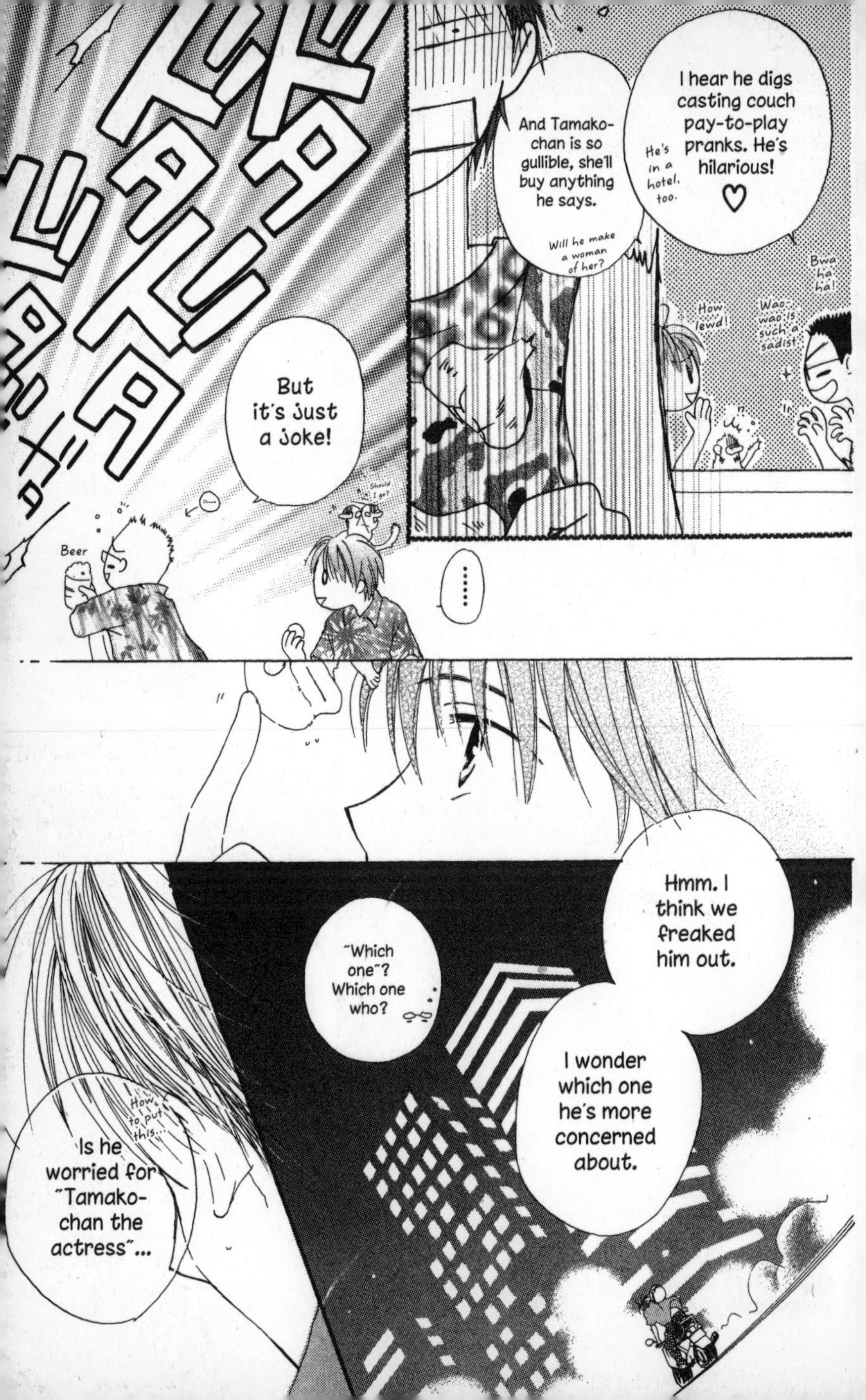
I hear he digs casting couch pay-to-play pranks. He's hilarious! ♡
He's in a hotel, too.
And Tamako-chan is so gullible, she'll buy anything he says.
Will he make a woman of her?
Bwa ha ha!
Wao-wao is such a sadist.
How lewd!
But it's just a joke!
Should I go?
Beer
......
Hmm. I think we freaked him out.
I wonder which one he's more concerned about.
"Which one"? Which one who?
Is he worried for "Tamako-chan the actress"...
How to put this...

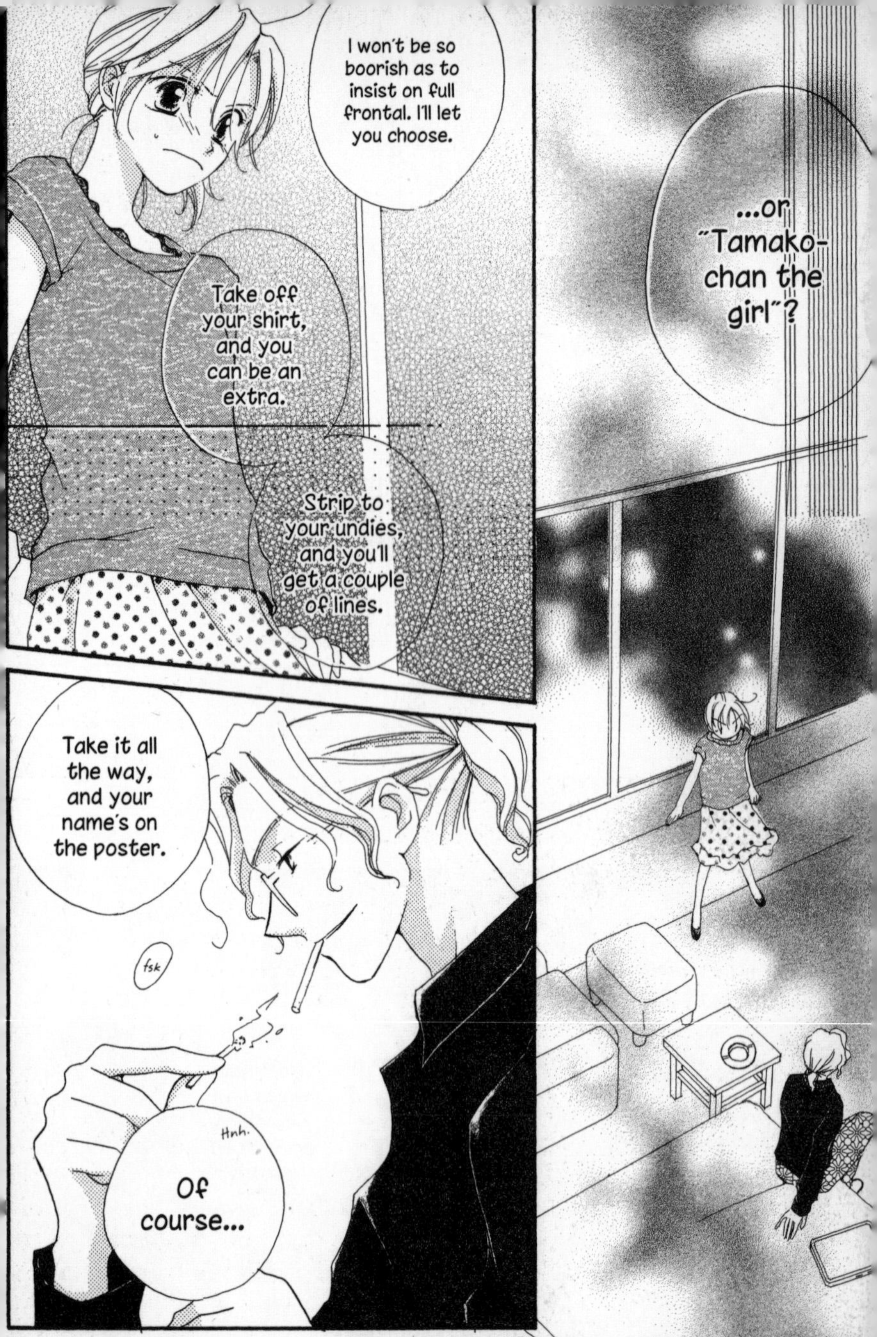

...or "Tamako-chan the girl"?
I won't be so boorish as to insist on full frontal. I'll let you choose.
Take off your shirt, and you can be an extra.
Strip to your undies, and you'll get a couple of lines.
Take it all the way, and your name's on the poster.
fsk
Hnh.
Of course...

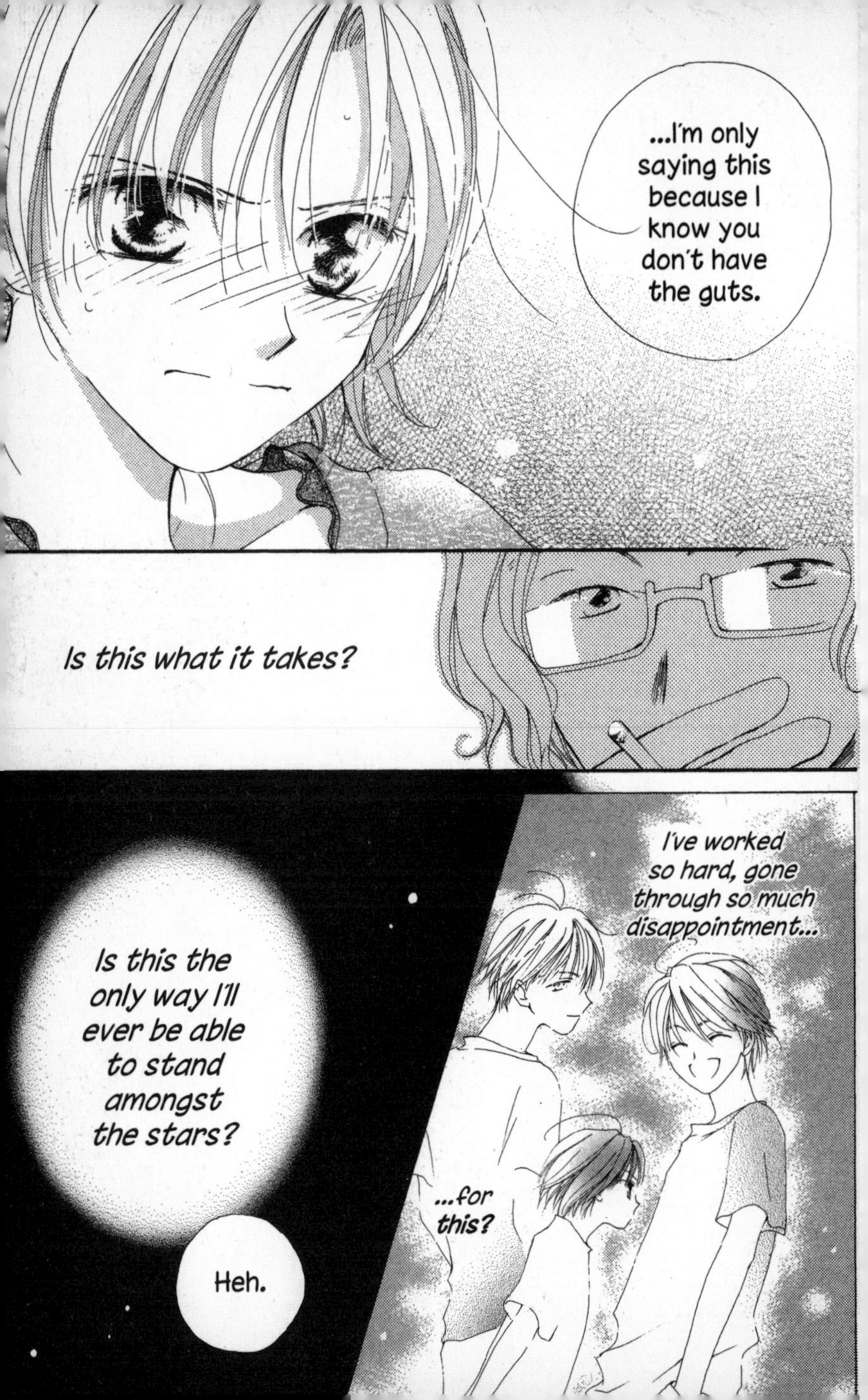
...I'm only saying this because I know you don't have the guts.
Is this what it takes?
I've worked so hard, gone through so much disappointment...
...for this?
Is this the only way I'll ever be able to stand amongst the stars?
Heh.

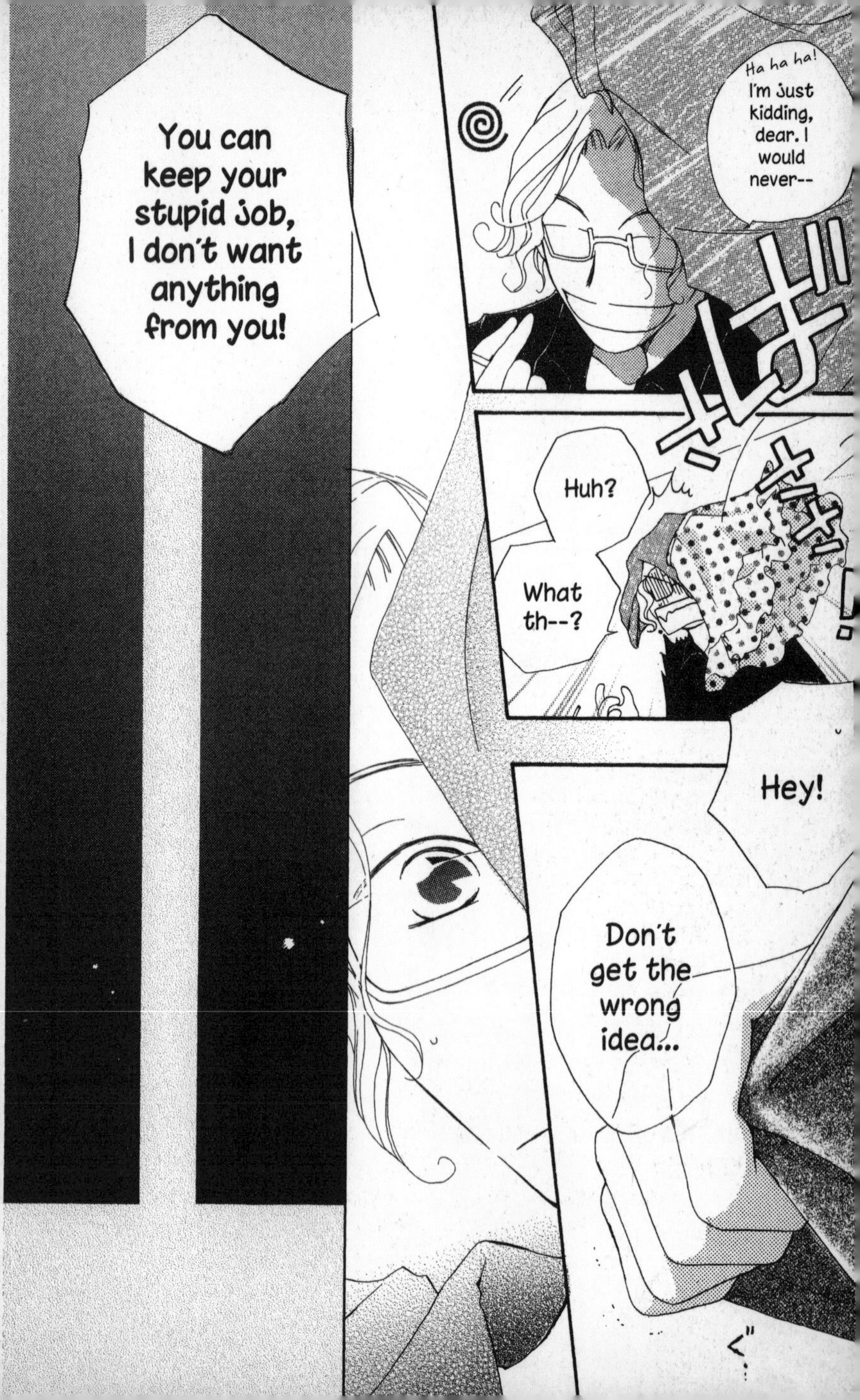
Ha ha ha! I'm just kidding, dear. I would never--
Huh?
What th--?
Hey!
Don't get the wrong idea...
You can keep your stupid job, I don't want anything from you!

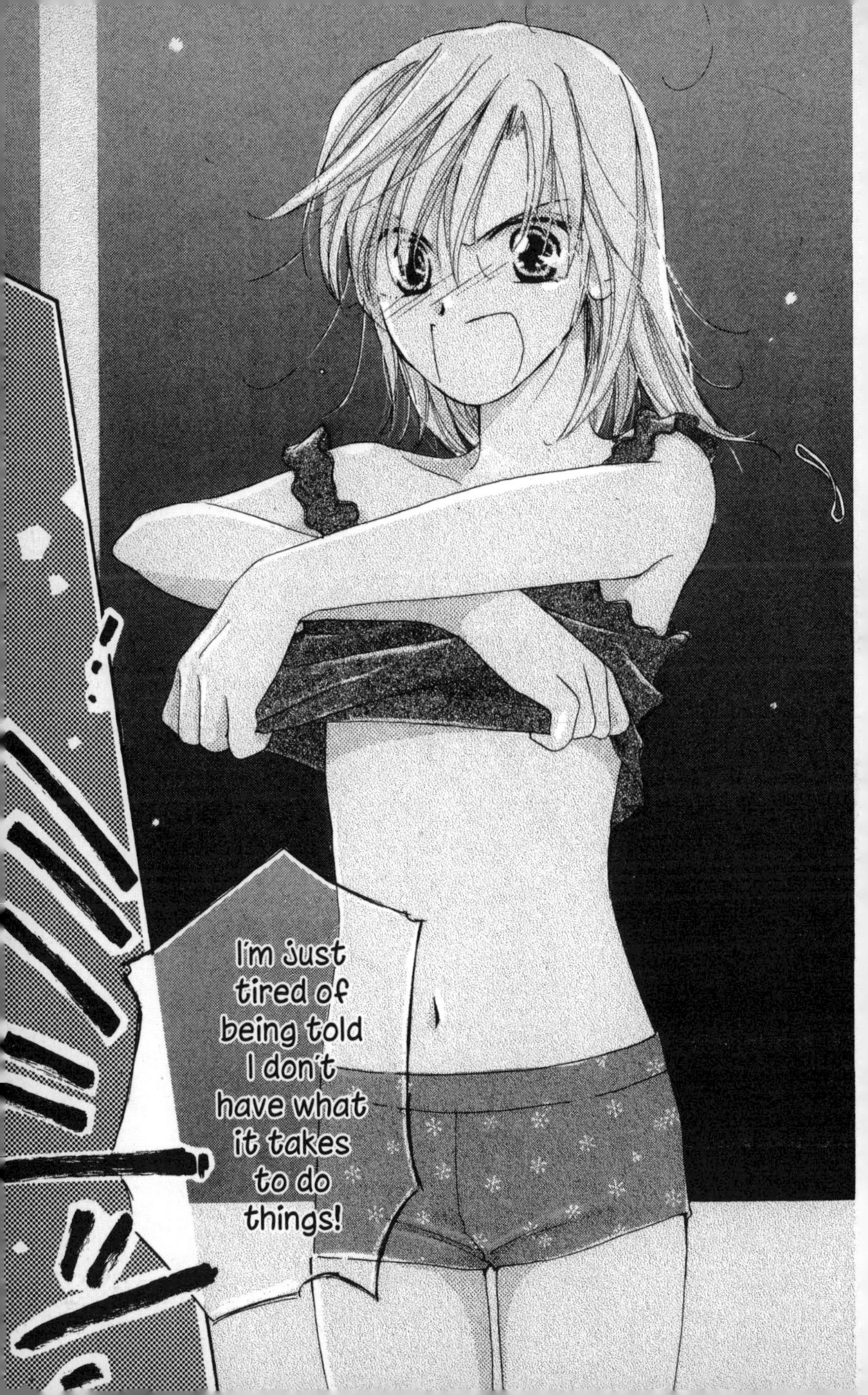
I'm just tired of being told I don't have what it takes to do things!

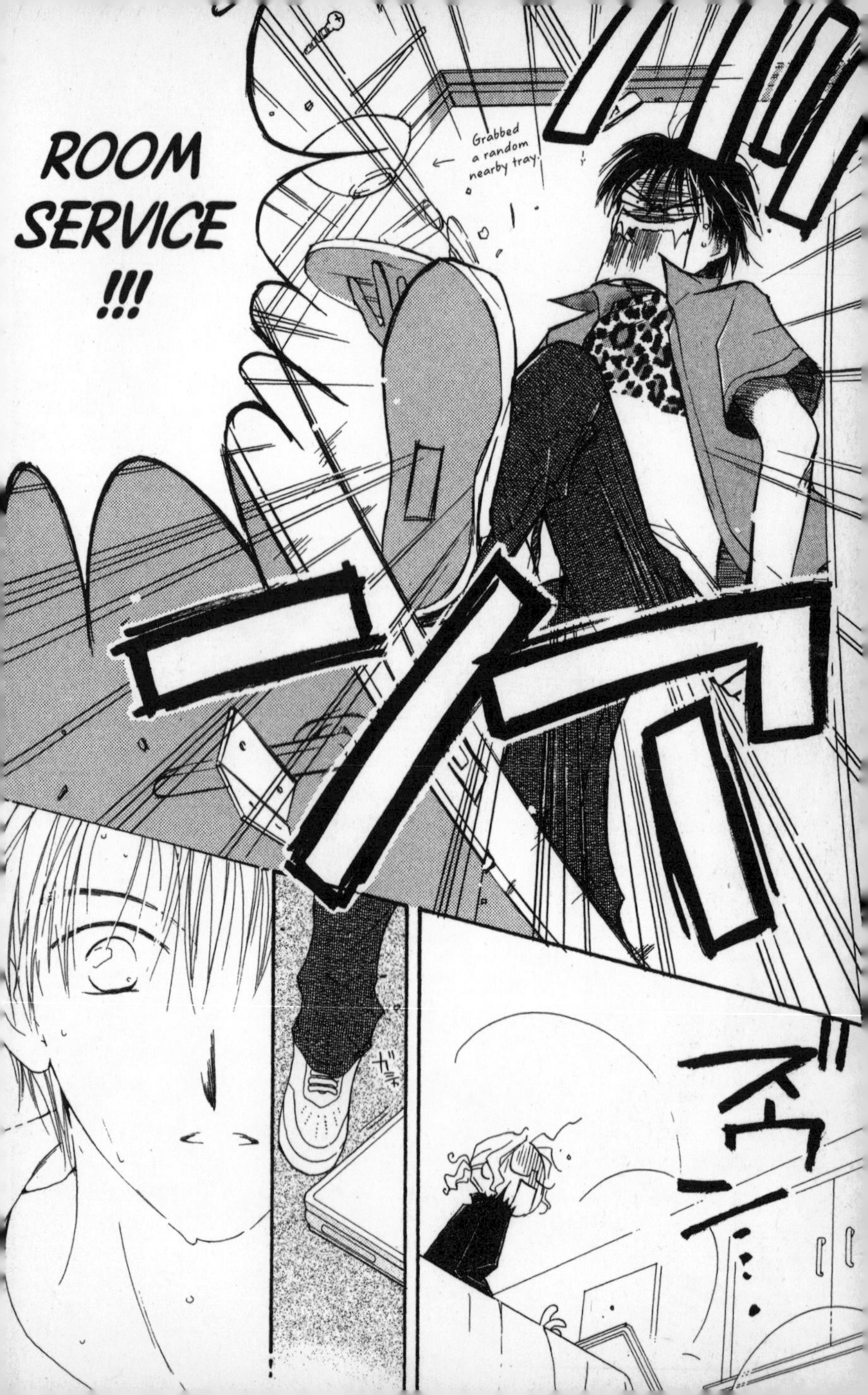
Grabbed a random nearby tray.
ROOM SERVICE !!!

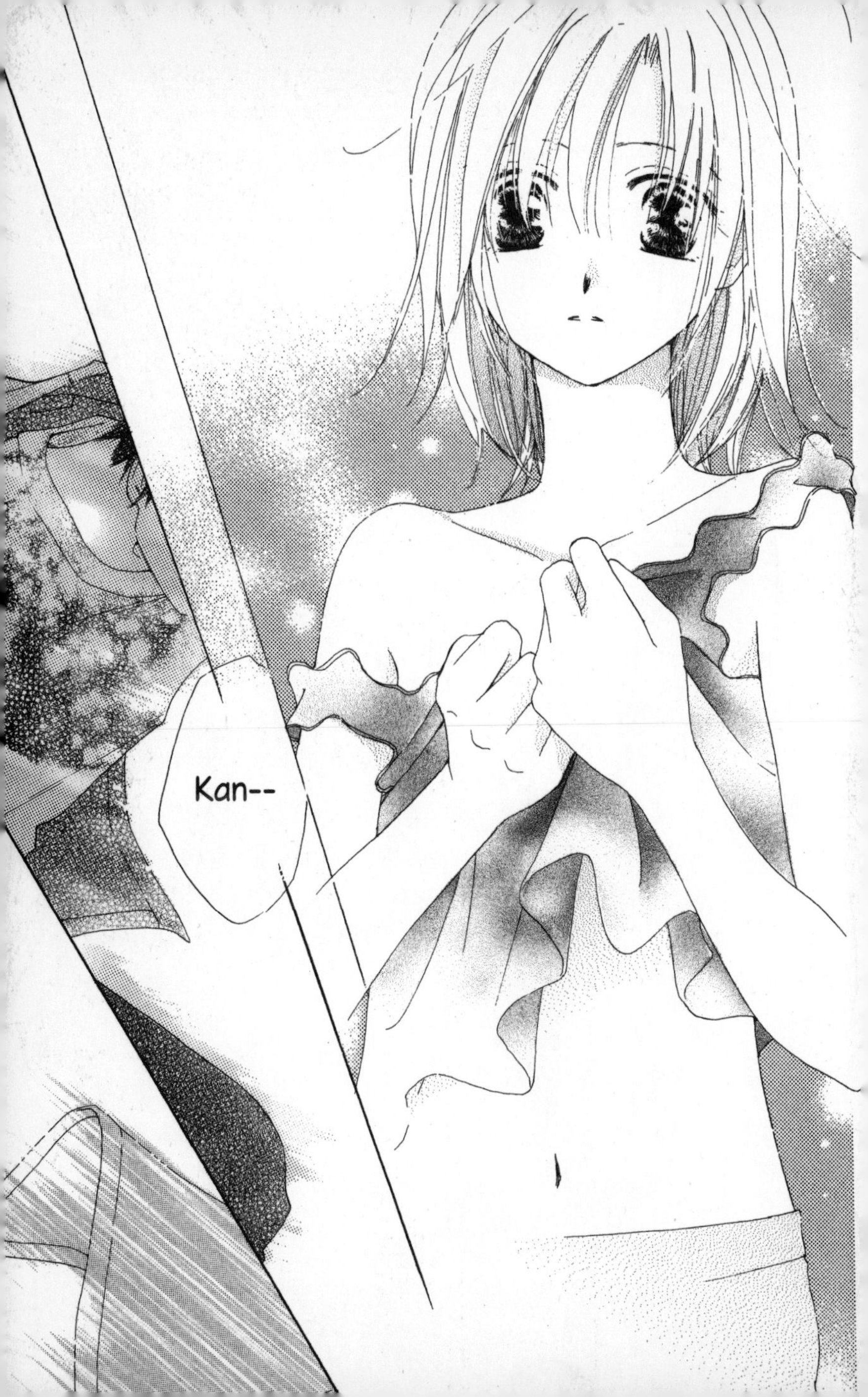
Kan--

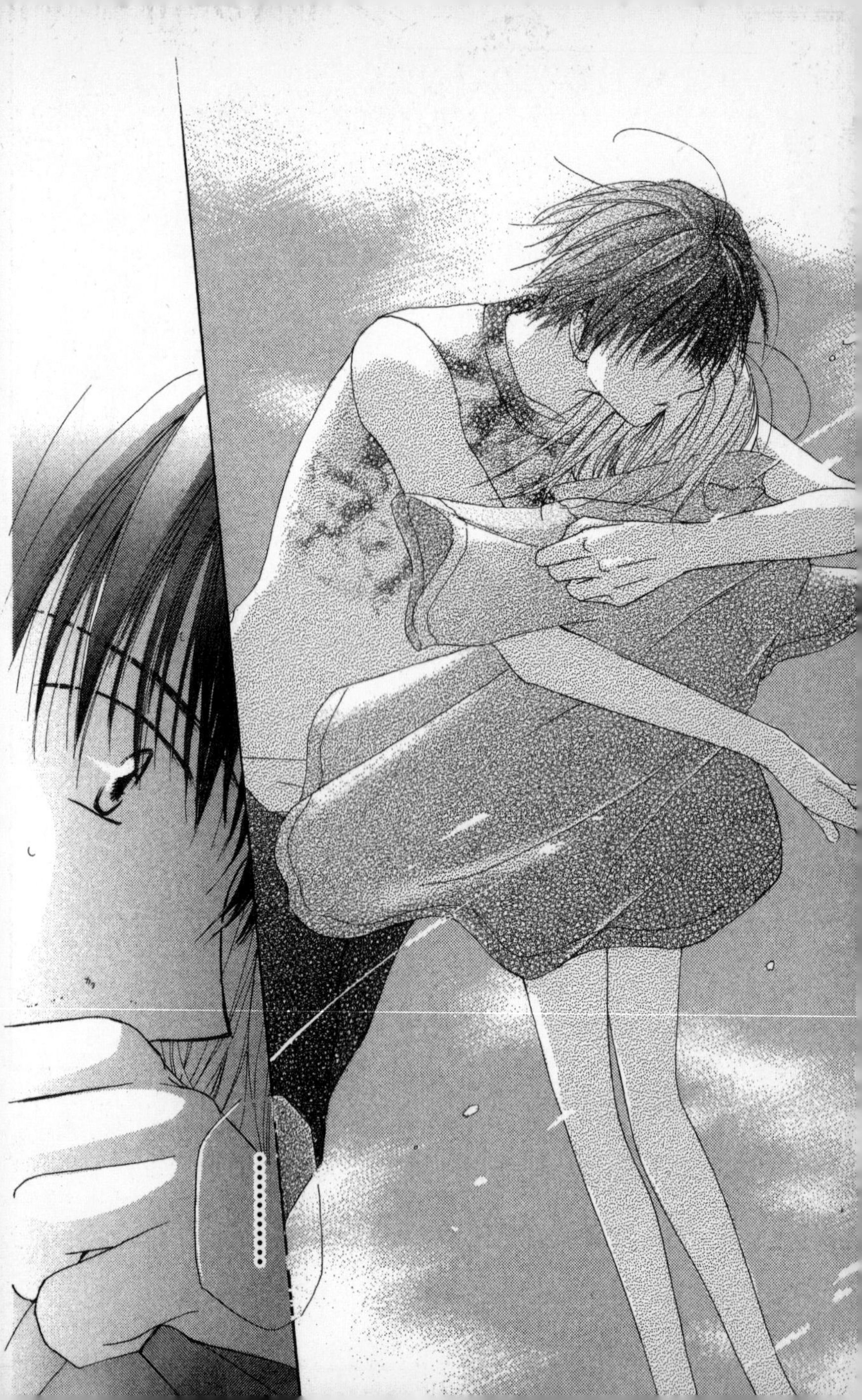
……

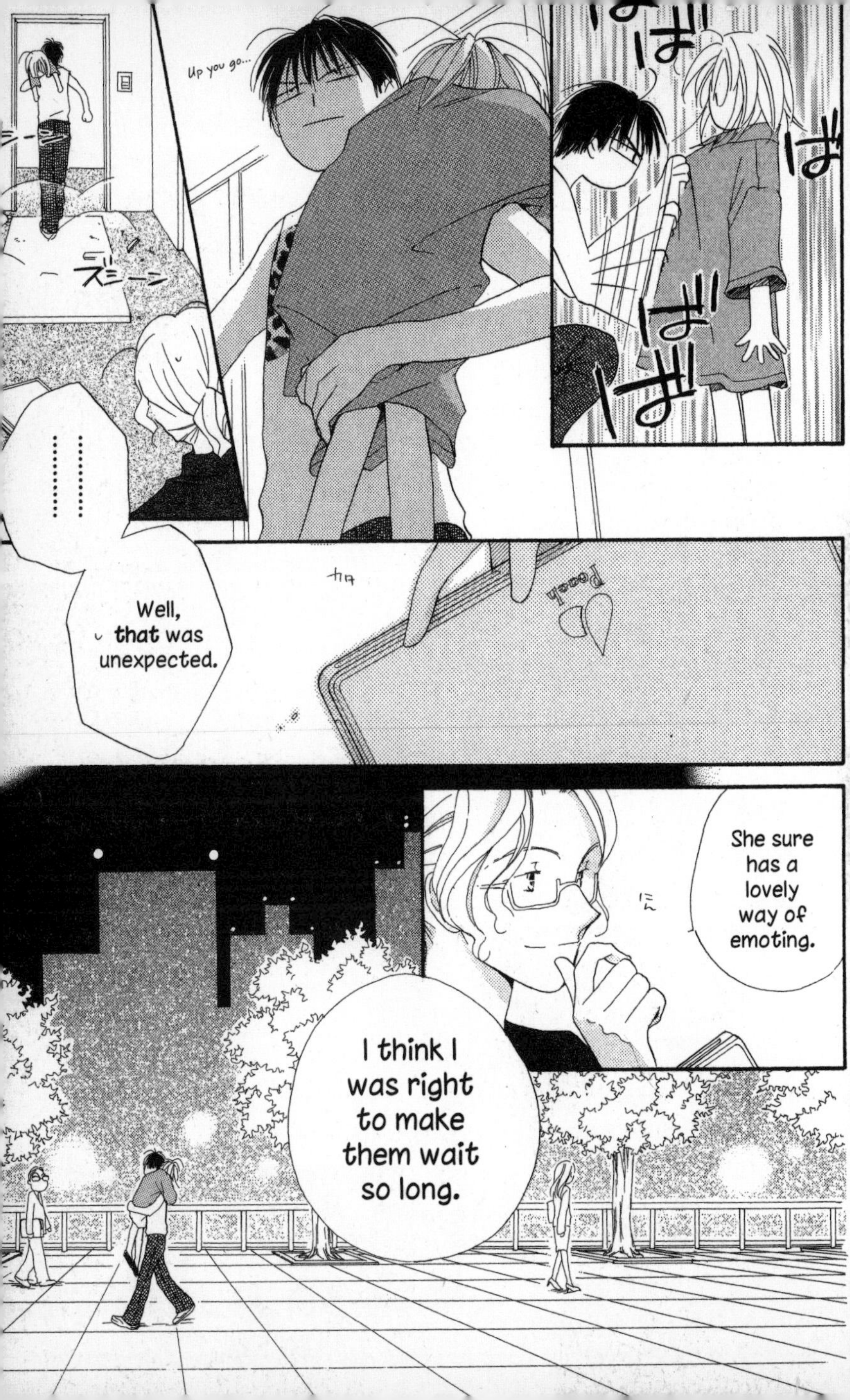
Up you go...
ズシーン
......
Well, that was unexpected.
She sure has a lovely way of emoting.
I think I was right to make them wait so long.

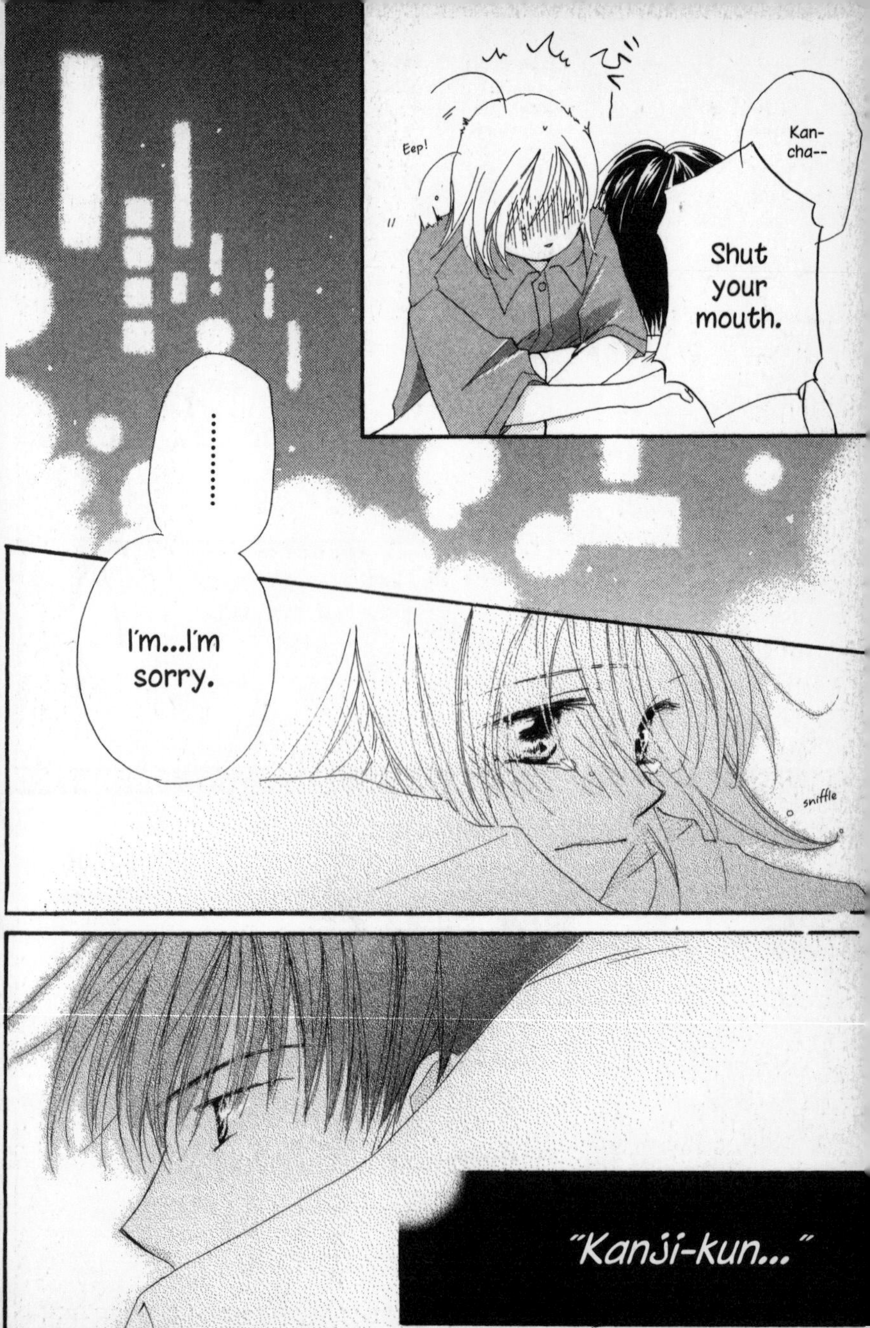
Kan-
cha--
Shut your mouth.
Eep!
....
I'm...I'm sorry.
sniffle
"Kanji-kun..."

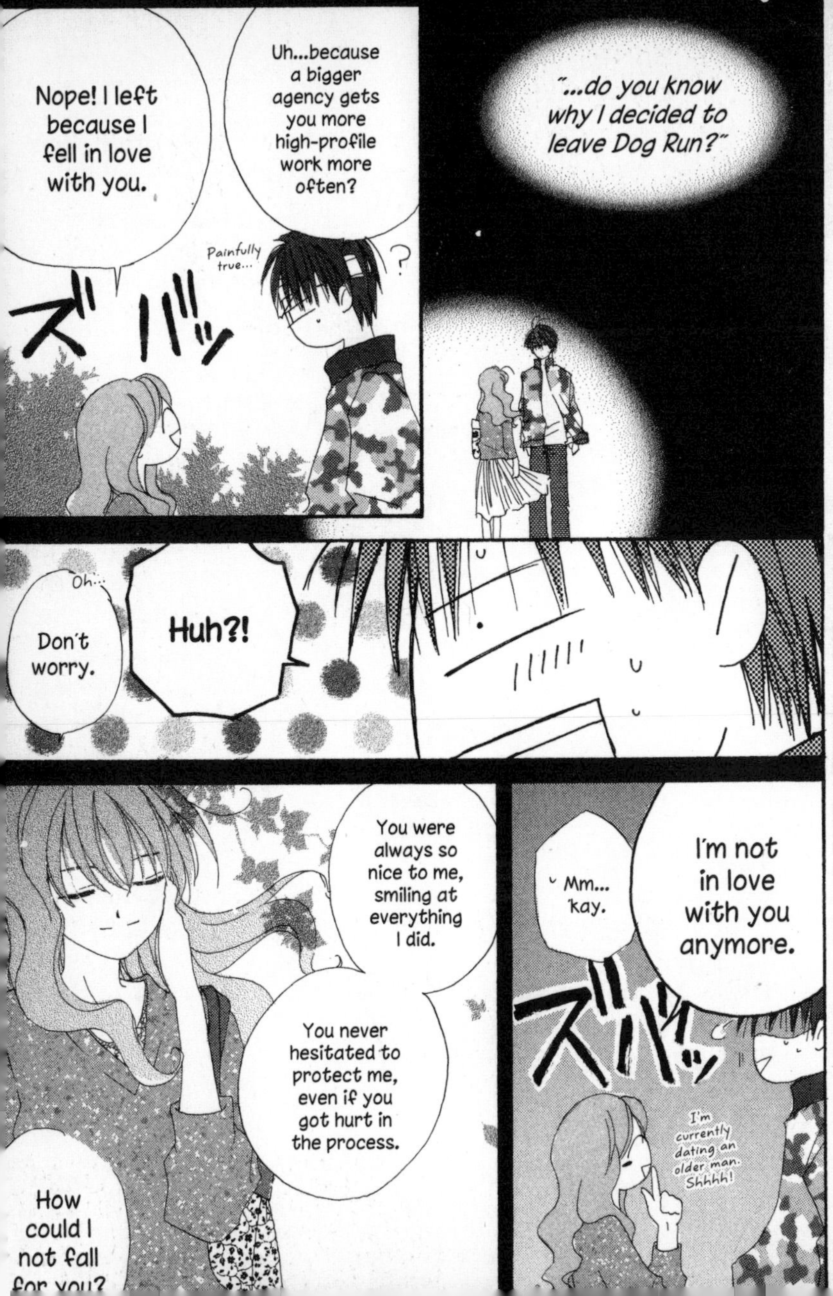
"...do you know why I decided to leave Dog Run?"
Uh...because a bigger agency gets you more high-profile work more often?
Painfully true...
?
Nope! I left because I fell in love with you.
ズバッ
Huh?!
Oh...
Don't worry.
I'm not in love with you anymore.
Mm...'kay.
ズバッ
I'm currently dating an older man. Shhhh!
You were always so nice to me, smiling at everything I did.
You never hesitated to protect me, even if you got hurt in the process.
How could I not fall for you?

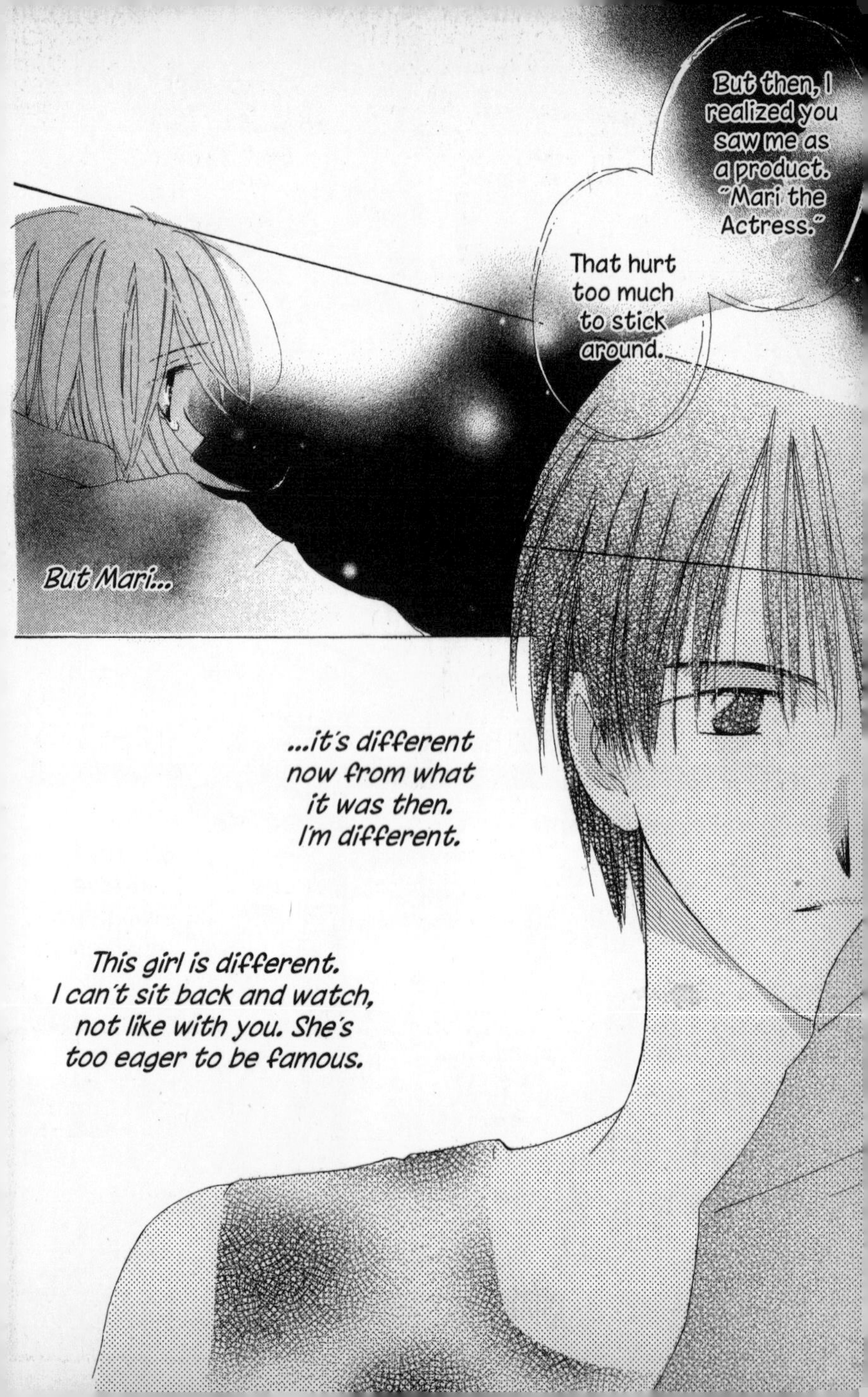
But then, I realized you saw me as a product. "Mari the Actress."
That hurt too much to stick around.
But Mari...
...it's different now from what it was then. I'm different.
This girl is different. I can't sit back and watch, not like with you. She's too eager to be famous.

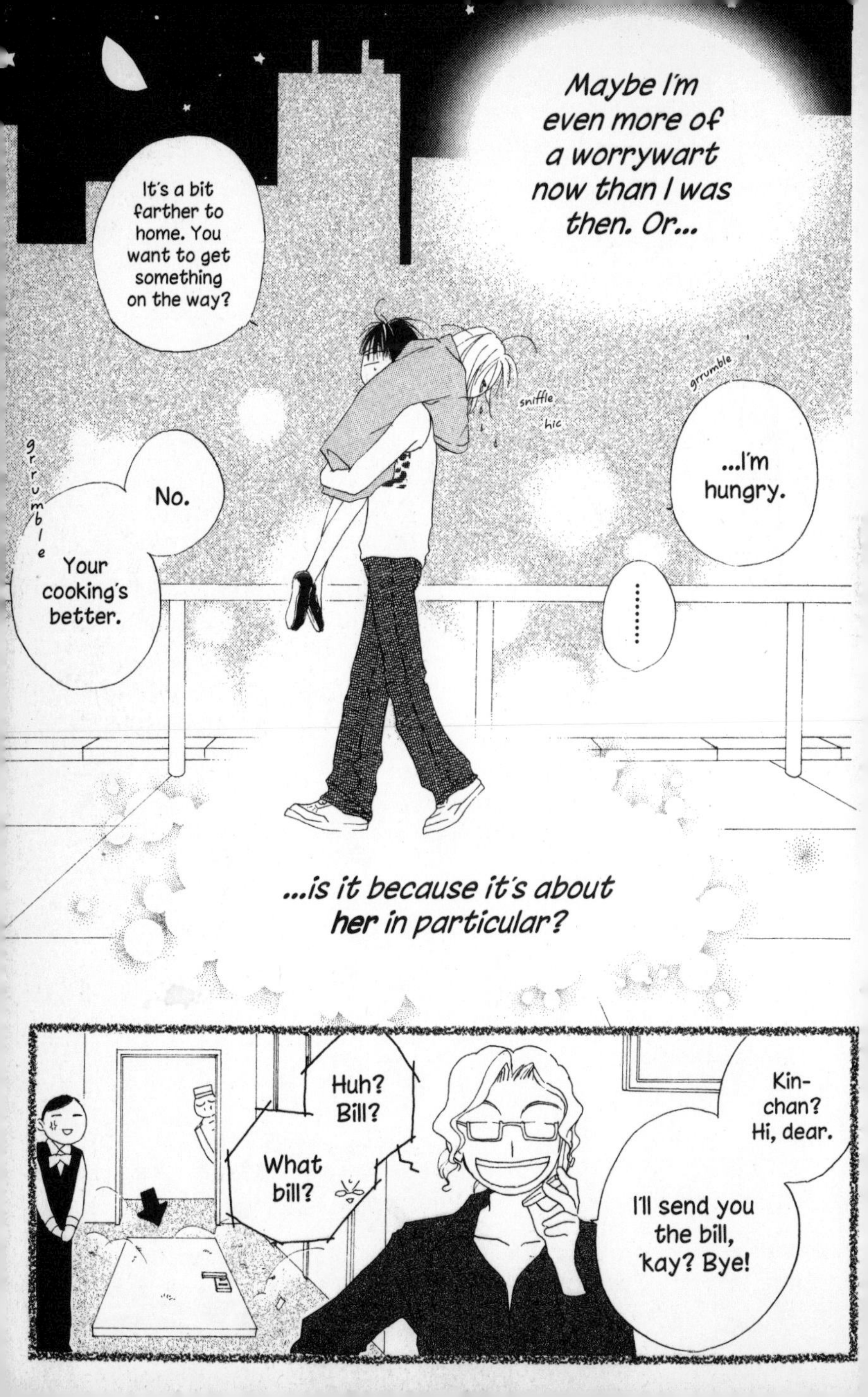

Maybe I'm even more of a worrywart now than I was then. Or...
It's a bit farther to home. You want to get something on the way?
grrumble
...I'm hungry.
sniffle
hic
......
No.
grrumble
Your cooking's better.
...is it because it's about her in particular?
Kin-chan? Hi, dear.
I'll send you the bill, 'kay? Bye!
Huh? Bill?
What bill?

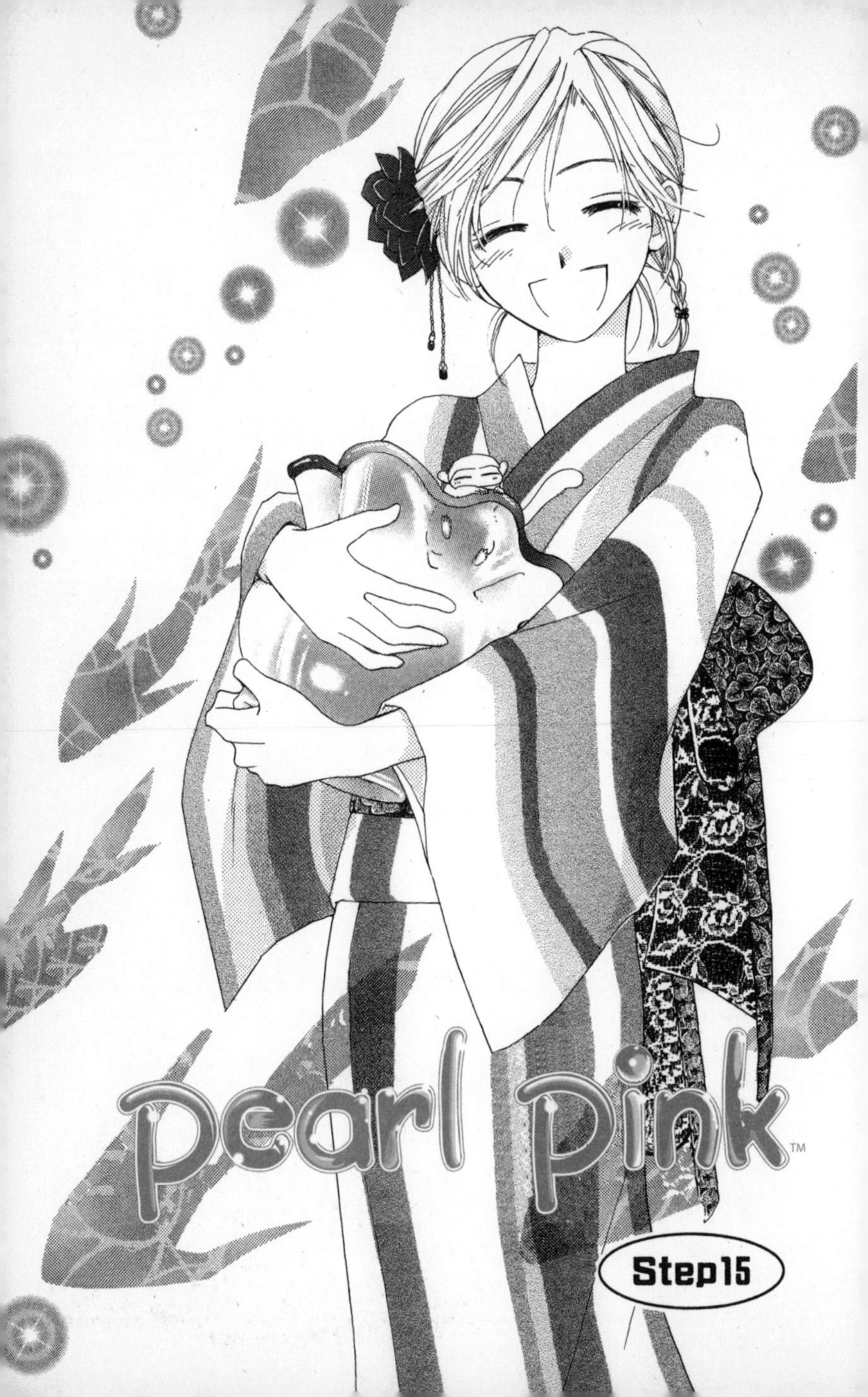
Pearl Pink™
Step 15

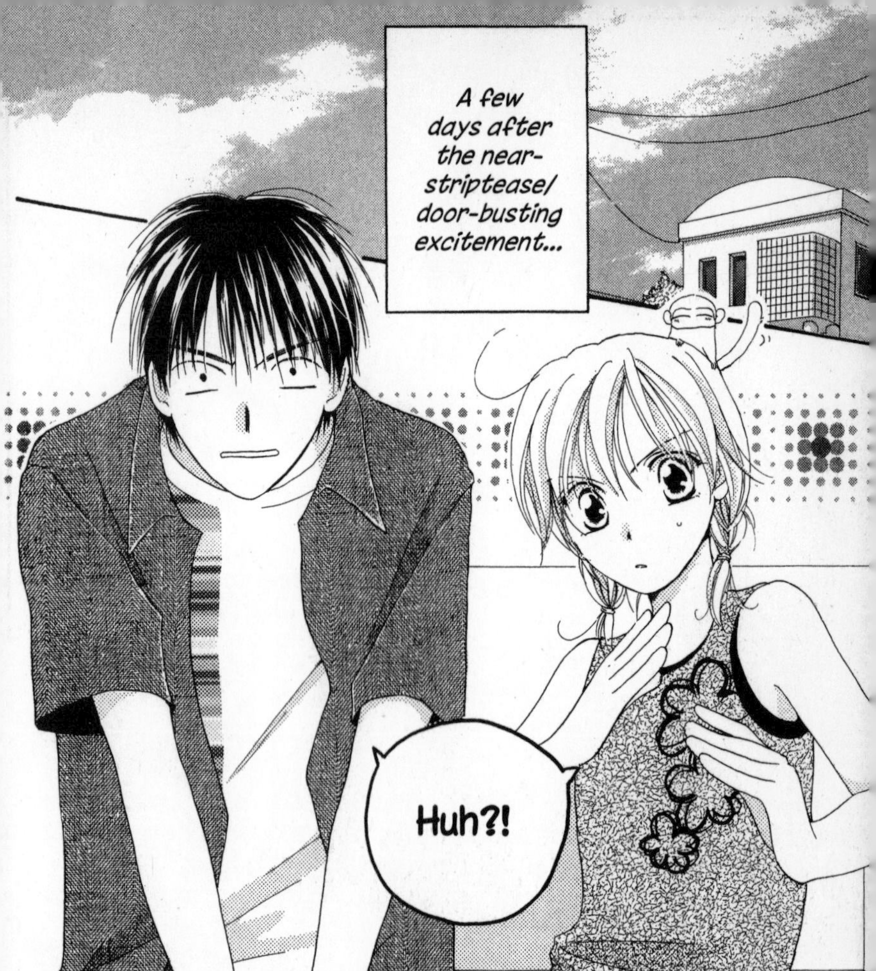
A few days after the near-striptease/ door-busting excitement...
Huh?!

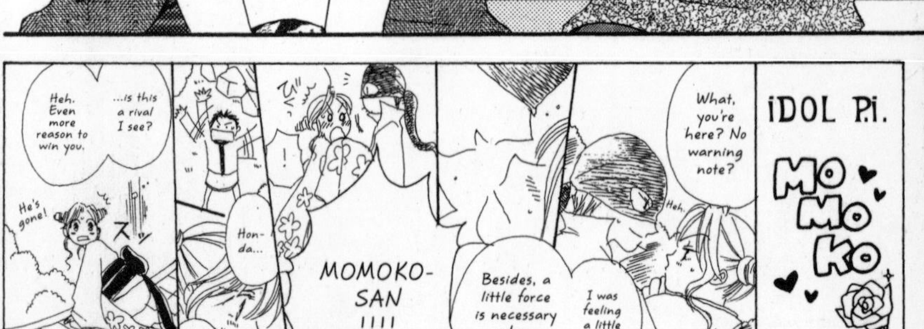
iDOL P.i.
MOMOKO
6
What, you're here? No warning note?
Heh.
I was feeling a little anxious.
Besides, a little force is necessary when stealing a heart...
MOMOKO-SAN!!!!
Hon-da...
My, my...
...is this a rival I see?
Heh. Even more reason to win you.
He's gone!
What's this?! A love triangle between Momoko, Honda, and Thief Handsome?!

Y'know, there aren't many gags this volume. Guess I got too serious... (Tanaka)

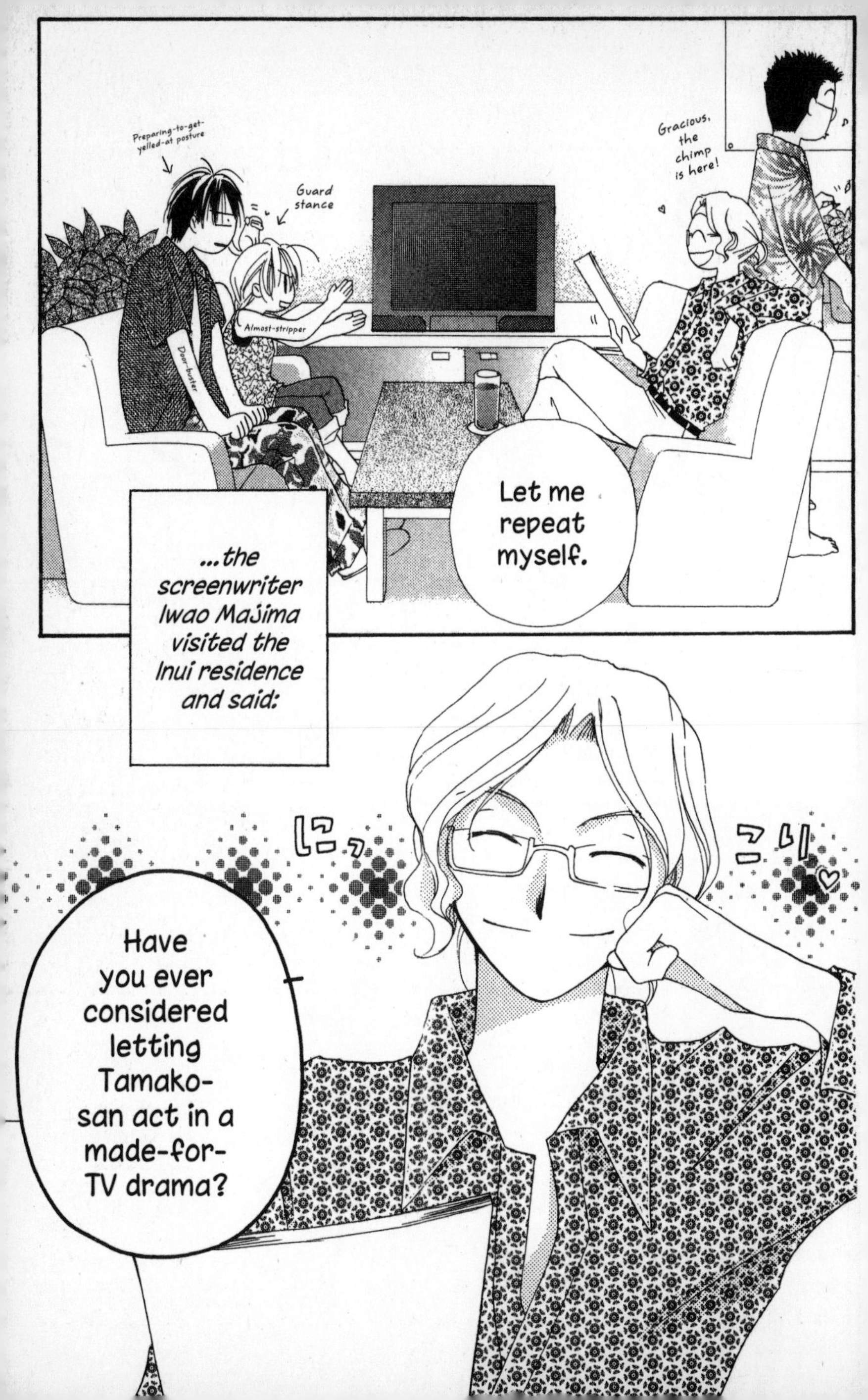
Gracious, the chimp is here!
Guard stance
Preparing-to-get-yelled-at posture
Almost-stripper
Door-buster
Let me repeat myself.
...the screenwriter Iwao Majima visited the Inui residence and said:
Have you ever considered letting Tamako-san act in a made-for-TV drama?

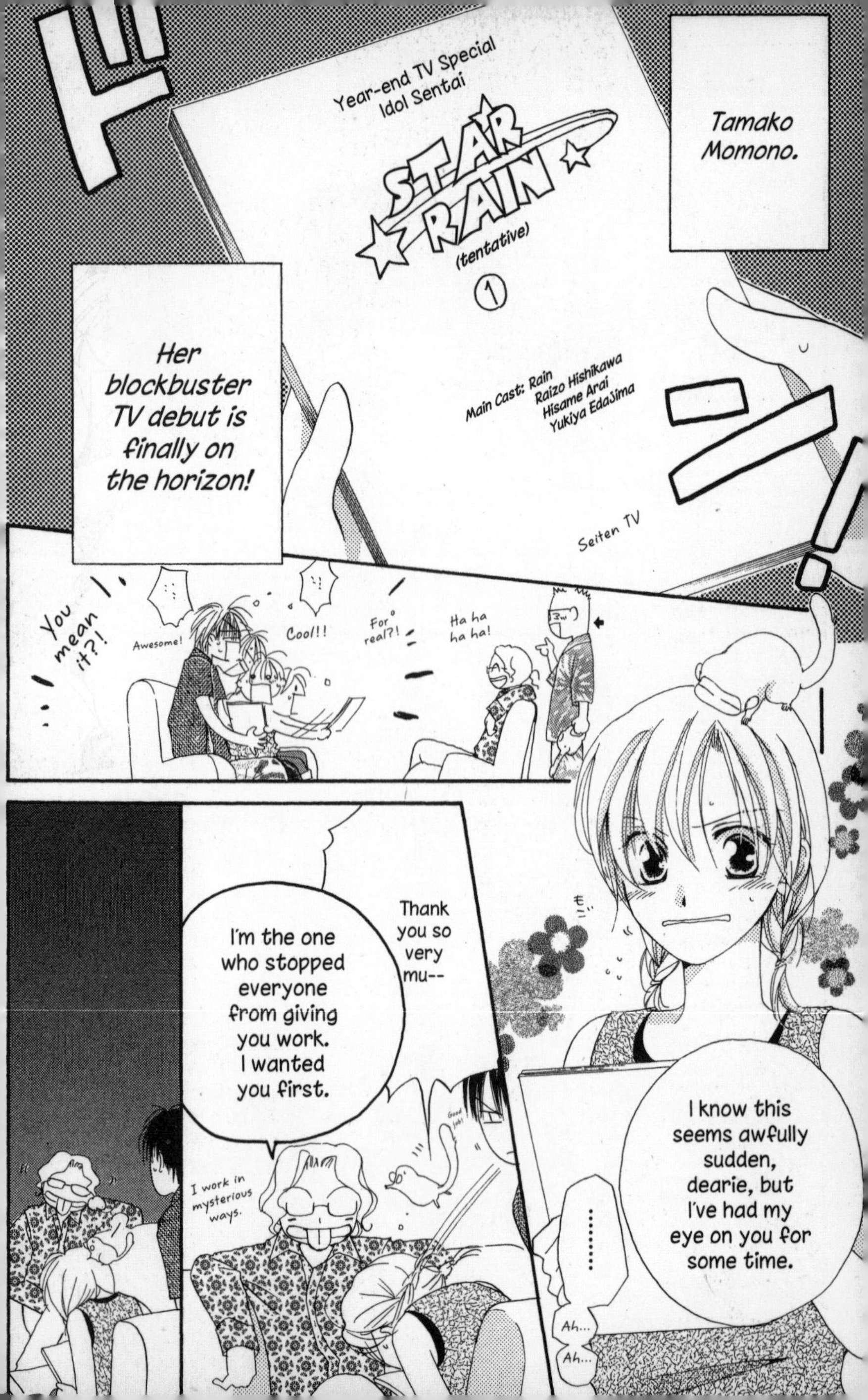

ン!
Tamako Momono.
ド
Year-end TV Special
Idol Sentai
STAR RAIN
(tentative)
1
Main Cast: Rain
Raizo Hishikawa
Hisame Arai
Yukiya Edajima
Seiten TV
Her blockbuster TV debut is finally on the horizon!
Ha ha ha ha!
For real?!
Cool!!
Awesome!
You mean it?!
I know this seems awfully sudden, dearie, but I've had my eye on you for some time.
......
Ah...
Ah...
Thank you so very mu--
I'm the one who stopped everyone from giving you work. I wanted you first.
Good job!
I work in mysterious ways.

Thanks.

Last volume, I kinda let it slip that I'd hurt my hand. Soon after, I started getting lots of fan mail full of get-well wishes. Thank you so much! My hand is all better now! For all you aspiring manga artists out there, a piece of advice: take good care of your drawing hand. Apparently, stress can build up over time and it's easier to get hurt than you'd think.

Lots of stretching and massages!

Please send thoughts and comments to:

Pearl Pink Mail
c/o TOKYOPOP
5900 Wilshire
Blvd, Suite #2000
Los Angeles,
CA 90036

Recently, I found out somebody made an Image CD for this manga.

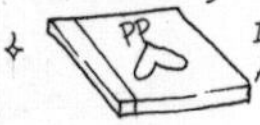
PP
Image Album

I can hardly believe it. I didn't know there were Image CDs for manga. Thank you, thank you, thank you!!

Mari Yagi

See you next volume!

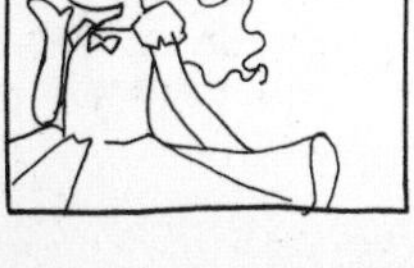

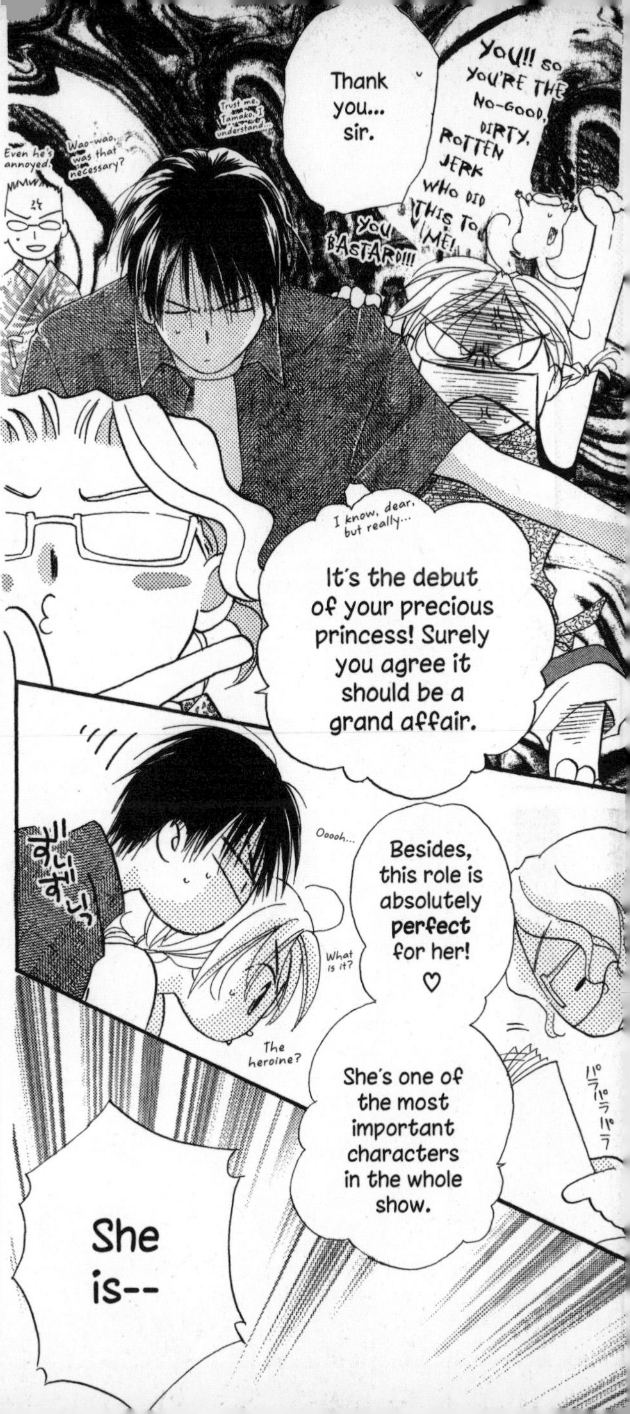
YOU!! SO YOU'RE THE NO-GOOD, DIRTY, ROTTEN JERK WHO DID THIS TO ME!
YOU BASTARD!!!
Thank you... sir.
Trust me, Tamako, I understand...
Wao-wao, was that necessary?
Even he's annoyed.
I know, dear, but really...
It's the debut of your precious princess! Surely you agree it should be a grand affair.
Besides, this role is absolutely **perfect** for her! ♡
Ooooh...
ずいずいっ
What is it?
The heroine?
パラパラパラ
She's one of the most important characters in the whole show.
She is--

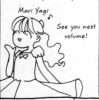

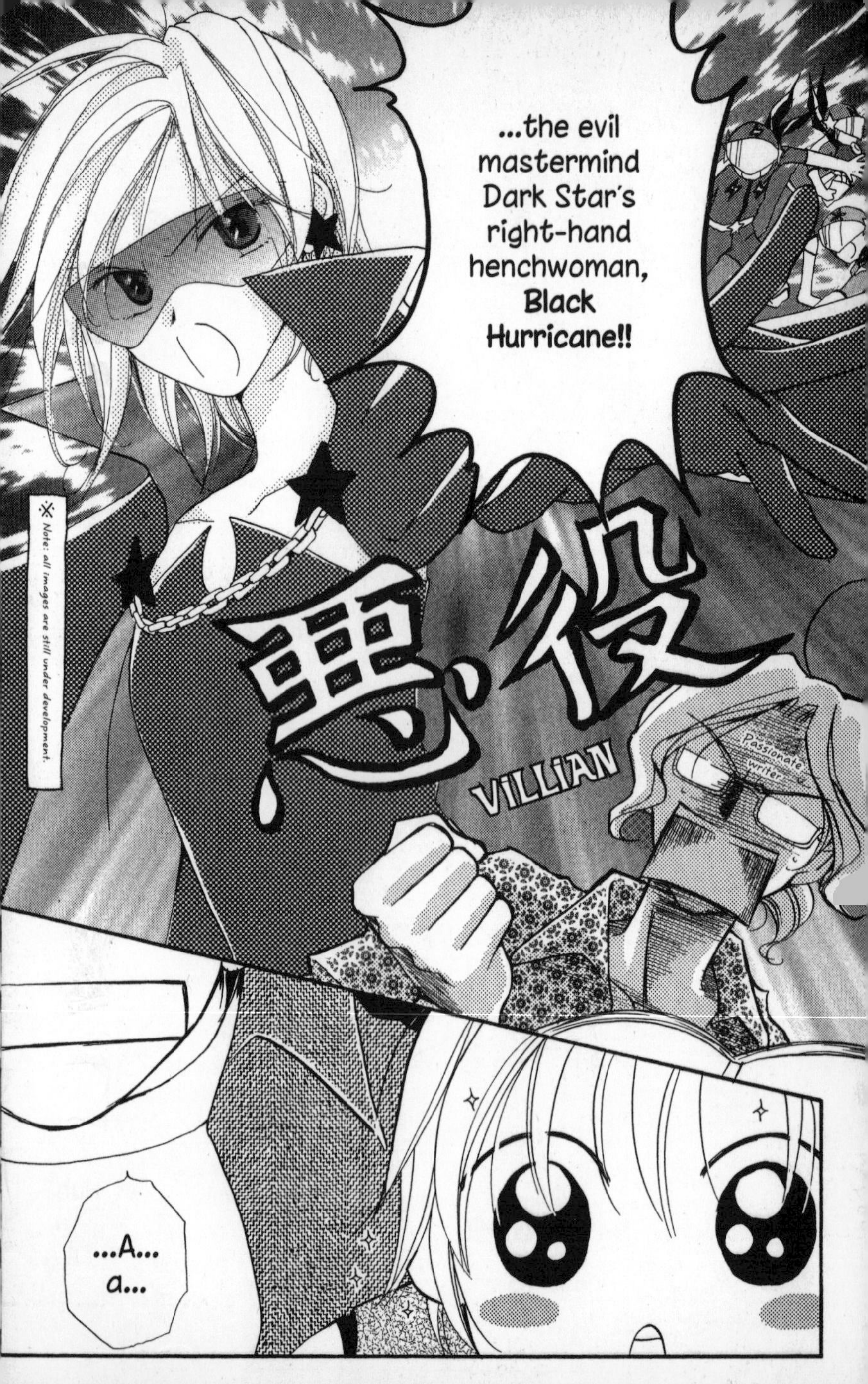
...the evil mastermind Dark Star's right-hand henchwoman, Black Hurricane!!
※ Note: all images are still under development.
悪役
VILLIAN
Passionate writer
...A... a...

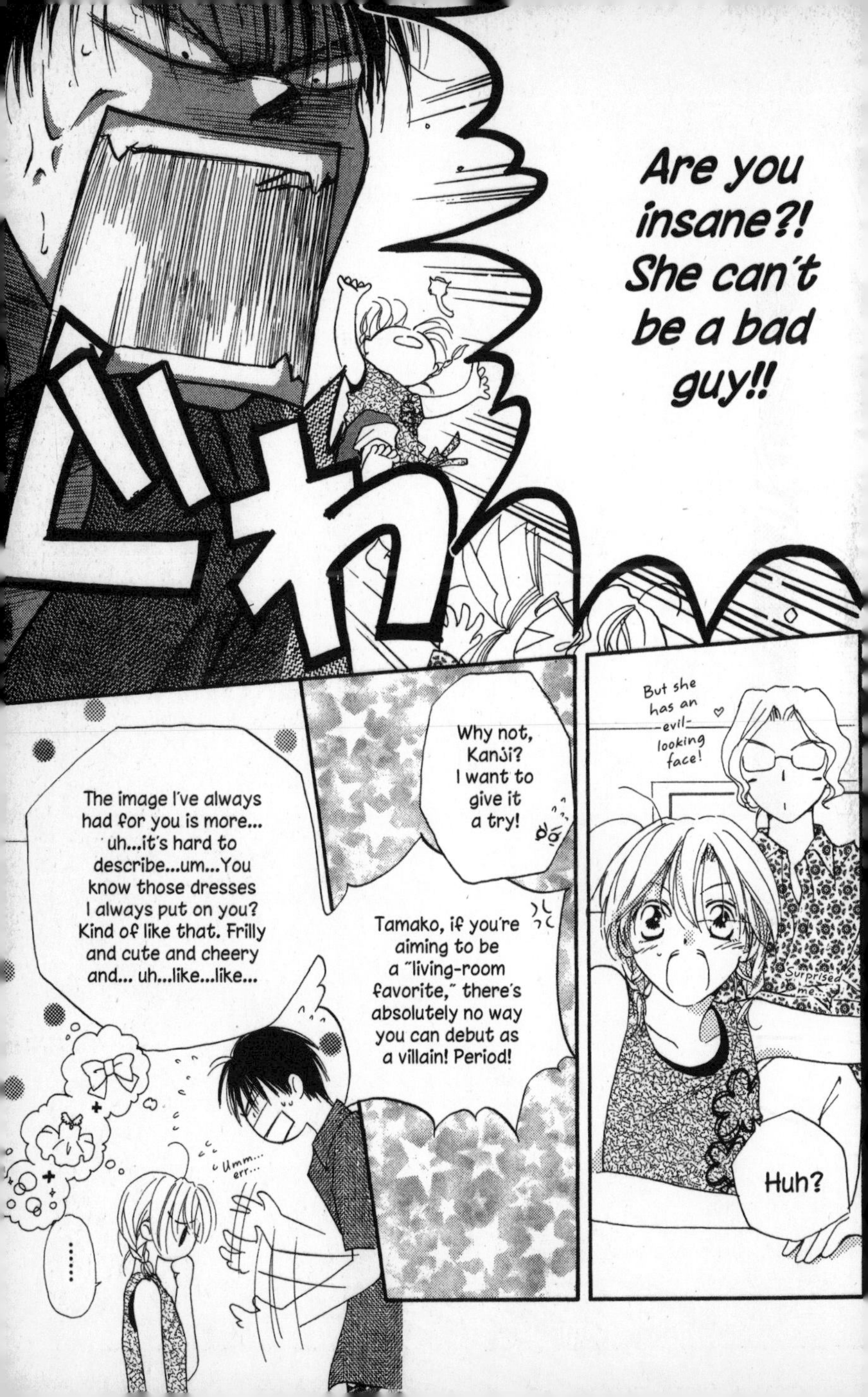
Are you insane?! She can't be a bad guy!!
But she has an evil-looking face!
Surprised me...
Huh?
Why not, Kanji? I want to give it a try!
Tamako, if you're aiming to be a "living-room favorite," there's absolutely no way you can debut as a villain! Period!
The image I've always had for you is more... uh...it's hard to describe...um...You know those dresses I always put on you? Kind of like that. Frilly and cute and cheery and... uh...like...like...
Umm... err...
......

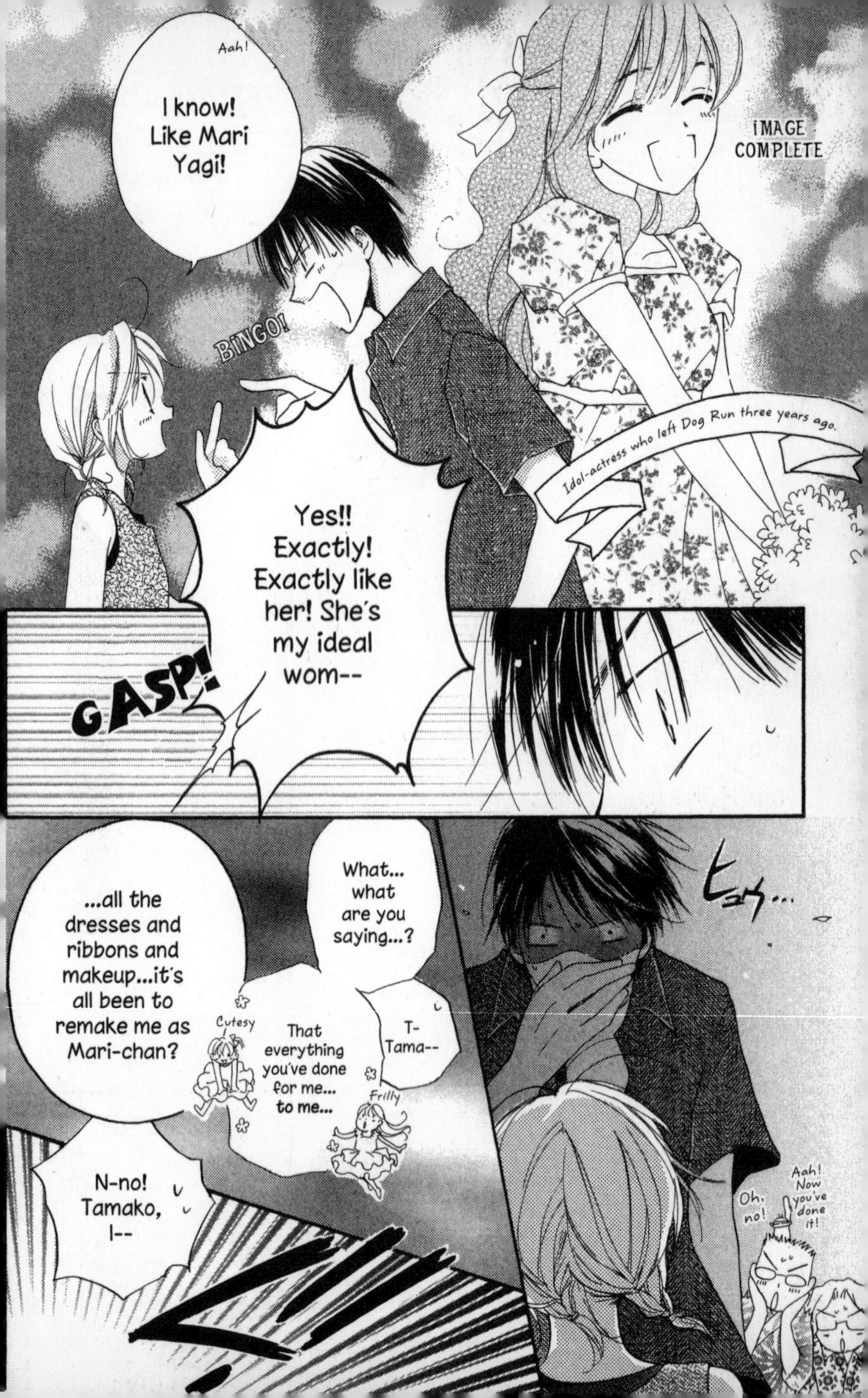
IMAGE COMPLETE
Aah!
I know! Like Mari Yagi!
Idol-actress who left Dog Run three years ago.
BINGO!
Yes!! Exactly! Exactly like her! She's my ideal wom--
GASP!
Aah! Now you've done it!
Oh, no!
What... what are you saying...?
T- Tama--
That everything you've done for me... to me...
Frilly
Cutesy
...all the dresses and ribbons and makeup...it's all been to remake me as Mari-chan?
N-no! Tamako, I--

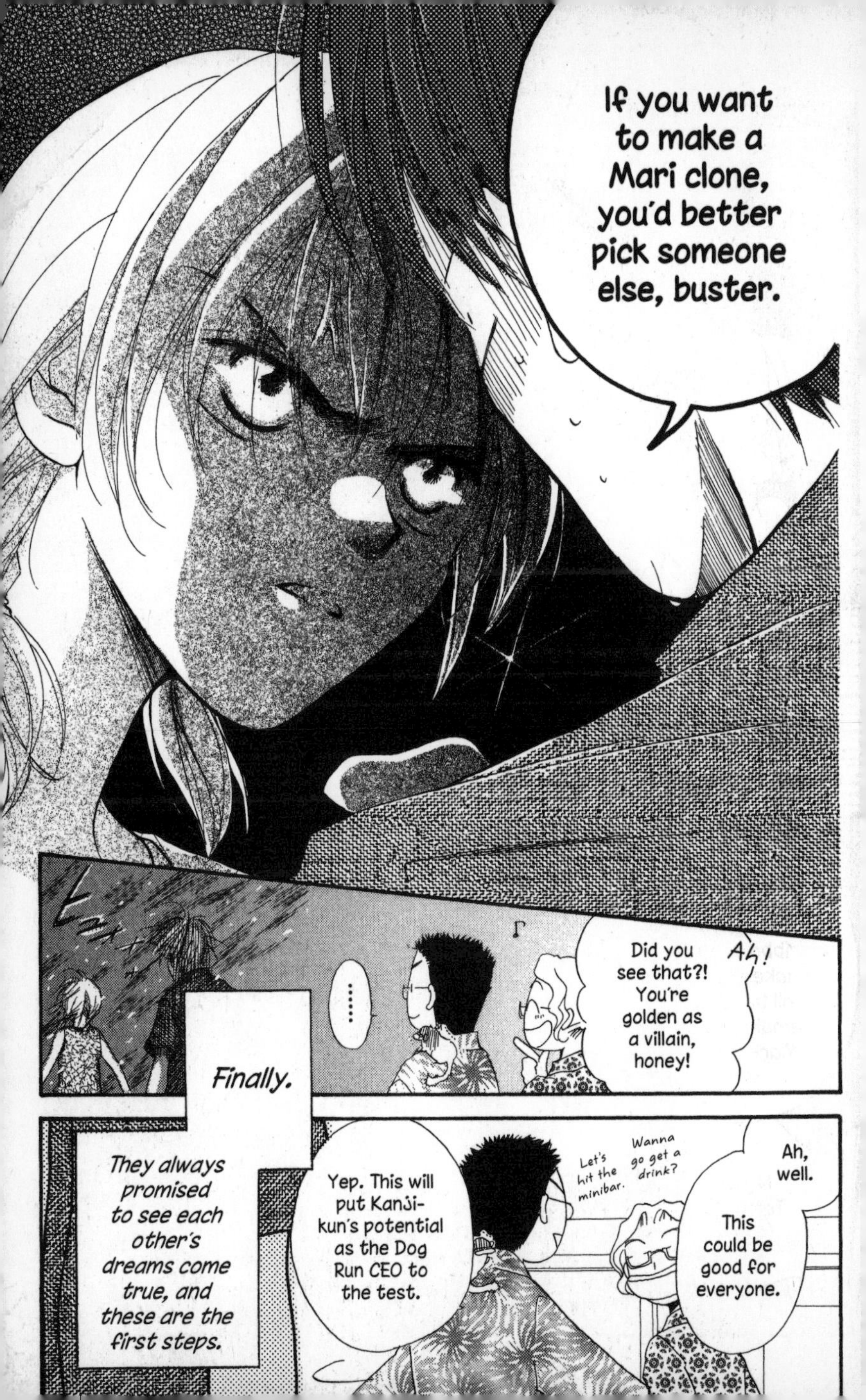
If you want to make a Mari clone, you'd better pick someone else, buster.
Ah!
Did you see that?! You're golden as a villain, honey!
......
Finally.
Ah, well.
This could be good for everyone.
Wanna go get a drink?
Let's hit the minibar.
Yep. This will put Kanji-kun's potential as the Dog Run CEO to the test.
They always promised to see each other's dreams come true, and these are the first steps.

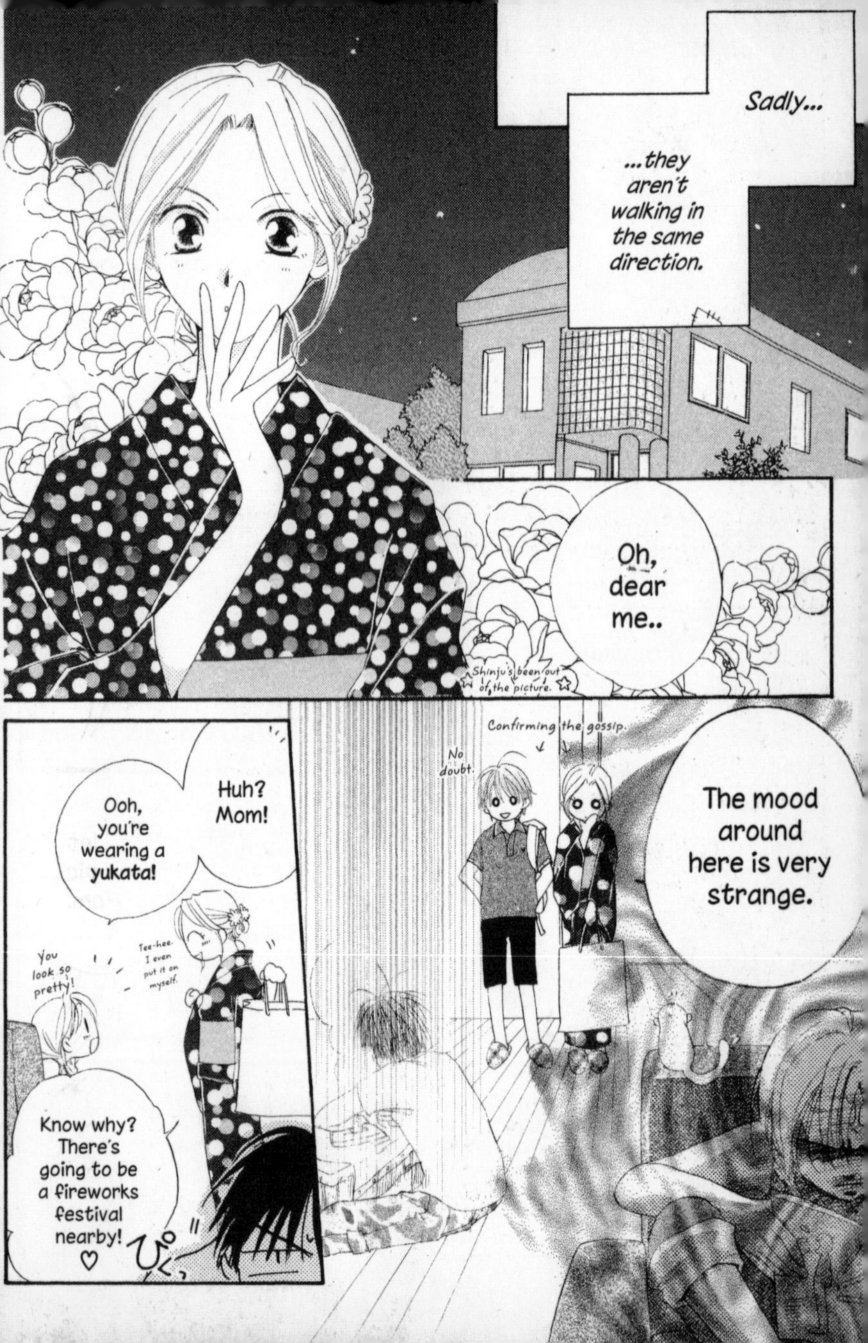
Sadly...
...they aren't walking in the same direction.
Oh, dear me..
Shinju's been out of the picture.
The mood around here is very strange.
Confirming the gossip.
No doubt.
Huh? Mom!
Ooh, you're wearing a yukata!
Tee-hee. I even put it on myself.
You look so pretty!
Know why? There's going to be a fireworks festival nearby! ♡

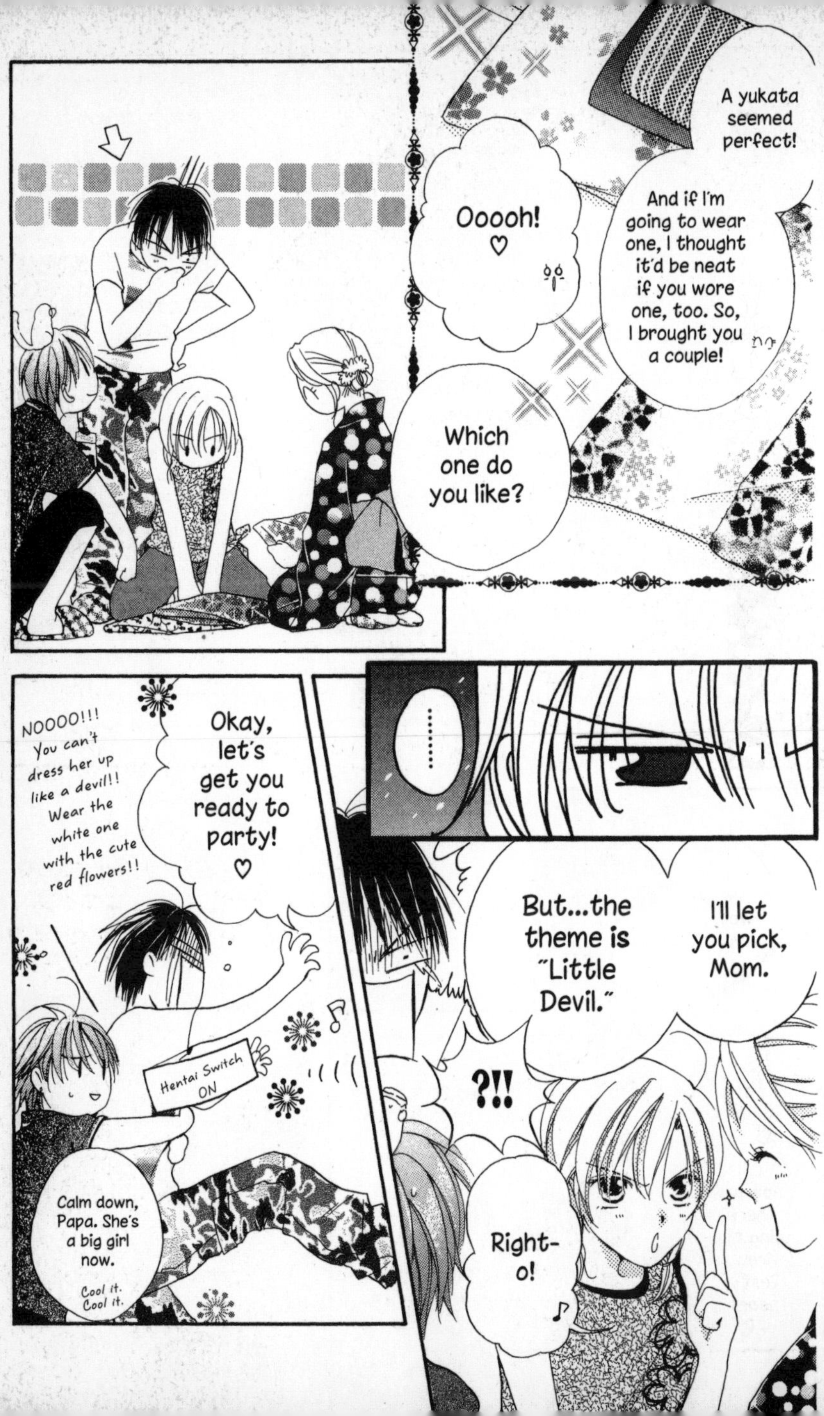
A yukata seemed perfect!
And if I'm going to wear one, I thought it'd be neat if you wore one, too. So, I brought you a couple!
Ooooh! ♡
Which one do you like?
......
I'll let you pick, Mom.
But...the theme is "Little Devil."
?!!
Right-o!
Okay, let's get you ready to party! ♡
NOOOO!!! You can't dress her up like a devil!! Wear the white one with the cute red flowers!!
Hentai Switch ON
Calm down, Papa. She's a big girl now.
Cool it. Cool it.

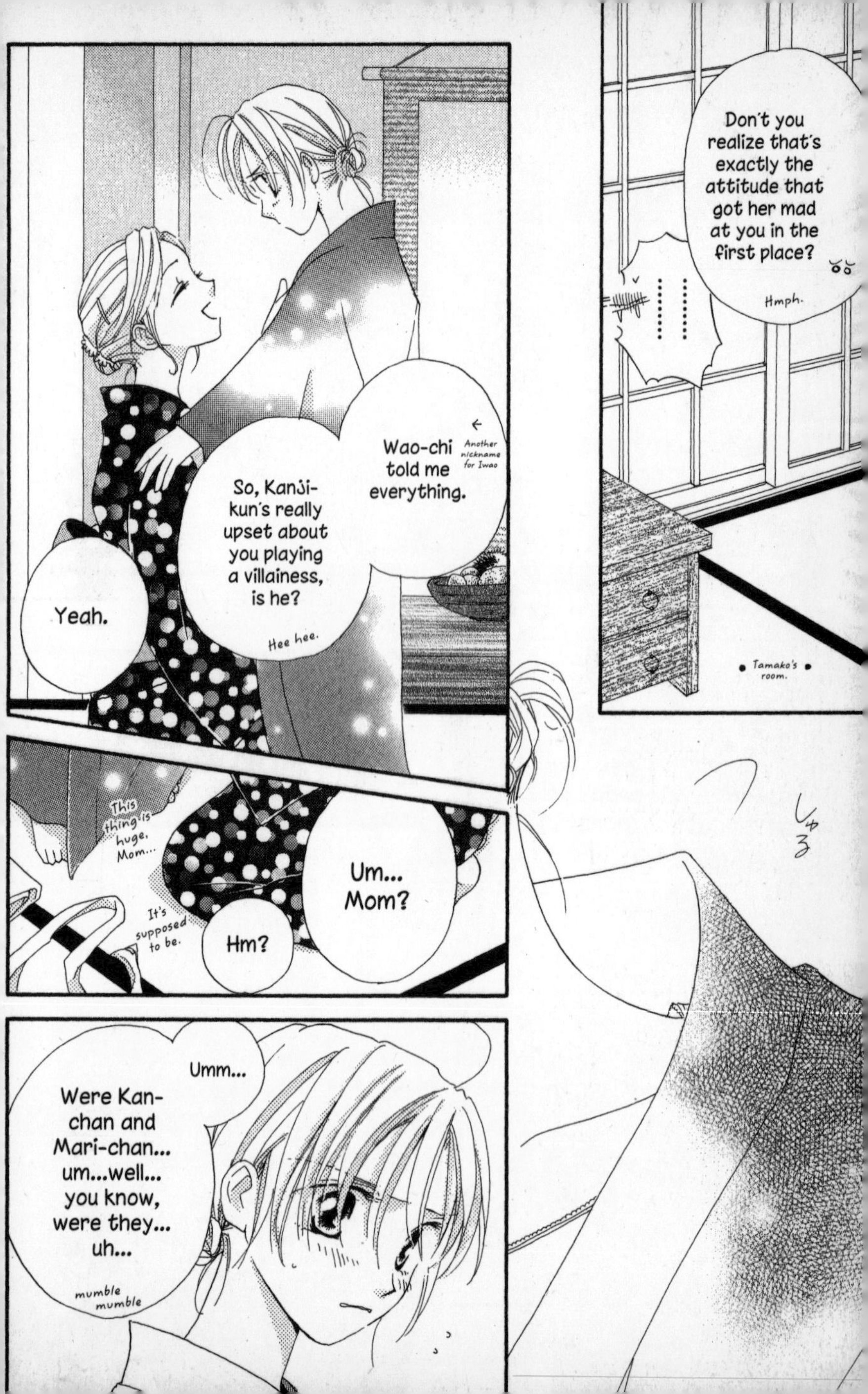
Don't you realize that's exactly the attitude that got her mad at you in the first place?
Hmph.
......
Tamako's room.
Wao-chi told me everything.
← Another nickname for Iwao
So, Kanji-kun's really upset about you playing a villainess, is he?
Hee hee.
Yeah.
しゅる
Um... Mom?
Hm?
This thing is huge, Mom...
It's supposed to be.
Umm...
Were Kan-chan and Mari-chan... um...well... you know, were they... uh...
mumble mumble

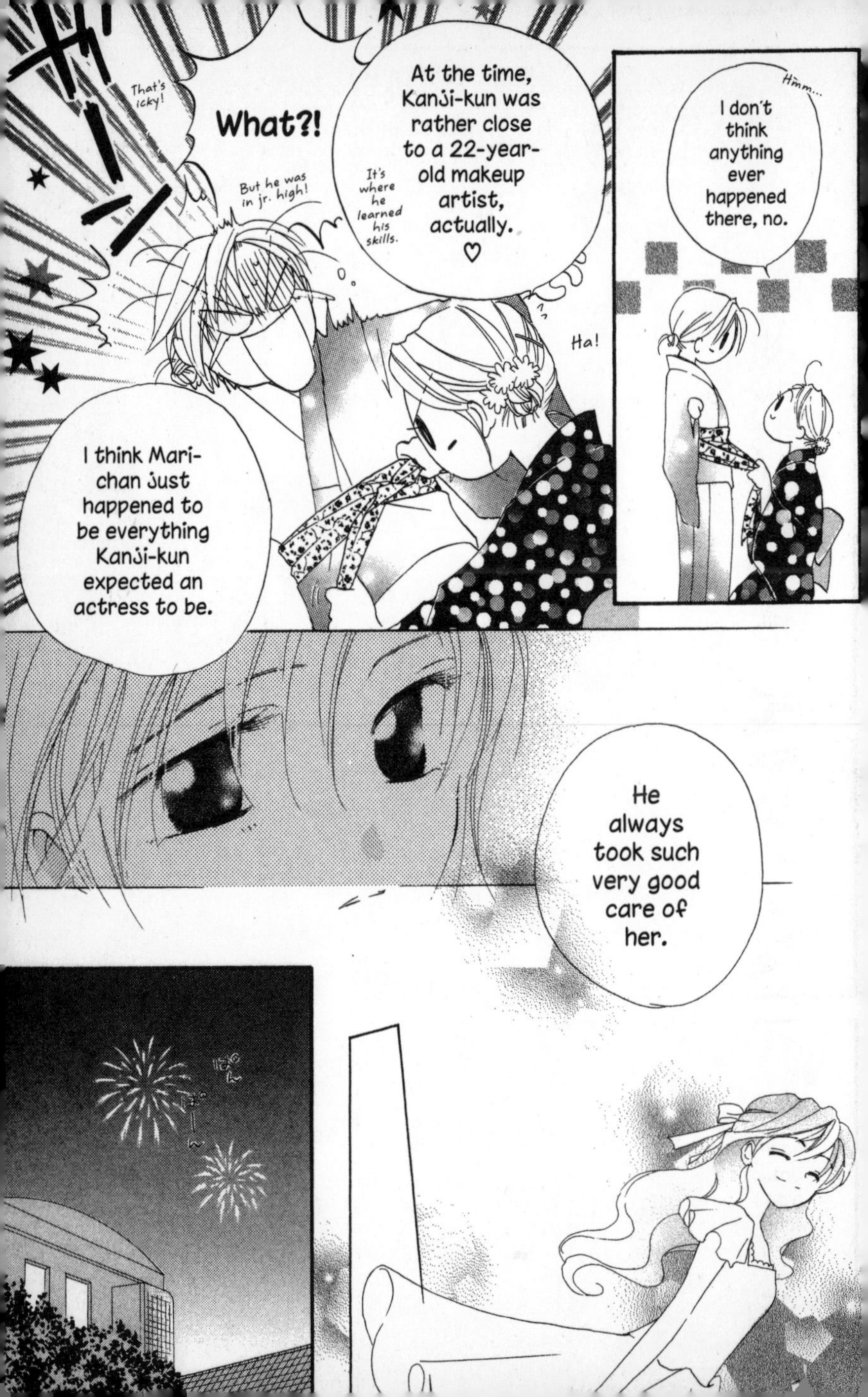
Hmm...
I don't think anything ever happened there, no.
Ha!
At the time, Kanji-kun was rather close to a 22-year-old makeup artist, actually. ♡
It's where he learned his skills.
What?!
But he was in jr. high!
That's icky!
I think Mari-chan just happened to be everything Kanji-kun expected an actress to be.
He always took such very good care of her.

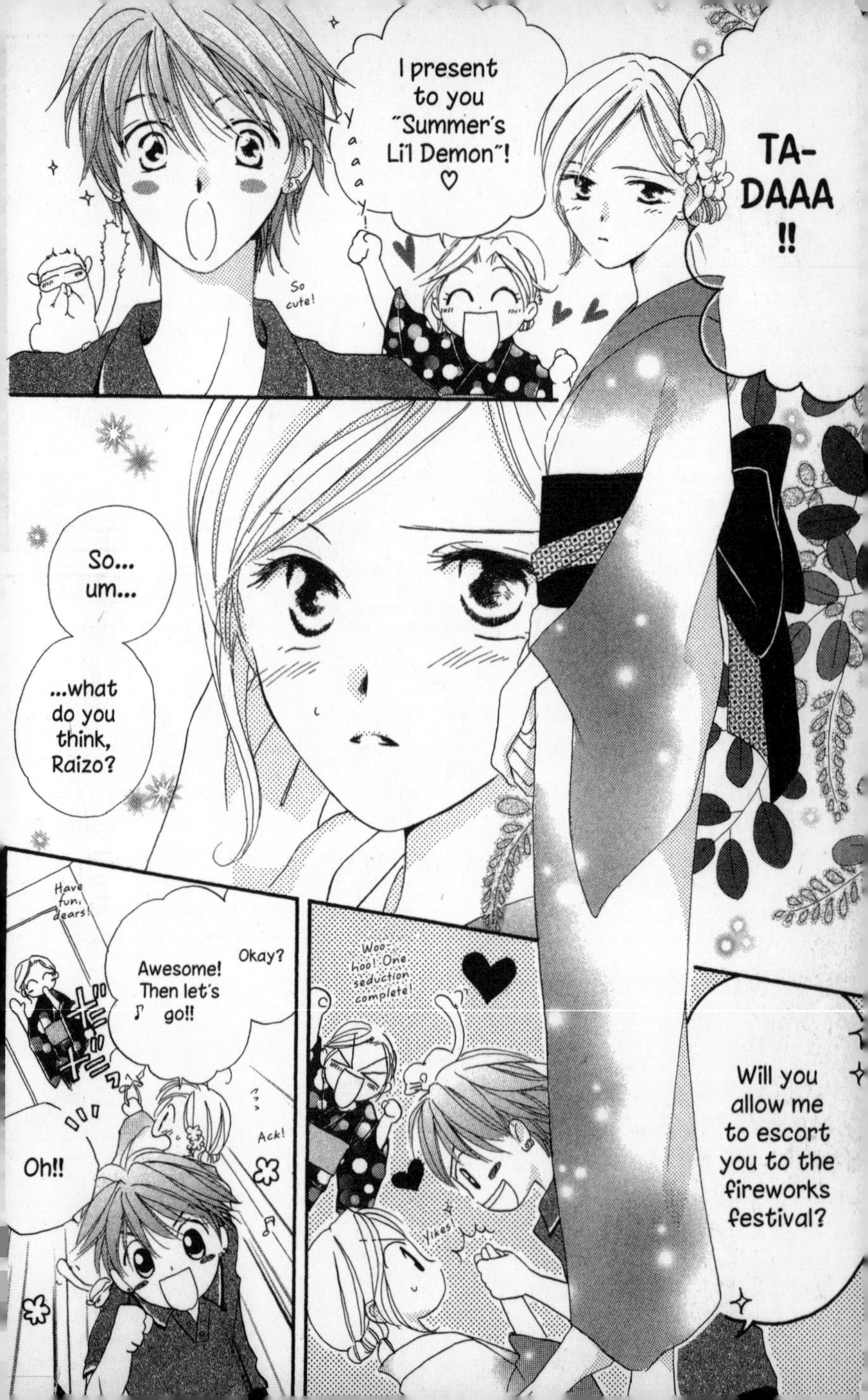
TA-DAAA!!
I present to you "Summer's Li'l Demon"! ♡
Yaaaay!
So cute!
So... um...
...what do you think, Raizo?
Will you allow me to escort you to the fireworks festival?
Woo-hoo! One seduction complete!
Yikes
Okay?
Awesome! Then let's go!!
Have fun, dears!
Ack!
Oh!!

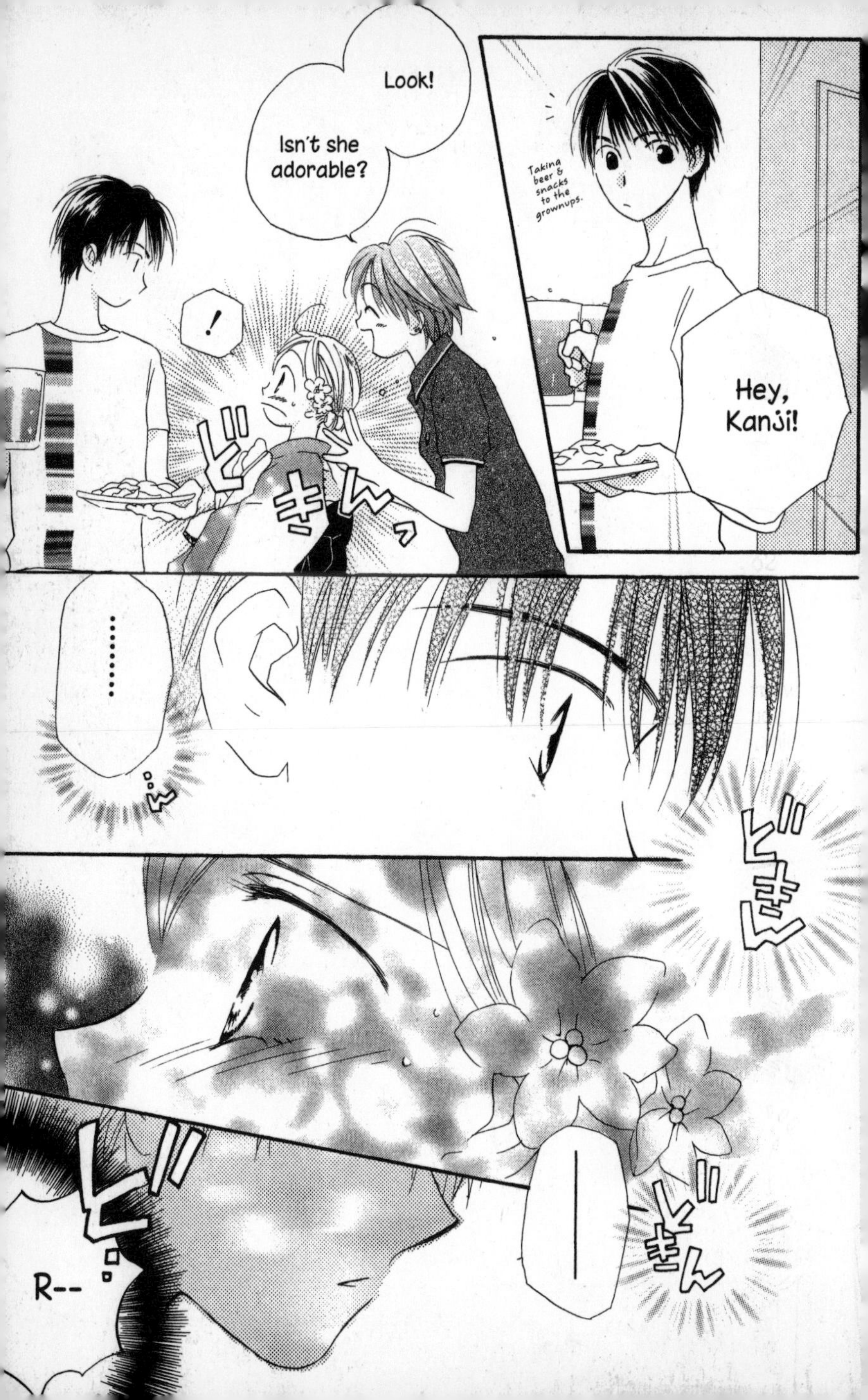

Taking beer & snacks to the grownups.
Hey, Kanji!
Look!
Isn't she adorable?
!
どきんっ
……
どきん
—
R--

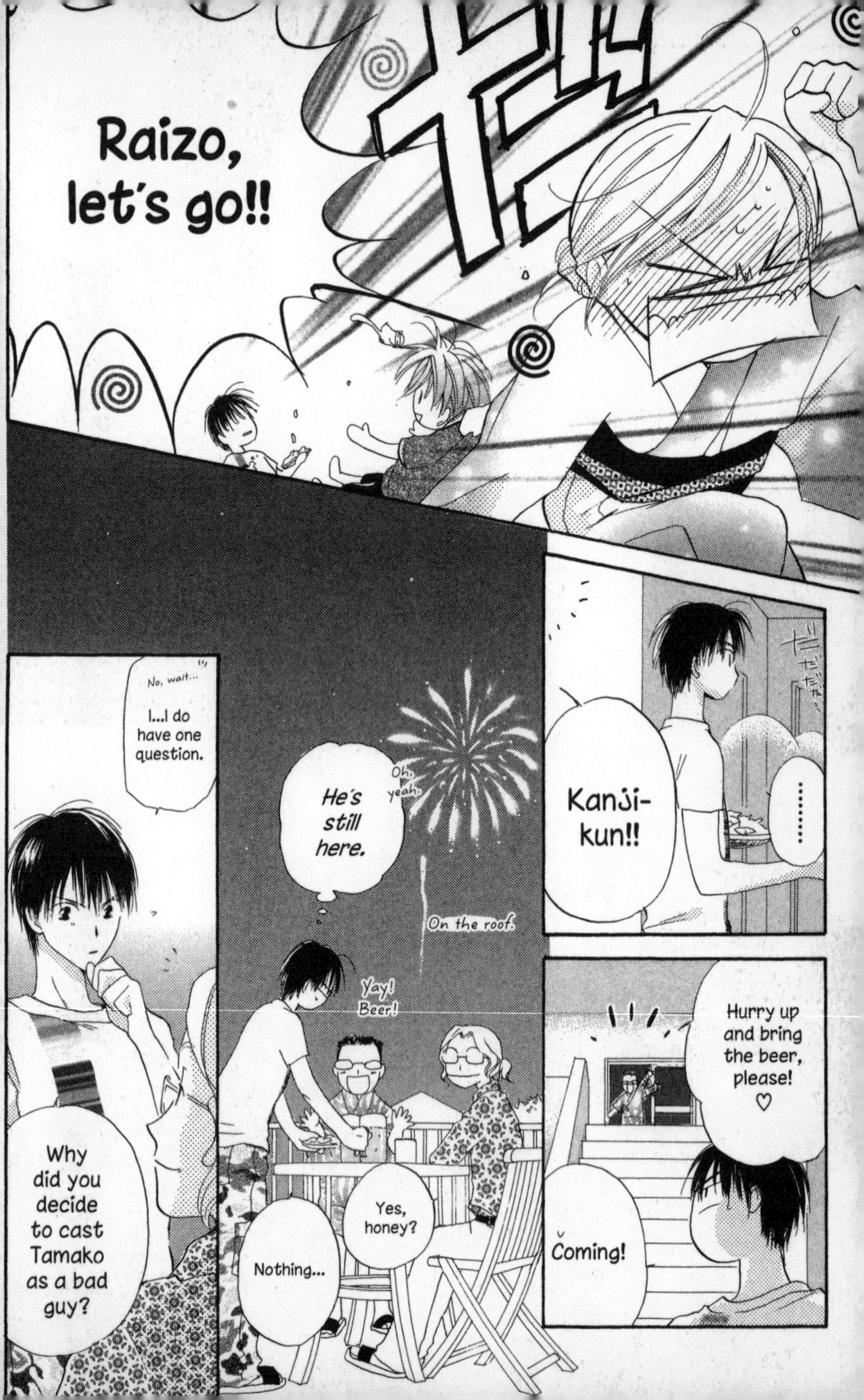
Raizo, let's go!!
Kanji-kun!!
......
Hurry up and bring the beer, please! ♡
Coming!
Oh, yeah.
He's still here.
On the roof.
Yay! Beer!
Yes, honey?
Nothing...
No, wait...
I...I do have one question.
Why did you decide to cast Tamako as a bad guy?

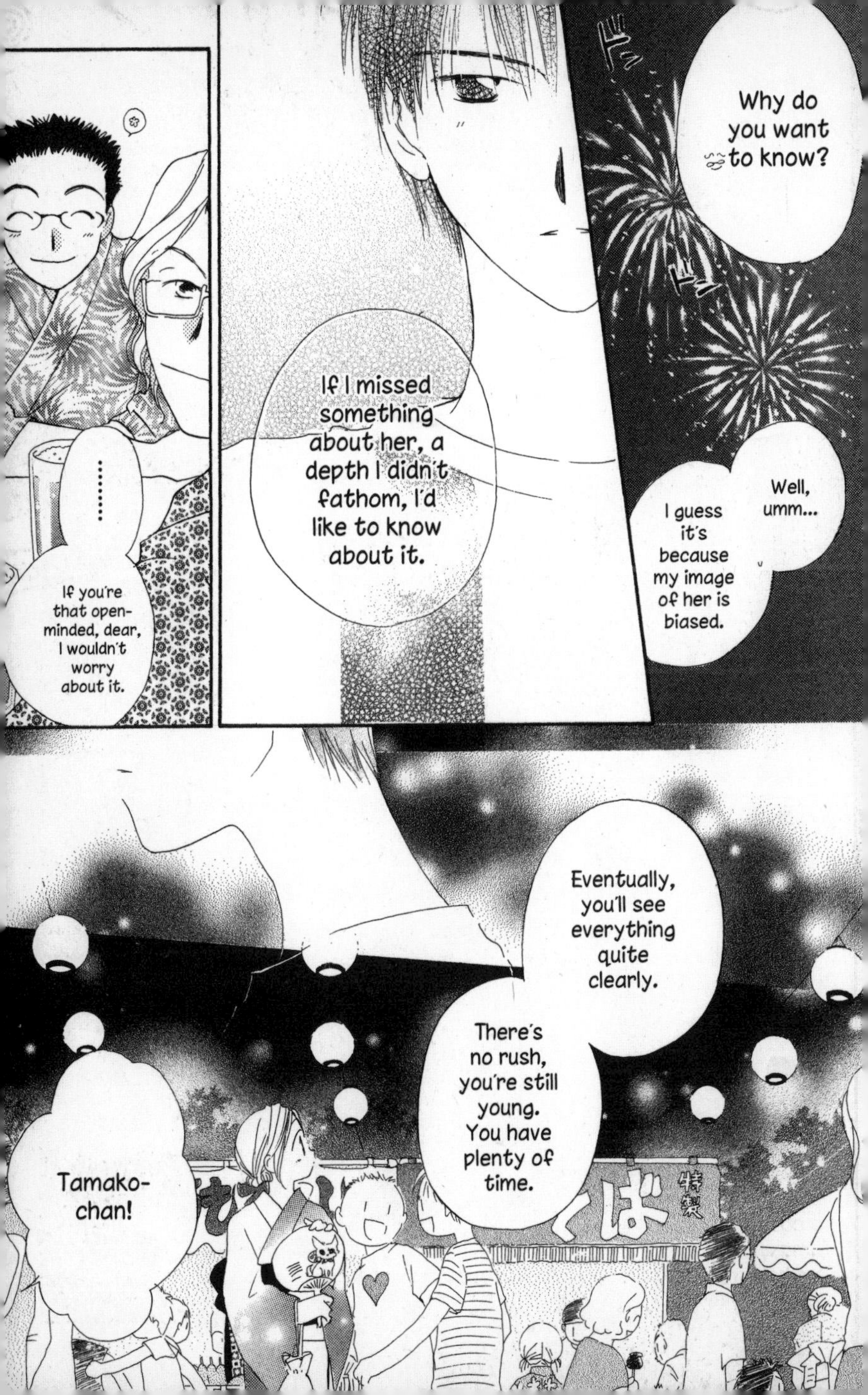
Why do you want to know?
Well, umm...
I guess it's because my image of her is biased.
If I missed something about her, a depth I didn't fathom, I'd like to know about it.
....
If you're that open-minded, dear, I wouldn't worry about it.
Eventually, you'll see everything quite clearly.
There's no rush, you're still young. You have plenty of time.
Tamako-chan!

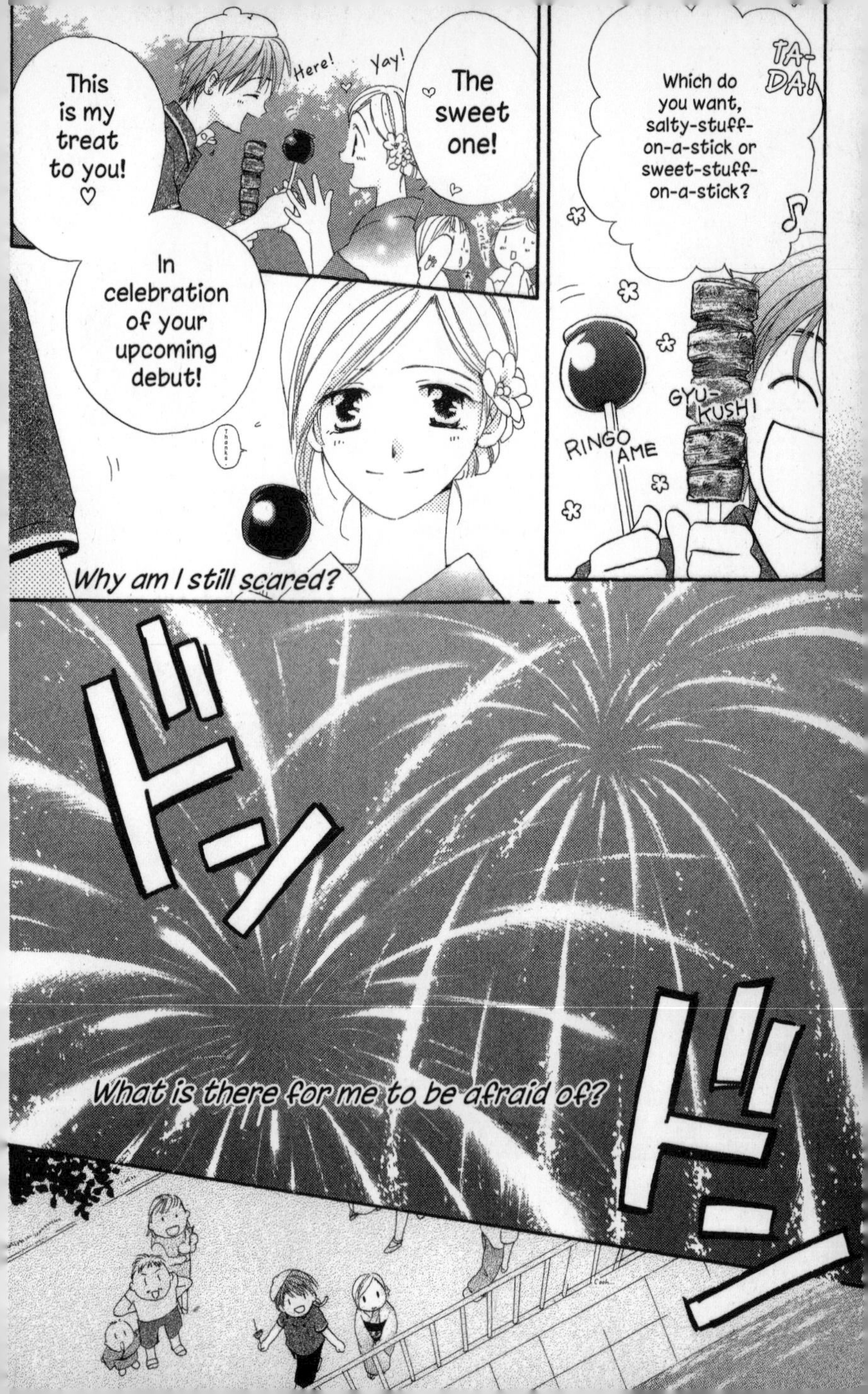

TA-DA!
Which do you want, salty-stuff-on-a-stick or sweet-stuff-on-a-stick?
GYU-KUSHI
RINGO AME
Yay!
The sweet one!
Here!
This is my treat to you!
In celebration of your upcoming debut!
Thanks...
Why am I still scared?
ドーン
ドーン
What is there for me to be afraid of?

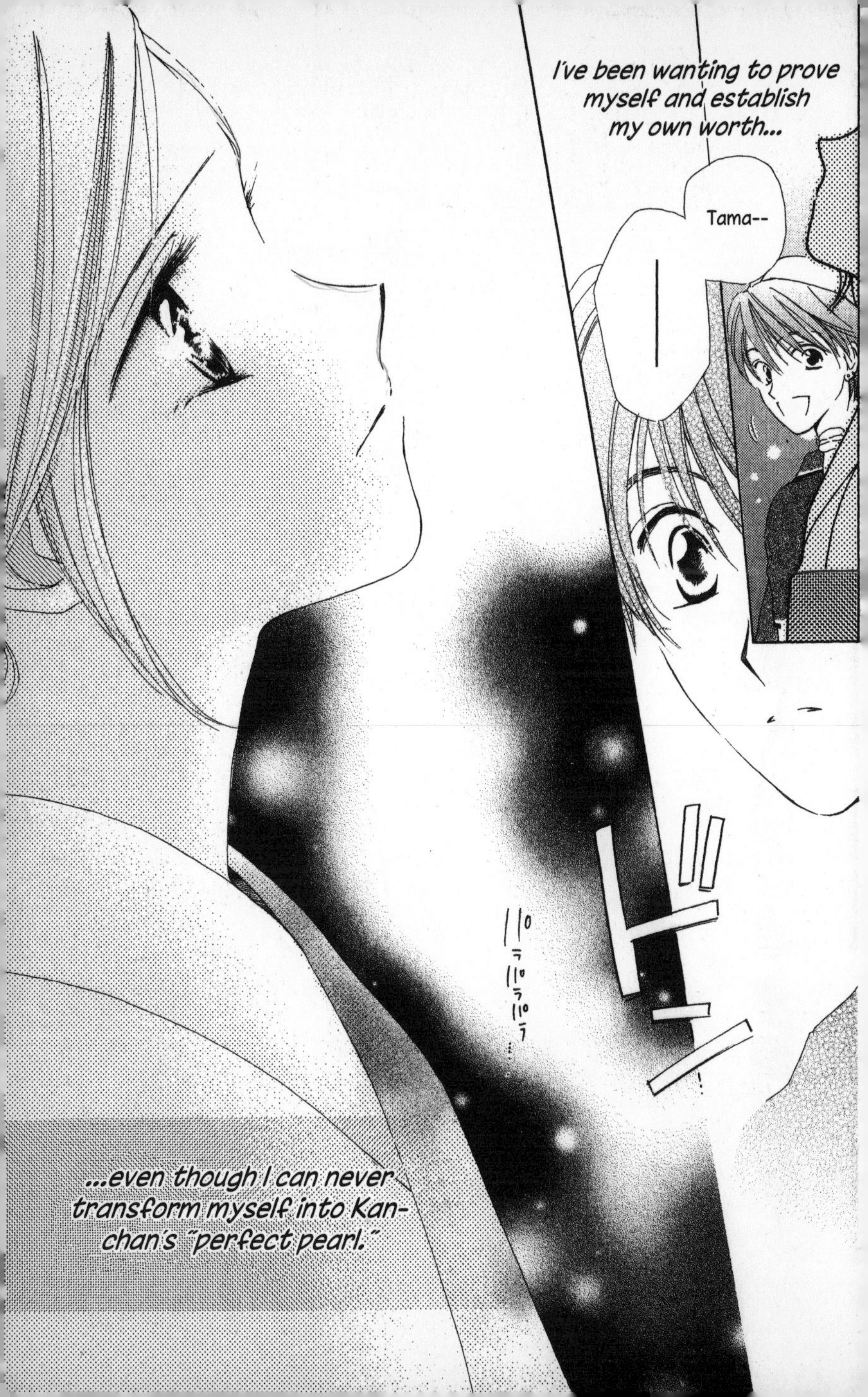
I've been wanting to prove myself and establish my own worth...
Tama--
...even though I can never transform myself into Kan-chan's "perfect pearl."

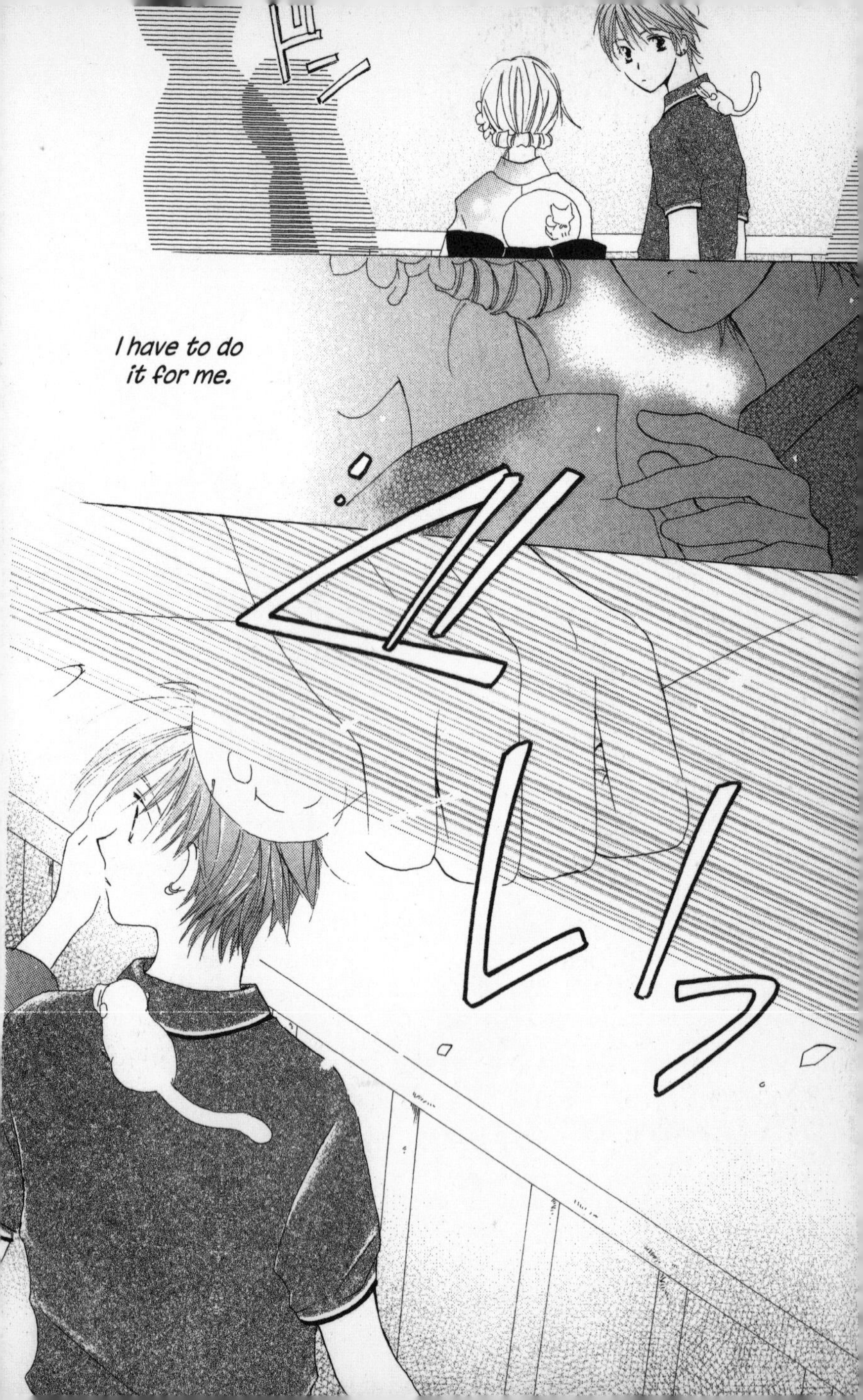
I have to do it for me.

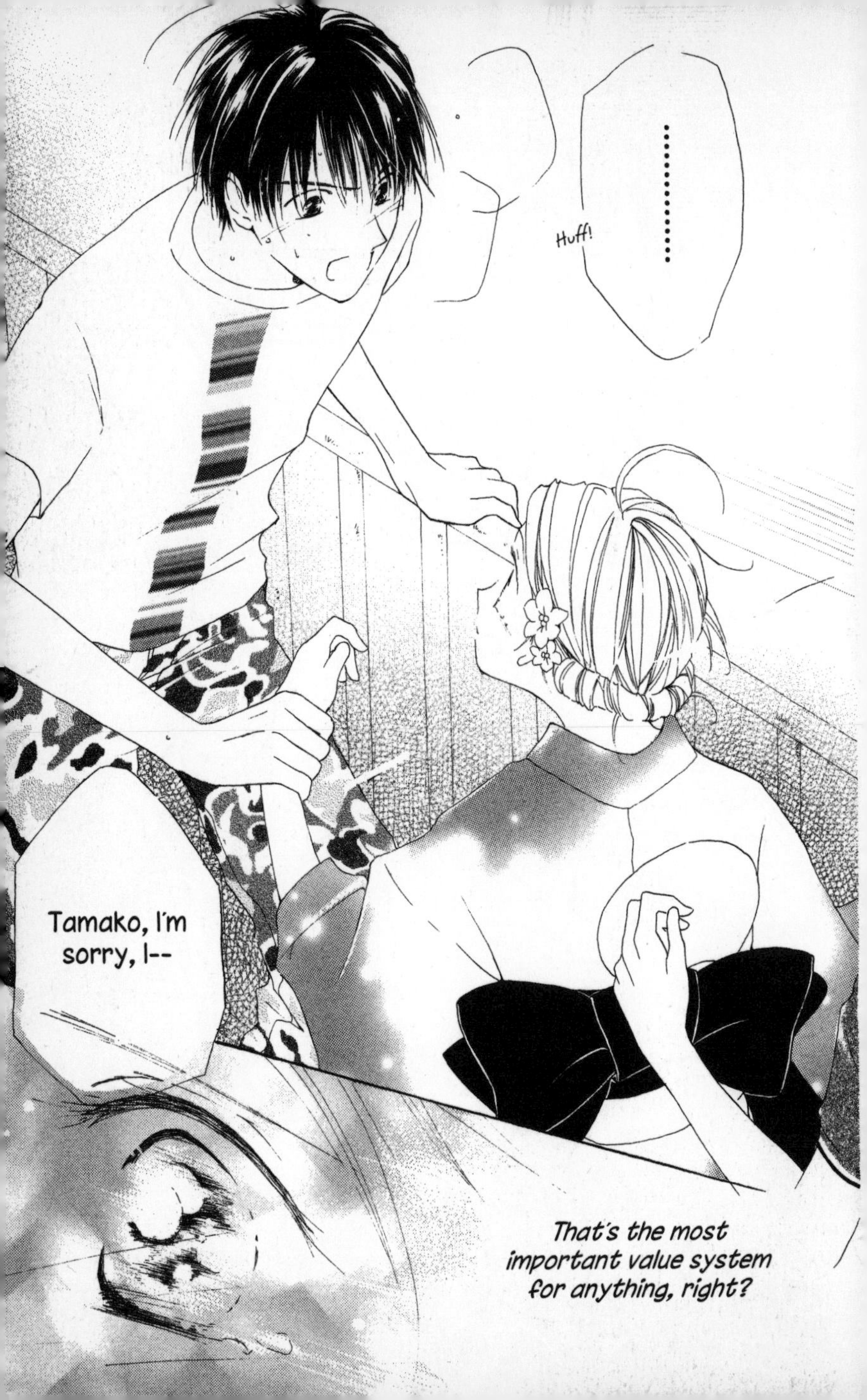
......
Huff!
Tamako, I'm sorry, I--
That's the most important value system for anything, right?

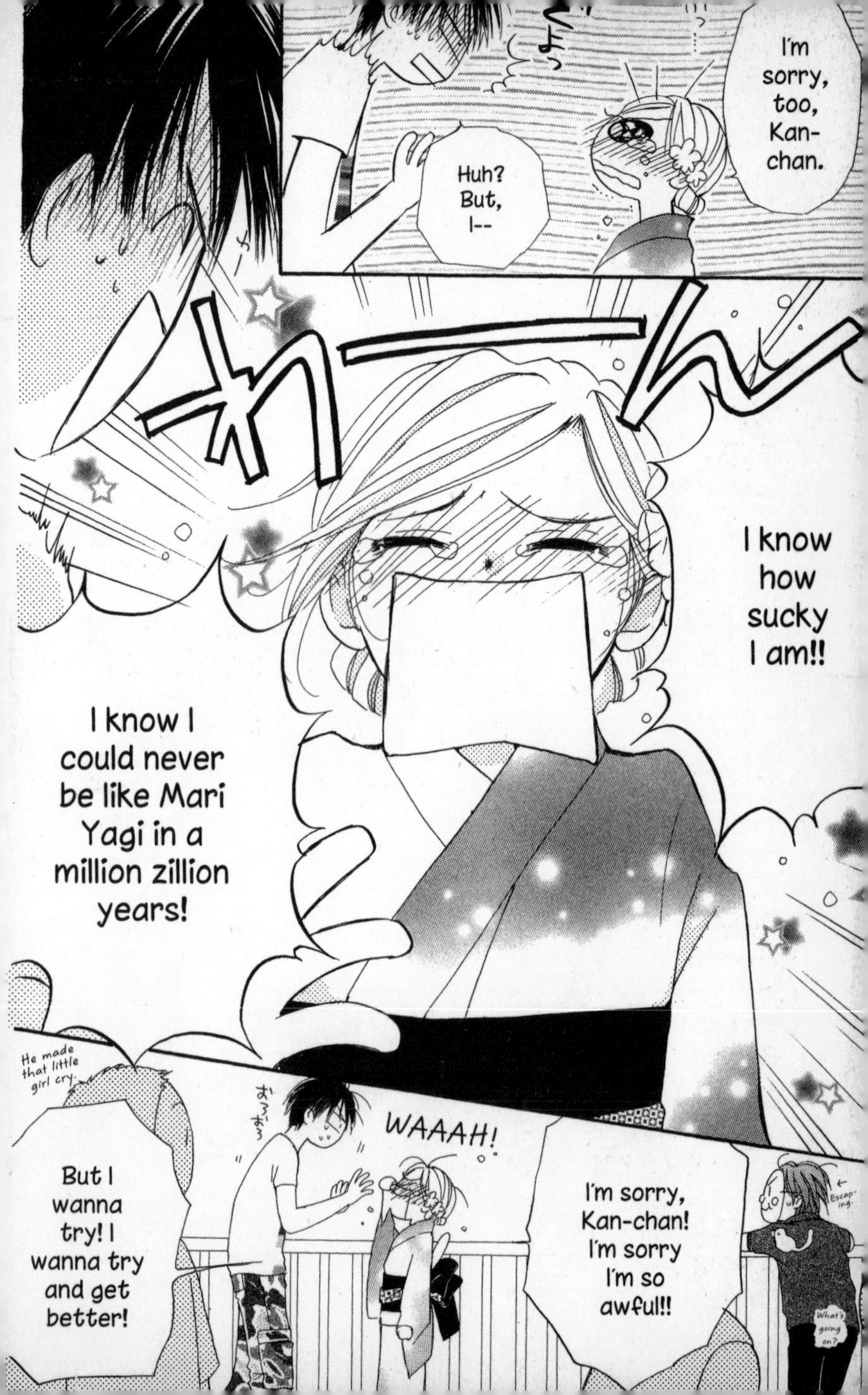
I'm sorry, too, Kan-chan.
Huh? But, I--
I know how sucky I am!!
I know I could never be like Mari Yagi in a million zillion years!
← Escaping.
I'm sorry, Kan-chan! I'm sorry I'm so awful!!
What's going on?
WAAAH!
He made that little girl cry.
But I wanna try! I wanna try and get better!

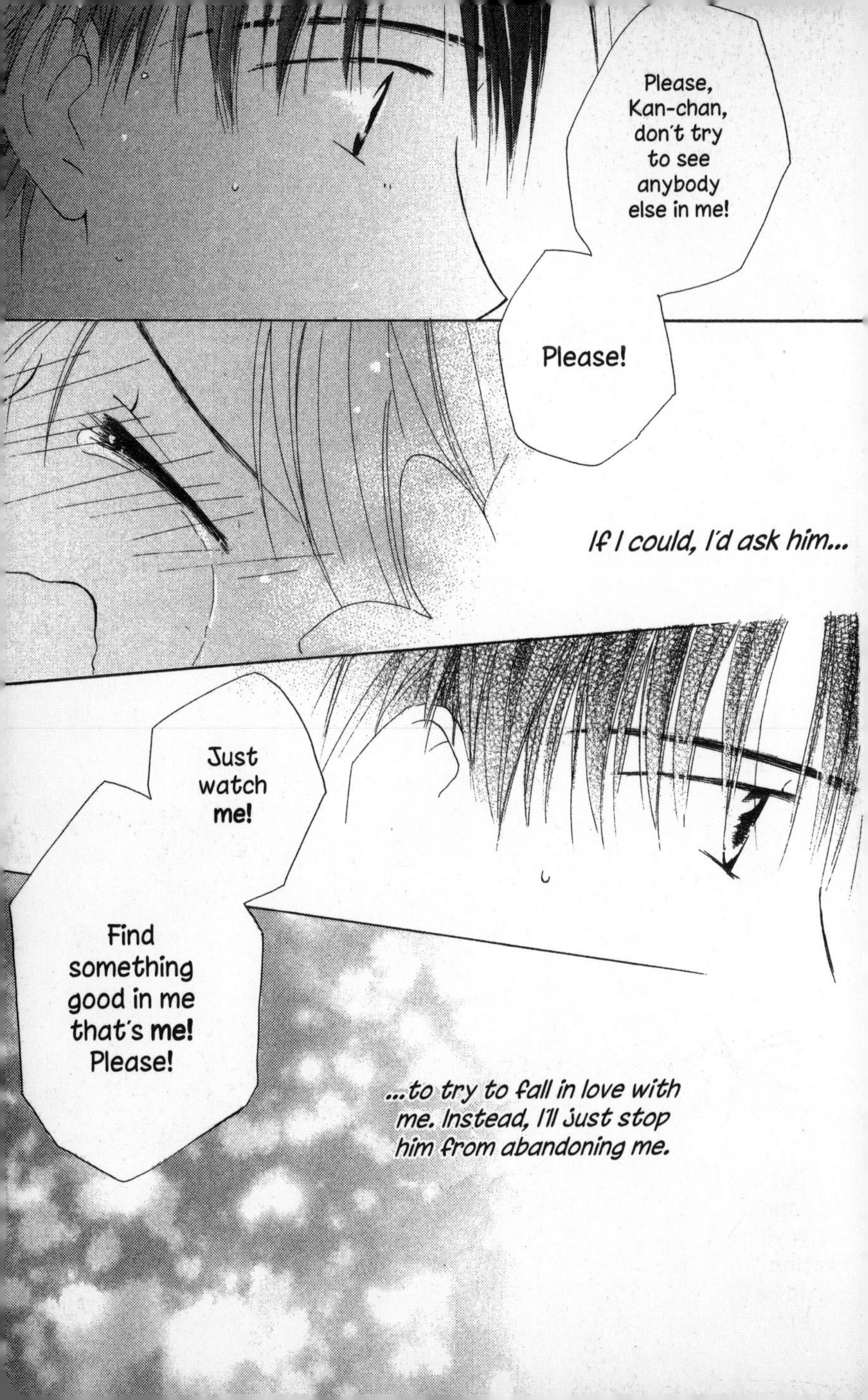

Please, Kan-chan, don't try to see anybody else in me!
Please!
If I could, I'd ask him...
Just watch me!
Find something good in me that's me! Please!
...to try to fall in love with me. Instead, I'll just stop him from abandoning me.

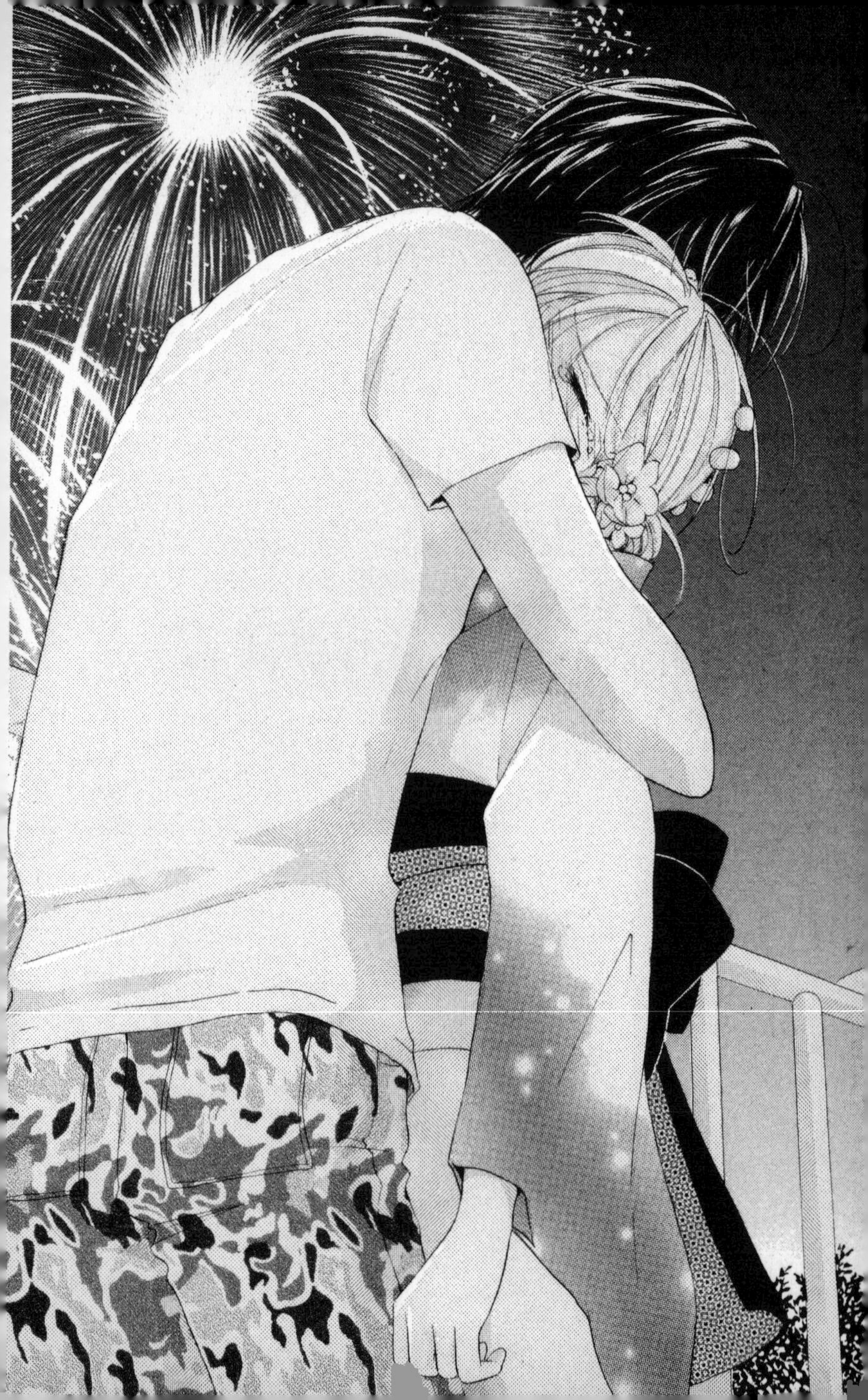

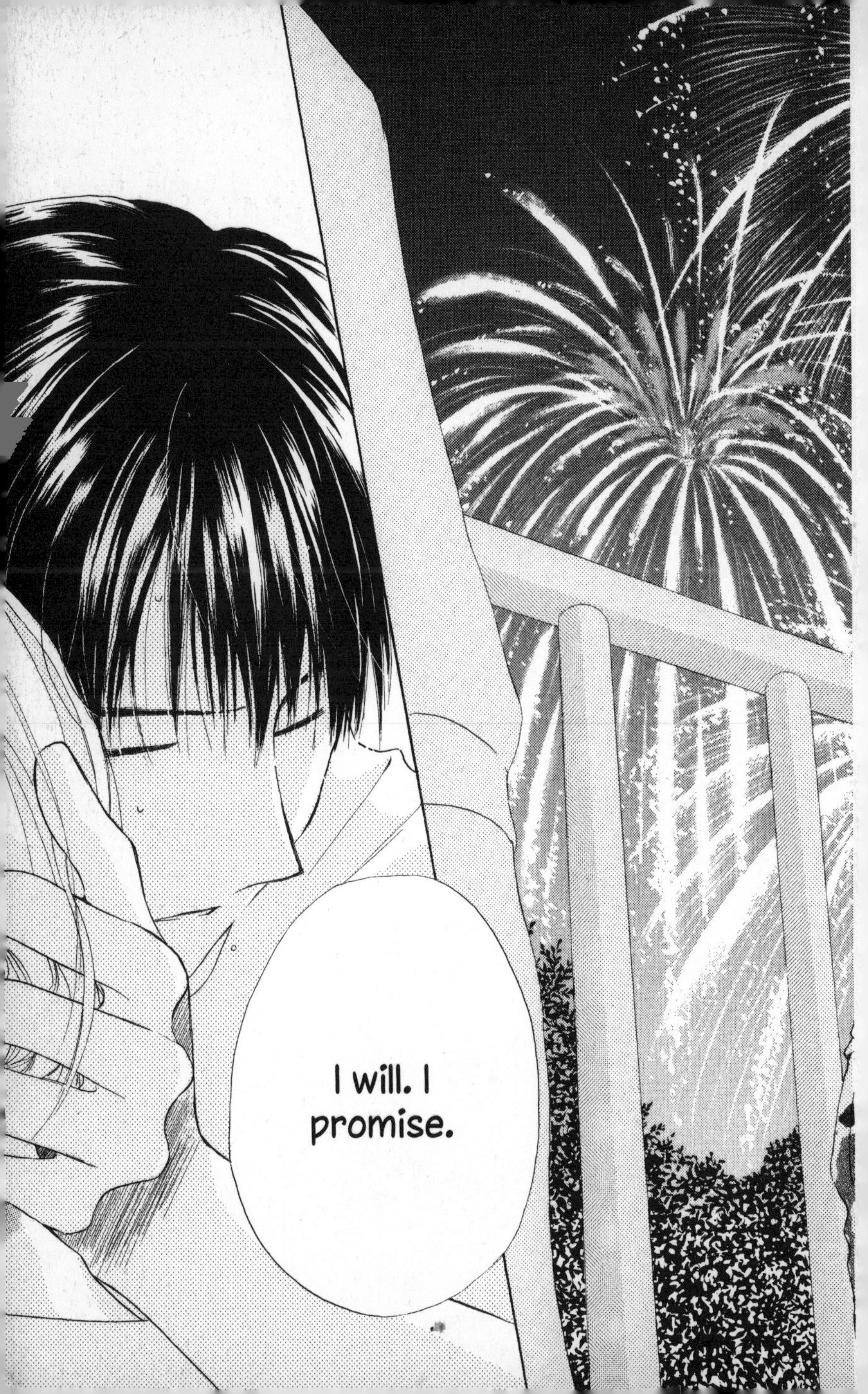
I will. I promise.

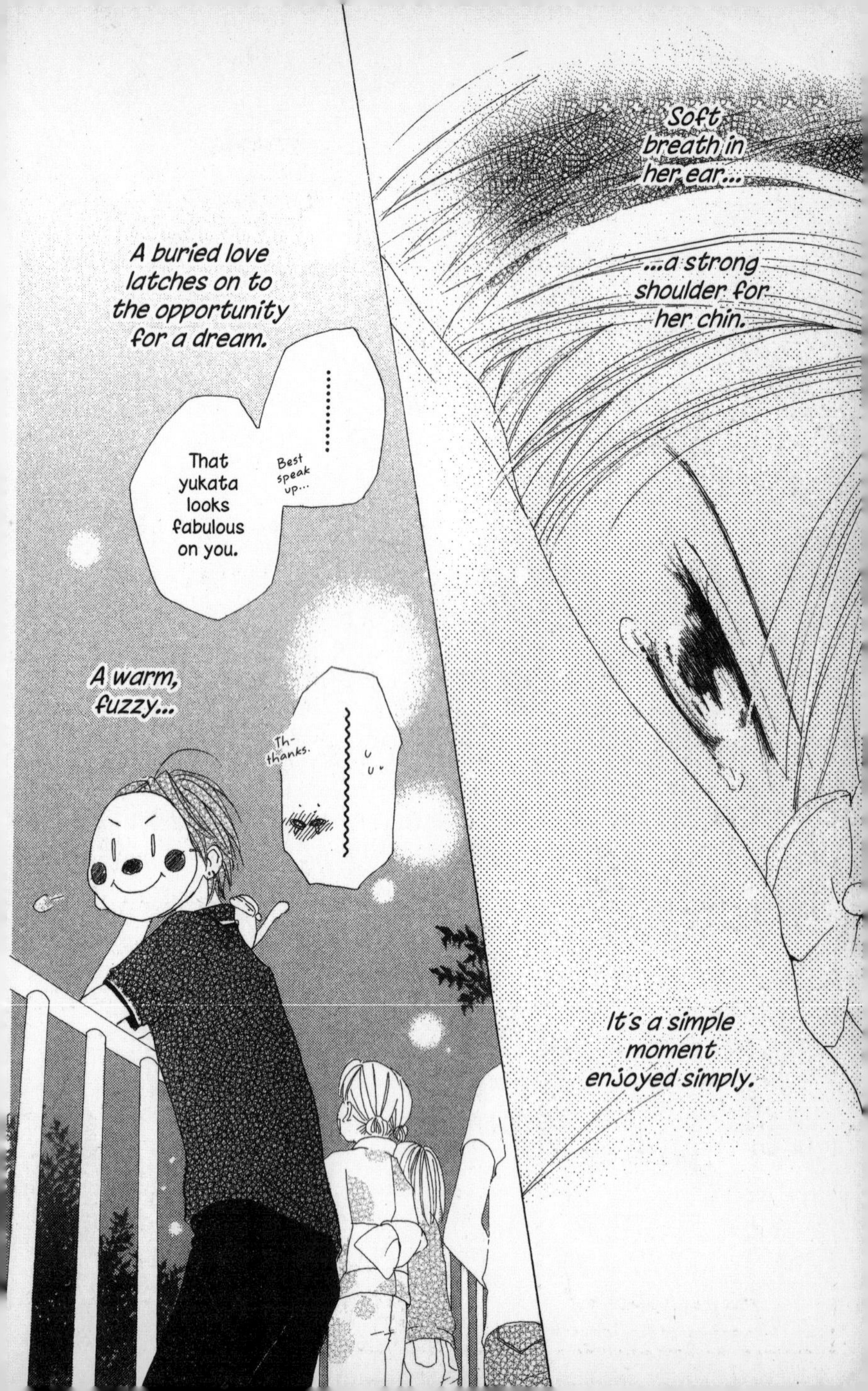
Soft breath in her ear...
...a strong shoulder for her chin.
It's a simple moment enjoyed simply.
A buried love latches on to the opportunity for a dream.
......
Best speak up...
That yukata looks fabulous on you.
A warm, fuzzy...
Th-thanks.

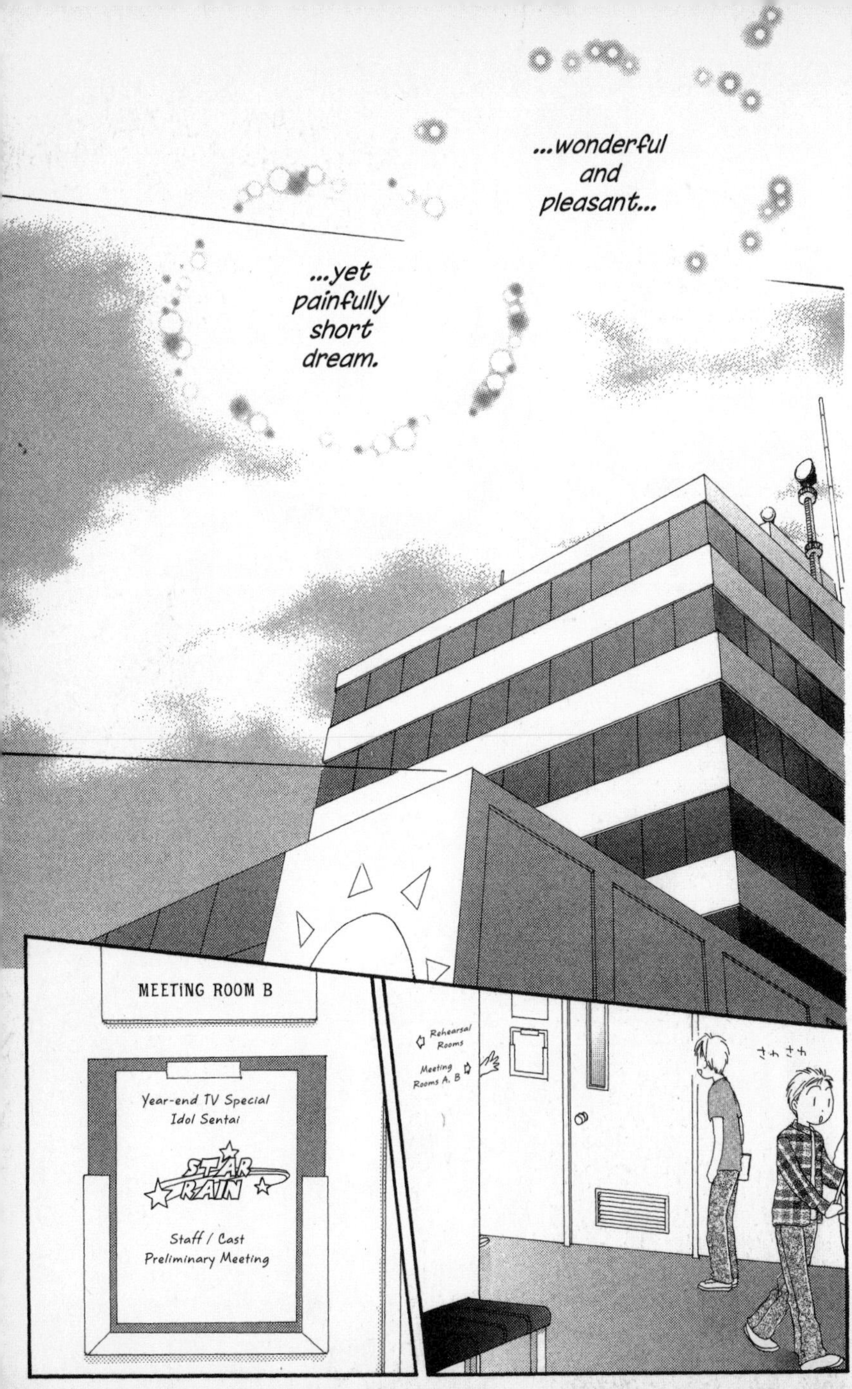
...wonderful and pleasant...
...yet painfully short dream.
Rehearsal Rooms
Meeting Rooms A, B
さわさわ
MEETiNG ROOM B
Year-end TV Special Idol Sentai
STAR RAIN
Staff / Cast Preliminary Meeting

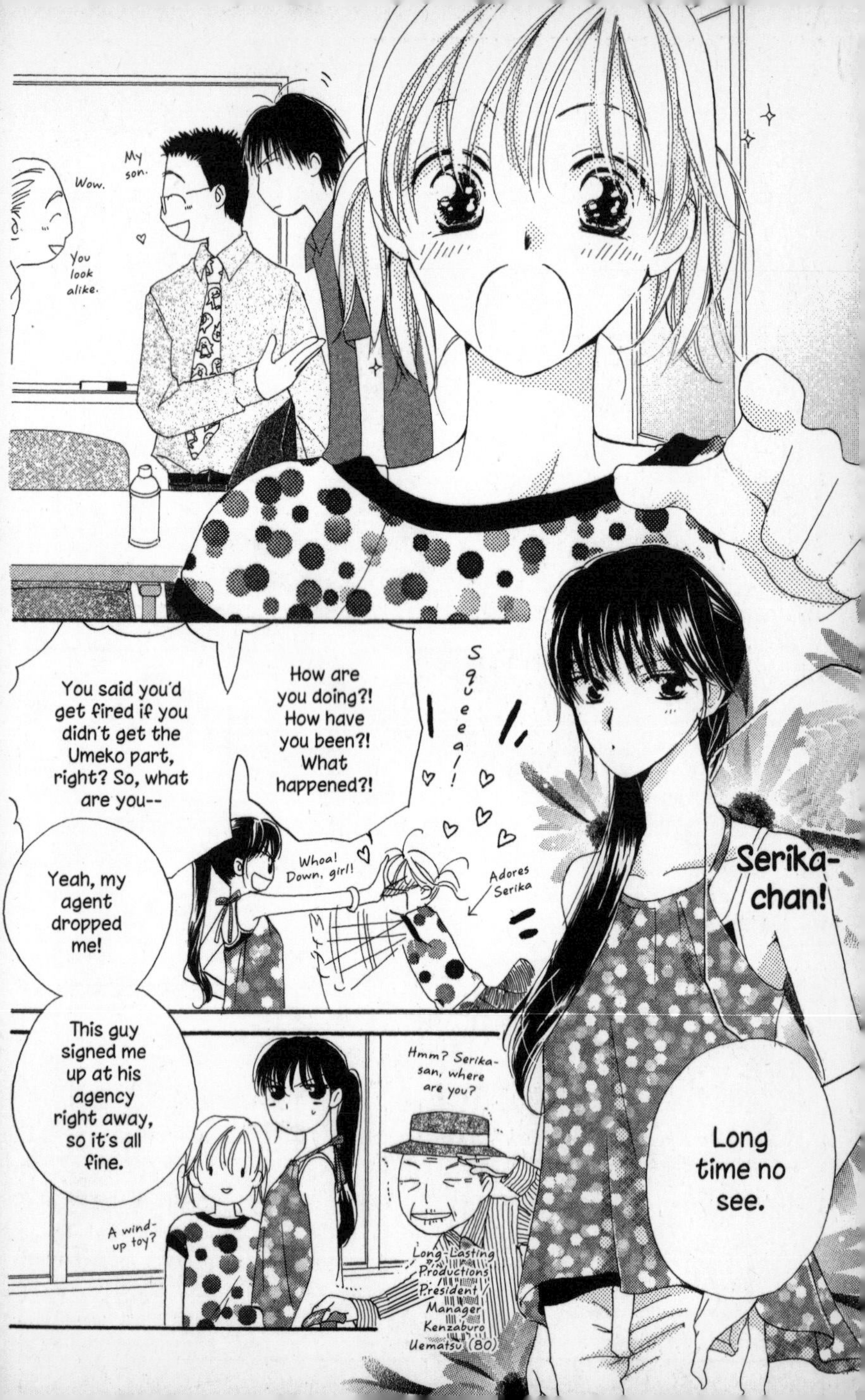

My son.
Wow.
You look alike.
Serika-chan!
Long time no see.
Squeeea!
How are you doing?! How have you been?! What happened?!
You said you'd get fired if you didn't get the Umeko part, right? So, what are you--
Adores Serika
Whoa! Down, girl!
Yeah, my agent dropped me!
Hmm? Serika-san, where are you?
This guy signed me up at his agency right away, so it's all fine.
A wind-up toy?
Long-Lasting Productions President/Manager Kenzaburo Uematsu (80)

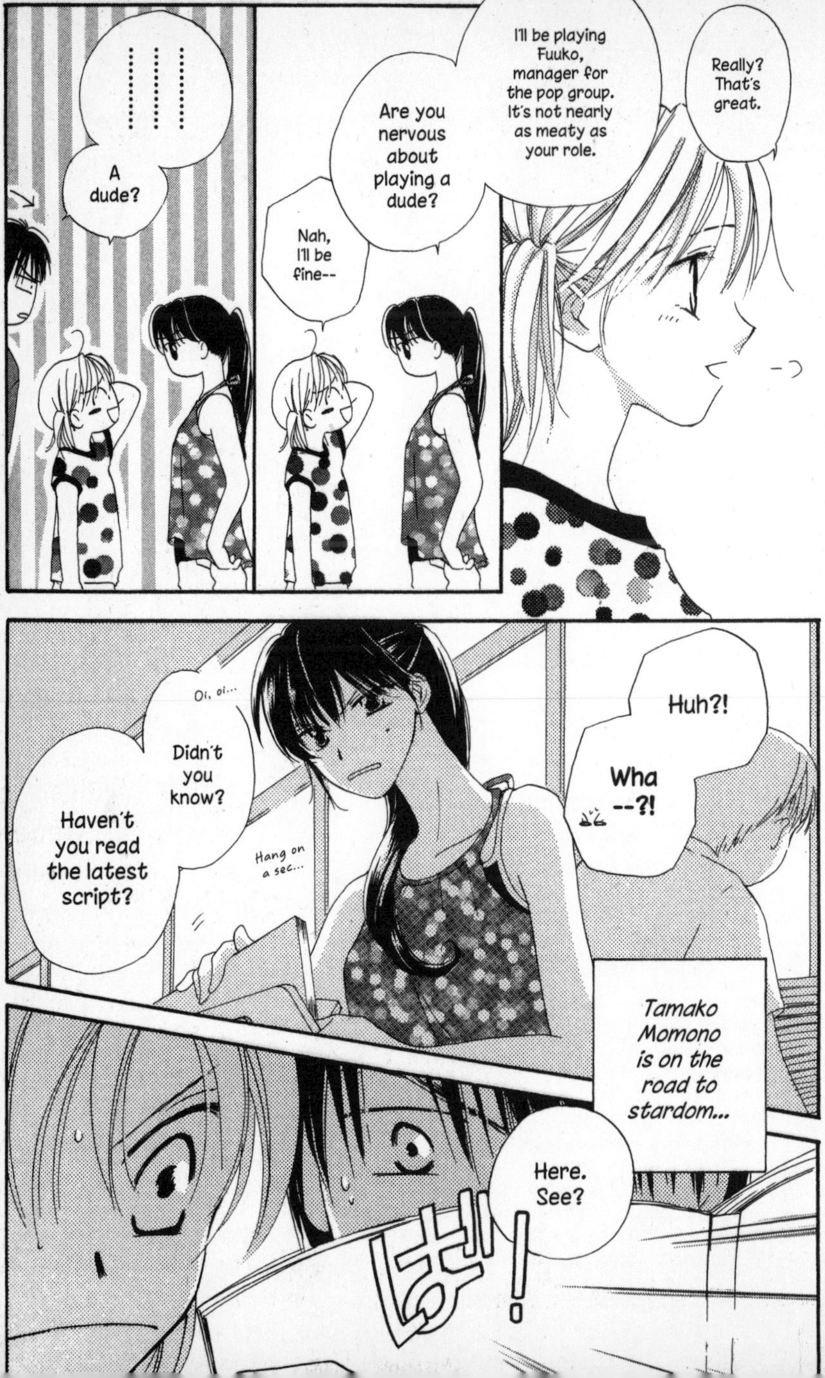
Really? That's great.
I'll be playing Fuuko, manager for the pop group. It's not nearly as meaty as your role.
Are you nervous about playing a dude?
Nah, I'll be fine--
......
A dude?
Huh?!
Wha--?!
Oi, oi...
Didn't you know?
Hang on a sec...
Haven't you read the latest script?
Tamako Momono is on the road to stardom...
Here. See?

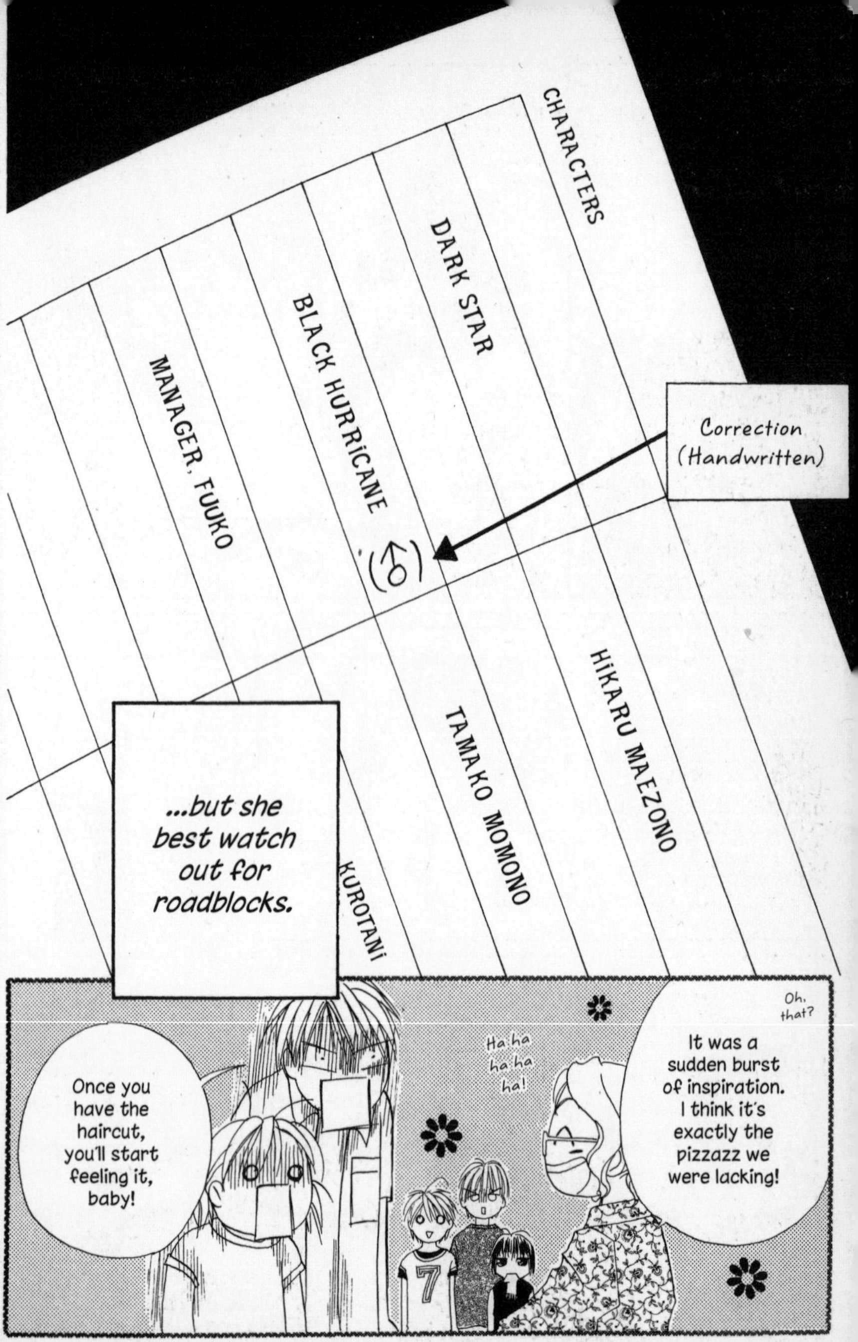
CHARACTERS
DARK STAR
BLACK HURRiCANE
(♂)
Correction (Handwritten)
MANAGER, FUUKO
HiKARU MAEZONO
TAMAKO MOMONO
KUROTANi
...but she best watch out for roadblocks.
Oh, that?
It was a sudden burst of inspiration. I think it's exactly the pizzazz we were lacking!
Ha ha ha ha ha!
Once you have the haircut, you'll start feeling it, baby!

Pearl Pink Volume 3 / End

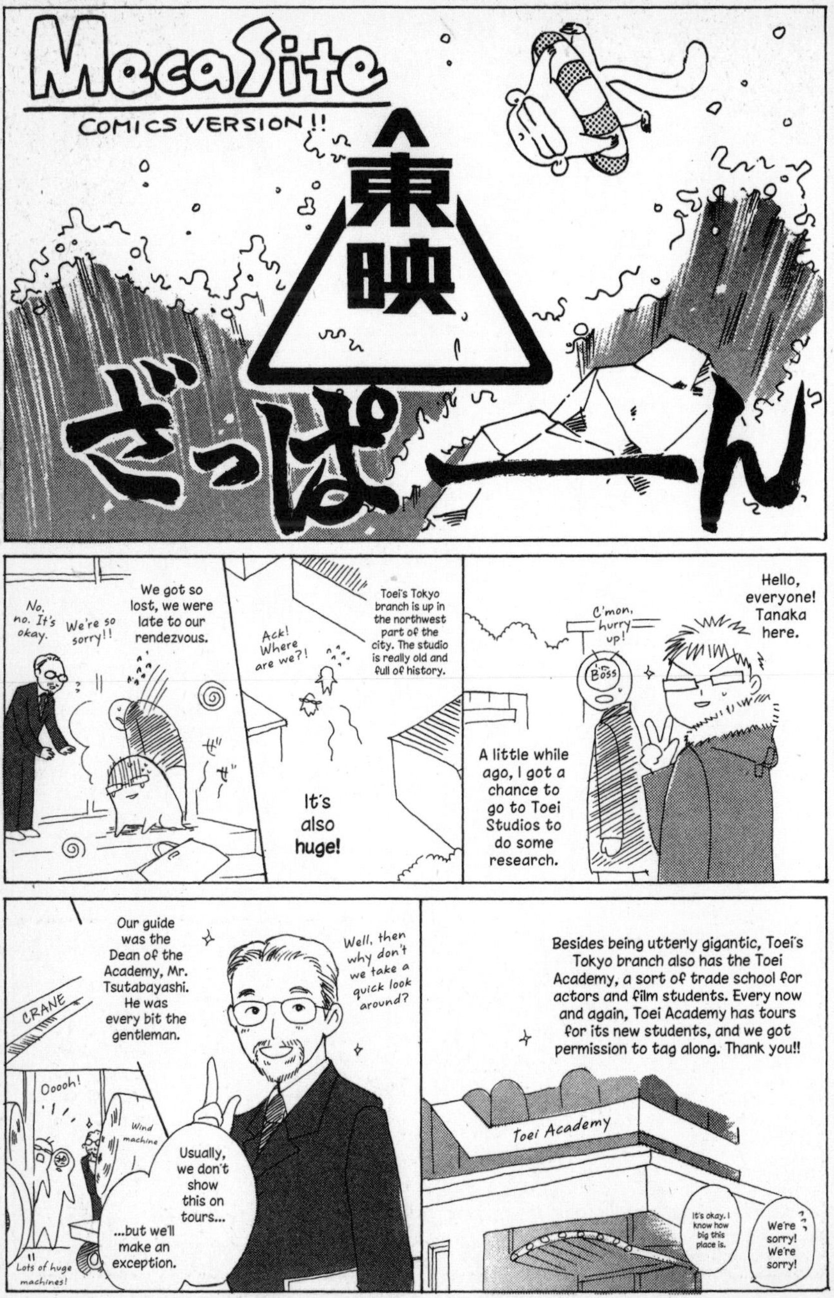
MecaSite
COMICS VERSION!!
東映
ざっぱーん
Hello, everyone! Tanaka here.
C'mon, hurry up!
Boss
A little while ago, I got a chance to go to Toei Studios to do some research.
Toei's Tokyo branch is up in the northwest part of the city. The studio is really old and full of history.
Ack! Where are we?!
It's also huge!
We got so lost, we were late to our rendezvous.
We're so sorry!!
No, no. It's okay.
Besides being utterly gigantic, Toei's Tokyo branch also has the Toei Academy, a sort of trade school for actors and film students. Every now and again, Toei Academy has tours for its new students, and we got permission to tag along. Thank you!!
Toei Academy
We're sorry! We're sorry!
It's okay. I know how big this place is.
Well, then why don't we take a quick look around?
Our guide was the Dean of the Academy, Mr. Tsutabayashi. He was every bit the gentleman.
CRANE
Usually, we don't show this on tours...
...but we'll make an exception.
Wind machine
Ooooh!
Lots of huge machines!

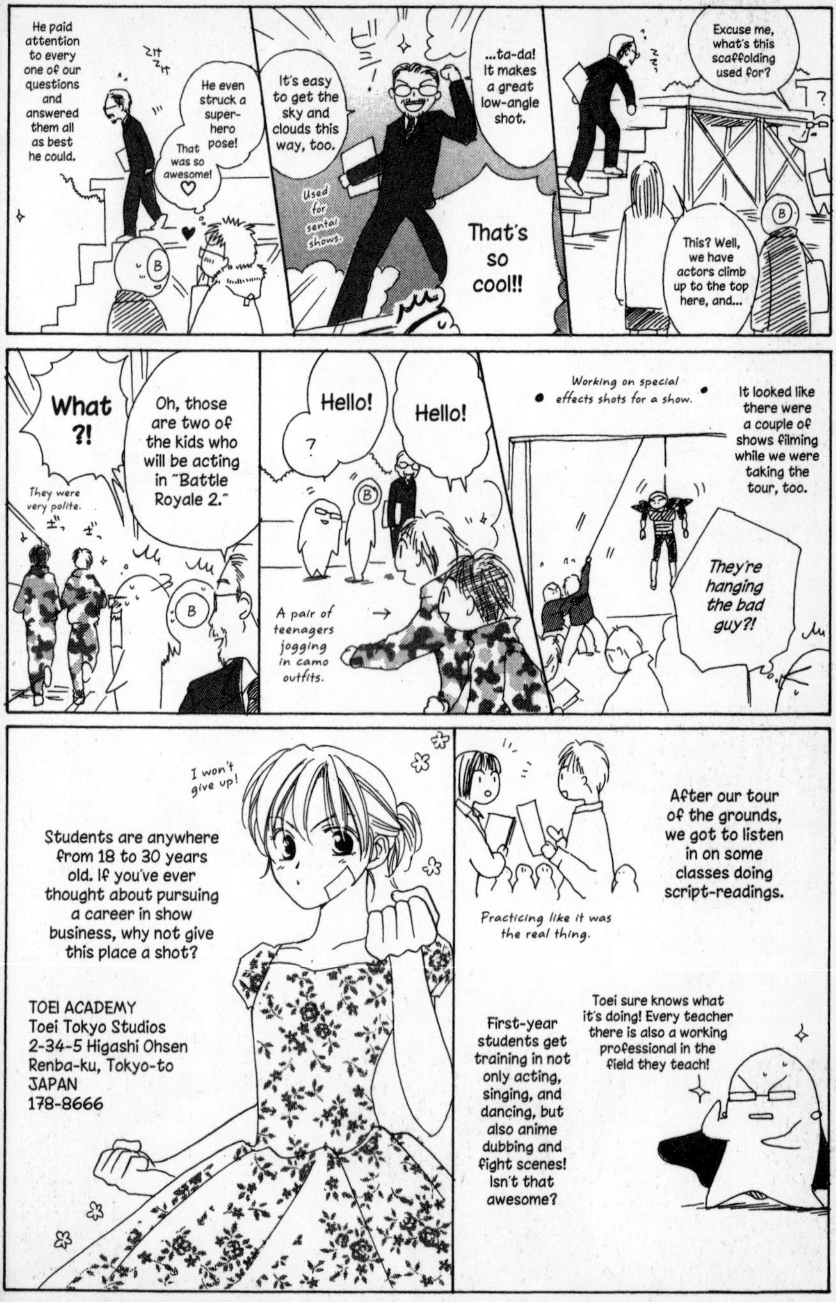

Excuse me, what's this scaffolding used for?
This? Well, we have actors climb up to the top here, and...
...ta-da! It makes a great low-angle shot.
It's easy to get the sky and clouds this way, too.
Used for sentai shows.
That's so cool!!
He even struck a super-hero pose!
That was so awesome! ♡
He paid attention to every one of our questions and answered them all as best he could.
Working on special effects shots for a show.
It looked like there were a couple of shows filming while we were taking the tour, too.
They're hanging the bad guy?!
Hello!
Hello!
A pair of teenagers jogging in camo outfits.
Oh, those are two of the kids who will be acting in "Battle Royale 2."
What?!
They were very polite.
After our tour of the grounds, we got to listen in on some classes doing script-readings.
Practicing like it was the real thing.
Toei sure knows what it's doing! Every teacher there is also a working professional in the field they teach!
First-year students get training in not only acting, singing, and dancing, but also anime dubbing and fight scenes! Isn't that awesome?
I won't give up!
Students are anywhere from 18 to 30 years old. If you've ever thought about pursuing a career in show business, why not give this place a shot?
TOEI ACADEMY
Toei Tokyo Studios
2-34-5 Higashi Ohsen
Renba-ku, Tokyo-to
JAPAN
178-8666

A few new characters have stepped into the limelight this volume. Serika-chan was originally supposed to be a selfish, stuck-up idol who was in love with Kanji, and Mari was supposed to be an utter klutz on the verge of getting fired. As you can see, they both ended up being almost the exact opposite. Still, there weren't that many girls for me to draw in this manga before, so I'm happy.

They'll be the two girls who give our dense, slowpoke main characters a push in the right direction. At least, they should. I think. Well, I'm really hoping they will! Please?

Oh, and when I draw Wao-wao...

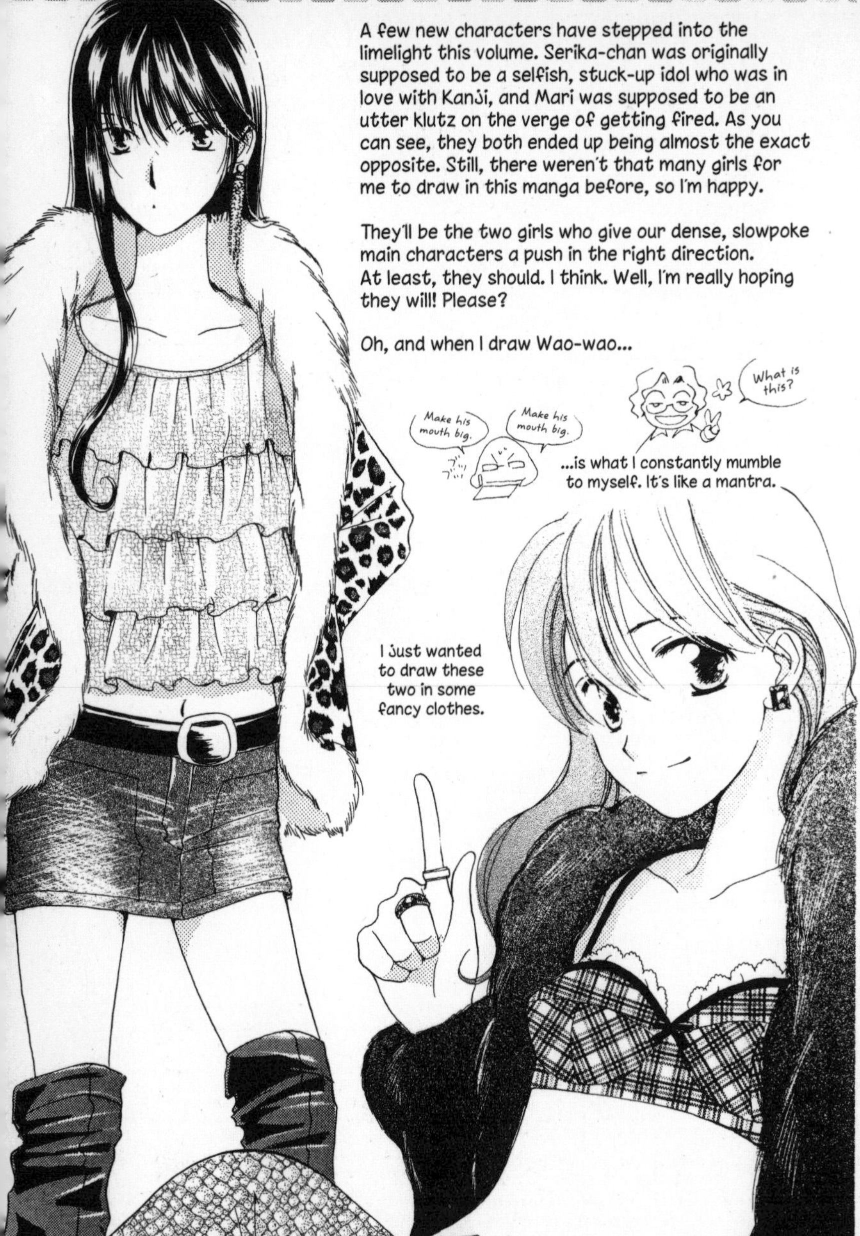
What is this?
Make his mouth big.
Make his mouth big.

...is what I constantly mumble to myself. It's like a mantra.

I just wanted to draw these two in some fancy clothes.

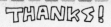

THANKS!

Mr. Yamamoto
Koyasu Uchida
Sano
Midori Ono
Toei Academy
My boss
Everyone who supported me.
Everyone who's reading this manga (you!)
Thank you so very much, everyone!!!

Well, that's all for this volume!

Meca Tanaka

Kanta's Past   Read this way ⟶

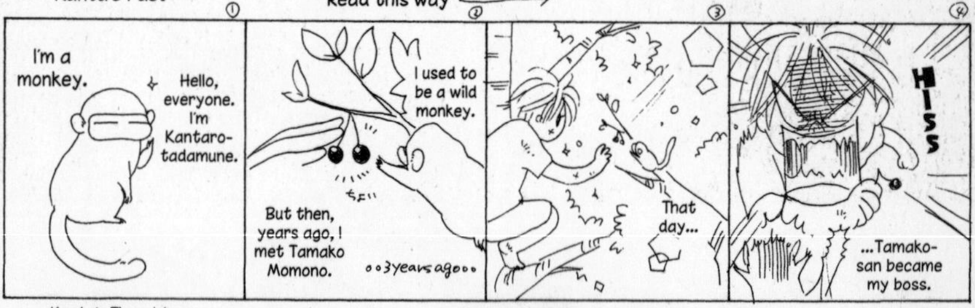

① I'm a monkey.

← Hello, everyone. I'm Kantaro-tadamune.

I used to be a wild monkey.

But then, years ago, I met Tamako Momono.

○ ○ 3 years ago ○ ○ ○

② That day...

③ HISS

...Tamako-san became my boss.

Kanta's Thoughts

Tamako-san didn't try to "train" me "or force me to do anything.

I pretty much live exactly how I want.

Hiya, Kanta!

I used to play with Raizo-san a lot...

...but he's gotten really busy, and I've been kind of lonely without him.

Kanji-san is the human Tamako-san crushes on, and he makes really good food...

But...

Yo...

...I wonder if he's ever going to call me by my name?

Have a banana.

:...

...here's your lunch, monkey.

Mecasite Comics Version / End

in Volume 4

TAMAKO's on her way to success...

...who's this mysterious man?!

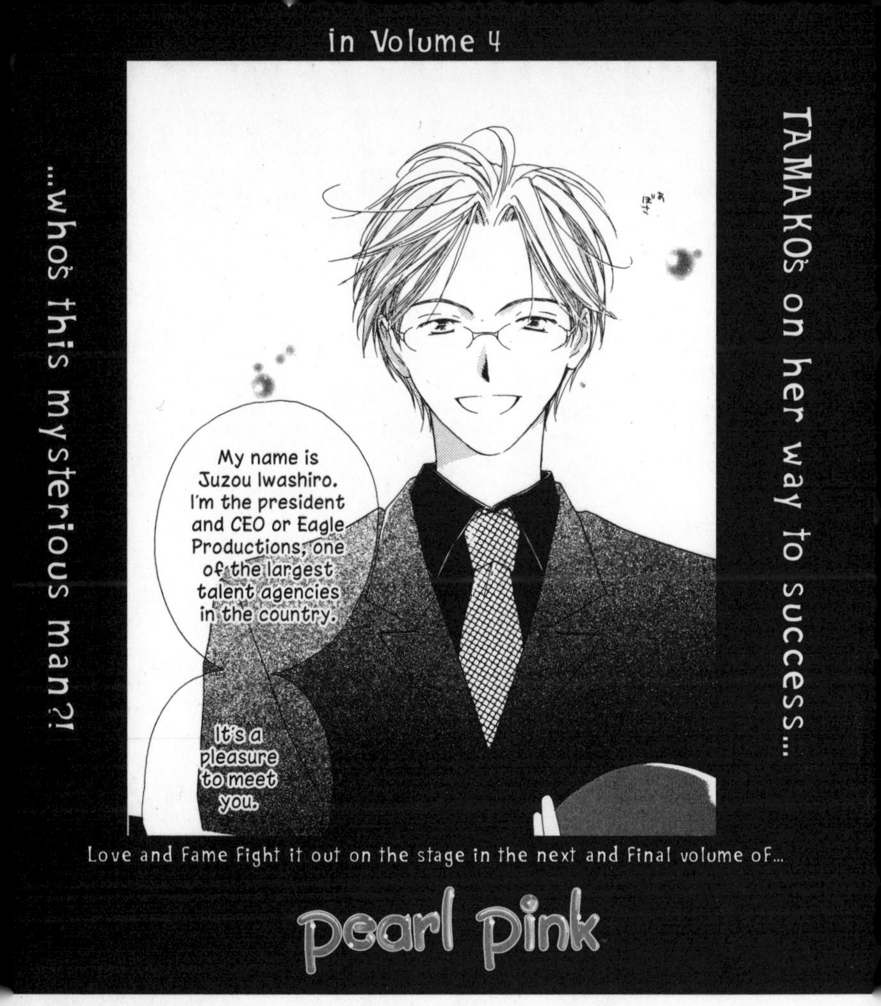
My name is Juzou Iwashiro. I'm the president and CEO or Eagle Productions, one of the largest talent agencies in the country.
It's a pleasure to meet you.

Love and fame fight it out on the stage in the next and final volume of...

pearl pink

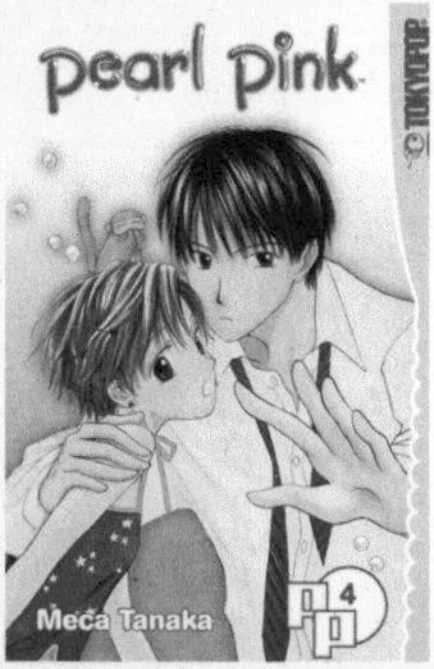
pearl pink
TOKYOPOP
4
Meca Tanaka

Out little heroine's passed the guantlet of auditions and been given the chance to star (as a villain) in a new television drama, and this is where the real drama begins! Explosions, fighting...and a kissing scene? With Tamako growing closer to Kanji everyday, will she put her career or relationship first? As the curtains come to a close, will the audience get a happy ending...?

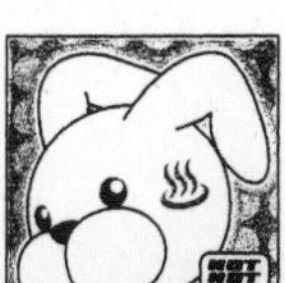

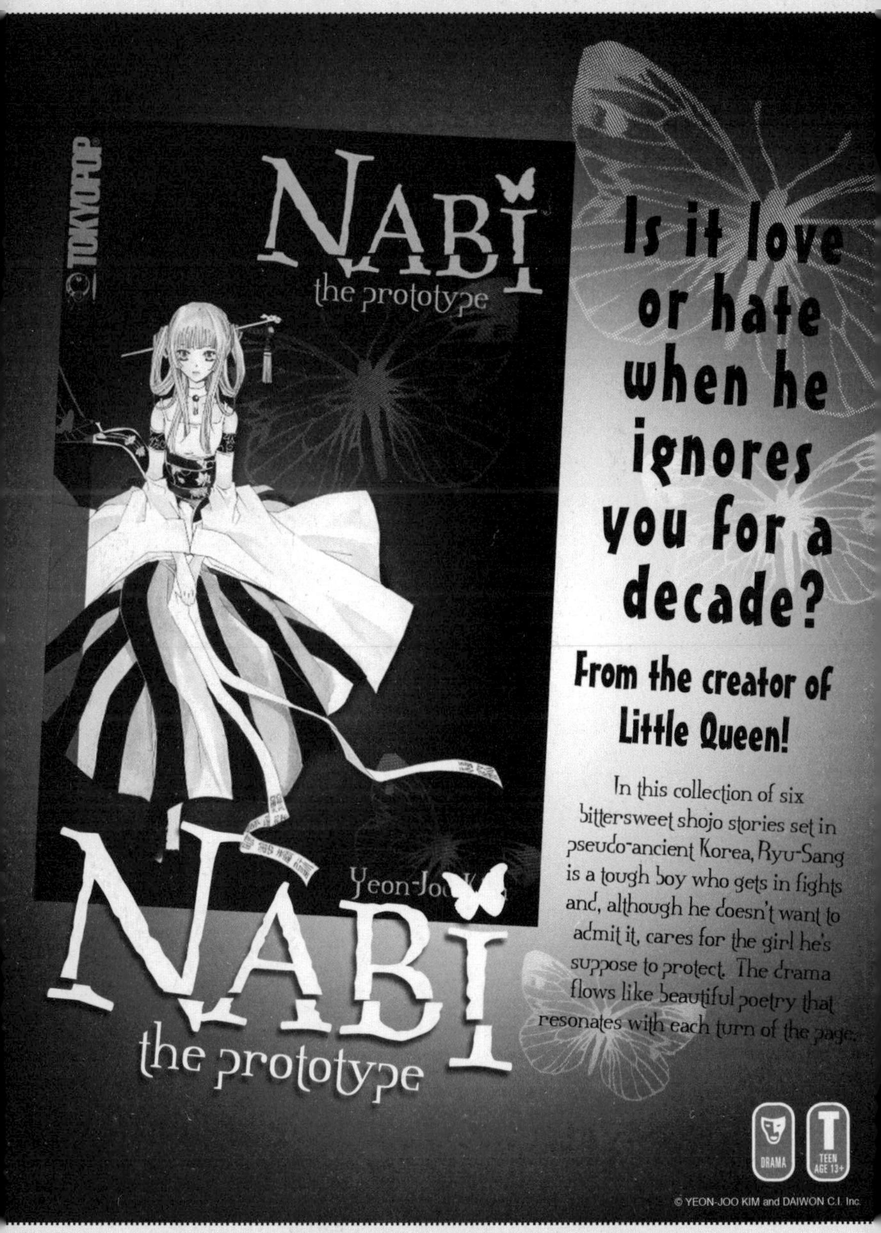
TOKYOPOP
NABI
the prototype
Is it love or hate when he ignores you for a decade?
From the creator of Little Queen!
In this collection of six bittersweet shojo stories set in pseudo-ancient Korea, Ryu-Sang is a tough boy who gets in fights and, although he doesn't want to admit it, cares for the girl he's suppose to protect. The drama flows like beautiful poetry that resonates with each turn of the page.
NABI
the prototype
DRAMA
T
TEEN AGE 13+
© YEON-JOO KIM and DAIWON C.I. Inc.

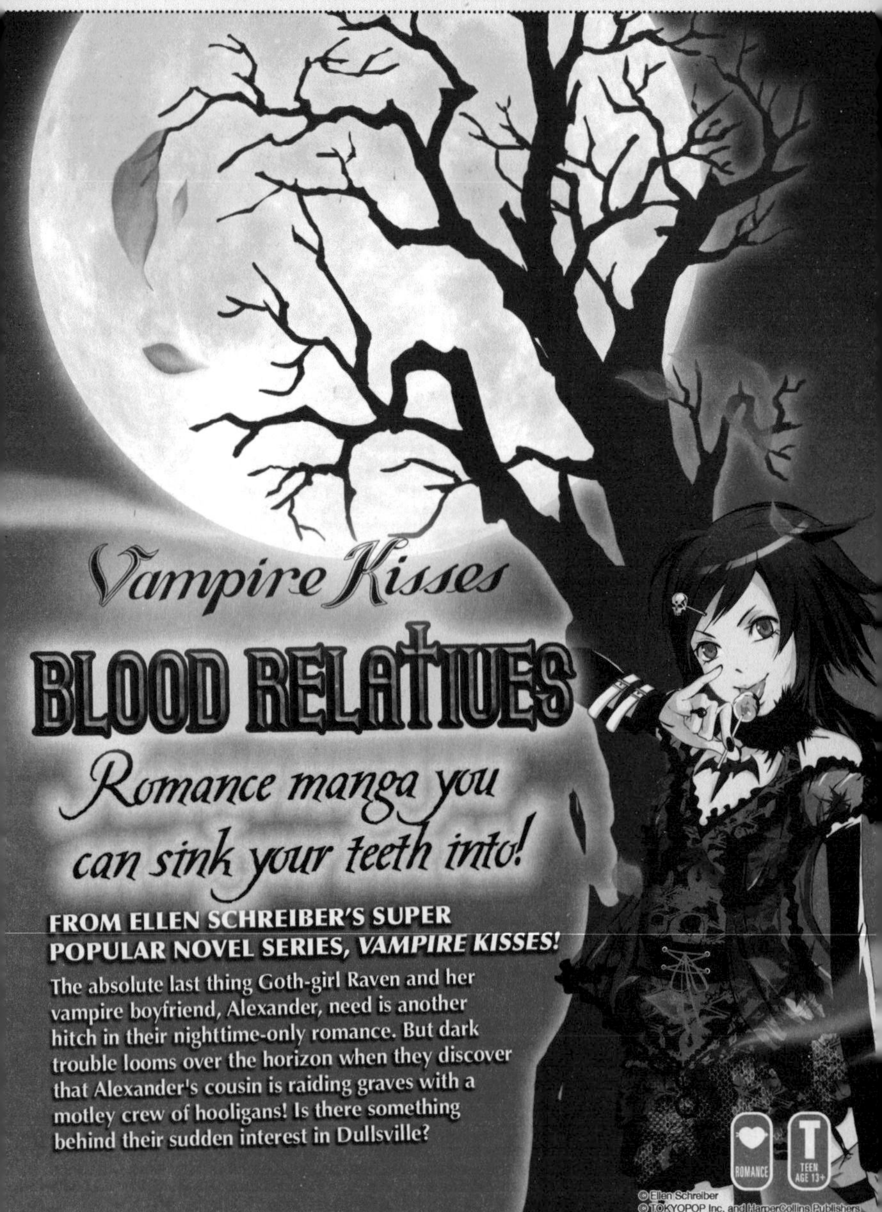
Vampire Kisses
BLOOD RELATIVES
Romance manga you can sink your teeth into!
FROM ELLEN SCHREIBER'S SUPER POPULAR NOVEL SERIES, VAMPIRE KISSES!
The absolute last thing Goth-girl Raven and her vampire boyfriend, Alexander, need is another hitch in their nighttime-only romance. But dark trouble looms over the horizon when they discover that Alexander's cousin is raiding graves with a motley crew of hooligans! Is there something behind their sudden interest in Dullsville?
ROMANCE
T
TEEN AGE 13+
© Ellen Schreiber
© TOKYOPOP Inc. and HarperCollins Publishers

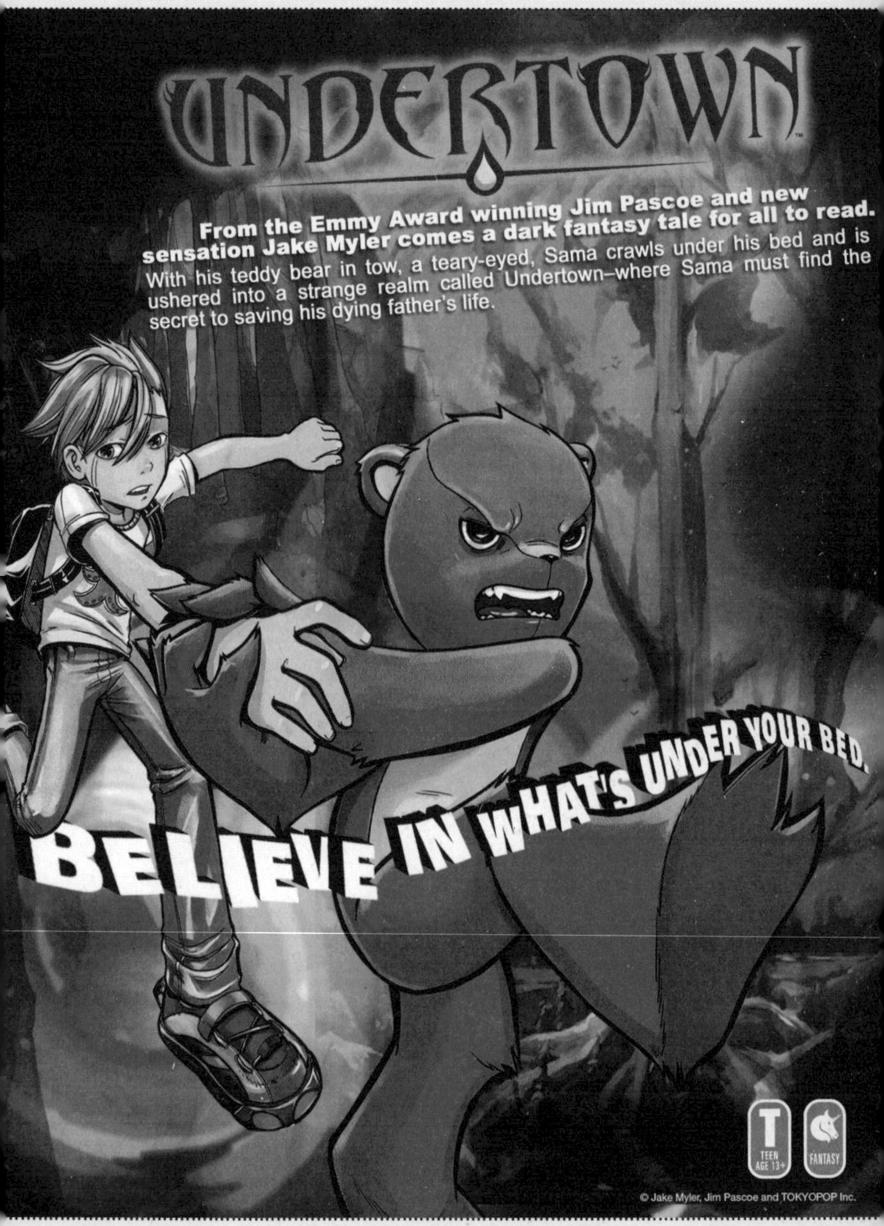
UNDERTOWN™
From the Emmy Award winning Jim Pascoe and new sensation Jake Myler comes a dark fantasy tale for all to read.
With his teddy bear in tow, a teary-eyed, Sama crawls under his bed and is ushered into a strange realm called Undertown–where Sama must find the secret to saving his dying father's life.
BELIEVE IN WHAT'S UNDER YOUR BED.
T TEEN AGE 13+
FANTASY
© Jake Myler, Jim Pascoe and TOKYOPOP Inc.

FROM DAVID HINE, CRITICALLY ACCLAIMED WRITER OF *SON OF M*, *SILENT WAR* AND *SPAWN*, AND HANS STEINBACH, CREATOR OF *A MIDNIGHT OPERA*

EVERYBODY WANTS HIS POWER BUT HIM

POISON Candy

毒飴

The SKAR virus infects a handful of adolescents worldwide, giving them superhuman, telekinetic powers along with a death sentence. The government and the private sector have both set out to find a cure for the deadly illness, but this humanitarian effort belies a powerful race that could set up an entirely new world order. When the young Sam Chance finds himself SKAR-positive, the imminent end of his life just might be the beginning of an entirely different world.

SCI-FI OT OLDER TEEN AGE 16+

© David Hine and TOKYOPOP Inc.

FOR MORE INFORMATION VISIT: WWW.TOKYOPOP.COM

STOP!

This is the back of the book.
You wouldn't want to spoil a great ending!

This book is printed "manga-style," in the authentic Japanese right-to-left format. Since none of the artwork has been flipped or altered, readers get to experience the story just as the creator intended. You've been asking for it, so TOKYOPOP® delivered: authentic, hot-off-the-press, and far more f

DIRECTIONS

If this is your first time reading manga-style, here's a quick guide to help you understand how it works.

It's easy... just start in the top right panel and follow the numbers. Have fun, and look for more 100% authentic manga from TOKYOPOP®!